AS TIME GOES BY

The Life of
INGRID BERGMAN

Laurence Leamer

D1197651

HAMISH HAMILTON
LONDON

First published in Great Britain 1986
by Hamish Hamilton Ltd
Garden House 57–59 Long Acre London WC2E 9JZ

British Library Cataloguing in Publication Data

Leamer, Laurence
    As time goes by: the life of Ingrid Bergman.
    1. Bergman, Ingrid, *1915–1982*
    2. Moving-picture actors and actresses—United States—Biography
    I. Title
    791.43'028'0924   PN2287.B435
    ISBN 0-241-11871-9

Typeset by Rowland Phototypesetting Ltd, Bury St Edmunds, Suffolk
Printed and bound in Great Britain by Butler & Tanner Ltd, Frome, Somerset.

To Vesna

CONTENTS

PHOTO CREDITS

Following page 118

The transcendent beauty of Ingrid Bergman (*Theater Arts Library, Harry Ransom Humanities Center, University of Texas at Austin*); Ingrid and her father (*Svenska Filminstitutet*); Ingrid as an extra (*Svenska Filminstitutet*); At the Swedish Royal Dramatic School (*Svenska Filminstitutet*); Ingrid and Petter at the Lutheran church in Stode, Sweden (*Sture Geuert*); Ingrid and Petter as man and wife (*Sture Gewert*); In *The Count of the Monk's Bridge*, with Edvin Adolphson (*Svenska Filminstitutet*); In the Swedish *Intermezzo*, with Gösta Ekman (*Svenska Filminstitutet*); Ingrid in 1937 (*Svenska Filminstitutet*); A pregnant Ingrid making a film in Nazi Germany in 1938 (*private collection*); In *The Four Companions* (*Svenska Filminstitutet*); Taking direction from Gregory Ratoff in the American *Intermezzo* (*Theater Arts Library, Harry Ransom Humanities Center, University of Texas at Austin*); In Hollywood in 1939 (*Selznick archives*); Publicity shot, 1939 (*Selznick archives*); With Leslie Howard in Selznick's *Intermezzo* (*Selznick archives*); With Burgess Meredith in *Liliom* (*Phototeque*); With Humphrey Bogart and Dooley Wilson in *Casablanca* (*Memorabilia*); The most famous goodbye (*Memorabilia*), Sam Wood directs Ingrid and Gary Cooper in *For Whom the Bell Tolls* (*A.M.P.S.*); Cooper, Ruth Roberts, and Ingrid during the making of *For Whom the Bell Tolls* (*A.M.P.S.*); Petter and Pia (*private collection*); Behind Alfred Hitchcock's back, Ingrid jokes for the camera (*private collection*); With Gary Cooper and Clark Gable on the ski slopes (*private collection*); Gable with an eagle shot on a trip with Ingrid and Petter (*private collection*); Ingrid and Pia in the house on Benedict Canyon (*private collection*); Ingrid and Petter's bedroom (*private collection*); Pia, Petter and Ingrid (*private collection*); A very rare publicity shot (*private collection*); A costume test for *Saratoga Trunk* (*private collection*); Reunited with Cooper in *Saratoga Trunk* (*Memorabilia*); With Gregory Peck in *Spellbound* (*Selznick archives*); With Cary Grant in *Notorious* (*Selznick archives*).

Following page 278

At Hampshire House during *Joan of Lorraine* (*Svenska Filminstitutet*); With Sam Wanamaker in *Joan of Lorraine* (*Phototeque*); Director Victor Fleming adjusts Ingrid's armor for *Joan of Arc* (*A.M.P.S.*); Joan burns at the stake (*A.M.P.S.*); With *Arch of Triumph*'s director Lewis Milestone (*A.M.P.S.*); With Charles Boyer in *Arch of Triumph* (*A.M.P.S.*); Ingrid and Roberto as she arrives in Rome (*Wide World Photos*); With Roberto at the Excelsior Hotel (*Wide World Photo*); Shooting *Stromboli* (*Phototeque*); a pregnant Ingrid leaving her apartment (*Wide World Photos*); With Giulietta Masina in *Europa '51* (*Aldo Tonti*); In the Honegger-Claudel oratorio *Joan at the Stake* (*H. Roger-Viollet*); With Pia Lindstrom, 1957 (*Wide World Photos*); With Oscar, 1957 (*Wide World Photos*); Reunited with her children Isabella, Isotta, and Robertino (*Wide World Photos*); New York press conference, 1957 (*Paris Match*); With Helen Hayes in *Anastasia* (*Phototeque*); With Lars Schmidt, 1958 (*Paris Match*); Accompanying her three children back to Italy (*Wide World Photos*); With Lars (*Associated Press*); With Pia and Hugh O'Brian (*Wide World Photos*); With Goldie Hawn in *Cactus Flower* (*Larry Edmunds*); With Anthony Quinn in *A Walk in the Spring Rain* (*Larry Edmunds*); With Isabella, Pia, and Edgar Lansbury at premiere of *Godspell* (*Wide World Photos*); With Lauren Bacall in *Murder on the Orient Express* (*The Memory Shop*); Rossellini in his last years (*Francesca Rodolfi*); Directed by Ingmar Bergman in *Autumn Sonata* (*Svenska Filminstitutet*); With director Alan Gibson (*Harve Bennet*); Ingrid in April 1982 (*Paris Match*).

THE STAR
WHO HAD EVERYTHING

The plane soared high over the Atlantic Ocean, carrying Ingrid Bergman towards Rome, to make a movie with Roberto Rossellini, the master of the new Italian cinema.

In recent years, Ingrid had become the most popular movie star in America and perhaps the world. She stood above the scandals and gossipmongering of Hollywood and had become a symbol of goodness, a vulnerable woman full of moral strength.

When Ingrid played women of questionable virtue, such as Clio Dulaine in *Saratoga Trunk* or Alicia Huberman in *Notorious*, her innate goodness seemed to show through; when she played virtuous women, such as Maria in *For Whom the Bell Tolls* or Sister Benedict in *The Bells of St Mary's*, she appeared to be displaying aspects of herself. At a time when the moral standards of Main Street America were being challenged, here at least was one star with whom decent people could identify. Everyone who read the movie magazines or the columnists knew that Ingrid lived happily in Hollywood with Petter and their daughter, Pia.

But now she was taking an enormous chance. A month before, Rossellini had visited Hollywood to arrange for the film that he and Ingrid would make now on the island of Stromboli, off the coast of Italy. Roberto had stayed with Ingrid and Petter in their house in Beverly Hills. Ingrid was mesmerised by him. Until now she'd always been able to control her affairs, ending them when she wanted to end them, often using her lovers to help perfect her roles, always returning to her husband and daughter. This time, too, she wanted to use Roberto to make a fine film on Stromboli; but without a word to Petter, she had cleared out many of her clothes and furs, jewellery and clippings books. When she left, she hadn't let on to Pia that it might be months before she returned. She had no idea that she was about to become the centre of the greatest celebrity scandal of the postwar period. More than that, she would become part of contemporary social history, helping to define an era.

Here was a woman who had everything that the most powerful

country in the world could give – a star whose adopted country had made of her the symbol of female virtue and beauty. And she was about to abandon America, leave her husband and daughter and run off with a married Italian director. If Ingrid Bergman could leave all that, then what was happening in the United States? She had betrayed America, and to many Americans she would become a moral bell-wether of the McCarthy period. She would be viewed as a symbol of Hollywood's social and moral betrayal, part of a third column under-mining America's traditional values.

In Italy, Ingrid would become an even more complicated symbol. A huge crowd was already gathering at Ciampino airport, outside Rome. To the Italians there was no Hollywood star like Ingrid Bergman. She was flying into Rome to make not a Hollywood film but an Italian film. And she was making not a big film at Cinecittà, the new 'Hollywood on the Tiber', but a modern neo-realistic Italian film on location on one of the most remote islands in Italy. Further, she was making the film not with just any successful director but with Roberto Rossellini, a man whose love affairs were discussed almost as avidly as his films.

As the TWA clipper taxied on the tarmac, the crowd pushed forward. All the other passengers filed out. Then Roberto marched up the portable stairs and greeted Ingrid with a kiss and a bouquet of roses that would have engulfed a smaller woman. Ingrid stepped out of the plane and smiled, and it was as if she were a searchlight, illuminating the night. She looked at the great crowd that stared upward, cheering and yelling. Then she descended, and within a few weeks nothing was the same.

CHAPTER 1

'PAPA, PAPA, THAT'S WHAT I'M GOING TO DO'

On Saturday afternoons much of Stockholm paraded along Strand-vägen, the most elegant of the capital's avenues. Young children hopped across the cobblestone quays. Old men, who had been young in the 1880s when the avenue was still a rude seafront, ambled along. Now burghers who had made fortunes in herring, coal, lumber, and steel lived in the great new apartment houses along Strandvägen. Well-known actors and actresses from the Royal Dramatic Theatre, whose sumptuous new performance hall stood at the head of the avenue, strutted past; lovers strolled towards the Gröna Lund amuse-ment park, across the bridge in Djurgården.

Strollers who glanced into the window of the photography shop at No. 3 Strandvägen saw a display that contrasted with the resolutely impersonal tone of the street: a silver baby shoe, and a picture of a mother and her small daughter. The robust, full-bodied young matron had broad eyebrows over small, quizzical eyes, and a mouth that seemed to be smiling at some secret joke. As for the angelic little girl, she had her mother's eyebrows, and a face that peered out on the world with serenity. It was a scene of such domestic bliss that a passerby might be forgiven a moment of envy. But the silver shoe and the photo constituted a kind of shrine, a memorial to a family scene that had lasted not much longer than the clicking of a camera. For the mother now was dead.

Ingrid Bergman was only three years old when her thirty-four-year-old mother, Friedel Adler Bergman, died of a liver ailment. Ingrid had no real memories of her – only photographs, grainy film footage, a portrait, love letters, and the anecdotes of others. She could under-stand, though, why her German-born mother had fallen in love with her father.

Justus Samuel Bergman was the eleventh of thirteen children; his father had been a schoolteacher and an organist in Slätthög. *Berg* means 'rock' in Swedish, and the Bergmans were for the most part practical, responsible people. Ingrid's father was an exception, a bohemian with the sensuous eyes of the boulevardier. Friedel Adler had been holidaying in Sweden shortly after the turn of the century when she had come upon Justus painting in the woods outside Stockholm. She'd been born in Lütjenburg, near the Baltic Sea; her father was a wheelwright, and she was the second of three daughters. Friedel was a pretty woman, as resolutely practical as her husband-to-be was impractical and whimsical. In the most out-of-character act of her short life, she fell in love with Justus.

Back in Hamburg, where they now lived, Friedel's family issued a threefold objection. Justus was not German; he was Friedel's senior by thirteen years; and in all those years he had achieved no position or wealth.

But love is love, and Justus gave Friedel an engagement ring. In order to fool her family she wore the ring around her neck during the day and on her finger only in the privacy of her room at night. When the Adlers discovered the ruse, they exacted their harsh price; the couple could marry only when Justus had achieved a position of responsibility and substance worthy of an Adler. And thus Justus opened his photographic store at No. 3 Strandvägen, where he worked for seven years before he was deemed worthy to marry an Adler.

Ingrid believed that if her father had developed his artistic abilities, he might have become a painter of stature. Her belief testified more to a daughter's loyalty than to artistic judgment. Justus was perhaps fortunate to be able to dream what he might have been, while prospering in a business that allowed his artistic bent a certain freedom. Some of his paintings remain; that he gave many of them away was possibly not as much a measure of generosity as absence of patrons.

Whatever his limitations as a painter, Justus was a man of charm and culture. Despite his lack of business acumen, his shop prospered. He took pictures, developed film, sold cameras and frames. He even had a device by which a customer could snap his own passport photograph. Justus was eventually successful enough to hire two full-time employees, playing the *grand patron*, visiting the store when he saw fit.

The Bergmans lived in a large apartment on the sixth and top floor above the store. No. 3 Strandvägen is not quite as grand a structure as No. 21, modelled after a palace in Zaragoza, but nonetheless is imposing enough, with small balconies facing the water, a smooth plaster front, and a tarred roof bordered by copper trim and great turrets; Justus's bohemian friends derided it as hopelessly bourgeois.

The Bergmans' apartment was large and comfortable. There were half a dozen large rooms, an atelier for Justus's painting, and a small kitchen, space enough for a family far larger than the three Bergmans. Friedel had, in fact, been pregnant two times before the birth of Ingrid. One child had died at birth, the second after a week of life.

Ingrid was a gift, and from her birth, on 29 August 1915, her parents adored her. She was named after the two-year-old Swedish princess. On her first birthday, Justus took his family to a park to film them. Little Ingrid in a white dress kissed her kneeling mother. Then her father walked down the path, debonair in a three-piece suit, hat, and cane. He knelt down too, and she kissed him, her face hidden behind the brim of his hat. For her second birthday, Justus made another film. Ingrid stood in a white dress. She placed her arms around her kneeling mother's neck, touching the hem of her long, full skirt. Her mother kissed her. Ingrid shook her hand and curtsied, and then curtsied again, as if she had learned a new trick.

The next time Justus took home movies, three-year-old Ingrid wore a dark coat and carried white flowers. And as her father filmed her, she placed the flowers on her mother's grave.

Justus might have reverted to a more unconventional life style, but a good Swedish daughter had to be brought up with all the strictures of the bourgeois life. Thus Ingrid's forty-nine-year-old Aunt Ellen descended on No. 3 Strandvägen. Ellen was the only one of Justus's twelve siblings not to marry; she had turned to God and to a life of service to her brothers and sisters. Ellen had a heart condition and rarely left the apartment. She was a stern Lutheran who could smell the taint of sin in the most innocent of passions. One afternoon, a number of years after Friedel's death, the mother of one of Ingrid's school playmates telephoned to invite her daughter's friend to play.

'Is Mrs Bergman there?' she asked.

'She's gone to God,' Aunt Ellen answered, as if the sod were still fresh on her grave.

In the summers Justus left his daughter in Hamburg with her grandparents and aunts; they disciplined their grandchild like Prussian drill sergeants. When her father returned from his summer wanderings, she fled into his arms as if only there could she find respite from imposed order and routine.

Her father was not the patriarch of their tiny family. He was her mentor and friend and companion. He doled out affection and treats in grand dollops; she was one of Justus's favourite photographic subjects. When she was about six or seven, she dressed up in her father's coat, hat, and glasses, and was photographed reading the daily paper, a slight smirk on her face.

Justus was a man of many interests. He was in a choir that made two trips to America. He loved music so much that he dreamed his daughter might become an opera singer. In Sweden, as elsewhere, there is a whole industry based on parents' artistic aspirations for their children, one that gives far more pleasure to parents than it does to children; but Ingrid enjoyed taking piano lessons and singing for her father, as he sat puffed up with pride.

Better yet, Ingrid loved to act in front of Justus. To her acting meant joy and pleasure for herself and for those around her, a journey out of the mundane rites of daily existence. When she was alone she acted too, creating a world of wondrous characters and stories.

Ensamhet, loneliness, is a great theme of Swedish culture. In the twentieth century, when people complained of isolation and aliena- tion as they would of toothache, the greatest Swedish playwrights and filmmakers seemed to be speaking a peculiarly modern idiom. But in Sweden that *ensamhet* has roots not only in the psyche but in the land. It is a land of vast empty spaces, of stark panoramas, of foreboding that might have made another people huddle together. For the most part, though, Swedes have lived as apart from one another as possible. In the villages and countryside where most of them dwelt, the houses were usually set apart. Into the growing towns and cities the Swedes brought their loneliness with them.

Justus sent his daughter to the Palmgrenska Samskolan, the most prestigious girls' school in Stockholm. The five-story yellow-brick structure was a solid building for a solid education. Ingrid was not a good student or a particularly popular one.

'She was a sad child and so shy,' remembers Disa Lauhren, one of her classmates. 'But when she played she always played like a star. We had a little playhouse at my house. We made a fire in the stove and we played with the food and made little pancakes. But all the time Ingrid was outside by herself, acting.'

Then when Ingrid was nine Greta Danielsson arrived in the apart- ment on Strandvägen to be her governess. Justus wanted a happy person, and in eighteen-year-old Greta he had found that and more. 'Her father wanted me to be an older sister to her,' Greta says. 'And I think we were sisters. She was very happy.'

Greta came from Norrtäije, a little town outside Stockholm. She had dreams of being an opera singer. She helped Ingrid not only with schoolwork but with her piano lessons. In the evenings, Greta, Ingrid, and her father sat around the piano, playing and singing.

'He had a beautiful voice,' Greta remembers. 'I accompanied him. And we would go for walks, the three of us.'

Greta had a fresh beauty and gentleness. She was the youth and laughter that the house so lacked. Greta was always there waiting when Ingrid walked home from school.

'Where have you been?' asked Greta one day when Ingrid arrived late.

'There was a little bird that died, and we had to bury it in the park. And we had to sing.'

'What did you sing?' Greta asked.

'The only song I knew was "Glad as a Bird in the Morning."'

Justus was fifty-three years old when the teenaged governess entered the house in 1924. He flirted with her, and under Aunt Ellen's nose a romance began. In the summer, Justus, Greta, and Ingrid went to Aunt Ellen's tiny summer house outside Stockholm and swam in the lake. They were a happy threesome – her father, who was not a strong, disciplining parental figure but, as she said later, 'like a big brother'; and Greta; not a figure of authority either, but, as she saw it, 'an older sister'; and Ingrid, who accepted this ménage as natural and good.

As soon as Aunt Ellen and the other relatives learned about it, they were outraged. Justus's love cost Greta dear.

'We fell in love and it was very difficult,' Greta says. 'He was so handsome. We had so much to talk about. I cared for him very much, but I was much younger. He wanted to marry me. It was very difficult for me. If we had married, her aunt said that she would not have stayed. She wanted to stay with Ingrid, and I understood that. I said marriage was impossible.'

In the name of propriety, Aunt Ellen and the others drove Greta out of the house. And with it they drove out most of whatever lightness and gaiety there had been in Ingrid's home.

Soon afterwards, when Ingrid was twelve years old, her father developed cancer of the stomach. He'd heard of a doctor in Bavaria who had a miraculous new cure and he wanted to go there. Even if this trip was futile, he would save Ingrid from observing the agony of his decline. He asked Greta to put aside the singing career to which she had returned and go off with him.

'He was very, very sick,' Greta recalls. 'The doctor said he didn't have a long time to live . . . I travelled to Germany with him . . . He could only eat a little bouillon. We lived on a farm, but they had no chickens and I wanted to cook bouillon. I found chickens on another farm . . .'

When Justus and Greta returned, Ingrid's chubby, prosperous-looking father was replaced by a thin old man. The end was near, but Aunt Ellen and the other Swedish relatives would not have Greta hovering around. Not until Ingrid's aunt from Germany, Frau Elsa Adler, arrived for the death watch was Greta allowed to return. Frau Adler was a formidable woman, not used to being contradicted. Ingrid called her Aunt Mutti, and she was indeed like a mother to Ingrid.

In his last weeks Justus set his life in order. He had Greta and Aunt Mutti round up all his paintings so that he could give them away. He handed Greta the key to his atelier and asked her to destroy his papers. Greta burned the documents without reading a page of what she thought were personal journals.

Ingrid and Greta sat at his bedside. 'I remember my father turned his head to look at Greta, and then he turned his head to look at me, and I smiled at him,' Ingrid said. 'And that was the end.'

For six months Ingrid lived with her fat, ageing Aunt Ellen alone in the large apartment. Then one night Ingrid heard her aunt calling out in the dark: 'I feel really ill.' She asked Ingrid to telephone her brother.

Ingrid was supposed to throw the key out of the window, but she had forgotten. And when her uncle finally burst into the room, Ingrid was holding Aunt Ellen in her arms. The old lady, gasping her last, was the black colour of death.

Ingrid moved in with her Uncle Otto and Aunt Hulda and five cousins. The apartment was within walking distance of her home on Strandvägen, but it was a world apart. Her father had been an artist; to a loving daughter, the fact that he rarely sold a painting didn't matter. Theirs had been an artistic home, with the smell of oil paint drifting out of the atelier, and singing frequently sounding from the living room. The only singing at her aunt and uncle's was of Lutheran hymns.

Uncle Otto had a frameshop and fancied himself an inventor. Hulda was the mainstay of the family, a genius at making the soup go further, and patching a winter coat. She slept on a tiny portable bed in a windowless corridor, while her two girls shared one bedroom and her three boys slept in others. Ingrid had the largest bedroom to herself, furnished with pieces from the old home, including the piano.

The family depended upon Ingrid's father's business; thus Ingrid merited the biggest room. Even the family's summer vacations were spent at the small house on Lake Mälaren that Ingrid had inherited from her Aunt Ellen. Her closest friend was her cousin Britt, two years her junior, who would remain a friend all her life. 'She was like a sister,' Britt reflects. 'She was very sensitive as a girl . . . She lived in another world.'

When she was about eleven, her father had taken Ingrid to the theatre. At the first interval, she had announced, 'Papa, Papa, that's what I'm going to do.' Her home on Strandvägen had been no more than a hundred yards from the greatest Swedish theatre, the Royal Dramatic. The magical theatrical world had begun not in the theatre but on the marble steps of the gracious building where there arrived each evening gentlemen in evening dress, and ladies in long gowns.

Ingrid's new home was not far from Stockholm's film palace, the Röda Kvarn (Red Mill). Built in 1915, the year of Ingrid's birth, the great movie theatre was as elegant as an opera house; music for the silent films was provided by one of the best orchestras in Stockholm. The well-dressed audience sat watching not only Charlie Chaplin, Mary Pickford, and other foreign performers, but films by the two Swedish masters Victor Sjöström and Mauritz Stiller.

While other girls dreamed of boys, Ingrid dreamed of the stage. Increasingly, she retreated into her fantasy world. She went to her room, shut the door, and played different roles, as if she were trying on costumes.

Often on Sundays, Ingrid went to supper at the home of her father's old friend the florist Gunnar Spångberg. After dinner Spångberg would ask her to perform for his friends. She enjoyed the attention and looked forward to these soirées. At school one Christmas, the students in her class could not do their exercises because the gymnasium had been turned into a stage for the senior play. As they sat waiting out the hour, Ingrid leaped to the stage and offered to put on a play for her peers. With six of her classmates drafted into subsidiary roles, Ingrid performed *The Green Elevator*, a play about a love triangle. Partway through the drama, the teacher returned and ordered the students outside. Ingrid finished her performance in the park, standing on a bench. 'If you remember Ingrid as a child, you remember her as an actress,' says Disa Lauhren, her classmate. 'When it was raining outside, one girl played the piano and Ingrid read poems. She was very quiet, but when she did it, that was the real Ingrid.'

Uncle Otto tried to dissuade Ingrid from becoming an actress. 'My father was a very religious man,' Britt said. 'He thought they met bad people in the theatre. He tried to get her interested in other things.' He might well have thought that Ingrid's prospects as an actress were woeful, and wanted to shelter her. After all, she was too unassuming, too timid, ever to grace a stage. She had even developed a nervous condition. Sometimes her lips, eyelids, and fingers became so terribly swollen that she was almost grotesque.

In later years Ingrid insisted that she had begun her journey upward from a pit of loneliness. Although her Uncle Otto and Aunt Hulda could not provide an idyllic family life for their orphaned niece, her memories of unhappiness were partially an actress's gift for self-dramatization. Those who knew her most intimately during those years do not remember such desperate unhappiness. 'I never had the feeling she was unhappy,' recalls Britt. 'I think Ingrid exaggerated.' Greta Danielsson, a more dispassionate observer, makes the same observation. 'I think she was happy as a child. But she was at a difficult age when she went to her uncle's. There were so many children, and before that she had been the only one.'

Greta was the only person Ingrid knew who had made even a modest start in her chosen métier. Greta had gone back to studying music, hoping for a career in opera, but someone at a film studio had offered her work as an extra and even a few small parts. Although she had the prospect of a larger career in films, she wasn't interested; she simply wanted money to pursue her singing. One day Greta offered to take Ingrid out to the studio, having arranged work for her as an extra; Ingrid was then fifteen.

The Svensk Filmindustri studios lay on the outskirts of Stockholm, on land that two decades before had been an ostrich farm. On that morning in late 1931 when Ingrid journeyed through the studio portals, the first golden age of Swedish film was as much a thing of the past as were ostrich feathers on ladies' hats. With the advent of sound most of the better films were from America. It was what a French film historian of Swedish film calls an 'age of lethargy'. Even the two masters of early Swedish films had journeyed to Hollywood. Victor Sjöström had made the classic western *The Wind* before returning to Sweden. Mauritz Stiller had travelled westward too, taking his protégée Greta Garbo with him. He had been as much a failure as Garbo would prove a success, and had come back to Stockholm to die in 1928.

Svensk Filmindustri was the giant of the industry, with a captive market in its own chain of theatres. Every little town and village had its movie theatre. For centuries the Swedes had been a poor farming people; but then there had been a great migration, not only to the cities but also to America. The first trickles of industrial wealth were reaching even the tiniest villages; people in rural areas sought entertainment and knowledge that the parish pastors could not provide. 'The cinema was the church in the village,' says Rune Waldekranz, the Swedish film historian.

If the cinema was the new church, it was primarily preaching comedy and tedious drama. For Ingrid's debut as an extra, she and a dozen other young women were doused in heavy yellow make-up. Wearing fur-trimmed wool coats, they were lined up along a brick wall, beside a sign saying: 'MODEHUSET ESTELLE' (Estelle Fashion House). The director told the pretty, well fed young women that they were playing desperate unemployed women applying for a job. They were to act appropriately hungry and fretful. Ingrid was in the second row. She was supposed to look forward. Instead, Ingrid turned slightly towards the camera. When the scene was shot, she was the only one of the thirteen extras whose full face appeared.

Ingrid was finished for the day, and it was only 10.30. She was not about to leave. She spent hours wandering about, visiting the various sets and films, still wearing her make-up. Late in the afternoon, when almost everyone else had left, a production assistant came upon her and gave her ten krona for her work.

'She was so fascinated that she didn't want to leave,' Greta says. 'She was so happy. She said, "I must be an actress now."'

If Ingrid was to become a great actress, there was only one place to begin: the school of the Royal Dramatic Theatre. Founded by King Gustavus III in 1788, the Royal Dramatic is Sweden's national theatre. The opulent four-tiered theatre was at that time a place where one came to be seen and fitfully amused. Indeed, during the early 1930s the theatre was playing primarily comedies and other light works. And yet Strindberg's *Master Olaf* had opened the new theatre in 1908, and Eugene O'Neill's *Strange Interlude* had premiered there in 1928. As an academy for actors, the Royal Dramatic School is almost unique in the western world. The school is so tiny, the competition so fierce, the training so rigorous, and the opportunities so great, that admission almost guarantees one a successful career in the theatre.

In 1933 there were seventy-five would-be actors and actresses competing for eight places. Entrance depended on an audition before directors and others of the Royal Dramatic Theatre. Ingrid was a young woman of resources, and she prepared for the audition with dedication. She had her own private drama teacher, Gabriel Alw, who prepared her for every aspect of her audition. She took private gymnastics lessons from Ruth Kylberg, who worked with the students at the Royal Dramatic School. She went to Ruth's apartment on Strandvägen and worked out in a room full of mirrors, bars, and paintings by her instructor's husband.

Ingrid's first audition was one of the great moments of her professional life, and in later years she loved talking about that day. When a great public performer makes an entrance, the audience *knows* that something has changed, that the play, the set, the auditorium, the stadium, is not the same. All this before a word is uttered. In her memory, her entrance onto the great stage became such a moment. In 1959 she told Joseph Steele, her biographer, that she had played the boy in Rostand's *L'Aiglon*. She was expecting applause from the twenty judges, but when she finished she was greeted only by silence. Two days later she learned that she had been chosen. Only much later did she learn that the jury was so moved by her stunning performance that they had been unable to applaud. 'They just sat there till the lights were turned on, and then the mood burst and they cheered,' Ingrid recalled. 'But I had already left the theatre.'

In her autobiography Ingrid had a different story to tell. She said that she had played a feisty, daring peasant girl in a play by a Hungarian playwright of such obscurity that she could remember neither the play nor the playwright. She ran on stage and boldly laughed, shouting her first line. The jury instructed her to stop. According to Ingrid, years later one of the judges told her that she had been stopped because they had at once recognized that she had stage presence and had needed to see no more.

Rarely, alas, is life so dramatic. Although there is no one left who remembers that August 1933 occasion, in 1946, when Ingrid was probably the most popular star in the world, an American reporter went to Stockholm to write about the Royal Dramatic School. He discovered that Ingrid had first performed a scene from *The Tower of the Conscience*, 'with only minor slips'. Like the other candidates, she went on to do two other pieces, choosing Rostand's *L'Aiglon* and Strindberg's *Dream Play*. One of the judges noted: 'While she has too much the appearance of a country girl, she is very natural, and is the type that does not use make-up on her face or on her mind.'

Ingrid had stood out well enough to be chosen one of the eight new students, but she had not stood out from her peers like a beacon in the night.

CHAPTER 2

'OH, SHE STARTS WELL, DOESN'T SHE?'

Two months after entering the Royal Dramatic School, eighteen-year-old Ingrid sat with one of her cousins and two other friends at the Grand Hotel. As a little girl Ingrid had looked out her window on Strandvägen and seen the tall spire of the greatest hotel in all Sweden, a noble building that would not have been out of place along the Grand Canal in Venice. Here the world's artistic greats and Nobel Prize recipients stayed when they came to Stockholm. But Ingrid had never entered the lobby, much less sat in one of the Grand's fine restaurants.

Her cousin had arranged a date for Ingrid with a successful young dentist, Petter Aron Lindstrom,* called Aron since childhood. It was a measure of how much, and how positively, Ingrid's life was changing that she was having dinner at such a place, even if her blind date was a half hour late. Since she had entered the Royal Dramatic School, her face had stopped puffing up, and her hands no longer looked distended. She had only a couple of years before appeared a gawky adolescent, but now she was beautiful, glowing with youth and health. She was a full-bodied robust young woman five feet nine inches tall, weighing around 130 pounds. In many respects she looked like a thousand other pretty Swedish girls, but there was an extraordinary quality to her appearance. She seemed not only to look good but to be good, and to cry out for protection.

The revolving doors whirled once again, and through them walked a handsome six-foot-two-inch-tall young man. Petter Aron walked briskly towards them.

He was a forceful young man with a confident, even cocky, air. He had light-brown hair and exuded order and good health. As Ingrid discovered, he was a wonderful dancer. If he had burdened Ingrid with his accomplishments, he would have left her little room to talk. He had studied dentistry in Sweden and in Germany, and at the age of twenty-six had the only doctor of medical dentistry degree

---

* In the United States, Dr Lindstrom's first name was often to be rendered as Peter.

in Sweden. He had spent a summer in the Arctic Circle working in a tuberculosis sanatorium that provided dental treatment to Laplanders. He had published research papers, and was in private practice. He was also an associate professor at the Dental College of the Karolinska Institute in Stockholm. As if that wasn't enough, he was a medical student at the institute where he was an instructor.

Petter was known as a dedicated teacher; woe betide the hapless student who came to his class unprepared. Outside of his work he was good fun, with the ability to laugh at himself. He was an athlete, a champion boxer and skier, enjoyed hiking and challenging the unwary to arm-wrestling matches that he almost always won. He also knew artists and writers, and found time to go to concerts and the theatre.

Petter called Ingrid a few days later and they began dating. Their backgrounds were very different. Petter had grown up in Stöde, a large village of six hundred in north central Sweden. Most of the people in the village earned their living from farming or timber, but Petter's father was the provincial landscape architect. The family house was a simple two-storey structure, set off on several acres of land.

The Swedes are not given to ostentation, and the house was neither more nor less grand than the others in the village. 'When I was growing up there were many homeless, hungry people travelling through,' Petter says. 'My parents let them stay in the barn, sleeping in the hay, and gave them porridge to eat. It wasn't for religious reasons but because that was the family attitude. My mother did want me perhaps to become a priest because that was the most honoured position in the town.' There is an old Swedish saying, 'Neighbours are brothers', and though Petter did not become a priest, he was a man who was forever helping people. It was almost a compulsion with him. Even when Ingrid first knew him there were many people whom he was helping with advice, money, treatment, or time.

Petter was a man of great pride, the pride that the Lutheran priests railed against in their Sunday sermons. But pride was the sinew of all Petter's virtues. He was proudly virtuous, proudly generous, proudly humane, proudly caring, and proudly loving. He was a good man and he knew it, and the proof of his goodness was in his daily actions.

Petter was living in Stockholm now but remained in many respects a man of Stöde. Life there had been tough, simple, and good: a sauna at the town steam bath on the weekends, nude bathing in the summer (the men and the women separated), sports all the year round. Despite his degrees and his ambition, Petter still sought the simple life.

Ingrid had already had one involvement, with an artist, and she was suddenly being courted by many young men. 'She was absolutely natural in some things,' Britt reminisces. 'Many of the boys from the theatre fell in love with her. They called and stood outside the window. But her career came first.'

Petter was eight and a half years older than Ingrid and one of the most eligible bachelors in Stockholm; it was small wonder that she would be flattered by his attention.

Ingrid was not interested in mere boys; she had her career to think about. Petter was a good listener; he sat there as she went on endlessly about the theatre and the school. He liked to take care of things, and freed Ingrid from worrying about many of the boring details of life. He thought about her, advised her. He was there waiting for her when she needed him. He was funny, witty, caring; and endlessly solicitous of Ingrid.

If he was not a womanizer, it was as much because of his sense of his own worth as of his personal morality. He understood Ingrid's value. She had a loveliness beyond loveliness; she was an adornment for any man – sweet, and innocent, and alone. He could do no better. If she wasn't as broadly interested in the world as he was, that didn't matter. He was concerned enough about the world for both of them.

Even before they professed their love, Ingrid had the first crisis of her professional life. A month or so after her meeting Petter, one of the judges at her audition, Alf Sjöberg, offered her a large part in the play he was directing. At the Royal Dramatic School, acting was a profession that required several years of apprenticeship. Any third-year student would have coveted such a role. It was almost unheard of to give a freshman any role, let alone a big one.

The young actors and actresses behaved as if they were a band of brothers and sisters of the arts, sharing equally of the bread of theatre. Alas, there are good parts and bad parts and no parts at all. Ingrid's good fortune brought forth a plague of envy. To quell the uproar, the offer of the part was withdrawn. The sting of unfairness had wakened her to the realities of a world where there are more prize seekers than prizes.

Her classmates surely did not shower Ingrid with as much venom as she imagined; they were too involved in their own careers for that. Indeed it's striking how few memories her fellow students have of her. Signe Hasso, the Swedish actress, was one of those older girls who allegedly hated her. Yet Hasso states that she did not know her at all, a remarkable achievement in a school with less than thirty students. 'I was so busy I never saw anyone,' she says. Frank Sund-strom, the actor and director, was a schoolmate who was photographed with Ingrid in the class picture; he says that he never met her. Gunnar Björnstrand, the actor known best for his work with Ingmar Bergman, says that he has almost no memories of her.

When the school year was over, many of her fellow students went on an inexpensive tour to study theatre in Russia, but Ingrid stayed in Stockholm. Later she blamed Petter, saying that she had stayed because she was in love.

Ingrid had begun to use Petter as an excuse. She had other reasons not to go. She had few friends at the school; she surely could not relish spending twenty-four hours a day with young actresses who she felt hated her. She was growing bored and frustrated with mere classes. Probably she had other ideas for her career that she dared not talk of too openly.

Women were not supposed to parade their ambition nakedly; Ingrid had to garb her intentions in modest dress. She played the sweet ingénue, but she was full of fierce determination to succeed.

Ingrid went to see Gunnar Spångberg, in whose house on Sunday evenings she had once so happily performed. Many actors and actresses bought flowers at Gunnar's shop near the Royal Dramatic Theatre; Ingrid wanted Spångberg to ask one of these customers to help her get a small part at the film studio. Spångberg was delighted to help her, but he was a florist, after all, not part of the theatrical world. Ingrid, on the other hand, knew the customer to ask: Karin Swanström, the artistic director of Svensk Filmindustri. Wouldn't it be nice if Gunnar gave Miss Swanström a bunch of roses and then asked if young Ingrid might come out to the studio to seek advice? That was the neatest of touches: to ask not for an extra's role but only for advice. Gunnar told the artistic director that Ingrid was his little girl, the daughter of his best friend, and an orphan. It was a tale more poignant by far than half the melodramas being produced at the studio, and Miss Swanström agreed to see Ingrid the next day.

Ingrid knew how to make people want to help her, to make her success seem theirs as well. Miss Swanström fancied herself a *grande dame* and was not immune to the more subtle forms of flattery. The next morning she not only gave Ingrid 'advice', but listened to her reciting poetry, and set up a screen test the following day.

Before arriving at the studio for the ten o'clock screen test, Ingrid got off the tram at the small cemetery where her parents were buried. Ingrid was not sure that she believed in God, but she did believe in her own ability as an actress. She sat and prayed not to God but to her father, and not for success either, but merely that she not be nervous. When she arrived at the film studio, she was met by Gustav Molander, a leading director. Ingrid was flushed with excitement.

She had no lines to recite. She merely had to sit while the camera played over her, as she turned her head, smiled, or scowled.

A screen actor must concentrate absolutely and yet appear relaxed. Thus as Ingrid sat there, so sweetly, so obligingly, she was acting as much as if she had been standing reciting before a vast audience. She was exuding those inexplicable qualities that would make her a star: a femininity that was at once sensuous and innocent, a smile that was as warm as a winter's hearth, a fresh milky beauty that lay on her countenance like the morning's dew – a magical quality that enhanced the film with life, and seemed to enhance those who watched her.

The camera had the only eye that mattered. The film was the only judge and jury. Not until Molander saw the rushes the next day did he know for sure what a find this Ingrid Bergman was. As Ingrid sat watching herself, she was the professional criticizing her performance as if she were watching another person.

One of the films about to be shot that had a possible role for her was *The Count of the Monk's Bridge*, directed by Edvin Adolphson, who also played the lead. This was Adolphson's first chance to direct. He would have preferred a serious drama, and not a madcap comedy, a popular genre in Sweden during the 1930s. Adolphson assembled a fine group of comic talent; the only remaining role was the ingénue. The first-time director was seeking a hard-nosed girl with character.

Ingrid was one possibility, but Adolphson had unhappy memories of the studio's newest starlet. The previous year Adolphson had starred in a play in which Ingrid had been an extra. In his memoirs the director wrote that she and another student 'had destroyed a scene for Inga Tidblad and me in Sheridan's play *The Rivals*. Inga and I had a big scene on a park sofa with people walking in the background. Just when the important dialogue was taking place, two elegant ladies with umbrellas and wide eighteenth-century crinolines came and giggled in front of our sofa so that the public could see neither Inga nor me . . . One was Ingrid Bergman.' In theatre, an extra upstaging a lead character is a sin against the holy ghost. Ingrid was roundly reprimanded. But her behaviour certainly displayed hard-nosed character. Adolphson gave her the part.

When Ingrid arrived for her first day's work, no one at the studio was as curious about her as Birgit Tengroth. Although she was Ingrid's age, Birgit was already a popular actress with half a decade of filmmaking behind her. In almost any other profession, Birgit would have viewed the future with confidence, but she was haunted by the spectre of Ingrid Bergman and the dread thought that her own career might soon be over.

Two years before, Birgit's gymnastics teacher had told her about

a high school student who looked like her and who would be trying
out for the Royal Dramatic School. That had been enough to ruin
Birgit's day. Then, recently, when she had demanded a higher salary
for her current picture, she had been told that 'there was a girl enough
like me to be used to take my place'. And now this Ingrid Bergman
had a part that Birgit believed should have been hers.

Birgit was no paranoid but a perfect product of her chosen profession; for five years she had been pampered, made the centre of the
universe – now, suddenly, 'the new Birgit Tengroth' had arrived as
if Birgit had been only the caretaker. Even Ingrid's arrival that
morning had been spectacular. No star or would-be star had ever
wheeled into the studio on a bicycle, wearing sunglasses. It was as
dramatic as it was unexpected.

Ingrid seemed to be totally devoid of self-doubt. 'I was crushed, I
sat in my dressing room with my troubles and a feeling of anguish,'
Birgit wrote later. 'I heard her come up the stairs and into the dressing
room corridor, and then she picked up the telephone, called up the
restaurant and asked for two sandwiches, one with liver pâté and one
with veal, and then her strong laugh saying "I love to eat and sleep."'

If Ingrid had bicycled all the way from her apartment, she had got
up early indeed. Ingrid and Petter, in fact, later found it a wonderful
joke. Ingrid would drive out near the studio, park the car, and
then ride her bicycle the last few hundred yards, arriving with a
wind-blown, miraculous freshness.

In *The Count of the Monk's Bridge*, Ingrid played a maid whose
boyfriend and his disreputable friends lead the Stockholm police a
merry chase through the capital's bohemian districts. The plot was a
thin strand on which to drape one madcap scene after another. In
one scene on the first day of shooting, Tollie Zellman, a leading
comedienne, wrapped a fish for a customer while another customer,
Ingrid, looked on. While the shot was being set up, Ingrid proceeded
to show the talented and seasoned Miss Zellman how one properly
wraps a fish.

Tollie looked first at the director and then at Ingrid, her measured
glance more telling than speech.

'And who's this?' she asked as Adolphson looked on, richly
amused.

'Well, she's a young girl who's just started.'

'Oh, she starts well, doesn't she?'

Ingrid was merely another strand holding up the comic scenes, yet
she made the most of it. Starting well was a matter of how she looked
as well as how she acted. Åke Dahlqvist, the cameraman on this and

six of Ingrid's other Swedish films, was as responsible as anyone for creating what became the Bergman look. He had photographed the screen test that a decade before had led Greta Garbo to Hollywood. He had a tender, lyrical way of photographing women. 'More as an experiment than anything else, at the studio they took special still pictures of Ingrid to show that her face was evenly balanced,' Dahlqvist said. 'They then took two right sides and two left sides, and the face looked the same. When they tried that with other actresses, they often got horrifying results. But on photographing her one side of her face was lit stronger than the other side. I did that. You had to be careful. I tried to avoid one profile. I thought that if I did an extreme profile it was too sharp.'

As soon as Ingrid finished *The Count of the Monk's Bridge*, she was offered a studio contract. That would mean leaving drama school. In the 1920s Garbo had left the Royal Dramatic School early, but it was highly unusual. To make it even more difficult, Ingrid had been hired at the film studio by Gustav Molander, whose brother, Olof, was the new head of the Royal Dramatic Theatre and School. The fact that the Molanders were brothers was ironic; their competitiveness and jealousy bordered on hatred.

Olof was like an Old Testament patriarch who saw the true faith threatened by a false sect. He had begun to revitalize the Royal Dramatic Theatre, bringing it into one of its most creative periods. The year before, he had staged O'Neill's *Mourning Becomes Electra*, and he was preparing a new, more realistic version of Strindberg's *Dream Play*. He considered it unthinkable that a serious student of acting should give up *this* for his brother's fiefdom: mere money, celebrity, and the ersatz Swedish film industry.

If Ingrid had remained in school, she would have learned the disciplines of the theatre and might have become a great stage actress. At least that is what Olof Molander told her when she went in to tell him her decision not to return in September. He ranted at her, in turns threatening, flattering, and cajoling; but Ingrid's mind was made up.

Ingrid left with Olof's prophecies ringing in her ears and it is true that, although she took private drama lessons, she never did acquire the grounding of so many of her contemporaries that makes the Swedish acting community so brilliant. She had to rely on her instincts, on whatever technique she could pick up as she went along, and on her personality.

Ingrid had hardly finished *The Count of the Monk's Bridge* when she began her second film, *Ocean Breakers*, a melodramatic tale in which she played a fisherman's daughter, seduced and impregnated by a married minister. *Ocean Breakers* was considered one of the best Swedish films of the year, good enough to be sent as a Swedish entry to the Venice Film Festival in the summer of 1935.

'One did believe in her tenderness and faithfulness,' said the critic of the *Stockholm Daily*. Around her image on the screen there was a penumbra of goodness and caring that stayed no matter whom she played.

In her third film, *The Family Swedenhielms*, Ingrid played alongside Gösta Ekman, one of the most distinguished names in Swedish cinema, and Ingrid's idol. For the first time Ingrid saw how the image and the reality could be totally at odds. Ekman appeared a good family man, but he was homosexual and a drug addict. 'Ekman told Ingrid that it didn't matter what people say about you; what matters is that they talk about you,' Petter says. 'She learned that from her idol, and she said it all the time.'

In *The Family Swedenhielms* Ingrid was cast as the rich girlfriend of a brilliant scientist, played by Ekman. The scientist, falsely accused of forgery, turns down the Nobel Prize, but love and truth triumph, and Ingrid carries on, noble and selfless. She seemed to glow with character, as if her beauty grew out of intrinsic goodness. In *Walpurgis Night*, Ingrid's fourth film, her role had similarities to that in *Ocean Breakers*. Once again Ingrid found herself innocently involved in an illicit affair with her married boss. Her lover's wife becomes pregnant, gets an abortion, kills her blackmailer, and commits suicide. Loyal Ingrid is waiting when her lover returns from the Foreign Legion, where he has fled, and they marry and raise a family.

For her fifth film, a comedy called *On the Sunny Side*, Ingrid was cast as an orphan from a good family who marries a rich older gentleman and goes to live on his estate. Her husband, played by Lars Hanson, fears that his young bride may be bored by the tranquil country life. He invites her old flame, a bohemian writer played by Edvin Adolphson, to liven up Ingrid's days. The triangle creates enough friction to light a fire, but inevitably love and virtue triumph.

Day after day Ingrid journeyed out to the studios, playing one role after another. Fame was still a mystery that had not touched her. There is a time gap in a film career, and Ingrid had already completed three films when *The Count of the Monk's Bridge* premiered at Stockholm's Skandia Theatre on 21 January 1935. Ingrid received respectable reviews, but none of her early films were sensational successes, though she was becoming a figure of major importance at the studio, and a favourite among Stockholm moviegoers. Her name and face were familiar to audiences in the far villages of Sweden.

Even Hollywood was taking its first small notice of Ingrid Bergman. *Variety*, the entertainment industry's leading trade journal, noted in its review of *On the Sunny Side* on 16 September 1936, that Eva Bergh, played by Ingrid, was 'one of the better characterizations in the play . . . pretty and capable, rating a Hollywood berth.'

By far the most important of Ingrid's movies was *Intermezzo*, so much so that she considered it one of the three films on which her career was based (*Casablanca* and *Autumn Sonata* were the others). Not only was *Intermezzo* a much deserved success, but it indelibly defined Ingrid's film persona. Gösta Ekman played Holger Brandt, a world-famous violinist who falls in love with Anita Hoffman, a beautiful young pianist, played by Ingrid. Brandt leaves his family and runs off with Anita. The couple travel through Europe, where Anita serves as Brandt's accompanist. Much as she loves him, Anita realizes that their love cannot go on, so she steals away and Brandt returns to his eternally patient wife and family. His daughter is struck by a car when she runs across the street to meet her errant father, but she presumably recovers.

Gösta Ekman had by far the largest part in the film. *Intermezzo* should have been *his* film, but from the moment Ingrid appears on the screen *Intermezzo* is her film. The haunting, poignant strains of the theme music become her theme, the music of her soul. She haunts the screen even when her scenes are finished. 'It wasn't just a *pilsnerfilm* [beer movie],' Ingrid told a Swedish interviewer at the end of her career. 'It was so well written that you felt pity for everybody.'

The exquisite melancholy of *Intermezzo* is irresistible. When the film opened on 16 November 1936 at the Red Mill Theatre, the Stockholm *Daily News* reported that at the end the audience sat silent, not wanting to break the spell with applause.

Ingrid had enraptured the audience in what was becoming a familiar role. In three of her first six films Ingrid played an innocent woman involved in an illicit affair. In the fourth she was the catalyst for what could have developed into an adulterous affair. In these films her innocence is based on a mixture of ignorance and the exoneration of pure emotion. For her audience she sanctified behaviour that the moral dictates of her time considered slightly sordid or improper. It was a role she would play again and again.

At the end of *Intermezzo*, Ingrid is off somewhere, pursuing her career. This, too, became the ending in so many Ingrid Bergman films: Ingrid running off, getting on a plane, leaving a school, her daughter's home, a royal appointment, running off, running away, running on.

★　　★　　★

As her career blossomed, she kept her personal and professional lives totally separated. Like most actors and actresses, Ingrid was always talking about her dear friends in the theatrical world, praising them extravagantly in public; but she had no real friends in films; her personal life meant one person – Petter Lindstrom. Ingrid was Petter's *fästmö*, a peculiarly Swedish word that means steady girlfriend but with at least some presumption of sexual intimacy.

There were those who felt that Petter was too prideful about Ingrid, too much the man of the world bestowing a precious heritage on a young woman. Ingrid did not take Petter out to the studio, or to her film openings. He was as busy as Ingrid, studying medicine while continuing to teach and practise dentistry. In the evenings, when Ingrid was busy learning her lines for the next day's shooting, Petter was studying medical books. But at weekends they often went off on long hikes.

Ingrid was only mildly interested in what went on outside the walls of the film studio. She constantly talked to Petter about films and the theatre. She rarely read books, and she knew practically nothing about the darkening political situations. She rarely cooked, and she threw up her arms at the idea of running the house. Petter took care of all the practical side of her life, leaving her free to do what she did best. She could be honest and open with him. And in his company she often became a radiant, childlike person.

On 4 July 1935, Ingrid and Petter left Stockholm on their first trip together, to drive to northern Norway. They bought a diary before their trip and intended to save it to read again in old age. In a pension they had dinner and rented two rooms with a door between them but used only the smaller bedroom. He called her 'Kat' (kitten), and a kitten she was. During the second night of the trip a black cat entered their bedroom. Ingrid felt like a true cat and she wondered whether the second cat meant good luck. She wrote in her diary that the black cat had the considerable nerve of trying to take her place, nestled up against her lover's stomach. Next morning Ingrid and Petter woke up and he told her that her competitor was still lying in bed with them. And she thought that Petter was nice not only to her but to the other 'cat'.

They drove to the northern lights. With each day's journey the roads grew more empty, until they were practically alone. Petter took pictures of Ingrid sunning herself on the rocks. They pitched their tent one evening next to a rushing stream and did not crawl out until noon the next day. Petter went to help a couple with car trouble. As she sat waiting for him to return, Ingrid wrote: 'He does that maybe to impress me, and that he's really doing to a high degree. I think he's so sweet, and I do love him so much.'

Petter did not make a formal proposal; nor did he have to, for it seemed to both of them that their fates were intertwined. Her mother's lucky number was seven. Ingrid wanted to become formally engaged the following year on the seventh day of the seventh month. She wanted to do it in Hamburg, her mother's birthplace. And so early in July 1936 they drove to Hamburg.

Ingrid's worldly, sophisticated relatives, the Adlers, were doing well in the first years of the Thousand Year Reich. 'They all were there and they raised their arms, saying "Heil Hitler,"' remembers Petter. 'So did Ingrid. I just said hello and I said to her, "If you do that again I am returning to Sweden." But she said, "Heil Hitler" is just a greeting.'

'The day after we arrived, the morning before we were to have an engagement party, Frau Adler took me aside and said, "I have to explain why we have to change your name." Then Frau Adler said, "We can't have a Jewish name in our family."

'"Oh," I said. What could I say?

'"I don't ever want to hear you called Aron again," Ingrid said.

'I went along because though I had been called Aron all my life, my first name was really Petter, on both my birth certificate and my passport.'

On the seventh day of the seventh month, Ingrid and Petter stood in the same church where Ingrid's parents had been married. They exchanged platinum engagement rings that had two wavering lines engraved on them, growing apart but then always converging again.

Ingrid had come to Hamburg almost every summer since she was a child. She especially admired and trusted her mother's older sister, Frau Elsa Adler. Unlike her Swedish Uncle Otto and Aunt Hulda, her Aunt Mutti was a sophisticated woman. Petter felt differently; a man of stern moral fibre he was upset by his German relatives-to-be. Aunt Mutti was married to a wealthy French planter, who lived in Haiti; she hadn't liked the Caribbean island and had returned to Germany, leaving her two sons with their father. A good Swedish Lutheran, Petter believed that when you were married you were married. 'Ingrid was brought up in an atmosphere where sex wasn't important, and not only in her immediate family,' Petter reflected years later. 'When I came to visit, Frau Adler hadn't seen her husband for ten years. She was living with a man. He took us to show his bedroom. There was a bedroom with the biggest bed I've ever seen, the bed shaped like an enormous heart.'

What troubled Petter far more were the family's political attitudes. 'The man Frau Adler was living with was a high Nazi who was selling uniforms to the SS. Ingrid was brought in with these people who heiled Hitler and in Hamburg she would heil Hitler herself. Frau Adler had left a mark on her. I wanted her to read a book about Nazism, but she wouldn't. She had no real interest in politics.'

On 29 August, for Ingrid's twenty-first birthday, Petter bought her a spectacular present: a silver fox coat. Alone in her apartment, Ingrid opened the gift. She was not an extravagant woman and she hadn't dared to think that Petter would give her such a gift. Rushing to the phone to thank her fiancé, she tripped and broke her ankle.

At the Serafimer Hospital, Ingrid had many guests, including the actress Birgit Tengroth. The year before, Birgit had been in the hospital for a mysterious, though temporary, condition. Her face had swollen, and she had rested in bed looking despondently at her distorted image in a hand mirror. That was punishment enough, but what had truly exasperated her was the arrival of Ingrid in a yellow sweater as sunny as her mood. 'How happy I am,' Ingrid had said, hardly the desired greeting. 'This is for you.' She pushed a tin of cookies at Birgit.

War is war, and today Birgit brought Ingrid an enormous box of chocolates. 'Thank you,' Ingrid said. 'I've already got lots of boxes.' Just then Ingrid's lunch was brought in. 'How nice it smells,' Ingrid said, never one to belittle the obvious. 'And how dangerous it is with good food.'

Ingrid proceeded to eat a full meal, before turning to her knitting. 'How happy I am now, knitting a sweater for my cousin,' Ingrid said, as if there was nothing in the world she would like better than to be sitting here in a hospital bed, her plastered leg up in the air.

'I was [jealous] but it was not just a case of simple "*jalousie de métier*",' Birgit wrote later. 'I was envious of her coolness and freshness, envious that she was so bright and real, envious at her wonderful ability to meet problems with a ringing laugh. She said to me once, "I will never survive a bad review." But she never got a bad review. And she knew she wouldn't get one. How on earth did she do it? She had a secret knowledge about success of which every friend had to be envious.'

Ingrid had already far outdistanced her erstwhile rival. They were both members of a small company of leading actors and directors who formed a theatrical company to keep busy during the winter. Ingrid was busier than most of the others. She was the only member of the group in an active production at the film studio, yet not only did she take part in the first production, *Jean*, a political comedy by the Hungarian playwright Bus-Feketes, but she played the lead.

In a profession where jealousy abounds Ingrid was able to make people want to help her, to lift her high above them. Birgit Tengroth watched this spectacle in awed wonder. Dressed in a prim outfit and frilly mini-apron, and carrying a silver calling-card tray, Birgit played Ingrid's maid. 'She [Ingrid] played a young girl of good family who falls in love with her man servant but has character enough to renounce her love,' Birgit recalled. 'The part was made for her. Ingrid was a child of the secure world. She didn't make any mistakes with servants. And she had nerves as strong as wires from the Royal telegraph.'

Like almost everything else Ingrid touched, the play was a great success and ran well into the spring. By then Ingrid was busy at the studio with her new film, *Dollar*, a romantic comedy directed by Gustav Molander in which she played an actress married to a successful businessman.

Edvin Adolphson was one of her co-stars. The actor/director had become a problem for her, making passes with unrelenting persistence. One evening the film company arranged a formal dinner after the play. Any young star would have known that attendance at such an occasion was mandatory; not Ingrid.

When Ingrid told Adolphson that she was not going, he was furious. Ingrid wrote Petter that Adolphson 'evidently planned a lot for this evening. He is so in love that he is half nuts already.' She had something else on her mind: her wedding. She wanted it for 7 July, but as the film production lagged on, the date had to be changed to the 10th.

She wrote Petter from the studio twelve days before the wedding, saying that she was 'devilishly lonesome'. She wrote intense, passionate letters calling Petter her own golden kitten, the only man that she would ever love. She told him that she dreamed of the moment when he would kiss and embrace her. She implored him never to leave her, for she said that she would never leave him. She was madly in love.

'How many hours do I have left as a miss?' Ingrid asked as she stood on the verandah of the Lindstroms' old house in Stöde.

'Three,' Petter said. Although they became engaged in Hamburg they would be married in Stöde, symbolizing Ingrid's entry into Petter's family; he was the small town boy who had gone to the big city and made good.

Though Ingrid and Petter shared visions of a rich married life, they had grown up with profoundly different experiences of the way men

and women live together. Petter looked no further than his own
family; his father was patriarch; he had never seen his parents quarrel.
Ingrid could not remember what it was to have a mother and father
and a happy home life. She had seen how happy her father had been
with Greta, but Greta was more an older sister than a mother figure.
And that wasn't a marriage anyway. At Aunt Hulda's, Ingrid had
been part of a real family, but she was treated as the rich relative and
given a private room. In Germany, Ingrid had seen her beloved Aunt
Mutti living in an adulterous relationship. Throughout her young
life, Ingrid had been emotionally uprooted. For her words like
'fidelity', 'loyalty', and 'devotion' might not have quite the same
meanings that they had to Petter.

In those years the villagers of Sweden were the most ceremonial
of people, as if rituals well performed will placate the gods. By the
appointed hour of 4 p.m. on 10 July 1937, the church was full. This
was one of the biggest events in Stöde's history. Villagers and
dignitaries squeezed into the pews. A few younger people stood
against the walls. All were in their best clothes; most of them had
known Petter since childhood. He looked elegant in morning dress.
As for Ingrid, she could have stepped off the screen, playing an
ethereal bride of transcendent beauty. She wore a long white silk
gown that fell to her white shoes. Her light-brown hair was crowned
by a Juliet cap from which flowed a veil of silky white mesh. In
her arm she carried a spray of orchids, lilies of the valley, and
stephanotises. Although the wedding was supposed to be private,
one young reporter, Barbro ('Bang') Alving, had shown up. Bang
thought that the congregation 'sometimes behaved as if it were in a
theatre', at this wedding in which 'the most popular film star in
Sweden was no longer Ingrid Bergman but Mrs Ingrid Lindstrom'.

The newlyweds went south on a honeymoon trip to Norway and
then to England. In Stockholm they discovered their picture on the
cover of the *Daily News*; they were shown leaving the church in
Stöde. 'MOST BEAUTIFUL AND PRIVATE BRIDE IN SWEDEN SHOWS A LACK
OF PUBLIC PRESENCE' was the headline of Bang's long article. If the
camera was one friend that never betrayed Ingrid, publicity was the
other. 'I think I should send this Bang a picture postcard,' Petter
remembers her saying. 'She may become important.' For all her
unspoiled qualities, Ingrid had the attributes of a politician, courting
her constituents. Mixed motives are often the most durable, and
Bang soon became a friend.

There was a seemingly guileless quality to the public Ingrid, and
her new husband didn't know quite what to make of it. He knew
the private Ingrid, who, as he remembered years later, was fiercely

jealous of Birgit Tengroth and Signe Hasso and other actresses. It didn't matter that Ingrid had outdistanced them as a movie star; she still, as Petter saw it, felt threatened. Petter knew an Ingrid, too, who could say the strangest things. According to him, a few weeks after they were married she turned to him and said, 'I'd like to make love with at least one man of each race.'

CHAPTER 3

DESTINED FOR HOLLYWOOD

'Men make women helpless by deciding and telling them what to do,' Ingrid reflected years later. 'Men in my life taught me to be dependent, beginning with my father, and after that Uncle Otto, who didn't want me to become an actress, and then Petter, even before our engagement – not that it was Petter's fault. I was the one who asked him for advice and help in those early days.'

Men had not taught Ingrid to be dependent as much as to create the illusion of dependency. Like many widowed or divorced fathers, Justus Bergman had lavished affection on his only daughter; Ingrid had learned that the best way to get things from her father was to make him think everything was his idea. As for Uncle Otto, here was a weak man full of moral precepts; she had listened politely to her uncle and then done as she pleased.

She'd learned to use people without appearing to use them, while maintaining an innocent façade. Much of this was done not consciously but instinctively. She grasped the fact that people in the arts enjoyed having protégés, boasting that they had 'made' a career. Ingrid had already had several mentors, among them Karin Swanström and Gustav Molander, both of whom at an appropriate moment she was willing to discard.

Petter was also her mentor. He was a strong, dominant man. He was also a slave to love. He had even given up his name Aron at Ingrid's demand. Ingrid had Petter help her to create *herself*, the person who became Ingrid Bergman. She had him chide her for overeating, slouching, and wrinkling her forehead. She even devised a signal so that he could alert her if she was talking too much at a party. In those early years Petter was only doing what Ingrid asked him to do. With their success in evolving Ingrid's persona, they were creating a star far different from the woman he thought he had married.

Petter handled the household affairs, looked after the money, and managed the house.

'I had the strong feeling that he admired her a great deal,' says Elsa Holm, a close friend, whose husband, Cyril, was Ingrid's lawyer. 'It was not my ideal of communication between man and wife. He admired her. And I wouldn't have liked my husband to be like that.'

If it is possible to love a woman too much, then he loved Ingrid too much, or rather her image, and he could no more communicate with that image than talk to one on the screen.

Ingrid couldn't stand unpleasantness, and was prepared to let others, including Petter, take the blame for her mistakes. Petter was forceful in protecting Ingrid, but he did not go to the studios, the openings, the movie parties, largely because Ingrid had segregated her life. 'Ingrid made nine pictures in Sweden,' Petter says. 'I never visited a set. I never met any of the actors and actresses. I never saw a contract. I never had anything to do with her films.'

In fact, in Ingrid's next film, *A Woman's Face*, Petter gave a technical hand to his wife's career. Ingrid played a young woman whose face had been hideously burned in a fire. Petter built a brace for her to wear inside her mouth, which distorted her left cheek. 'Gustav Molander, the director, wanted one side of the face normal, the other distorted,' remembered Dahlqvist, the cameraman. 'So the husband built this thing inside her mouth to twist her face. It punctured the inside of her mouth, so he had to change it.' According to Petter, his invention was not the problem; it was that Ingrid insisted on wearing the device all the time.

A Woman's Face, later remade in Hollywood starring Joan Crawford, was a film that Ingrid very much wanted to make. As Anna Holm, she portrayed a woman scarred internally far more than externally, a mean-spirited, graceless, mistrustful leader of a gang of blackmailers. It was an extraordinary role and Ingrid gave a performance touched with brilliance. As the scarred and tortured Anna, Ingrid holds her hand up to her face, shielding her ugliness from the world. Her back is slightly hunched, her head tilted. She sneers at the world, her pain palpable. Even after the successful operation, Ingrid holds her gleaming countenance in check, psychic scars still visible, a gash deeper than the physical. And then as she slowly enters into life and love and human concerns, her beauty begins to light up her face. A year later, when *A Woman's Face* played in New York, the *World-Telegram* wrote, 'Ingrid Bergman is another Garbo . . . as good as Garbo in her earliest efforts.'

In order to do *A Woman's Face*, a role that went so much against her usual casting, Ingrid had to agree to make *Only One Night*, a film that she considered 'junk', but one that was perfect typecasting. Ingrid had become known in Sweden as the *herrgårdsflicka*, the manor house girl, a phrase that may have been coined by Rune Waldekranz in a review. The manor house girl was an upper-class woman living on a country estate, beautiful but seemingly untouchable. *Only One Night* begins at a travelling circus where a handsome roustabout, played by Edvin Adolphson, leaves his mistress to claim his inheritance as the illegitimate son of an ageing, wealthy aristocrat. On his father's estate, Adolphson falls in love with Ingrid, who rebukes his crude drunken attempt at seduction. Realizing that he would be happier in the circus, he leaves the estate to marry his old sweetheart.

Only One Night was largely turgid melodrama, but Ingrid's mere presence seemed enough to make a film memorable. Her beauty was now fully mature, a breathtaking, ethereal beauty that seemed to exist beyond time and space. It was a beauty that would have proved irresistible to most leading men, and Adolphson's seduction scenes may have existed not only on the screen. 'Adolphson put his two arms around her to protect her,' said another actor in the film, 'but I knew his motives. I thought it was awful. He was well known as just taking the girls. He was big and strong and she fell for it. Ingrid always wanted someone strong.'

'I remember when Petter and Ingrid were newly married and we went out to their flat,' says Elsa Holm. 'Ingrid was upset because Edvin Adolphson was trying to flirt with her. She told Petter that he should say that if they were going to continue with the film he should act properly. She was very upset. And she told Petter to take care of things. She didn't want to meet the problem herself. She pushed Petter to do it.'

Ingrid was one of the most popular stars in Sweden, but her aspirations extended beyond Scandinavia. Hollywood was the greatest capital of cinema, but the new Germany was a major and growing power in filmmaking, seeking to supplant Hollywood in the world's imagination. Ingrid knew German, indeed, she was half German. Early in 1938, despite what Petter calls his strong opposition, Ingrid signed a three-picture contract with UFA, the major German film company. Her first role was to be in a fluffy, rather mindless comedy, *The Four Companions*, but then she would star in a role she richly coveted: Charlotte Corday, the eighteenth-century Frenchwoman who assassinated Jean-Paul Marat, the revolutionary leader.

Ingrid was pregnant, and another woman might have taken time off. She saw no reason, however, why she couldn't have her career and her child. When she arrived in Berlin to begin filming, Hitler's troops had just marched into Austria, German planes were flying against Loyalist Spain; George Orwell wrote in that summer of 1938 that it was an age of 'rubber truncheons and concentration camps'.

But Ingrid noted little – and understood even less – of what was going on around her.

She was not the only Swedish actress to make films in Germany. Sarah Leander was a major UFA star. Kristina Söderbaum, who later made the notorious *Jew Süss*, had married a German director and was more German than Swedish. Signe Hasso made a film for the Germans as well.

In later years Ingrid would say she had been frightened by what she had seen in Berlin. In her autobiography she claimed that when Fröhlich, the director, took her to a Nazi rally with Hitler, she refused to give the Nazi salute.

Petter has a different recollection of his wife's attitude. 'Ingrid knew that Goebbels was not only Minister of Information but the head of the studio. When Frau Adler took her to a Nazi meeting to hear Goebbels in Hamburg, she said it was a fantastic speech.'

Ingrid wanted to get on with her work. It was not an unusual posture for an actress. Movie stars are damned if they take political stands, pilloried for abusing their fame; and they are damned if they remain silent, indifferent citizens selfishly hoarding their celebrity. However, Ingrid's image made audiences want to believe that she stood on the right side regarding the great issues of her day.

The Four Companions was by no means a piece of Nazi propaganda. The film chronicled the adventures of four young women in an advertising agency, and was thin gruel, indeed, for an actress with Ingrid's aspirations. For the shooting Ingrid's stomach was bound up like a maiden's foot in imperial China. One weekend when Petter joined her, he and a clearly pregnant Ingrid walked the streets of Berlin, Petter surreptitiously taking pictures of the Third Reich, posing Ingrid in front of Jewish-owned stores slashed with swastikas, and other evidence of the new Germany. The shooting could not end soon enough for him.

No more than a month after their return to Sweden, on 20 September 1938, Ingrid gave birth to a daughter. They christened the baby Friedel Pia, the first name in honour of Ingrid's mother, the middle name taken from the initials of Petter, Ingrid, and Aron. Ingrid had never lived in a home with a baby. She had entered into her pregnancy with nonchalance, not thinking that a baby might dramatically change her life. She was not particularly maternal. She herself later admitted she was not a good mother to Friedel Pia. Studio photographers took romanticized pictures of the star with her child, but Petter caught one shot that came closer to the reality of Ingrid the young mother. The star whom the cameras so adored stood there a bewildered young woman, appearing almost a child bride, the baby crooked awkwardly in her arms. It was as if she did not know what to do with this tiny bundle.

Ingrid could always flee into her roles, exchanging the tawdry robes of reality for finer things. After the birth of Friedel Pia, she was planning to return to Germany for another film. She imagined that she could float between film capitals, above the clang of swords and the martial shouts. She could not see that early in 1939, a film made in Berlin was a political act.

Petter was obsessed with the idea that his wife should not return to Nazi Germany. 'I had told her not to go before she went the first time,' Petter says. 'This time I told her, If you go back to Berlin it's the end of our marriage.' Petter understood Ingrid well enough to know that the one way to prevent her fulfilling the contract was to find better film prospects elsewhere. Thus without telling Ingrid he contacted Helmer Enwall, a leading theatrical booking agent, and asked him to find Ingrid roles in England or America.

Ingrid was already known in America, at least among those who searched the film world for talent. When *Intermezzo* opened at the Cinema de Paris in New York in December 1937, the film and its female lead made a decided impression. 'It is poignant, full of pathos, and above all, has shown, in Ingrid Bergman, a talented, beautiful actress,' *Variety* noted. 'Miss Bergman's star is destined for Hollywood.'

Ingrid always credited Kay Brown with discovering her for America. In the late 1930s and early 1940s, Kay worked in New York as movie producer David O. Selznick's East Coast story editor. Ingrid loved to tell how Kay had first learned about *Intermezzo* from an enthusiastic Swedish elevator boy in her office building at 230 Park Avenue. Kay does not remember the episode, but it did not require the divine intervention of a young Swede for Selznick International to stumble across Ingrid Bergman. 'As I recall it, David sent one of his famous memorandums to the office saying to look at foreign pictures for remake purposes,' Kay says. 'Elsa Neuberger, my assistant, and I went and saw *Intermezzo*. I didn't appreciate the story, but there was this wonderful girl in it.'

If anyone can be credited with first discovering Ingrid for America, it is not Kay Brown at all but a woman whose role has been completely forgotten: Jenia Reissar. Jenia was Selznick's London representative, a position that she held into the 1950s. Kay wrote to Selznick on 26 July 1938: 'Miss Reissar has long been after me to look at a picture in which Ingrid Bergman appears. Today, I had the opportunity of seeing *Intermezzo* . . . Quite frankly, I don't know what to say about Miss Bergman. She is absolutely enchanting in some parts of the picture and so terribly ugly in other parts . . . The story of *Intermezzo* is very contrived but . . . if you are interested in Miss Bergman after seeing the picture, I have got all the data on her in the New York office.'

Kay shipped a copy of the film west to Selznick the next day. In the movie industry, the term 'genius' is an accolade that is bestowed with about the same frequency that the Boy Scouts award merit badges. But Selznick deserved the term as much as anyone. Still in his thirties, he had already been a major producer, a top studio executive at RKO and MGM, and now, as head of his own studio, Selznick International, he was in the midst of producing the most anticipated film in Hollywood history, *Gone With the Wind*. The phrase, 'Produced by David O. Selznick' over a film's title was almost a guarantee of a quality production. He was proud of his extraordinary attention to details, be they the publicity stills for *A Tale of Two Cities*, Marlene Dietrich's hair in *The Garden of Allah*, or the sound of the surf in *A Star Is Born*.

Selznick was enthusiastic about all the elements of *Intermezzo*: the script, the director, and Ingrid. 'Keep it most confidential,' he wrote in a memo on 15 August, 'but so that you can be guided, I want to make a deal to remake the picture; for the director; and for the girl.'

Selznick considered it an enviable prospect to remake *Intermezzo* with its female star. The producer was so enthusiastic about Ingrid that he wired Kay Brown the next day that he 'would be still interested [in Bergman] even if she does not start until next year'. Selznick's personality was richly laced with paranoia, however, and he was already figuring out what could go wrong. Having noticed that the credits gave top billing to Gustav Molander and Gösta Stevens, Selznick wired that 'a cold shudder has just run through me on the realization that maybe we are dealing for the wrong girl. Maybe the girl we are after is Gösta Stevens.'

When Selznick set his mind on something, he spewed out memos and directives and ideas with frenetic energy, forging ahead heedless of time or cost. Within three days he learned that Svensk Filmindustri wanted $25,000 for the rights to *Intermezzo*. He wasn't about to wait until he had formally bought the rights. Within the space of a few weeks he had thrown out the names of many possible actors and actresses for the film: Charles Boyer, Leslie Howard, William Powell, or Ronald Colman for the lead; Nazimova or Gloria Swanson for the wife; Lionel Barrymore for the violinist's manager; and Freddie Bartholomew for the son. A translator was hired at seventy-five dollars a week, and an English draft of the original screenplay written by 24 September.

The Swedish film was shown to representatives of Joseph Breen, the industry censor, by Val Lewton, the West Coast story editor. The Production Code administrator's main concern was that 'the "girl's punishment" will have to be made a little heavier'.

Ingrid heard about the *Intermezzo* offer through Jenia Reissar in London when she was eight months pregnant and Jenia cabled Kay in New York: 'BERGMAN NOT KEEN ANYWAY CANNOT WORK NEXT SIX MONTHS AS HAVING BABY AND MUST MAKE LAST PICTURE FOR UFA.'

In late September, Reissar journeyed to Stockholm, hoping to sign Ingrid to star and Molander to direct *Intermezzo*, to finalize the deal for the film with Svensk Filmindustri, and to explore signing another young Swedish actress: Signe Hasso. The hotels were almost empty of foreigners. Placards in the streets announced that the British fleet was mobilizing. Newspaper headlines stated that Hitler demanded an answer from Prague by 2 p.m. In the middle of Reissar's meeting with Selznick's Swedish attorney, the lawyer received a call saying that he was to join his artillery unit in southern Sweden the next day. Even neutral Sweden was mobilizing.

'This feeling of uneasiness is beginning to engulf even me!' Reissar wrote Kay. Nonetheless, she managed to buy the rights to *Intermezzo* for $12,500. She thought that Signe was a natural for America, but she had less luck with Ingrid. She met with Petter, who told her 'it was pretty useless to talk business with her [Ingrid] at the moment, as she was not interested in pictures away from home, but that she did want to meet me . . . He made me promise, though, not to worry her by insisting upon some answer or discussing terms.'

In the afternoon Reissar went to the Lindstroms' residence. 'It was as soon as she got home with the baby,' Reissar remembers. 'She was so proud and delighted with her baby. She brought it in to show me. She said she couldn't come to America or consider anything at the moment. She said the baby must be older. I told her they were thinking of casting Leslie Howard for *Intermezzo*. She was mad about him, and that was one of the things that I think made a great impression on her and she wanted to work with him. But she was still at the stage of not talking business.'

'It is a very bad moment psychologically to talk to the girl,' Reissar wrote Kay. Molander had been pressing Ingrid to sign. He had told her that his deal to direct the American *Intermezzo* depended on her going with him. Ingrid had resisted Molander's entreaties and Jenia assured Ingrid that the Molander negotiations were totally separated.

'Under no circumstances would she consider another picture engagement until 1940 except in Sweden,' Reissar wrote Kay on 4 October. 'She was very flattered by Mr Selznick's interest, and I think genuinely so. Though she seemed very scared of Hollywood she is anxious to go, but in a new role and preferably *not Intermezzo* . . . I think the time to talk to that young woman would be after she has finished her UFA picture and got back into her working mood. At the moment she is quite satisfied with her home and her husband and her child.'

Here once again was an Ingrid who could appear timid, yet was sure enough of her professional status to ask the Selznick people to wait. And she was right. Selznick was no longer interested in Hasso or Molander, but he still wanted to sign Ingrid, even if she couldn't co-star in *Intermezzo*. He was not the only Hollywood producer interested in her; Hal Wallis of Warner Brothers had been in Stockholm recently and had seen *A Woman's Face*.

Selznick was having a devilish time casting his new movie. He had even thought of getting Jascha Heifetz, the great violinist, to play the lead. He tried to get Loretta Young, but that didn't work out, and by January he had reluctantly concluded that 'there is seemingly no way of casting it properly, apart from showmanship, that would warrant the cost of the picture. I am commencing to feel that the way to handle this subject is to wait for Bergman, ballyhooing her debut in it.' He was, by his own admission, getting 'rather frantic . . . because we have no picture planned between *Wind* and *Rebecca* and *Intermezzo* seems much the most likely.' Selznick was a gambler. He didn't care about Ingrid's commitment to do Charlotte Corday for UFA. He decided to push her to come to Hollywood almost immediately, even if that risked losing her for good.,

In London, Jenia Reissar was having an impossible time trying to deal with Ingrid by phone. She wrote Kay: 'To almost every question I put to her she replied: "Perhaps. I am not sure. I will write." *And that is all* – except that she *doesn't* write.' But Reissar's persistence paid off.

The next time she called Stockholm, Ingrid was enthusiastic. She was even more interested when, late in January 1939, she learned that her role in UFA's *Charlotte Corday* was cancelled for political reasons. (In retrospect, it is hard to see how a sympathetic portrait of a demagogue's assassin could ever have been made in Nazi Germany.)

Ingrid immediately wrote Reissar that she was available either in the autumn of 1939 or the following year to make a film for $3000 a week with a six-week minimum. But Selznick wanted Bergman *now*. He sent Kay to Europe to try to close a deal. As Kay was braving the Atlantic in late winter, cables were going back and forth between

London and Stockholm, further refining the details of Ingrid's contract. Reissar wired Ingrid, asking her to come to London to negotiate
the final details. Ingrid was not amused. 'I am very astonished –
and not quite pleasantly astonished – about your sudden changing
of dispositions,' Ingrid wrote, flatly insisting that Kay come to
Sweden.

In the second week of February, Kay flew into Stockholm through
a snowstorm. If there was any doubt of the seriousness of Kay's
quest, she had beside her a London lawyer, Joynson Hicks, to handle
the legal details. Kay had girded herself against the winter winds in
her inevitable fur coat, but she had become sick in the unpressurized
airplane. Her neck glands had swollen, and she sat in a dressing gown
in her suite at the Grand Hotel, hardly the image of the high-powered
Hollywood representative.

Kay had received no call from Ingrid and Petter, but suddenly
there was a knock at the door and there stood 'these two lovely
people. She looked absolutely beautiful. She had on a beaver coat
and hat, and was carrying yellow and blue flowers for me.'

'Welcome to Sweden,' Ingrid said, and then apologized that she
and Petter had a dinner engagement and would not be able to stay.
If the Lindstroms were apprehensive about the meeting it was a
shrewd move not to be slavishly attentive to Kay. Before they left,
however, Petter called a woman doctor and arranged for Kay to
receive treatment. The next day Petter laughingly admitted that
they had had no dinner plans. They merely wanted to take Kay's
measure.

Though she acted indifferent, Ingrid was very excited about the
prospect of making films in Hollywood. Kay had promised her
William Wyler as director and Leslie Howard as co-star, two names
that she knew and admired. Petter was even more committed to
getting Ingrid away from Germany and German films.

With Ingrid's cool Swedish demeanour and Petter's savvy, Kay
had no idea how badly they wanted the negotiations to succeed;
indeed, as she wrote the Selznick office, 'when I arrived in Sweden
I found Miss Bergman so utterly confused about our various requests,
changes of dates, etc., that it looked as though there was no chance
to make a deal whatsoever.' Ingrid and Petter weren't sure how
strong Kay's mandate was to bring Ingrid to Hollywood, so for three
days negotiations went on between Helmer Enwall – the Swedish
booking agent contacted by Petter – Cyril Holm, Ingrid's attorney,
and Kay and her London lawyer. Ingrid sat watching, saying
little.

Kay realized that 'Ingrid wanted to go but under her own conditions'. Kay wanted Ingrid to sign a standard seven-year contract, a gilded form of indentured servitude, which would give Selznick the right each year to drop her. Soon after the negotiations Kay wrote Daniel O'Shea, Selznick's top executive: 'I suggested that her husband look over our draft contract.' According to Kay, Petter would not agree to a seven-year contract. Petter, however, says that he was not present at the negotiations and had nothing to do with the contract. In later years, Ingrid and Kay both asserted that what Ingrid signed was a one-picture contract with an option for a second picture. Ingrid did, indeed, sign for *Intermezzo* at $20,000 ($2500 a week for eight weeks). But the contract also gave Selznick the option to make one or two pictures a year with Ingrid for five more years, with the salary increasing finally to $40,000 a picture. At the same time, the contract gave Ingrid the right to make two outside pictures a year in a language other than English. Ingrid, then, had made a serious commitment to a life of international stardom, hoping to make at least two more films in Germany, films in Sweden, and of course films for the next five years in Hollywood.

Selznick didn't like Ingrid's name. He cabled Kay at the Grand Hotel that once the contract was signed, she might explain to Ingrid about the 'SOMEWHAT UNATTRACTIVE AND EVEN SEMITIC SOUND OF NAME TO ANGLO-SAXON AUDIENCE'. A week later, when Selznick still had not heard about a possible name change, he cabled Kay again: 'I DO HOPE NOTHING WENT WRONG WITH THE CABLE.'

Kay said later that Ingrid was as innocent as a young child. It was as if Ingrid and Petter were living in a land of gingerbread houses. In fact, at the age of twenty-three, Ingrid was already the veteran of eleven movies; in her circumscribed world she was a sophisticated professional. Kay did in fact catch glimpses of a more worldly Ingrid. In Stockholm, Kay had talked to Signe Hasso. 'I was afraid that Bergman might find out that I had seen Hasso,' Kay wrote Selznick, 'and so casually brought her into the conversation to which Bergman replied that although she did not know her, she knew that she was an actress in Sweden. Bergman has a wonderful quality of arrogance about her which I personally like.'

Kay claims that she almost tried to talk Ingrid out of going, telling her that she had a beautiful baby and a fine home.

That was a curious remark for Selznick's representative to make. After all, Kay was not about to return to the States empty-handed to tell Selznick that she would not be a partner in subverting Ingrid's innocence. Kay's 'terrible qualms about what I was doing to this

wonderful young couple' were not so much disingenuous as paying
proper obeisance to that 'childlike air of innocence' that was the
essence of Ingrid's appeal.

'Well if there are people as nice as you in Hollywood, then I'm
sure I shall like it, so I shall go, and take the risk,' Ingrid responded,
perfectly in character.

Before a month was up, Kay learned that when it came to her
career, Ingrid was strong-willed and unyielding. Because of problems
on Selznick's big film, *Gone With the Wind*, Leslie Howard was no
longer available to play the lead in *Intermezzo*. Charles Boyer was a
possibility, if the starting date could be postponed until June. Ingrid
cabled back: 'UTTERLY DISAPPOINTED BASIS OF AGREEMENT ABSOLUTELY
DESTROYED . . . INSIST ON HOWARD AS PROMISED OR EQUAL STAR.
REMIND YOU THAT HAVE ALREADY SACRIFICED TWO PICTURES EUROPE
FOR HOWARD INTERMEZZO   GREETINGS.'

Ingrid was partially placated when Howard was reinstated as her
co-star, but she was ready with other requests. Petter, the family
emissary, says that at her request he wrote a long letter to Kay.
Petter's English was far from fluent, but he made it clear how Ingrid
should be greeted in America. He worried about people bothering
Ingrid: 'My wife, who since her childhood has been left to her own
devices, avoids preferably foreign people and society life . . . In
Hollywood, she is afraid, that a similar crowd of Scandinavian people
and nowadays even German people will disturb her, invite her etc.'
He wanted her to have proper lodgings: 'This may be situated near
the studio, if possible on a height and with some outlook. No luxury
apartment! More than 2 á 3 rooms might not be necessary. On a
hotel she might be disturbed.' Petter says that Ingrid wanted to do
nothing anti-German: 'She will, of course, not even in the future,
work in film, which has any tendency or propaganda against a
country, which has taken her services and showed her hospitality
. . . Of course, I will be very glad if we could inform the UFA that
you have let us know, that Selznick Int. for inst. does not intend to
give out German Hostile films.'

Kay's approach was to try to soothe Ingrid, and not worry her
over a possible later starting date for *Intermezzo*. Ingrid decided that
she wanted to sail to New York on the ship with John Hay ('Jock')
Whitney, the immensely wealthy socialite and vice-president of Selznick's new company. Whitney decided that he didn't want to spend
time alone with Selznick's new discovery, and that was a problem
too. 'IF WE ARE GOING TO HAVE TO HANDLE HER WITH AS MUCH USE OF
GLOVES AS THIS MAYBE WE SHOULD SEND HER BACK TO THE CUTGLASS
FACTORY', Selznick cabled Kay.

But finally Ingrid set out from Stockholm, leaving her husband and six-month-old baby behind. Her plans were to complete the filming of *Intermezzo* by July. But her future in Germany still lay ahead of her as well.

CHAPTER 4

'A FIGURE TO TAKE INTO ACCOUNT'

Ingrid sailed on the *Queen Mary* from Southampton. The New York newspapers and columnists would have vied for a story about the arrival of the newest 'Selznick star', but when the ship docked in New York on 20 April 1939, only Kay Brown greeted Ingrid and quickly shuttled her to the Chatham Hotel.

Selznick had told Kay that he wanted no publicity. He was still thinking of changing Ingrid's name. Moreover, he sensed that the public was satiated with the endless hyperbole about new foreign stars. They came in an endless parade – Pola Negri, Anna Sten, Miliza Korjus, Luise Rainer, Luli Deste, Isa Miranda, Tilly Losch, Lya Lys – to be promoted, photographed, and in most cases forgotten. 'I think that the best thing to do would be to import her quietly into the studio,' Selznick wrote Kay. He had an indisputable genius for publicity. Even before meeting Ingrid, he had hit upon the essential ingredient that would make her unique. He would sell her by seeming not to sell her. He would tinker with her name, if need be let her be Ingrid Bergman in Europe and something catchier in the States, but he would nonetheless promote her 'naturalness'.

Ingrid knew nothing of this, and if she found it strange that there wasn't someone to interview her on her arrival, she didn't say anything. She had little time to worry, for Kay kept her very busy. At dinner parties Ingrid was a hit. Kay delighted in setting her up with what she called 'eligibles', a service that Petter would have found less than amusing. One extremely wealthy escort was ready to hire a plane so that he and Ingrid could fly over New York. Ingrid said no to that offer, and to others as well.

In talking of her past, Ingrid usually emphasized the simpler aspects of her life, but what was striking was how she could go happily from the mundane to the exclusive, from beer to champagne, from hot dogs to caviar. Ingrid's discovery was that emporium of the culinary arts known as Schrafft's. She had the appetite of a lumberjack, and her favourite new American food was the hot fudge sundae. The Selznick people did not like their angelic property slurping down vanilla ice cream and fudge at Schrafft's. 'I got in trouble taking her to Schrafft's,' says Elsa Neuberger. 'She was simple in the way few actresses are. She wanted to know about America. She wanted to go on a bus, so I took her on a bus.'

Ingrid couldn't get enough of plays and movies. She went to the smash hit *Tobacco Road*, Erskine Caldwell's steamy excursion into the byways of poor Southerners. She could not make out the hillbilly dialect, a handicap she probably shared with some of the New Yorkers in the audience. The next night she went to see Raymond Massey playing *Abe Lincoln in Illinois*. The baroque nineteenth-century language was as foreign to her as Swahili. She was a foreigner in America, speaking a strange tongue. In many respects she had been a foreigner all her life. She had been brought up half German in a Sweden that had very few foreigners. She had married not an urban Stockholm man but a man with the puritan values of small town Sweden. She had just made a film in Germany, where she had often strained for the subtleties of language and gesture. Now she was in the United States, for her the strangest land of all.

Kay travelled westward with her by train. A Wellesley graduate with a husband and two children, she was the classic 'career woman' of her time. Born thirty years later, she would probably have become a producer. She had pestered Selznick to buy the rights to *Gone With the Wind*. She considered Ingrid her discovery and she watched over her jealously, but with affection.

In Los Angeles the Selznicks had offered to take Ingrid into their house for a few days – an extraordinary gesture. David and Irene Selznick almost never had overnight guests at their Georgian-style white brick house on Summit Drive, near the Beverly Hills Hotel. Now in the midst of finishing *Gone With the Wind*, Selznick was under considerable strain. Mixing booze and Benzedrine, he was functioning on very little sleep.

The *Super Chief* arrived in Pasadena on Saturday 6 May 1939. Ingrid was surprised when Selznick didn't meet her at the station, an offence more to her European sense of civility than to her ego. A publicity man drove her to the Selznicks' home.

Ingrid and Kay walked across the lawn to where Irene sat listening to a horse race on the radio.

Ingrid said hello, but Irene motioned her to be quiet. Irene was less than delighted at having had Ingrid foisted upon her. The daughter of Louis B. Mayer, the early film mogul, this dark-haired young mother with sharp, narrow eyes was a snob in a subtle and distinctly Hollywood way. This was a society based not on heredity but on success. Out here success could come and go; it might even come to this tall, big-boned woman who was squatting on her lawn.

Ingrid sat quietly. Finally, Irene greeted her and offered her some food, the Jewish hello.

As Ingrid went to her room to freshen up for lunch, her hostess noticed that she had only one suitcase and asked when her trunks would arrive. Ingrid did not understand the word 'trunk'. She finally made it clear to Irene that this one suitcase comprised her entire luggage. She had come to Hollywood for three months to make a film, and on the set would be provided with a wardrobe.

Irene changed the subject to the dinner party the Selznicks were giving the following Saturday night in Ingrid's honour. Ingrid explained that her suitcase contained an evening dress that she would wear to the party. Irene told her that the party was 'informal', one of the more unfathomable words in the bizarre lexicon of Hollywood; but as Ingrid appeared determined to wear her evening gown, an insistence based on necessity, Irene called the guests and told them to dress 'formally'.

That evening Ingrid made her first sally into the Hollywood world, at a dinner party at Don the Beachcomber's, a prominent restaurant that looked like a set for a Hawaiian musical. The dinner was hosted by Elsa Maxwell, an inveterate celebrity seeker. She didn't know who Ingrid was, an ignorance she shared with practically everyone else in Hollywood. But Elsa did not corral the famous by supping with largely unknown Swedish actresses with limited English. While Irene tried to keep up a conversation with her guest, she painfully noted that Elsa hardly spoke to Ingrid, nor did Grace Moore, Miriam Hopkins, and Richard Barthelmess, the three stars who shared the table. Later, when Ingrid remembered that dinner, she did what she always did, splicing away the unpleasantness, remembering only the exotic coconut drinks and a few snippets of conversation.

After dinner, the group went to Miriam Hopkins's house for a screening of a yet unreleased film. Ingrid was still most anxious to meet the mysterious David O. Selznick, but as she sat on a cushion in the living room, she soon became lost in the performances on the screen.

A hand grasped her shoulder. She was told that Selznick was in the kitchen and would see her.

Finally she was going to meet the man who would make her a star. In the kitchen, Selznick was seated at a table, devouring food. He looked like a neurotic teddy bear who had been dressed in Savile Row.

Selznick took one long look at his newest discovery and complained about her height and her Germanic-sounding name.

Two months before, Selznick had been concerned about the 'semitic' sound of Bergman; now he found it too German. Ingrid's relationship with Germany and the German film industry was a legitimate concern, since Petter had written Kay for assurance that Selznick would not do anti-German films.

Selznick did not go into detail about the German situation. What was so striking about this first meeting, as remembered by Ingrid, was that it was devoid of social graces. The two got down to business immediately, as if they were agents discussing a client. Ingrid might have appeared shy, but when she was discussing her career she was single-minded. She insisted that Selznick did not change her name; she saw herself as an international star, doing films in Sweden, Germany, and probably England.

According to Ingrid, Selznick complained about her teeth, and her thick eyebrows, but Ingrid insisted that she would not change them. She also remembered telling him: 'Let the movie come out, and then if people decide they like me, you can do the publicity and I'll give interviews. But let me try and creep into the affection of the American public.' To this, Selznick purportedly meekly concurred.

Since, months before, Selznick had already decided not to publicize Ingrid, the words that Ingrid claimed were probably Selznick's. In later years the producer bitterly contested Ingrid's assertions that the wearing of simple make-up was her idea. In 1945 he wrote an angry letter reminding her of his 'revolutionary instructions about your make-up and about leaving you alone in all your pristine beauty, eyebrows and all (although I now read in the press that you had a job with the studio to keep yourself intact).'

For the Saturday evening party much of Hollywood's elite had been chauffeured up to the Selznick home. The big stars: Gary Cooper, Katharine Hepburn, Tyrone Power, Greer Garson, Joan Fontaine. The big directors: King Vidor, Victor Fleming, Ernst Lubitsch. Almost everywhere Ingrid looked, there was a famous face. In most social circles it would have been considered not only polite but obligatory to talk to the honoured guest, but in Hollywood life rotates around the established stars, and almost no one talked to Ingrid. The guests appraised her coldly as if the Selznicks had set down an exotic piece of artwork in their living room; the women, in particular, were less than charitable in their evaluation.

'We have enough trouble getting jobs as it is,' Joan Bennett said. 'Do they have to import kitchen maids?'

'She's such a big peasant,' said Lubitsch.

It was a measure of Ingrid's uniqueness that her mere presence created such virulence. Most of the people in the room had their origins in the ghettos of Russia or Poland, the farms of the Plains states, the small towns of the Southwest. They reeked of insecurity and delighted in throttling the aspirations of such as this Swedish interloper. If Selznick was right about his new discovery, then what would happen to them?

Ingrid was dazzled by the parade of celebrity that passed before her. She had no idea that she was being summarily ignored. After dinner, as she sat before the fireplace on a settee, Ernst Lubitsch sat down next to her. Most of the actresses in the room would have been delighted to have a tête-à-tête with the director of such films as *The Love Parade* and the current *Ninotchka*.

Lubitsch, who before dinner had been one of those roundly savaging Ingrid, now told her not to be discouraged. Ingrid replied that she wasn't discouraged at all, she was delighted to see so many famous people.

Irene had been watching closely as the guests ignored Ingrid. She saw now, as Ingrid's charm began to work, that Lubitsch seemed 'beguiled'. By the time the last expensive auto was wending its way down to Sunset Boulevard, Irene had decided that Ingrid had proved herself 'a figure to be taken into account'.

The studio rented a small house for Ingrid at 260 South Camden Drive in Beverly Hills. Within ten days of arriving in Hollywood, she was already at work doing a screen test. The make-up people had been ready to rouge, pluck, fluff, and powder Ingrid until she looked like a Dresden doll. But Selznick would have none of that.

Ingrid had her screen test with her co-star, Leslie Howard. For all the gentlemanly demeanour, indeed nobility, of his onscreen image, Howard was often impetuous, arrogant, and demanding. To placate him, Selznick had agreed to make him associate producer on *Intermezzo*, and pay him $10,000 a week, as against the $7500 he had received for acting in *Gone With the Wind*. Furthermore, Howard had expressed himself adamantly opposed to Gregory Ratoff as director, and Selznick had signed William Wyler instead.

Selznick was intensely busy finishing *Gone With the Wind*, but he still found time to watch over the making of *Intermezzo*. Soon after the picture began shooting, Selznick fired Wyler and replaced him with the Russian-born Ratoff. Howard concurred with the change, leaving Ingrid confronted with a director whose accent was as thick as a porterhouse steak. She would have had a hard time understanding him if it had not been for her new English coach, Ruth Roberts, the sister of George Seaton, a writer and director. Ruth was bringing up three sons alone on the income she garnered teaching English to foreign-born stars, such as Hedy Lamarr. When she read that Ingrid was coming to Hollywood, she managed to be hired by Selznick. She knew that if Ingrid was to pick up English quickly, she had better not know that her teacher spoke Swedish.

On one of the first days of shooting, Ingrid had to speak the line 'I am glad to meet you, Mr Brand.' It was hardly a line to stretch the limits of dramatic art, and Ingrid approached it with her usual professionalism.

'Yi! Yi!' Ratoff shouted. 'Soch han hawkcent! Deez way say heet: "I ham glad zu mit you, Meeser Brunt."'

As an Englishman, Howard had to get in his twopence at this violation of his native tongue. Hearing this, Ruth came rushing over to intercede.

'Soch han hawkcent! Yi! Yi!' Ratoff repeated.

Ingrid learned to ignore Ratoff's accent, but it was difficult for her to understand him. Joe Finnochio, the soundman, took perverse pleasure in listening in on his earphones to the fractured exchanges, a veritable tower of babel. At one juncture, Ruth broke into Swedish to explain Ratoff's meaning. Ingrid cried out 'why hadn't Ruth told her before.'

When Selznick saw the first rushes, he was unhappy at the way Ingrid was being filmed. The unspoiled naturalness that she projected on screen was neither unspoiled nor natural. Selznick told Harry Stradling, the director of photography, to do whatever he had to do, to give Ingrid 'the combination of exciting beauty and fresh purity' she had achieved in the Swedish *Intermezzo*. Stradling couldn't do the job the way Selznick wanted it done so Selznick fired him.

Ingrid was momentarily distraught. She had been on the set only a few days and already the director and the chief cameraman had been fired. When Selznick told her about Stradling leaving, the producer noticed tears in her eyes. She asked whether the firing would hurt Stradling's career, and said that rather than hurt him, she didn't care if she photographed a little worse.

The first rushes under the new director of photography, Gregg Toland, didn't please Selznick either. 'More than with any other girl that I know of in pictures, the difference between a great photographic beauty and an ordinary girl with Miss Bergman lies in proper photography of her,' he lectured Toland. 'This in turn depends not simply on avoiding the bad side of her face; keeping her head down as much as possible; giving her the proper headdress, giving her the proper mouth make-up, avoiding long shots, so as not to make her look too big . . . but most important of all, on shading her face and in invariably going for effect lightings on her.'

He considered young Ingrid 'the most completely conscientious actress' he had ever worked with. She had already done *Intermezzo* once; she was full of ideas about how to film it. She knew the image she wanted projected; she worked with compulsive energy. On the set during rehearsals for a dramatic scene with Howard, she insisted on complete silence. Every detail of her role had to be right. She was almost always on time, in vivid contrast to Howard, who was late twenty-six of the fifty days of production and retakes.

In Ingrid, Selznick had come upon a person like himself, who found in pictures a life beyond life, one that could confer the gift of immortality. Selznick was not only a creator of Hollywood myths but a believer. He *believed* in Ingrid's pure image, the magic that Ingrid could project on the screen. He was in short maniacally devoted to developing her as a star.

When Selznick asked Ingrid to sign a photograph to him, she wrote: 'For David, I have no words.' And indeed, what David meant to Ingrid was beyond words.

Ingrid consulted Selznick about everything. She called him out of meetings to discuss such monumental matters as a pair of shoes. She asked him about all the minutiae of publicity. In most other societies Ingrid would have seemed almost pathological in her self-centredness, but not in Hollywood.

Despite all Ingrid's effort, there was none of that inexplicable groundswell of rumour that in Hollywood is the first sign of a hit. Indeed, Selznick continued to be unhappy with the rushes on Ingrid, though he remained confident in her. But others were not so optimistic. 'I don't hear particularly good reports about Ingrid in *Intermezzo*,' Kay wrote Val Lewton, her counterpart on the West Coast, on 17 July 1939. 'And I'm awfully sorry about this, as she's been so happy with us that I know she'll want to return.'

Although Ingrid was not yet to be heavily promoted, Selznick's publicity department did make some efforts on her behalf. They tried to get Ingrid an invitation to meet Garbo on the set of *Ninotchka*, but her legendary compatriot had no interest in greeting Ingrid. As an alternative the publicists were thinking about releasing a rumour 'that Garbo herself has been trying to see this glamorous, new import from Sweden but Ingrid, by God, had been too busy to see her, because she is working day and night in *Intermezzo*.'

One of the few interviews Ingrid gave was with Ake Sandler, a Swedish journalist and son of the Swedish foreign minister. 'I was told that I could not in the article report about Ingrid making films for UFA,' Sandler said. 'When I did mention it in articles published in Sweden, I was banned from the Selznick studios and from covering her again.'

As the last weeks of shooting drew near, Ingrid's departure for Berlin was imminent. She was tentatively planning to sail on the *Bremen*. Then in early July, Daniel O'Shea told her that Selznick considered it potentially harmful. She agreed to sail on another ship.

Selznick had hoped that Ingrid's German commitment could be postponed indefinitely. He had contemplated buying out her contract, but wanted to see how *Intermezzo* would do first. Now he was faced with a public relations problem so serious that it could ruin *Intermezzo*. In March, Germany had invaded Czechoslovakia, stilling the oracles of appeasement who the year before had lauded the Munich Pact as peace in our time, and Selznick had a new star on his hands who thought that she could go blithely from an American film to a German film to a Swedish film, totally unaffected by the political world in which she lived.

The Selznick people warned Ingrid that she was 'to say nothing whatsoever about going to Germany or making a picture in Germany'. Despite the precautions, on 28 July a story appeared in the *Hollywood Reporter*, headlined: 'INGRID BERGMAN IN LEAD OF NAZI "COMMANDANT".' The article stated that as soon as Ingrid finished *Intermezzo* she would be off to Berlin to film a picture about a Tibetan expedition. Selznick took the matter sufficiently seriously to decide that Ingrid should give no more interviews at all before she left the States, and in New York register in a hotel under another name.

'She was the most surprised person in the world to learn the extent of the anti-German feeling in this country, but she maintains, and I personally feel that she has every right to, that she has no grievance against the Germans,' Selznick wrote Kay, the day the *Reporter* article appeared. 'She is a characteristic Scandinavian isolationist and I think we might as well let it go at that.'

In the last weeks of shooting, Ingrid's primary desire was to finish up in Hollywood and go on to make her German film, even though it meant travelling directly to Berlin without seeing Petter and the baby. At the end of July, as she was finishing retakes, Petter wired that her UFA film had been cancelled because of problems getting Ingrid's fee paid in Sweden. Ingrid could have stayed a few extra days in Los Angeles, but now she was anxious to get back to Stockholm.

On 3 August, her next-to-last day in Hollywood, Ingrid had her first colour screen test on Stage 3, in Rhett's bedroom on the set of

Gone With the Wind. A stagehand put a card in front of her face.
'Ingrid Bergman – No Make-up – Test One.' She had no part to
play, but merely turned her head this way and that and said a few
words. She looked shy, and utterly feminine, exuding a gentle
fawnlike quality. It was a remarkable piece of film, partly because
Selznick edited it, cutting out shots in which Ingrid appeared to have
harsh lines. *Intermezzo* had been photographed in black and white,
but when Kay saw the test she understood: 'Once she's photographed
in Technicolor, then my darling's freedom is gone.'

Even though Ingrid was leaving, Selznick was still not satisfied
with all her shots in *Intermezzo*. He thought that she looked 'dreadful'
in slacks from the rear. He was obsessed with creating a brilliant new
image. On her final day in Hollywood Selznick shot Ingrid's first
scene again and again.

And then she was off at 8 p.m. on the *Super Chief*, arriving at the
station just as the train was pulling out. As she rushed through the
station, a little boy ran up to her and pressed a package into her hand,
a gift from Selznick: a recording of the voices of the people with
whom she had worked on *Intermezzo*. Tired as she was, Ingrid did
not sleep very much that first night while the train headed eastward.

Ingrid knew that she was not supposed to talk to reporters when
she reached New York, but she probably did not know to what
lengths the Selznick organization had gone to isolate her. Although
the summer film at UFA was cancelled, Ingrid was scheduled to
make another German film later in the year; Selznick was taking no
risks. At one time there had been plans for a large press luncheon in
her honour and photo sessions with *Harper's Bazaar* and *Vogue*. That
had all been called off. To avoid even the possibility of reporters at
Grand Central station, Selznick borrowed Jock Whitney's yacht and
had it sailed up the Hudson.

At 5 a.m. on 7 August, Kay quietly took Ingrid off the train
in Albany. Ingrid sailed down the Hudson to New York City and
left the country on the *Queen Mary* with hardly anyone knowing.
From on board, Ingrid cabled Selznick that she was so sad she couldn't
see America any more.

CHAPTER 5

A WILFUL IGNORANCE

For the first few days that Ingrid was back in Stockholm, Pia cried and would not go to the mother she had not seen for over three months, but soon life was back to normal at the Lindstroms' rented house by the water in Djurgården Park. Ingrid was sitting sewing hems for the living room curtains when, on 1 September, she heard on the radio that the Germans had invaded Poland. World War II had begun.

A little more than a month before, Ingrid had been ready to go to Germany to make a film. If UFA had not cancelled, she would have been in Berlin. Ingrid would have become tainted merchandise to the French and British; most Americans would not have considered her much better. That would almost certainly have been the end of her contract with David O. Selznick, and with her career elsewhere thwarted, she might have felt compelled to make other films in Nazi Germany.

Ingrid's relationship with Germany was a continuing problem for the Selznick organization. In late September a dangerous item appeared in a column by Louella Parsons, who fancied herself Hollywood's moral arbiter, and whose power in the industry was almost unsurpassed. Parsons alleged that Ingrid had a relationship with a high Nazi official. Selznick was worried that 'this thing could spread into a campaign against Bergman if we are not careful'. Ingrid rebutted the charges in a cable to Selznick on 29 September: 'NO POLITICAL INTEREST AND ABSOLUTELY NO PERSONAL RELATIONS AMONG OFFICIALS ANY COUNTRY.' She might have gone further and said that she would not make films in Nazi Germany, but she did not do that. Kay reported that Ingrid told her by telephone that UFA felt 'they have a claim on her for one picture at the end of the war'.

Kay was less than impressed with Ingrid's political sensitivities. 'As regards the international situation, you know as well as I do that Ingrid's not too well informed,' Kay wrote O'Shea. 'I asked her if it was true that they were having black-outs in Stockholm as reported in the paper and she said that everything is fine there and that you'd never know a war was going on. It was an extremely stupid remark but knowing Ingrid, quite understandable.'

Selznick realized that at any moment Ingrid's American image could explode. If he had not been so sure that Ingrid would become 'the greatest star in motion pictures', he might well have dropped her. As it was he had sought to tie Ingrid still more closely to him in a new contract even before the verdict on *Intermezzo* was fully in.

Selznick was fully occupied in perfecting every detail for the *Gone With the Wind* premiere in Atlanta on 15 December; nevertheless he gave to *Intermezzo* what for most other producers would have been a full-time effort. The film would open at Radio City Music Hall, the largest, most prestigious movie theatre in America.

Ingrid had heard that the preview audiences for *Intermezzo* had been positive. Yet she waited apprehensively for the premiere. She wrote Selznick that she was not even going to start her English lessons until she had heard what the 'frightening American critics' had to say. 'Perhaps I don't need to be so interested in English lessons any more!!'

When *Intermezzo* opened in October, the critics were not totally taken with the film. Had they seen the Swedish version, they would have realized that much of the exquisite melancholy of the original had been lost. About Ingrid, however, the critics seemed to be not writing reviews but playing violins in her honour. Frank S. Nugent of the *New York Times* wrote that 'there is that incandescence about Miss Bergman, that spiritual spark which makes us believe that Selznick has found another great lady of the screen'. He found her 'beautiful; not in any stylistic sense, through perfection of feature or the soft-focus lens, but in her freshness, serenity and wholesomeness'. Howard Barnes of the *New York Herald Tribune* called Ingrid 'the most gifted and attractive recruit that the studios have enlisted from abroad for many moons'. Wendy Hale wrote in the *New York Daily News*: 'It is extremely unfair to call her a second Garbo, just because she hails from Sweden. She has a combination of rare beauty, freshness, vitality and ability that is as uncommon as a century plant in bloom.'

Intermezzo was Ingrid's picture. When Selznick called to tell her the reaction, she cried. Ingrid's triumph was Selznick's triumph too, and he pressed forward to renegotiate their contract. He didn't care that outside the major cities *Intermezzo* did mediocre business at best. He wanted Ingrid back. He wrote to her, 'I always planned that the principal purpose of the picture was to introduce you to American and English audiences.' Typically the remark was at once gracious and manipulative. Ingrid found it wonderfully reassuring, particularly as she didn't know how many other actresses Selznick had sought for the part. It was also not a bad ploy, in the midst of difficult negotiations, to show her that she was indebted to him even more than she knew.

She wanted to return to the United States. She was also interested in going to England to make a film with Leslie Howard. Under the terms of the contract, Selznick would not allow Ingrid to make an English-language film for someone else. To placate Ingrid, Selznick wired Gabriel Pascal, the Hungarian-born producer, about her playing George Bernard Shaw's Saint Joan, a role that she deeply coveted.

Although Ingrid appreciated Selznick's effort, she was nonetheless a tough negotiator. She was proving, as Selznick wrote Kay, that 'her angelic nature is not above being tarnished by matters of mere money'. She was willing to add a third picture to the first fourteen months of their contract, but she was not about to make more than two pictures a year for Selznick. Nor would she unequivocally drop her work in Germany. She wrote Kay that 'at present' she did not feel like making films in Germany but hoped for better times. She said that while UFA had not accepted the cancellation of her contract, she did not think they would be able to act upon it.

By October 1939 Ingrid was already back at work in Sweden, starring in *A Night in June*. She played a decent, well-meaning young woman who becomes involved with a young sailor. The part was full of romantic subtleties and received excellent reviews. But for Ingrid *A Night in June* was a four-finger exercise. There was no challenge speaking Swedish; the crew and stage at Svensk Film-industri seemed small and almost amateurish compared with what she had had in Hollywood.

During the contract negotiations, Ingrid told Kay on the phone that if she came before June 1940 she would be coming without Petter. Ingrid had been gone for over three months, leaving Petter with an empty house and a new baby, but he had such confidence in his wife and their relationship that he was willing to bid her adieu once again. 'I wanted my wife and daughter safe,' Petter says. 'The Maginot Line was strong, but I was afraid that I was going to be called into the army.'

On 30 November the Soviet Union invaded Finland. The net of war was closing tighter around Sweden. Even though the Selznick organization did not have a film for Ingrid yet, they pushed for her to come to the United States. Selznick was genuinely concerned for Ingrid; he offered her enough money to live on while she waited for work.

And so in that December of 1939, Ingrid, Petter, Pia, and a young Swedish nursemaid begun the journey to the port of Genoa. They travelled by train through the blacked-out city of Berlin, through

Germany and Austria, down the coast of Italy to Genoa, arriving in time for New Year's Eve.

They went to a dance in the hotel dining room. And as Ingrid danced with Petter she thought that she might never see him again.

On 2 January 1940, Ingrid sailed on the *Rex* from Genoa to New York. She was crying as she stood on deck, Pia in her arms, waving to Petter as he ran along the dockside, waving back. Even on the high seas, the war was very much with the *Rex*. The ship docked unexpectedly at Lisbon and Horta, picking up ninety passengers whose plane flights had been cancelled. The passenger list was full of those haunted by the war. Anne Morgan, the head of the American Friends of France, had been preparing to help the civilian population 'if anything happened' to the French war effort. Dr Chaim Weizmann, the Zionist leader, was sailing to New York to enlist aid in developing Palestine 'as a haven and homeland for tens of thousands of Jews who have been uprooted and driven from their homes by the overwhelming wave of destruction now sweeping over Central Europe'. Martha Gellhorn, a prominent journalist, was returning to the States after covering the Finnish-Soviet war. She was full of stories of horror, heroism, and tragedy. Gellhorn noticed Ingrid, 'a woman with a baby on her back', and thought little more of it until months later.

Nine months earlier, Ingrid had sailed into New York unknown and unheralded. Now, on 12 January 1940, she was arriving with a full barrage of publicity. Among those scheduled to talk to her were representatives from the *New York Times*, the AP, the *New York Daily News*, *Screenland*, and *Harper's Bazaar*. Kay was there too, seeing to it that there would be no photographs of Ingrid with Pia in her arms.

'Don't talk too much about Joan of Arc – yes?' said Myer Beck, a Selznick publicist, before she met the reporters. He told her that the film had been postponed.

Ingrid had read about Joan of Arc when she was a little girl, and she had got down on her knees in the chapel on the ship to thank God for giving her *Saint Joan*. At the beginning of World War II, God may have had other things on his mind, for Ingrid learned upon arriving that the role was apparently just a publicity stunt. She was hardly in the mood to deal with the American press.

The reporters thronged around her. The cameramen got down on their knees, shooting up at her, getting as much leg as they could. The questions kept coming at her. Was she a jitterbug? Had she left her husband?

Ingrid burst into tears and ran out of the press conference.

★   ★   ★

She had been brought to America by the most celebrated, the most envied, the most admired producer in America. *Gone With the Wind* was ablaze on screens across America, the greatest triumph in Hollywood history, and perhaps the greatest Hollywood film ever made. In February 1940 it won the most Academy Awards ever given a single film. Selznick's new film, *Rebecca*, was not another *Gone With the Wind*, but with it he would win an unprecedented second Academy Award in a row for best film.

Ingrid imagined that Selznick was about to star her in his next great film, if not yet *Saint Joan*, then some other fine role. She was initially excited simply to be in New York, that great city she loved so much. It took hardly any time to settle into Kay's large apartment on Park Avenue, for, as Kay noticed, 'her wardrobe resembles her make-up kit – a large-sized tube of toothpaste'.

But Selznick had no work for her. To Ingrid, to be alive was to be busy. She couldn't understand. Her contract stated that she was to make one or two pictures in the year starting 1 April 1940, and by then she was sure she *had* to be at work. Kay told her pointblank: the contract didn't mean the first picture had to *begin* 1 April. As that sunk in, Ingrid's depression deepened.

On 22 January Ingrid took the train out to Los Angeles to perform *Intermezzo* on the *Lux Radio Theatre*, leaving Pia with the maid. She knew enough about Hollywood by now to realize how important it was for her to make her presence felt, to show herself at the proper parties, to meet the right producers and directors. After all, the year before, she had met Ernst Lubitsch at Selznick's house during her first week in Hollywood. And now, according to Selznick, Lubitsch was interested in working with her. Nonetheless, when Selznick attempted to take her around to parties, Ingrid would have nothing of it.

In her week in Hollywood, Ingrid did at least go to Selznick's house one evening for a screening. There she met Fredric March, who had played the has-been actor in Selznick's classic film *A Star Is Born*. March was so taken with Ingrid that he sought to have her star with him in his new film, *Victory*, based on the Joseph Conrad novel.

Selznick appreciated the qualities in Ingrid that allowed her to refuse to be hauled around to fancy parties. But he wondered whether he was in the early stages of creating a monster. He and Kay had filled her head with dreams of glorious roles. In New York, Kay had taken Ingrid to one party after another, where Broadway directors and producers dangled before her impressionable eyes all kinds of theatrical offers.

The surprising thing, however, was that there was so little demand for Ingrid's services at the other film studios. Indeed, although Selznick gave the impression that Lubitsch was after Ingrid, it was Selznick who was courting Lubitsch to make a film with his Swedish discovery.

'I noticed a distinct difference in her attitude . . . from what it had been when she left for Sweden,' he wrote Kay after Ingrid returned to New York City. 'I still think she is an angel . . . and I mention this only to indicate that there is the danger that we will succeed in accomplishing nothing except to create future trouble for ourselves if we get her thinking that everybody in the world wants her, and we are doing nothing with her. In fact, it may already be too late to correct this impression.'

Ingrid at first considered Selznick her professional father in America, a man who could do no wrong. He could speak with brutal frankness in his memoranda about her but to her face he was her mentor, spinning dreams of a glorious future. When she arrived back in New York on 4 February she told Kay that she intended to begin work on *Saint Joan* right away, studying the play and taking drama lessons.

Regardless of what Ingrid thought he had said, Selznick told Kay that he did not want Ingrid 'spoiled or stylized' by drama coaches, and that *Saint Joan* was far from a certain thing. Kay was left with the unenviable task of trying to keep Ingrid's spirits up as she shepherded her around New York.

Selznick lived by the memo and the letter, and Kay wrote Selznick frequently. 'I can't see that I have spoiled Ingrid the slightest bit,' Kay wrote Selznick on 9 February 1940. 'I can't keep her cooped up in her apartment and not have her meet anybody, and she's not the slightest bit interested in meeting anyone outside of the theatre . . . I have a great feeling of affection and friendship for Ingrid. On the other hand, it's like having four children to manage instead of two, and it's not all roses.'

Ingrid was not the number one star at Selznick International; far from it. Kay took her to see an early television broadcast of a play about Charlotte Corday starring Vivien Leigh. Afterwards, Ingrid talked enthusiastically about playing the part in a movie. As soon as the Selznick people heard that, they were worried about a 'cat fight' between their Swedish acquisition and the star of *Gone With the Wind*. Selznick told Kay to inform Ingrid that *Charlotte Corday* had first been Vivien Leigh's idea. That was true, but long before Vivien had become interested in the part, Ingrid had been scheduled to play Charlotte Corday for UFA in Germany.

What brought Ingrid out of the doldrums was the offer of a stage role in *Liliom*. The classic play by the Hungarian playwright Ferenc Molnár became even better known later as the basis for the Rodgers and Hammerstein musical *Carousel*. Molnár's play tells the story of Liliom, a barker for a merry-go-round, and his love for Julie, a housemaid. Liliom is a brutal, seemingly uncaring man who beats Julie. Caught stealing, he kills himself, and then returns sixteen years later to seek atonement.

When Ingrid read the play, she said later, she assumed that she was to play not Julie but the second lead, Julie's friend Marie. Ingrid was not reluctant to attempt great parts such as Joan of Arc or Charlotte Corday on film, and it was a curious kind of professional modesty that Ingrid had suddenly developed. According to Kay Brown, Ingrid's story was pure mythmaking. The only question was whether Ingrid's English was up to a major stage role; indeed, two days after Ingrid returned to New York, Kay was already wiring Selznick about the role of Julie for Ingrid. Her English was still not good; she could speak adequately in a film, where she performed only a few lines of dialogue at a time. In a Broadway play her English and her acting would be put to a severe test.

Ingrid was game and Kay thought it would be a good idea, but Selznick at first opposed the project. He worried that Ingrid's value in films would diminish if she received bad notices in *Liliom*. Few men, however, were a match for Ingrid when she was dealing with her career. She discussed the offer with him by telephone and talked him into letting her play the part.

During rehearsals, Ingrid learned that the producer had initially confused her with another Swedish newcomer, Signe Hasso, who had far more stage experience. As if that wasn't bad enough, she was playing opposite a young actor, Burgess Meredith, whom she towered over. Nonetheless, like most of her co-stars, Burgess was taken with Ingrid, and their chemistry played out on stage during rehearsals.

Then came opening night, 25 March 1940. Some actors have only a few shivers of stage fright before the curtain opens; for others there is a moment of pure dread. As the audience began to enter the theatre, Burgess sat in his dressing room while a group of gypsy musicians played, helping the young actor to get in the proper mood. Ingrid had no musicians, and though Kay felt that she was 'not unduly nervous about the opening', Ingrid said later that she was petrified.

Then suddenly, she was on stage. She was speaking. She was someone else. She was all right.

Many fine movie actors are a total failure on stage, but as Brooks Atkinson wrote in the *New York Times*, Ingrid kept 'the part wholly

alive and lightens it from within the luminous beauty'. She com-
manded the stage that evening. By the time she spoke her last lines,
the audience was hers. She received as many curtain calls as the
better-known Meredith.

Most of the reviews were positive, but there were several detractors, most vehemently John Mason Brown of the *New York Post.*
Brown found the performance as a whole 'shoddy'. Although he
admitted that Ingrid was 'charming to look at' and could act well,
he was the first American critic to sound the one theme of doubt that
would follow her for years. 'Miss Bergman fails to endow her love
for Liliom and her power to treasure even his blows with the wan
quality of abnegation for which the text calls and which is the source
of much of its tenderness . . . Her make-up does not help. She is so
ruddy, well fed, and apple cheeked throughout that it is hard to
believe in the passive proofs of Julie's devotion.'

'Thank God it is all over and you don't need to be ashamed of me!'
Ingrid wrote David in a short note after the opening. She had felt a
burden not only for herself but for Selznick.

There are few excitements in the public arts to compare to a starring
role in a hit play. For the first time in Ingrid's life there were fans
surrounding her who saw a magic in her beyond the magic on the
screen or stage. After some performances, as she sat in her small
dressing room wearing a peasant dress and apron and high-top boots,
she had to barricade the door from the onslaught of well-wishers.
'The theatre was my mother and my father,' she told an interviewer
one evening after her performance, and it was indeed as if she had
come home. Now for six weeks life was the routine of the play.
There was nothing, or next to nothing, to worry about: no time for
dinner parties, sitting next to New York gentlemen who burdened
her with their charm and whose words she sometimes only half
understood; no time to fret endlessly about her career, haunting the
movie houses and theatres; no time to have to spend tedious days
with Pia, but time simply to see her for a delightful hour or so,
squeezed in between performances, English lessons, interviews, singing and dancing classes, and meetings; no time but for the exhilaration
and challenge of each performance, the applause flowing over her.

Success in America was different, though; people thought they
owned you. You were public property to be pawed over and whispered about. In stores strangers suddenly struck up conversations,
not necessarily because they thought Ingrid a star, or beautiful;
sometimes simply because such instant intimacy was the American
way. The reporters were no better. They asked her if she had run

out on Petter, and suggested the names of possible lovers. One evening a little boy pestered her for autographs. One signature wasn't enough. When she got in a cab, he jumped in after her and began beseeching her for more autographs. The Selznick representative seated next to Ingrid picked the unruly tyke up by his neck and heaved him out of the door.

'Oh, you've hurt him!' Ingrid cried out.

'Hurt him, nothing,' said the representative, alert to the ways of New York. 'I've killed him. So long as I didn't use a gun or crown him, it was legal. You're going to like America. It's a great country!'

Ingrid considered America a great country, but she was still worried about what her next role would be in Hollywood. She was at the mercy of whatever Selznick and Kay decided to tell her, and they treated her like an adolescent whom they were protecting from the rude realities of existence. Moreover, Selznick was still trying to renegotiate Ingrid's contract, and he was not about to give her information that would make her bargaining position stronger.

Selznick was at the top of his profession, and he might have devoted part of his creative energies to producing Ingrid's second film, but he wasn't going to do that. He had done the ultimate with *Gone With the Wind*, and the Hollywood gossips said that he was burned out. His problem went deeper than that. He was constantly coming up with new ideas for Ingrid and his other stars, squandering his money, time, and enthusiasms on scores of projects that never quite worked out. He was like a rich little boy in a room full of toys, so jaded by the array before him that he simply sat there unable to move.

As Selznick considered various projects for Ingrid, he treated her like a piece of property to be bought and sold and rented. It was like any other property in Los Angeles; as speculative fever took hold, it might increase geometrically in value, but it might fall to next to nothing too. The producer couldn't tell Ingrid about all the wheeling and dealing. He didn't tell her that he had turned down the role in *Victory*, a decision that a few months later he regretted. He didn't tell her that the problem in loaning her out for another role was that he had been offered only $50,000, not the $75,000 he wanted, and he wouldn't settle for a mere $25,000, or double what he paid her.

Ingrid did learn about some film projects. In May she read the script for *So Ends Our Night*, based on the novel *Flotsam* by Erich Maria Remarque, famous for his antiwar novel, *All Quiet on the Western Front*. *So Ends Our Night* was an anti-Nazi film. Hitler's troops had invaded Denmark and Norway and were marching through the Netherlands, Belgium, and France, and the film was hardly full of revelations about the brutality of Nazism. But even at this late date O'Shea wrote Selznick that although Ingrid expressed herself as having 'reluctance about playing anything so decidedly anti-German, Kay feels that she can be talked into it easily'.

Ingrid's one worry beyond her career was Petter. She was emotionally halfway between Hollywood and Stockholm. When reporters talked to her, they found that when they asked of him, her blue eyes filled with tears. Sad as she was about the ending of the six-week run of *Liliom*, she was excited about Petter's arrival in June for a visit. She left Pia and the maid at Kay's summer place on Long Island, and took a room on the thirty-fourth floor of the Hotel Pierre, overlooking Central Park.

Petter forcefully assumed the role in Ingrid's career that his wife wanted him to play: the mentor and protector. In the few weeks that Petter was in the States, he and Ingrid had some crucial decisions to make. Selznick was trying to renegotiate Ingrid's contract, tying her up for more films, a longer period, and doing away with her right of cancellation. The producer succeeded in keeping Ingrid away from any agent who would seek to represent her; in this he made a big mistake. Petter tended to be suspicious of the fast-talking, Hollywood types who had brought his wife to the States to make movies but instead had plunked her down in Manhattan. Although he denies that he ever discussed contracts with O'Shea or Selznick, both Ingrid's recollection and communications within the Selznick organization suggest otherwise. Daniel O'Shea found him 'stubborn as a mule – he has a whim of iron'.

Ingrid's contract gave her a right to make films in languages other than English in Europe. Although Denmark and Norway had been invaded by the Germans, Petter thought that Sweden would be able to remain neutral. And he wanted his wife back in Sweden by Christmas. After meeting Petter, O'Shea wrote Selznick: 'He keeps harping on the fact that having brought her over here and not having made a picture with her for six months, and with a situation indicative of the fact that we will not be making one too shortly, we have cost her her German market and greatly interfered with and damaged her Swedish market . . . I very frankly told him that the Hollywood and German situations were not reconcilable. That if she were going to be a star in Germany, she would not be a star in Hollywood.'

When Selznick read O'Shea's letter he was infuriated. 'It is outrageous that they should consider accepting the hospitality of civilized nations and want to work with the Nazis,' he replied. 'I have no right to compel her or her husband to have any international morals – but I would like it to be made very clear that since they are always talking in terms of ethics and morality, I am shocked that they would even discuss working in Germany . . . I think you ought to make it very clear to Ingrid and her husband that if the only terms they can understand are commercial terms, and they persist in talking in terms of money, they might as well face the fact that if she makes one more picture in Germany she will not make another picture in any of the few civilized nations still left . . . They would probably stone the theatres in which her films played, and I wouldn't blame them.'

One essential fact remained: Ingrid wanted to stay in the United States and to do what had to be done to become a major star. And Petter agreed to return to the United States to pursue his medical studies.

CHAPTER 6

'THE BARS OF MY CAGE ARE BROKEN'

Petter was soon sailing to Europe, leaving Ingrid to spend most of the summer of 1940 alone. Nine months ago her American film debut had seemed a harbinger of grand success. Just a month or so ago she had been heralded on Broadway. Yet here she was living an unsettled life in hotels and other people's houses.

The one immediate film possibility was a loan-out to Columbia Pictures to do *Adam Had Four Sons*, directed by Gregory Ratoff. She read the book on which the film would be based. She and Kay found Ingrid's part as a governess too negative.

Ingrid had no illusions that the film would be a box office triumph, but there was no immediate alternative. Her main problem was Ratoff. The director had no idea of what his Swedish star truly thought of him. To his face Ingrid cooed words of sweet appreciation. She flattered him so much that later he addressed her as 'my sweetest Swedish baby'. But privately she and Kay were bitterly disdainful of Ratoff and the performance he had got out of her in *Intermezzo*.

Ingrid was not sure she should do the film. At a party that summer at the William Paleys, she asked Selznick's advice. As Selznick remembered the conversation, he told Ingrid that he didn't think the part was good enough, and that he would prefer to pay her for remaining idle, waiting for the proper role. But Ingrid could not stand to be idle. She was eating compulsively, and had already gained five pounds. She felt that she had to work, even if it was in a film that would do her career little good. And so she headed west from New York once again to play a part in a movie that she knew wouldn't be very good, under a director in whom she had little faith.

She knew that *Adam Had Four Sons* would not be much of a movie, but she hadn't been prepared to find the production a shambles. Every day new dialogue was written. Ratoff had no idea how his film was going to end, and indeed, after the film was finished Selznick spent by his estimate 'probably the equivalent of a solid week's work' editing a film that was in no way his responsibility. He did so solely so that *his* star would not appear in a debacle.

★　　★　　★

Ingrid liked – indeed, needed – her professional life to be as neat and orderly as her apartment, and she had some difficult times on the set. What helped immensely was that she had Ruth Roberts working with her again. Ingrid had written regularly to Ruth from the East Coast, primarily about her professional life. Ruth was becoming more than a mere language coach to Ingrid; she was her confidante, her friend. She insisted that from now on Ruth be written into the contract for each picture. Ruth was becoming, in the words of her housemate, Rae Pober, 'addicted to Ingrid'. She was a talented woman, but shackled her own aspirations to Ingrid's. Ingrid often dropped by Ruth's home. There, sitting laughing on the sofa, or washing dinner dishes together, they did not seem like employer and employee, but on the set or in the gatherings of Hollywood, Ruth knew enough not to pretend that they were equals.

Ingrid finished work on *Adam Had Four Sons* one morning at three o'clock and began work on her next film, *Rage in Heaven*, seven hours later. This time, Selznick had loaned Ingrid out to MGM for $34,000 to do a conventional story based on the James Hilton novel. Concerned about the quality of the production, he spent a Sunday going over the script before the film went into production. Ingrid played a young woman who finds that she has married a man (Robert Montgomery) who is a borderline psychotic. Her husband's friend (George Sanders) attempts to help him, but he is too riddled with jealousy and self-hatred. He commits suicide, making it look as if his friend has killed him.

One of the people Ingrid met on the set was the co-screenwriter Christopher Isherwood who went to the set every day to go over scenes with her.

'There are people who in the best sense of the word are amateurs, who due to their beauty and charm become stars,' Isherwood says. 'But she was a real pro. I feel at home with real pros the way Hemingway liked bullfighters. They're very tough and have a kind of glamour.

'She was absolutely charming. In some ways she was the most beautiful woman I ever met – not that women are my speciality. She wasn't a woman that you'd spend time with unless you were involved with her. She had a certain aspect of her that was almost masculine. She was so professional. When studio people would pinch her ass or something, she would give them a dry smile as if they were men in a locker room.'

In her Swedish films Ingrid had played the suffering, innocent, misunderstood young woman often enough that *Rage in Heaven* should have been a mere exercise for her; but like *Adam Had Four*

Sons this new production was plagued with one problem after another. MGM fired the first two directors, finally bringing in W. S. Van Dyke II, whose most distinguished attribute as a director was his fancy name, and whose main claim to fame was that he got films finished, come hell, high water, or temperamental actors.

Van Dyke dressed like a martinet, in high leather boots and military breeches. He berated the actors as if they were recruits in boot camp. Ingrid felt that she could not work with such a man, and she went to Selznick to complain. Selznick had no control over MGM. Moreover, he didn't want *his* Ingrid to get a reputation as a temperamental actress. So he sent her back to the studio to complete the film.

When it came to her work, Ingrid was relentless. During the shooting she was not happy with a certain scene.

'I know I can do it better,' Ingrid said, asking for another take.

'We're going to circle it,' Van Dyke said, ready to move on.

'We're moving too fast,' Ingrid insisted, making a scene in front of the crew.

Even while *Rage in Heaven* was in the first days of production in December 1940, Ingrid was looking for a better part for her fourth American film. She knew already that once again she was caught in an inferior, forgettable film. Once again she was playing under a director with whom she was far from comfortable. If she did not get into higher-quality productions soon, she would end up like so many other foreign stars, her career run aground upon the tricky shoals of Hollywood.

Ingrid had believed in Selznick, but he was shopping her around instead of starring her in 'A David O. Selznick Production'. Even Selznick could admit privately – though certainly not to Ingrid – that he had made at least two major mistakes; he had turned down *Victory*, and instead of purchasing the rights to *A Woman's Face* for Ingrid, he had let it become a vehicle for Joan Crawford.

Whatever Selznick was doing, he almost always had some other motive, some other scheme in mind. A year and a half earlier, when he and Victor Fleming looked at the daily rushes of *Gone With the Wind*, he had the daily scenes of *Intermezzo* shown as well. Selznick wanted him to see Ingrid 'over and over again so that I would have the opportunity for my campaign'. Fleming was sufficiently impressed with Selznick's Swedish protégée to want her to co-star in his new film at MGM, *Dr Jekyll and Mr Hyde*, due to begin shooting in February, a few weeks after *Rage in Heaven* was finished. Of course, Ingrid would play Beatrix Emery, the sweet, virtuous fiancée of Spencer Tracy as Dr Harry Jekyll. The sensuous Ivy Peterson was a natural for Lana Turner, but Ingrid wanted to play Ivy.

First, Ingrid had to convince Victor Fleming. The handsome, six-feet-two-inches-tall Fleming was, as Spencer Tracy called him, 'the Clark Gable of directors'. Fleming lived with his wife and family on a two-acre farm in Brentwood. Part Cherokee Indian, fifty-seven-year-old Fleming was a romantic figure who had travelled the world and piloted his own plane. As a director he was a consummate professional, who had made such diverse films as *Test Pilot*, *The Virginian*, and *Gone With the Wind*.

Ingrid went to Fleming and, as she remembered, asked if she could play the part of Ivy. According to Ingrid Fleming said that it was out of the question: no one would believe Ingrid as an amoral bar maid.

In her autobiography Ingrid wrote that she asked to do a screen test, but that Fleming told her Selznick would never put *his* star through the humiliation of trying out for a part. And so she and Fleming did the test secretly, and showed it to an incredulous Selznick.

Ingrid treated each man with whom she was involved as if the two of them were in a conspiracy against the rest of the world. Selznick felt that he was Ingrid's mentor, leading her upward, gently wooing Fleming so that he would want to work with her, while Fleming felt that he and Ingrid were artists, creating beauty and fame and wealth.

At one point Fleming may have believed that he and Ingrid were working together almost against Selznick; but in fact Selznick knew about the screen test from the beginning. He thought that Ingrid could indeed play a 'sexy bitch'. Early in December he even called Fleming to discuss being present for the screen test; Ingrid was the one worried about the risk of an unsuccessful test. Before shooting, she wanted to read for the part so that if it didn't work out, 'we won't have any bad tests floating around'.

Ingrid got the part of Ivy, a wonderful Christmas present, and a marvellous antidote to her experience on the set of *Rage in Heaven*. That Christmas of 1940 was special in another way. Petter had arrived from Sweden, after six weeks in a freighter from Portugal. A couple of weeks after he arrived, Petter and Ingrid flew to Sun Valley, Idaho, for skiing. Petter was a marvellous skier; Ingrid was more interested in the ski lodge or sitting in the sun, but the vacation was a welcome respite between films.

Ingrid had other matters on her mind. There was not only her forthcoming role in *Dr Jekyll and Mr Hyde*, but the possibility of acting Maria in the film version of Ernest Hemingway's new novel, *For Whom the Bell Tolls*, which in a few months had already sold over half a million copies.

Hollywood was in the midst of the biggest hoopla over a film since the search for Scarlett in *Gone With the Wind*. When Selznick read *For Whom the Bell Tolls*, he thought that Ingrid was a natural for Maria, the young, emotionally anaesthetized victim of Fascist rapists. So did Ingrid, who picked her way through the novel with the help of a Swedish-English dictionary. A few years before, Selznick might have bought the rights himself. Selznick had an entrée to Hemingway through his brother Myron, Hollywood's premier agent. Myron had sold the rights to the book to Paramount for $150,000, the highest amount yet paid for a novel, and Hemingway was grateful. Blood is blood and business is business, and Selznick commissioned his brother to help get the part for Ingrid.

Hemingway was as celebrated and publicized a figure as any movie star, and he was said to be mentioning Ingrid for the part. That was extraordinary, even if Ingrid and Selznick didn't think so. After all, in his novel Hemingway had a very specific idea of his Maria . . . 'Her teeth were white in her brown face and her skin and eyes were the same golden tawny brown . . . Her hair was the golden brown of a grain field that had been burned dark in the sun but it was cut short all over her head so that it was but little longer than the fur on a beaver pelt.' The description didn't sound quite like Ingrid Bergman, though it didn't sound like any other Hollywood star either. Moreover, Ingrid was not a major star. *Intermezzo* was her only American film yet to open.

Ingrid had one great stroke of luck. The year before, when she sailed on the *Rex* from Italy, the journalist Martha Gellhorn had been a passenger. Since then Gellhorn had married Hemingway, and the image of Ingrid on the ship had stayed with her. 'I suggested Ingrid for *For Whom the Bell Tolls*,' says Gellhorn. 'I had seen her on the boat, a woman with a baby on her back. And then I saw her in a film. And then I made the suggestion to Hemingway.'

Hemingway mentioned Ingrid as a possible Maria in an article in *Life*. That was enough for Selznick to try to set up a meeting for Ingrid with the novelist. Hemingway was about to sail for China from San Francisco. So on 30 January 1940, Ingrid and Petter cut short their vacation to meet the novelist. They drove through the night to Reno to catch the morning plane. The winter weather in the San Francisco area was treacherous. The airport was fogged in, and the plane landed at Oakland, across the bay. Hemingway and Ingrid met on a street corner outside Jack's Restaurant, along with their respective spouses. The foursome then proceeded inside for a private tête-à-tête, the intimate moment duly immortalized by a reporter and a photographer for *Life*.

Twenty-five-year-old Ingrid was no longer an innocent at the Hollywood publicity games. To play at the highest level did not mean cheesecake pictures and interviews with the fan magazines; it meant lunches like this one, where calculated, public performances were made to seem like private moments, where *Life* was made to seem like life.

'If you don't act in the picture, Ingrid, I won't work on it,' Hemingway told Ingrid, who, as reported by *Life*, was 'shy' but 'finally laughs'.

He was in favour of Ingrid, but he did not tell her what he had told Selznick by phone earlier in the day: that among other things, Paramount considered Ingrid 'dumb', 'wooden', and 'untalented'. During the flight to Los Angeles, Ingrid read the inscription on the copy of *For Whom the Bell Tolls* Hemingway had given her: 'To Ingrid Bergman, who is the Maria of this story.'

Hemingway had done all that could be expected to help Ingrid get the part. He had richly repaid his debt to Myron Selznick; now it was up to David Selznick and Ingrid to make her choice as Maria inevitable. That would take some time, for Paramount was luxuriating in all its possibilities, relishing the windfall of publicity. Ingrid was mentioned as a possible Maria, but so were Paulette Goddard, Betty Field, Annabella, and others.

Petter was excited about Ingrid's career. He enjoyed skiing and tagging along on the visit with Ernest Hemingway, but he liked sitting around as little as did his wife. Petter was already in his mid-thirties; he was making a sacrifice that few men of his generation and professional position would have made. But he was not going to become Mr Ingrid Bergman, hovering around the Hollywood set. He began applying to medical schools so that he could finish up his degree and become a doctor in the United States. 'I could have stayed in Los Angeles and gone to USC, but I wouldn't be able to enter for a whole other year,' Petter says. 'I had an honorary fellowship with the American Scandinavian Foundation. They suggested that I visit and select one of three medical schools in the East. So I left California and travelled east, visiting medical schools at Yale and Rochester and Chicago.'

Petter would be the one, this time, to establish himself for many months far from Ingrid and her work. A mark of Petter's confidence in himself and in his relationship with Ingrid, it was also a sad commentary on the nature of their marriage. Here was a man who believed in the sanctity of marriage, yet he and his wife had lived apart for almost half of their three-and-a-half-year marriage. Theirs was a marriage of the special moment, of meetings in hotels or on vacation, or between films and projects; they had still to test the mettle of their relationship in day-to-day living. These were the war years and millions of married couples were living separate lives; but it was not the war that kept Ingrid and Petter so much apart.

Ingrid had what most women, even other stars, would have considered an enviable life: starring role in an exciting new film, and a husband who adored her and was unquestionably loyal. But that was not enough. 'Ingrid told me often that she couldn't work well unless she was in love with either the leading man or the director,' Petter says. Another husband would have asked his wife in no uncertain terms what 'love' meant, and whom she was talking about. Petter did not ask. He seemed not to want to know too much about the woman who was his wife.

As an actress, Ingrid was always playing aspects of herself. She knew that when she made love to a man as the cameras rolled, she would give a better performance if she was making love to him offscreen as well. It was not a question of morality. Nor was it a matter of profound romantic passion, a fact that it would take several men a good while to understand. She had enormous professional cunning. That was nowhere more apparent than in her relationship with her new director, Victor Fleming, and her co-star, Spencer Tracy. *Dr Jekyll and Mr Hyde* began shooting on 12 February 1941; in it, she was playing a woman of wanton sexuality, who in one scene wallows in mud, in another rests voluptuously upon a bed of flowers. When she was acting in a part, her whole life was that part, and it was no wonder that she should become involved with both Fleming and Tracy.

On the set waiting to perform, she was, as Charles Schram, the make-up man, remembers, 'shy and bashful and blushing a lot and very quiet and a little scared', but once the camera started, Ingrid appeared the personification of naughty, amoral Ivy. Fleming got a stunning performance out of her, in part because she was playing the sensuous, hedonistic woman offscreen as well as on it. He had a long-standing reputation as a ladies' man; indeed, in 1934 he had been accused by Paul A. Lockwood, a cameraman, in a $150,000 alienation of affection suit. Lockwood alleged that Fleming had promised his wife a career; she had agreed to go with the married director to Honolulu, but Fleming had left her in San Francisco, where she suffered a nervous breakdown.

Fleming was more than twice Ingrid's age, but in her presence all his youth and vitality seemed renewed. In the scene in which Spencer Tracy was to carry Ingrid up to the bedroom, Fleming showed his star what to do by sweeping Ingrid up into his arms, and carrying her upward as if the stairs were not part of a set but the entry to his private quarters. Tracy was not about to attempt to replicate the director's effort. He insisted that a sling be used to help hoist Ingrid's body aloft.

At times, Fleming could be almost sadistic. In a scene in which Ingrid was to cry hysterically, he slapped her across the face. If Van Dyke or Ratoff had tried such a stunt, Ingrid would have berated them endlessly, but as she admitted she 'was deeply in love with Victor Fleming', in love, too, with the performance he was coaxing out of her.

Ingrid was also involved with Spencer Tracy during the filming. 'I watched her relationship with Spencer on *Dr Jekyll and Mr Hyde*,' remembers John Houseman, the director and actor. 'But that's not uncommon in this business.' During the filming Tracy was extraordinarily enthusiastic about Ingrid. He came up to Selznick at a party and told him 'that in all his career he had never seen her equal, either on stage or on screen . . . that she is clearly destined to be the greatest star in pictures'. When Thornton Delehanty, a newspaper reporter, came to talk to Tracy on the set, the actor insisted that the reporter interview her as well.

Ingrid was exceptionally lucky on *Dr Jekyll and Mr Hyde*; she had both her director and her co-star slavishly devoted to her. They helped her to achieve a performance that brought more glory and acclaim to her than to either of them. To Ingrid, a good role was freedom and ecstasy, and good work (as opposed to love affairs) made her happy.

On the set of the movie, Ingrid lived a whole life, and when the movie was finished the affair with Fleming was finished as well. She said later that Fleming ended it because he wasn't in love with her. However, a love letter that Fleming wrote Ingrid six years later suggests that the reasons were more complicated ('Six years is twice as long for me for what I've lost is lost for ever'). Ingrid apparently maintained a longer-term interest in Spencer Tracy. According to Petter, months later he prevented her from going off with the actor for two weeks in San Francisco to discuss 'future roles'.

After *Dr Jekyll and Mr Hyde*, Selznick had no new movie immediately on the horizon, but in August he was planning to star Ingrid in Eugene O'Neill's *Anna Christie* at the Lobero Theatre in Santa Barbara. Before rehearsals, she had a chance to go east and spend some time with Petter and her friends. Ingrid's long, restful days were made doubly tranquil because she had a challenging role ahead of her. She appeared to be happy, but she was full of her familiar insecurities. Selznick didn't comment quickly enough after seeing a screening of *Dr Jekyll and Mr Hyde*; Ingrid was sure that his silence meant that he didn't like the film.

In June, Petter, Ingrid, and Pia stayed a few days in upstate New York at a guesthouse on a property owned by Burgess Meredith. One of the other guests that weekend was Olivia de Havilland. She had met Ingrid only once before, at the Selznick studios during the making of *Gone With the Wind*. Olivia remembers Petter and Ingrid sitting in canvas chairs in front of the guesthouse; Petter read books, and Ingrid chatted and looked over scripts. 'He adored her and I think she knew it, but I think every man adored her,' de Havilland says.

Ingrid was soon travelling west once again, alone. Petter had been accepted at the University of Rochester Medical School, and he journeyed to upstate New York, where Ingrid would soon be joining him. Pia would stay with Kay Brown on Long Island, the first extended period that the child was without either parent.

Selznick took credit for getting Petter into Rochester through his acquaintance with Dr Alan Valentine, the president of the university. Petter's credentials and training were first rate, and he states adamantly that he got into medical school on his own; Selznick may have helped facilitate matters, but in acting as if Petter was nothing without him, he was seeking to show Petter and Ingrid how much they needed him.

In *Anna Christie*, Ingrid was facing the most challenging theatrical role of her life. 'Anna was a whore,' said John Houseman, who directed the O'Neill play that two decades before had won a Pulitzer Prize. 'And that was difficult for Ingrid. When she tried to be evil, it usually didn't work.' At the play's opening on 30 July 1941, there were far more stars in the audience than onstage. 'Gimme a whisky and make it a double!' Ingrid said to the barman as she stepped onstage, and the audience howled with laughter. It was hardly the reception a thespian would have wanted, but she was soon fully into the part. Four days later, when the play opened a short run in San Francisco, the critic of the *Call-Bulletin* reported that he 'hadn't heard [such applause] in a decade'.

By the middle of August, Ingrid was on the train back to New York for yet another short run of *Anna Christie*, at the Maplewood Theatre in New Jersey. *Dr Jekyll and Mr Hyde* had just opened, and as she travelled eastward, the first reviews were appearing in the papers. The common consensus, as the *New York Times* expressed it, was that 'only Miss Bergman had emerged with some measure of honour'. Ingrid had hoped to enjoy Sunday at Amagansett with Pia, with whom she was spending so little time, but as her train arrived Sunday morning and she had to begin rehearsals Monday morning, she decided that wouldn't work out. Instead, Miss Olsen, the nanny, brought Pia into New York on the train.

Ingrid prepared diligently for the new summer stock production in a bare rehearsal room at 16 West 46th Street, but she had time one weekend afternoon to stand in line and see herself in *Dr Jekyll and Mr Hyde*. She saw other movies too and gave interviews to the local papers. New York reporters wore their cynicism like crowns; they were less than amused when they discovered that they had all been given 'exclusive' interviews with the Swedish star; but as soon as they sat down with her they were taken with her, and proceeded to fill their columns with paens of praise.

Before Ingrid, there had been Garbo. Garbo the inaccessible, Garbo the mysterious, Garbo the incomparable, slinking in and out of the city in dark glasses. And here was Ingrid, another Swede, sitting apparently without make-up, looking 'like the Ideal American Senior at Vassar, low-heeled edition complete with saddle oxfords'. Here was Ingrid not only physically accessible but seemingly accessible emotionally, a star whose great mystery was her seeming lack of mystery, a star about whom there were no rumours of scandal, a star who was a happily married twenty-five-year-old mother, a star who when she wasn't working intended to live not in Palm Springs, or Hollywood, but with her medical student husband in, of all places, Rochester, New York. This, then, was the Bergman the reporters met, a Bergman who, as the *New York Post* headlined its article, was the 'Garbo of the 40s'.

For Ingrid, everything was going well, and she seemed to glow with well-being. The reporters adored her, but so did the public, and so did Selznick and Kay, and so did Petter. He came down from Rochester to see the Maplewood production, an even bigger hit than *Anna Christie* had been in the West. He cabled Selznick:

... EVERY EVENING HERE SOLD OUT IN ADVANCE AND ONLY FIRE DEPARTMENT WITH THEIR DIRTY TRUCK COULD STOP THE CROWD FIGHTING THEIR WAY IN ... WE ARE SO GOOD AND WE ARE SO BEAUTIFUL AND THE MORE WE THINK OF EUROPE AND COCA COLA THE MORE WE LIKE AMERICA.

PETTER

CHAPTER 7

MONEY, FAME, AND POWER

After the close of *Anna Christie* in New Jersey, Ingrid travelled to Rochester. The move seemed to confirm all the hype about Ingrid's naturalness, her disdain for the glamour of Hollywood.

After a couple of days in the Lindstroms' rented house at 985 South Avenue, Ingrid pronounced herself 'really happy'. The house was 'really sweet', almost a 'dream house'. She became a Swedish housewife, for whom life is eternal spring cleaning.

She was soon discontented. Rochester was a farming centre, and there was wonderful food – goat cheese, fresh apples, sausage. Petter had told her it was all right to eat, but she was gorging herself. The compulsive eating that frequently overcame her could have been viewed as a psychological problem requiring attention, but neither Ingrid nor Petter had such insight.

She was almost as fat as she had been in the spring in Hollywood. Next year how would she ever play the nun in *The Keys of the Kingdom*, the next role David had promised her? And what if after all this time she should get the role of Maria in *For Whom the Bell Tolls*?

No one like Ingrid had ever lived in Rochester, and articles about her arrival appeared in the local papers. One writer, Howard C. Hosmer, who had not interviewed Ingrid or Petter, described an extraordinary scene: crowds standing two deep in front of the Lindstroms' house; fans camped out on the front lawn; the curious peering through the windows. 'The Lindstroms had been living in their house only two days when someone broke in, ransacked their bedroom, took lingerie . . . and several articles of value . . . little keepsakes for celebrity hunters,' Hosmer wrote. 'The next night, someone broke into the house again. The bedroom was turned upside down again. No money was taken, just small personal articles, souvenirs for someone of a screen actress' attempt to become a Rochester housewife.' The article said the situation was so bad that she was going to leave Rochester.

The two breakins never took place, though Ingrid would tell the story repeatedly, and included it in her autobiography. To Selznick, however, on 29 September, she sent the newspaper clipping with a note: 'Don't get upset, because nobody actually got into the house and none of my "dear precious things" disappeared.' There had been one minor incident when a window was left open, but that was all. Nor were there crowds outside the house or swarms of relentless fans. Ingrid had received occasional pestering phone calls, but Petter had installed an unlisted phone, and the calls were no longer a problem. If anything, the problem in Rochester was that life was too tranquil.

Ingrid didn't have to tolerate her life in Rochester very long. She had hardly been there a couple of weeks before she was off again to Hollywood for a screen test in *For Whom the Bell Tolls*. Ingrid had strong insights into her own ambition. In Hollywood, Dan O'Shea reported that she had said that she was 'a very poor loser and when she undertakes a thing like this it is much worse for her to be turned down than if she never undertook it'.

Ingrid was 'frantic' about doing a poor test. Selznick understood his star's mentality. To get her to go along with the test at Paramount, he insisted on all sorts of conditions. He wouldn't allow a full screen test, but a silent version, supposedly simply to show how Ingrid looked in a short wig. Only those producers and directors at Paramount directly involved with *For Whom the Bell Tolls* would be permitted to look at the film, then the negative and all prints would have to be given to Selznick. O'Shea added a further precaution; Ingrid would do the test under an assumed name, Marie Devoe.

Ingrid waited for days while the Selznick and Paramount executives negotiated the specific conditions for the test. Finally, at the end of October, Selznick telephoned Sam Wood, the film's director, to learn what was holding up the test. Wood told Selznick that he thought Ingrid 'was all wrong for the role . . . He did not think she could wear trousers properly, that is without looking like a girl, and he thought she was too tall.' Ingrid got on the train and headed back to Rochester. She had heard Wood's excuses – her height, her look in slacks – but she realized that 'another reason (perhaps the real one) would have hurt me more'.

Ingrid had no agent and the Selznick people attempted to deal with Petter in renegotiating Ingrid's contract. In July, Petter had warned Kay that she had 'better count on the possibility of an agent's voice loudly calling from Rochester in the future'. He was a man of his word.

'I really feel a great responsibility,' he wrote Kay Brown. 'I have been fortunate to meet the finest character and one of the greatest actresses, both in the same person. We do not know very much about

the future of that person, and actress, but . . . she probably will go
on some years ahead . . . If not, the reason most likely is that the
people around her – including myself – failed and misled her.'

Selznick wanted to tie Ingrid up in a longer-term contract, and add
an extra movie each year. He had wanted to do it while *For Whom
the Bell Tolls* hung in the balance. If she was offered the part of Maria,
he had planned to refuse to lend her out until she signed a new
contract. Although Ingrid knew about Selznick's plan, she found it
useful to feign innocence and play the sweet ingenue. On 7 November
she wrote from Rochester: 'With your wisdom and my intuition we
should go far!'

Those were sentiments with which Selznick would not have dis-
agreed, but he found her letter disquieting. He was worried that
Ingrid's English wasn't improving, because she was spending so
much time with Petter, speaking Swedish. According to Petter,
however, he and Ingrid always spoke English together. That was
another extraordinary comment on the quality of their marriage.
What they had in common above all else was that they were Swedish.
To give up the language that they spoke with ease was to make even
their most intimate moments a learning exercise, like not slouching.

Yet the ending of Ingrid's letter *was* incomprehensible enough to
justify Selznick's concern. In her clear, large handwriting, Ingrid
wrote: 'It will please you to know that I understand, that my cabbage
head should know you can't catch the larks by being in cahoot with
hoodlums even for a C-note cash on the nail every day because there
is always the danger of passing in your cheques unexpectedly!'

Rochester was far from Sweden, but one could lead a very Swedish
life in the upstate New York city. Petter, the boy from small town
Sweden, enjoyed much of his life in Rochester, and he thought that
Ingrid could enjoy it as well. 'She was working only eight weeks a
year and I thought she would stay in Rochester,' Petter says. 'I
thought she could be there just as well – we had skiing, swimming,
and steam baths.'

Petter had what he thought was quite a realistic vision of his
marriage. 'She was a healthy girl. I was a healthy boy. She had a
sense of humour. As marriages go – and I saw a lot of young doctors
and their wives – I was always hopeful. We always thought that she
would work until she was about forty. That's when as a doctor I
would really start to be at the top.'

Back in Stockholm, Kay Brown had thought that Petter and Ingrid
were naive. There were, indeed, things about life that neither of them
understood. Ingrid breezed in and out of Rochester, in and out of
her marriage, in and out of motherhood, as if this were just one of

many roles; she didn't see that life is not a series of episodes but a continuum. If one was in endless motion, then one risked becoming nothing but memories, anecdotes, clippings, and reels of film.

Ingrid had been back only a few weeks before she was off to New York early in December to do a radio programme with Spencer Tracy. If anything, she was only looking for a diversion, a little attention. When she saw an attractive man, she needed to know that he wanted her. It was like looking in a mirror, and if she sometimes ended up in bed it was proof of nothing more than her own desirability.

Winter arrives early in upstate New York. By mid-December Ingrid and Petter had already gone skiing in Rochester. Petter was very busy, though, and for long hours Ingrid was by herself. Mabel, the maid, did the shopping, but occasionally Ingrid took Pia grocery shopping at Loblaw's in South Avenue. Sometimes they went ice skating on Riley Pond in Cobbs Hill Park or for a romp through the snow in Highland Park. Sometimes, too, Ingrid sat by the window looking out at the snow, listening to the radio, knitting sweaters for Pia's dolls, and thinking that she seemed 'so very, very far away from a camera eye'.

Petter decided to have a dinner party for the dean and a dozen or so of his colleagues at the school and their wives. 'Ingrid stopped talking and just sat there,' Petter remembers. 'She said afterwards, "Don't ever invite physicians again to our house. They don't know anything about film." She refused to have anything to do with doctors from then on. I never had them in the house again. I was invited time and time again, and I could never invite people. I had to take people out or give gifts or flowers.'

One of those Petter took out to dinner was Dr Ella McCann, a biochemistry professor, who tutored him in scientific English. 'We talked about his work,' McCann said of her dinners with Petter and Ingrid at Rochester's Sagamore Hotel. 'We didn't talk about her very much. He used to tell her she talked too much. He said, You have a good brain on you but you talk too much.

'I think that he thought a great deal of her. He was very proud of her career. I thought it was one of these European marriages that would never break up. They were unalike. There was no question. They were not alike.'

All the same there were good moments in the house on South Avenue. She was so proud of three-year-old Pia, whom she considered an 'extraordinary child'. She didn't want her daughter to be spoiled. She told her that for Christmas they would give away all Pia's unwanted toys. Pia sorted through her possessions.

Selznick sent Ingrid expensive topaz jewellery for Christmas, but not the gift that she wanted above all others: a role in a new film. All she had in the offing for 1942 was the role of Sister Veronica in *The Keys of the Kingdom*. Even Selznick thought privately that the predicament was 'a frightening one from the standpoint of her career'.

Ingrid went to New York to do *The Kate Smith Show* on radio in January. Back in Rochester, she maintained her regimen of reading and writing and walking with Pia. Then in mid-February she began sitting in a corner by herself. She didn't care about anyone or anything, and she felt that Petter didn't even notice. She wouldn't even take Pia for her walk. She wouldn't exercise.

Everything seemed to be going wrong. She was dying to make an American version of the British *Gaslight*, but Selznick was threatening not to buy the rights unless she signed a longer-term contract. She was losing all the parts she wanted. She had told Kay that 'she would forgive [her] everything in the world, except the loss of *Strange Woman* to Bette Davis'. And now Warner Brothers had announced that Bette Davis had the role. On the question of the renegotiated contract, Petter wrote to Kay, 'I should be very happy if you would discuss the present situation with me again ten years hereafter.' The Selznick organization found him proud, self-righteous, and unyielding.

Ingrid and Selznick had always exchanged adoring letters, no matter what brutal denunciations they might occasionally make in private. That façade collapsed now. When Ingrid met Kay in March, she wrote Ruth that she had sworn and yelled, and hoped that Selznick would drop her option. According to Selznick documents, Petter and Kay spent a marathon seven straight hours in unsuccessful negotiations, a meeting Petter says he never attended. Kay was nonplussed at Petter's 'genius of no-yessing everything'. Petter did not renegotiate Ingrid's contract. Instead, Ingrid signed a non-exclusive agreement with Charles Feldman, a top Hollywood agent, a solution that pleased both Ingrid and Selznick. It was, nonetheless, a mark of Petter's unfamiliarity with Hollywood that he didn't understand that an agent was paid out of his client's share; Petter wanted the agent to be paid by the studio.

On 24 March, when Ingrid appeared on the Book-of-the-Month Club radio programme, she managed a subtle dig at Selznick. 'I've heard some curious accents come out of Hollywood,' the interviewer said, 'and from native-born actors and actresses, and I would say that they were further from the King's English than yours.' 'I hope Mr Selznick is listening,' Ingrid replied.

A week later Ingrid played Jenny Lind on the *Cavalcade of America* programme: Selznick was not listening. Afterwards he heard reports that Ingrid's accent was overwhelming. He wrote Kay: 'I wish you would tell Ingrid . . . that she will be the prime sufferer from her laziness and indifference.' Selznick was tired of Ingrid's 'squawking about my not making pictures with her', when he was planning to star her in *The Keys of the Kingdom*, a movie that 'from the standpoint of cast, exploitation and pretentiousness will be second only to *Gone With the Wind*'.

Selznick wanted Ingrid to know that she wasn't the only actress in Hollywood. Rosalind Russell had read *The Keys of the Kingdom* and 'was insane about it'. Ingrid simply didn't appreciate him. 'But for the terrible way I have treated her, she might be happily in Sweden waiting for the Germans . . . I suppose it's time I grew up and learned that all actresses are alike whether they are born in Brooklyn or Stockholm.'

Kay was getting tired of Selznick's outbursts; still, she sat Ingrid down and conveyed Selznick's criticism. Ingrid couldn't understand. She had worked hard on the role of JennyLind. The New York critics had praised her performance. The *New York Daily Mirror* called it 'the greatest acting from a Hollywood star we have ever had on radio'.

Kay also informed Ingrid that Rosalind Russell had called Selznick, seeking the lead in *The Keys of the Kingdom*. After hearing all this, Ingrid cancelled her luncheon with Kay, saying that 'she was so unhappy she wouldn't be fit company for anyone'.

When Ingrid had arrived in America, she had thought that she and Selznick shared the same dreams. She had believed in him and had been almost giddy in her enthusiasm, but Selznick hadn't made a film since *Rebecca*. He was at times ranting, irrational, and megalomaniacal. One day he would be talking about 'selling' Ingrid to another studio, with words that could have come from *Gone With the Wind*, the next he was elaborating on his glorious, golden dreams of films, spinning a web around Ingrid once again. 'She [Ingrid] is bewildered by the constant beating I am forced to give her,' Kay wrote Selznick. 'I am a little bewildered too.'

Selznick would have none of it. He railed against 'that Swedish genius Lindstrom' whom he considered graceless and ungrateful. 'Ingrid's devotion to me reminds me of Ronald Colman's friendship – both apparently give me the privilege of costing myself money,' he replied to Kay. 'I feel that from the outset all of us have failed to crash through that combination that Ingrid and Petter have shrewdly or innocently thrown together – a combination of stubbornness, irrational resistance to making the further development of her career easier, sweetness and light, and wounded animal cries.'

Money, fame, and power were the only salves that could soothe these wounds. But none of Ingrid's potential roles were working out for her. There had been talk for a while renewed interest in a screen test as Maria in *For Whom the Bell Tolls*, but that proved wrong. Moreover, Ingrid lost the other role that Selznick wanted strongly for her, starring with Spencer Tracy in *Keeper of the Flame*. George Cukor, the director, had wanted Ingrid, but MGM didn't. Nor did her old friend Spencer Tracy. He preferred Katharine Hepburn.

Ingrid had had so many disappointments, but finally, on 20 April 1942, she learned that she had a role in a new film. She was so excited that she couldn't sleep. She tossed so next to Petter that he couldn't sleep either, and three times she had to go downstairs to sit by herself in the living room. For weeks she had not allowed herself to *feel* how much she missed the film world. Now she could admit it. In a few days she would be gone, back to Hollywood, back to her world. She knew nothing about the film except its name, *Casablanca*, but that hardly mattered. She wired Selznick that she was 'fainting crying screaming' and preparing to return to Hollywood.

For four months Hal Wallis, the Warner Brothers producer, had been seeking the proper female lead to play the beautiful, tormented Ilsa Lund Laszlo opposite Humphrey Bogart as Rick, the cynical, world-weary saloon owner. In February, Ann Sheridan had been set for the part. Hedy Lamarr had been another possibility, but MGM wouldn't loan her out. On 1 April, Wallis decided to go ahead with plans to test yet another actress, Michele Morgan, and to talk to Selznick about Ingrid.

Wallis now considered Ingrid his 'first choice, ideal for the foreign girl with a slight accent'. Wallis was the kind of producer that Selznick once had been, with an almost compulsively detailed concern for his films. He was contemptuous of Selznick, whom he considered 'an agent at heart'. 'Selznick was always very evasive,' says Wallis. 'I put up with Selznick because . . . he had the ace card.' During a trip to New York, he called on Selznick at the Carlyle Hotel, where both were staying. Selznick was interested, but he wanted to hear more about the script.

Julius and Philip Epstein, the two screenwriters on the project, were assigned the unenviable task of telling Selznick the plot of an only partially written script. 'What will we tell him?' Julius asked. 'Tell him anything, but get Bergman,' Wallis replied. The Epstein twins were a highly successful team. They could tear a screenplay apart in a few hours, turning characters and scenes upside down, and they could wing it with David O. Selznick as well.

Julius talked while Selznick ate lunch at his desk, never looking up. Julius had been in enough story conferences to know that he was losing it. He had been there for a good while and he hadn't even talked about Ingrid's character. One device always worked in Hollywood: say you were going to do a film like the big hit of the day. So Julius mentioned *Algiers*, the Charles Boyer–Hedy Lamarr hit. 'I said *Casablanca* is going to have a lot of that *Algiers* schmaltz – lots of atmosphere, cigarette smoke, guitar music,' Julius remembers. 'Selznick looked up and nodded. We knew then we had Bergman.'

Now the deal had to be struck. Wallis had a touch of the agent in his soul too. He also knew that he had some good cards. Warners had recently bought the rights to Edna Ferber's novel *Saratoga Trunk*, a film that he had heard Ingrid very much wanted to make. He knew, moreover, that for one of his own pictures Selznick wanted Olivia de Havilland, then under contract to Warner Brothers. Selznick, however, was not going to tie Ingrid up in a two-picture contract. And so, for a promise of the lead in *Saratoga Trunk*, but no signed commitment, the loan-out of Olivia de Havilland to Selznick, and $25,000 in salary, Ingrid was signed for *Casablanca*.

According to Wallis, Selznick didn't even bother perusing the still-unfinished script before signing the contract. One of the reasons Selznick was so anxious to sign Ingrid to a film right away was that he had heard that Sweden might soon be forced into joining the Axis; he had told O'Shea confidentially that made it 'all the more important our bearing down on getting a picture for her immediately'.

With all his concerns, it didn't appear to matter to Selznick that by signing Ingrid to do an anti-Nazi film, he was dumping upon Wallis and Warner Brothers a public relations problem that could have been devastating to the success of *Casablanca*. Doubly ironic was the fact that a year before, Ingrid might well have rejected *Casablanca* as too anti-German.

Michael Curtiz, her new director, had a background as clouded and mysterious as that of Rick Blaine, Humphrey Bogart's character in *Casablanca*. He had an Eastern European face, with high cheekbones and forehead, thick eyebrows set tightly against sharp, inquisitive eyes. A Hungarian Jew, Curtiz claimed to have worked in a travelling circus as a juggler, strongman, and trampoline artist before beginning work in the nascent Budapest film industry. In 1919, during the filming of Molnár's *Liliom*, he'd fled from Béla Kun's short-lived Communist regime. Now he was the most successful director at Warner Brothers. He had his own estate, where he played the country squire; indeed, at the start of *Casablanca*, Curtiz's right hand was bandaged from an injury suffered on the polo field.

Curtiz might have his own polo field, but he could still remember hearing, as a boy on the street in Budapest, a policeman call out, 'Long live the king and beat the Jew'. His mother and two brothers had also fled Budapest; he had lived within modern history as few Americans had, and yet he had rejected that knowledge in Hollywood, making westerns like *Santa Fe Trail*, musicals like *Yankee Doodle Dandy*, films celebrating an idealized America, as if history were dirt that had been turfed over in America. He understood that 'we are not out here to preach with pictures, to take political sides or bring a great message. We are here to entertain.' He knew, then, that he was not making a *Casablanca* that was Casablanca, or Nazis that were Nazis. He was making an exotic romance, an *Algiers*, with a soupçon of reality thrown in.

Casablanca was shot sequentially. This was an unusual and expensive procedure, but since the script was not finished, Wallis had little choice. Most of the time the first day – 25 May 1942 – was spent rehearsing and waiting while the lighting was set up. Then, as Curtiz began shooting the first scene, the sound mixer announced that he could hear the hum of the sun arc, and in the end nothing was filmed.

The first day was an unhappy harbinger of the entire filming. Ingrid did not make her initial appearance until well into the film; before that she was busy with wardrobe tests. She was playing Hollywood's idea of a refugee, and it would not do for her to sit in Rick's café dressed less than elegantly. Much of the original wardrobe was thrown out. She didn't look good in most of the hats; all but one large white hat were got rid of. So was an evening dress that made her look bulky. Ingrid heard Selznick's admonition that 'the reason she has caught on is because of her lack of make-up and fresh appearance, so she should take the make-up off the eyebrows and stop using lipstick and go back to the way she was in *Intermezzo*'. Ingrid promised to 'be careful to use less' make-up, although as far as she could tell, she wasn't using any more than on her previous pictures.

Petter visited early in June, but most of his wife's time was taken up with preparation for *Casablanca*. Ingrid liked to prepare thoroughly for a role, but as she began work a full script didn't exist. Films are almost by definition the most collegial of arts, but even given that, *Casablanca* was unusual for the number of people who made major contributions.

It is based on an unproduced play by Murray Burnett and Joan Ali-son, *Everybody Comes to Rick's*, a fact that Ingrid didn't even know. Besides the Epstein twins, Howard Koch worked on the script; so did Casey Robinson, yet another Warner Brothers writer, who received no credit on the film, and who, according to Wallis, 'along with the Epsteins probably did the major part of it'. Ingrid knew the broad outline of the story. In the film, Casablanca is a station between the Nazis and the West, a dangerous, evil backwater. The hot spot in town is Café Americain, owned by Rick Blaine, a cynical American with a checkered past. Ingrid, as the Norwegian-born Ilsa Lund Laszlo, arrives in Casablanca on the arm of her husband, Victor Laszlo, a famous Czech anti-Nazi activist. They are seeking passage from the Vichy-controlled city to the West. To leave Casablanca on the plane to Lisbon, the Laszlos must obtain letters of transit. The nefarious Nazi officer, Major Heinrich Strasser, intends to prevent them from getting the documents.

At the Café Américain, Ingrid meets her old lover from her Paris days, Rick Blaine, whom she deserted the day the Germans arrived – the day, Rick reminds her, 'the Germans wore grey and you wore blue'. Rick is toasting his sorrow in champagne and cigarettes. Later, Ilsa tells Rick that when they were together in Paris she was already married to this 'great and courageous activist who opened up for her a whole beautiful world full of knowledge and thoughts and ideals . . . and she looked up to him and worshipped him, with a feeling that she supposed was love'. Ilsa says that in Paris she thought that her husband had died in a concentration camp; but when she learned that Laszlo was still alive, she fled from Rick, telling him nothing. Rick and Ilsa still passionately love one another. Rick has obtained the coveted letters of transit, the key to freedom; the plot turns on whether Ilsa will choose her lover or her husband, personal happiness or responsibility.

Among Hollywood male stars there is only one commandment: the hero gets the girl. Both Bogart and Henreid insisted that they be the one to walk off with Ingrid. Henreid had just finished *Now, Voyager*, in which he made romantic film history by putting two cigarettes at once in his lips, lighting them, and passing one to Bette Davis. After such a strong role, he was worried that the part of the heroic Victor Laszlo conversing with Nazis in a North African nightclub was not only a comedown but a foolish role deserving of comic opera. At Warner Brothers, Henreid was considered 'a bit of a ham'. His part was built up for him to agree to accept the role; it was, nonetheless, a role that could have seemed silly and naive against the brutal realities of Nazism. In real life *Casablanca* would have ended in the first reel – with Victor Laszlo's assassination.

Bogart was not much happier with his part than Henreid. An early reader of the play at the studio called the character 'two parts Hemingway, one part Scott Fitzgerald, and a dash of café Christ'. Bogart had snarled his way to stardom, as the bad guy in a series of Warner Brothers gangster films; only in his latest role, as Dashiell Hammett's tough, cynical detective Sam Spade in *The Maltese Falcon*, had he played a sympathetic leading man. No romantic star had ever had a face like Bogart's. He did for ordinary-looking men what Perrier did for water, but he wondered whether in *Casablanca* the audience would believe that a woman as beautiful as Ingrid would fall for a man with a mug like his.

Bogart's problems with the unfinished script were larger than that. When all Europe was aflame, Bogart wasn't about to play a broken-down former lawyer crying into his beer about a lost love. Rick was too much of a 'whiner'; he wasn't tough enough; he hadn't done enough. Wallis agreed to strengthen Rick's character.

When Bogart made his first appearance, sitting at a table in his Café Americain, the audience had already learned about him from other characters. Bogart's acting resonated with all that knowledge. He owned the film; yet when Ingrid arrived on the scene, he would have to make the audience believe that worldly, well-worn Rick could be so devastated by a mere love affair. Bogart, apprehensive about his female co-star, made a point of observing Ingrid's first scene.

Curtiz thought that Ingrid would be successful in *Casablanca* because she was playing a sympathetic, attractive woman. In fact, Ingrid was justifying, indeed making irresistible, behaviour that much of her audience would have considered immoral.

Ilsa radiates goodness and vulnerability; yet she is a woman who wants 'no questions' asked about her past – whom Rick accuses of being little better than a whore. An early reader of the play at the studio pointed out that 'the pre-action relationship between Rick and Lois [*sic*] . . . is one which does not seem permissible in a film'. After all, Ilsa had been involved in either an adulterous affair with Rick or, if she is telling the truth, a torrid romance soon after the assumed death of her heroic husband. On one level the whole question of the movie is whether she will take up with Rick again, hardly a morally elevating plot, particularly in a World War II setting. It would be no simple matter to make the character of Ilsa work so that the moral ambiguity and sensuousness become almost subliminal, deepening and broadening the part. The audience has to feel for Ilsa from the moment she appears onscreen.

If there is one definition of a great film star, it is that the world is different once he or she appears, different in a way that no one fully comprehends. Ingrid had much time to prepare her role before she made her first appearance, in the seventy-fifth shot of *Casablanca*. No other character had heralded the arrival of Ilsa Lund, telling of her beauty, vulnerability, or plight. Suddenly, Ingrid is there, dressed in white, walking with Henreid, in an off-white suit, into the shadowy world of Rick's Café. As she sits next to Henreid, Ingrid is not even the centre of the scene. But it is as if a ray of light has entered Rick's Café.

Ilsa notices Rick's black piano player and alter ego, Sam (Dooley Wilson), and asks him to play 'As Times Goes By'. Sam reluctantly agrees and sings in a voice charged with poignancy:

> You must remember this
> A kiss is just a kiss
> A sigh is just a sigh
> The fundamental things apply
> As times goes by.

Rick rushes into the nightclub, tormented by the romantic strains of the song he has told Sam must never be played again. Rick sees Ilsa. On an emotional level, the rest of the film does little more than elucidate the look in Ingrid's eyes, a look that manages to convey yearning, courage, uncertainty, bewilderment, love, melancholy, and pain.

'I didn't do anything I've never done before,' Bogart said afterwards of his role in *Casablanca*. 'But when the camera moves in on that Bergman face, and she's saying she loves you, it would make anybody look romantic.' Seeing the extraordinary chemistry between Ingrid and Bogart, many moviegoers assumed that their relationship must have continued off the set. But when asked about this, Ingrid always said, 'I kissed him but I never knew him.'

An actor is a scavenger, picking up his ideas and techniques from his own life and the lives of others, from past emotions and lives merely brushed against. Despite his screen image, Bogart was full of insecurity and self-doubt. When his scenes were finished, he wasn't flirting with Ingrid, tossing off bons mots that could have been used in the film; he was usually off by himself in his small trailer, talking about his part to buddies such as Howard Koch, getting advice, or playing chess.

Bogart had no trouble looking world-weary on screen. He knew all about a tragic romance, and it wasn't crying in a café over a sentimental song; it was life with his third wife, Mayo Methot, at 'Sluggy Hollow', his West Hollywood home. It was booze, blood and brawls, a butcher knife in the back, a fistfight in the living room, pistol shots in the living room ceiling. It was a wife so jealous of Ingrid that he didn't dare get near his co-star. It was life as a

forty-two-year-old balding actor with an alcoholic wife, a drinking
problem of his own, and a co-star so beautiful, so irresistible, so
shrewdly professional, that he was likely to lose the movie to her.

Ingrid didn't know much about Bogart's personal life. As part of
her own preparation for *Casablanca* she had screened *The Maltese
Falcon* over and over again. She could see that Bogart was a fine,
strong screen actor; she could still be star struck herself, and she had
been apprehensive about meeting Bogart. She discovered that he was
nothing like his image. On the set he was very professional; she did
not guess at his insecurities. Nor did she have any idea of the lengths
to which he was going to best her in their scenes together.

One of his advisers, Mel Baker, had told Bogart: 'This is the first
time you've ever played the romantic lead against a major star. You
stand still, and always make her come to you. Mike probably won't
notice it, and if she complains you can tell her it's tacit in the script.
You've got something she wants, so she has to come to you.'

Bogart did as he was told. It worked, not only for Bogart but for
Ingrid too, as the emotionally vulnerable Ilsa drawn back and forth
between the two men, the two focal points of her life. Here was Rick
Blaine: romantic, sexual, irresponsible, untrustworthy, witty. And
here was Victor Laszlo: trustworthy, conservative, responsible, pa-
ternal, solid. Blaine and Laszlo represented the two poles of male
attractiveness, poles that would prove as far apart in Ingrid's personal
life as in the film.

Ingrid worked best when she was in love with her leading man.
A romance might have developed if Bogart's wife had not been
watching so jealously. 'I think Bogart was in love with Ingrid,' says
Bob William, Bogart's publicist on *Casablanca*. 'He was kind of
jealous if I would bring anyone on the set, another man, to see her.
He would sulk. I had a feeling he was kind of smitten with her.'

As for having an affair with Curtiz, Ingrid had affairs with directors, but that did not include fornicating with a man of Curtiz's
reputation. She was perfectly aware that he almost always had at least
one 'starlet' on the set whose greatest performance took place in
Curtiz's dressing room. Indeed, one day during the shooting, Peter
Lorre secretly hooked up microphones in the director's love nest.
'Oh, God! Oh, no, no, no, . . .' Curtiz's impassioned voice came
surging across the set. 'Oh, yes, yes . . . Oh, God, yes . . .'

Ingrid's attitude towards the married Henreid was just as distant.
In the film he was her loyal, caring partner. Henreid looked very much
like Petter. Victor Laszlo had Petter's staid stability, his earnestness. In
creating her emotional attitude towards her husband in *Casablanca*,
she may well have drawn on her real marriage.

The set of *Casablanca* was a microcosm of the European world that seemed so remote for Ingrid now. To some of those on the set, a drama of refugees fleeing Nazism was as real as life. Henreid had fled Vienna after the Nazis marched in and had almost been interned in Britain as an enemy alien. Madeleine LeBeau, who had a featured role as a beautiful young refugee, had recently escaped from occupied France. The French technical director, Lieutenant Robert Aisner, had escaped from a German concentration camp and made his way to Hollywood via Casablanca. German-born Conrad Veidt, who played the villainous Major Strasser, was a prominent anti-Nazi. Another famous German star in the film was Peter Lorre. Few Americans who saw Lorre as the sleazy Ugarte knew that the Jewish actor had only a few years before stood on stage at a Berlin festival and daringly satirized the Nazis. S. Z. Sakall, who had a delightful cameo as a waiter at Rick's café was, like Curtiz, of Hungarian birth; one of the extras in a café scene, Trudy Berliner, had been a star at UFA in Berlin. Sitting next to Berliner was Dina Smirnova, once a great actress in her native Russia. In all, the Warners publicity office counted thirty-four nationalities among the cast of *Casablanca*.

Each one of these roles, then, was touched with a *vraisemblance* unusual in Hollywood films. It was as if in *Gone With the Wind* Vivien Leigh and Clark Gable had lived through the Civil War and the black actors had themselves once been slaves.

Ingrid liked her film life to be full of order, discipline, and certainty, but on the set of *Casablanca* she found herself often amid disorder, indiscipline, and uncertainty. Even with a finished script, Curtiz was not an easy director with whom to work. *Casablanca* seemed in trouble, and Curtiz knew what could happen if the film failed. 'In Europe, if an actor or director establish himself, he live forever,' Curtiz said later. 'Here, if he doesn't make dough, they kick him out. Hollywood is money, money, money.

'I work because I don't want to be kicked out. The only way you can stay on top is keep on smiling and show your teeth. You feeling lousy and they ask you how you feel. You say, "Okay, fine, just fine. Everything is wonderful."'

Curtiz conveyed his insecurity to everyone on the set. Nonetheless, he remained a courtly European who still clicked his heels when he met a lady. He was always civil to Ingrid. His English, though, was as difficult to understand as Ratoff's had been on *Intermezzo*. 'Don't play it hard,' he told her. 'Act easy-go-lucky.' During a café scene he directed: 'Now we will hear mutters from the natives and visitors in the café. And in the background I will have the low throbbing music of the native tom-thumbs.'

Even understanding Curtiz didn't always help. Ingrid had to know whom she was in love with: Henreid or Bogart. How could she play the part if she didn't know at least that? 'We don't know yet,' Curtiz told her. 'Just play it . . . in–between.'

Through most of the shooting, Ingrid didn't know which man had won.

Ingrid attempted to play the part down the middle. In doing so she became the emotional centre of the film, moving between the two other main characters. Ingrid is successful because Bogart and Henreid are successful. Rick Blaine could have been a silly Hollywood invention, a tough guy who cries over a song; but Bogart's Rick Blaine is indeed worthy of Ilsa's love, a man struggling with his own personal isolation, a metaphor for America herself in the days before Pearl Harbor. As for Henreid, he had good reason to fear that his part could be no more than comic opera; but he played Laszlo with dignity, nobility, and the high simplicity of the idealist. He, too, was worthy of Ilsa's love.

In a typical Hollywood melodrama, Ingrid would have flown off with Bogart, after Henreid died heroically, a conclusion that was indeed contemplated. But in an ending as perfect as a poem, both men live and Ingrid does not have to choose between them. 'I don't know what's right any longer,' Ingrid says. 'You have to think of both of us, for all of us.' Bogart chooses for her, telling Ilsa that she must leave with Laszlo, as he and his sidekick, Captain Renault, go off to fight the Nazis.

In perhaps the most famous farewell scene in films, Bogart bids goodbye to Ingrid on the grey tarmac on Stage 21, the fog machines blasting away with over a million cubic feet of vapourized oil. Standing in his rumpled trench coat and fedora, looking into Ingrid's tear-filled eyes, Bogart speaks: 'Look, I'm no good at being noble, but it doesn't take much to see that the problems of three little people don't amount to a hill of beans in this crazy world. Someday you'll understand that . . .

'Here's looking at you, kid.'

CHAPTER 8

A TIGRESS WHO HAS MADE A KILL

During the last days of shooting *Casablanca*, Ingrid prepared to return to Rochester, to spend the rest of the summer with Petter and Pia. Then she heard incredible news. The first rushes of Vera Zorina in *For Whom the Bell Tolls* were so bad that Paramount wanted to test Ingrid for the part of Maria. Paramount planned two full screen tests, one in the studio, the other on location. Hundreds of thousands of dollars were at stake, as well as the careers of several Paramount executives. There were rumours that if Ingrid didn't work out, Paramount might kill the film altogether.

Selznick felt that the idea of a screen test was 'absolute nonsense'. Hollywood was a sieve; once word got out that Ingrid had tested for the part, Zorina was finished. If Paramount insisted on going ahead, though, the producer felt it was imperative to try to keep the whole business quiet; Ingrid's reputation was on the line.

Ambition is a rude imperative. Selznick wanted the test to take place on location in California's Sierra Nevada mountains, where *For Whom the Bell Tolls* was being filmed. That would give Ingrid her best opportunity; there she could play opposite the other star of the film, Gary Cooper, with Sam Wood directing, all presumably while Zorina rested unknowingly in her cabin.

Stars usually consider a screen test a humiliation, suggesting a lack of confidence in the performer; Ingrid always insisted that she was given only a make-up test. In fact, she was put through a major screen test at Paramount on Friday, 31 July 1942. By then everyone in Hollywood knew about the 'secret' test. Two days before the 'Hollywood Rambler' column in the *Hollywood Reporter* had noted that 'Buddy DeSylva [the executive producer] and Sam Wood are really battling. It seems the director still isn't reconciled to the way Maria was cast . . . Ingrid Bergman is quietly testing, and if Zorina is replaced it'll be Ingrid.'

The stakes, then, were even higher now. If Ingrid lost the part, her humiliation would indisputably be public.

In *For Whom the Bell Tolls*, Maria is a long-limbed creature of the mountains. Ingrid had heard that in the early rushes Zorina had tiptoed through the rock-strewn passages of the Sierra Nevadas as if she were afraid that she might break her dancer's legs. For Ingrid, it was not her legs that she would always try to protect, but her face; and it was her face that would win her the part of Maria. Ingrid wanted to try one test with eyelashes, one without; one test without make-up but with her lips powdered down, and one with full make-up.

Maria's hair in *For Whom the Bell Tolls* has been cut off so that 'it was but little longer than the fur on a beaver pelt'. Vera's beautiful long hair had been so ungraciously cut that on film she looked like a freshly shorn lamb. Ingrid was not about to cut her hair until she definitely had the part. Nor, for the screen test, did she intend to wear a wig; she wanted Hazel Rogers, a prominent hairdresser to be there to pin back her hair.

Sam Wood had complained about Ingrid's looks in slacks, and as far back as *Intermezzo* Selznick had been unhappy with Ingrid's posterior. For the test Ingrid had the service of Miss Ray at Magnin's, a lady whom Selznick referred to inelegantly as 'the best girdle woman'.

Ingrid did the screen test on Friday. It would be Sunday, however, before Sam Wood, the director, returned from location and, together with Frank Freeman, a Paramount vice-president, and Buddy De-Sylva, made his choice. They would presumably look at both Ingrid's and Zorina's tests.

On Sunday, Ingrid sat next to the phone, waiting for Wood's call. And the phone never rang.

The next morning she was at Warner Brothers making publicity shots for *Casablanca* with Henreid. During the filming Henreid had sometimes wondered how someone as sweet, unassuming, and vulnerable as Ingrid could have become a star. He assumed that there had to be someone behind Ingrid, an éminence grise pushing and prodding her upwards.

Ingrid and Henreid stood posing together for the photographer, a not unpleasant chore for an actor. Yet Ingrid seemed ill at ease.

'Are you all right?' asked Henreid. Ingrid appeared on the verge of tears.

'All right? I'm heartbroken.'

Henreid was a man of the world. Though he knew about Ingrid's distant husband in Rochester, he assumed that she was involved in an unhappy love affair. He proceeded to try to cheer her up with a monologue on men, women, and love.

'No! No!' Ingrid interjected. 'I'm talking about *For Whom the Bell Tolls* . . . It's going to be a blockbuster of a movie, and I tested for it. It's a fantastic part.'

'Well, maybe you'll get it,' the actor replied.

'Oh, Paul, I lost it. They gave it to Vera Zorina! I wanted that part so badly, you've no idea. Picking Vera Zorina of all people. She can't act, Paul. She just can't and I'm good. I'm really good! I just hope they find out how bad she is.'

Ingrid talked with a conviction and energy unlike anything Henreid had ever heard. It was as if he was watching a great performance, though which was the act – the woman who stood before him now so proudly demeaning her successful competitor, or the modest woman he had known on the set?

The phone rang. Ingrid took the call.

Selznick was on the line.

Ingrid shrieked.

'I got it, Paul. I got it. I got it.'

'What happened?'

'I got the part of Maria. I just knew that if I fought hard enough they'd come to their senses . . . Paul, we've got to celebrate.'

Ingrid was her old self, but for an instant Henreid had seen the 'triumphant vitality and strength', the great secret engine that propelled Ingrid upward.

Selznick settled quickly with Paramount. He first wanted between $100,000 and $125,000 for Ingrid's services, three to four times what he received for her on *Casablanca*. He settled on a contract that paid him $90,666.65, as against the $31,770.83 that he paid Ingrid. Selznick felt that he was settling for less than he might have, but still it was a neat bit of business. Ingrid didn't care. She simply wanted to get on with it. She had just finished a strenuous film, and Selznick had requested two weeks' rest for her. She didn't want to rest. To Ingrid, working was rest.

Ingrid had read *For Whom the Bell Tolls*. She carried it with her now as if it were her book of prayer, underlining and making notations. She knew the story of Robert Jordan and Maria so well that she could recite it like a catechism. Jordan is an American professor fighting in the Spanish Civil War for the leftist loyalist forces against the Spanish fascists and their German allies. Jordan is assigned to blow up a crucial bridge in the mountains near Segovia before a Loyalist offensive. He enlists a group of guerrillas to help him. Among the peasants is Maria, a girl with no last name. Maria is emotionally disembowelled: her parents have been killed; she has been gang raped by the fascists, her head shaved in the prison at Valladolid.

Maria and Jordan fall in love. Their love is like a mountain flower, brilliant and short-lived. Jordan and the guerrillas blow the bridge, though the offensive has been betrayed. As they make their escape, Jordan is fatally wounded. He tells Maria that she must go forth and carry on the struggle; and so she leaves him to die on the mountainside.

Ingrid had just made a film in which at the end she left her lover to join the great struggle against fascism. But whereas *Casablanca* had been a patchwork of compromises that Ingrid considered simply a commercial venture, *For Whom the Bell Tolls* was literature. With a budget of close to three million dollars, it was the biggest production since *Gone With the Wind*, and it was being done with the same concern for the integrity of the original novel.

Ingrid's Hollywood movies had always required endless costume tests and fittings, hair stylings, and make-up tests, an aspect of film making that she liked least. This time, though, there were only simple make-up tests that showed Ingrid glowing with vitality, her countenance radiant. There were costume fittings, but for *real* clothes: a pair of man's trousers tied at the waist with a piece of cord, a long-sleeved shirt, a brown jacket. For the test Edith Head, the costume designer, used men's clothing that she had found in the extras' wardrobe, but for the film Head had new clothes bleached and dyed.

On Wednesday, accompanied by David and Irene Selznick, Ingrid went to Paramount for her Maria haircut. Selznick was going to have Ingrid disastrously shorn; the 'Ingrid bob' that Sydney Guilaroff, the MGM hair stylist, devised was charming, fashionable enough to become a minor fad.

On Friday, 7 August, only four days after she had learned she had the part, Ingrid left for the isolated highlands of the Sierra Nevadas. The location was 450 miles from Los Angeles, and two hours north of the nearest town, Sonora. Another actress might have been fretful and ambivalent about leaving the comforting confines of the studio, with its dressing rooms and endless solicitude, exchanging all that for rude primitive realities. Another wife and mother might have had her melancholy moments, realizing that it would be months before she would see her husband and daughter again. But Ruth Roberts, who was accompanying Ingrid, could see that her charge was 'happy to [the] bursting point'.

As soon as she arrived and saw the little cabin by the river where she and Ruth would live, she went to find the crew and actors. She had to drive a half hour more, then she took a horse farther up into the mountains, and when the horse could go no farther, she 'climbed on all four [*sic*] up to the cliff where the actors were working'.

When Ingrid met Gary Cooper, she blushed. 'Hello, Maria,' he said, and she blushed again. Up here one could almost believe that Ingrid was Maria and Cooper was Robert Jordan, and that in the wild beauty of this place they were living out their lives and love. Cooper had a face that was not merely handsome but seemed to be making a statement about human courage. Ingrid thought the lanky forty-one-year-old actor a 'beautiful man'. Cooper had just won an Academy Award for best actor in *Sergeant York*; he had starred in Hemingway's *A Farewell to Arms*, and went shooting and hunting with 'Papa' himself in Sun Valley.

Ingrid was married and so was Cooper. He was immensely attractive to women, onscreen and offscreen, and the fact that he was known as a womanizer did not hurt his reputation at all. Ingrid's image, though, was unsullied, and it would not do to have rumours in the gossip columns about her and Cooper. Luckily for Ingrid, the movie was being filmed away from the prying eyes of Hollywood.

Ingrid fell in love with Cooper, or was it that Maria fell in love with Jordan? They spent much of their spare time together. They prepared their parts together, and in the evenings they often ate together. In Hollywood, when the Paramount executives saw the rushes of the love scenes, they surmised immediately that a romance had begun.

Ruth Roberts was endlessly solicitous of Ingrid, concerned for her professional and her personal life. Ruth warned Ingrid that she should not look so much in love with Cooper. Although Ingrid did not fully confide in Ruth, her coach and companion knew more about her personal life than anyone else. Almost without realizing what was happening, Ruth had become part of a minor conspiracy, hiding the truth of Ingrid's love life, particularly from Petter. Ingrid was mesmerized by Cooper's personality: 'so enormous, so overpowering – and that expression in his eyes and his face . . . so delicate and so underplayed . . . the most underplaying and most natural actor I ever worked with.'

'Tell him [Selznick] that I am so happy even in the most tragic scenes my eyes are dancing with joy,' she wrote Dan O'Shea. 'I am stunned at the patience, the preparation, and perfection Wood spends on the story,' she wrote Irene Selznick. If Ingrid's eyes danced for joy even in the most tragic scenes, then the scenery danced as well, with too much life and colour. Black paint was sprayed on the streets and the boulders, the fields, and the road, to suggest something of the sombreness of the story, but even that didn't help. Ingrid's legs and feet were black and blue and scratched, hidden under Maria's trousers, her fingernails were broken, her ears were full of dust; but she wrote Irene, 'you don't hear any complaining from Maria', as if she and her fictional heroine had become one. After ten weeks on location most of the crew were overjoyed to go down the mountain for good. Ingrid would have stayed on and on.

Finally, early in September, everyone came down from the mountain, and the last twelve weeks of filming took place at the Paramount studios. Ingrid hoped that *For Whom the Bell Tolls* would prove the 'turning point' of her career. She had the greatest faith in the quality of the film; but it would take months to prepare such a monumental picture for presentation.

As for *Casablanca*, a product of the Hollywood studio system, ground out and packaged like another link of sausage, it was already opening, 26 November 1942, at New York's Hollywood Theater; allied troops had marched into Casablanca, and Wallis wanted to take advantage of the publicity. The film was an immediate popular success, playing to standing-room-only audiences.

For the purposes of the Academy Awards, *Casablanca* was considered a 1943 picture and received six nominations. The 1944 award ceremony would prove to be *Casablanca*'s night. The film received awards for best screenwriting from non-original sources, best director, and, most coveted of all, best film of the year.

In one of the abiding ironies of Ingrid's career, *Casablanca* became the immortal film, not *For Whom the Bell Tolls*. It was the film that helped make her the third most popular female star in America, according to the *Box Office Barometer* poll; it was the film that would be loved and admired and screened long after the reels of many of her other movies had been relegated to the vaults.

On the day before Ingrid left to go up to location for *For Whom the Bell Tolls*, Selznick dictated a long telegram to Petter, so brutal in its finality, so bitterly contemptuous, that if Ingrid had ever seen the document her relationship with the producer could never have been the same. All Selznick's attempts to sign Ingrid to a new contract had been foiled and he was fed up. 'In a lifetime in the picture business I have never encountered such a stubborn resistance to common sense, such a persistent attempt to out-trade and out-smart me and my associates, such ingratitude for unselfish effort.' If Ingrid did not sign a new, seven-year contract immediately, he would refuse to loan her out any more, limiting her to one picture a year.

Selznick did not send that telegram, but his venomous anger remained. The situation was made worse by the fact that Kay Brown was no longer there to mediate. She had left the producer in an acrimonious ending to their long relationship.

Selznick had been planning to force Ingrid to sign a new long-term contract before allowing her to do *For Whom the Bell Tolls*, but had given up on that, in part because he thought that he and Charles Feldman, Ingrid's new agent and an old Hollywood hand, would be able to negotiate a contract. That had not worked out either, and Selznick blamed Petter.

Petter was involved with other aspects of Ingrid's career. He wrote a broadcast for her to deliver over the BBC's Swedish service. When he was unhappy with an Office of War Information essay that a Warner Brothers publicist had written for Ingrid's signature, he edited the manuscript himself. 'I personally would have told Dr Lindstrom to go fly a kite,' Selznick told Whitney Bolton, his publicity director. 'I think a little bludgeoning might do the good doctor some good.'

At Strong Memorial Hospital in Rochester, where he was interning, Petter was proving himself to be an idealistic, dedicated doctor. He was concerned about patients as people and not just as receptacles for intriguing diseases. One day he had the unhappy duty of informing a middle-aged woman that her infected leg would have to be amputated. This was a task that many doctors would have dispatched as quickly as possible. Petter, however, performed the duty in such a way that over a quarter of a century later the woman's son still remembered. 'The way in which your dad broke the news to all of us was done with such feeling and compassion that somehow it made the whole experience a much easier one to take, especially for my mother,' Frank M. Kinsky wrote Pia Lindstrom in 1978. 'But that wasn't all! Your dad made it a point to visit my mother every day. One day, he asked my mother if there was anything special she wanted. She replied that she would like an ice cream cone. Would you believe your dad drove out of the hospital, up to a drugstore two blocks away that sold ice cream cones, and brought one back for my mother.'

In late 1942 Ingrid returned to Rochester to spend some time with Petter and Pia. She loved her husband and daughter, but they were at times a disconcerting intrusion that had to be subtly manipulated. 'I must handle my family with skill too,' she told Selznick's publicity people, equating Petter and Pia with photo sessions, interviews, and other obligations. She wouldn't let anyone do interviews in Rochester, and she shielded her husband and daughter from publicity. The reporters and columnists always wanted personal information that she did not like giving out. Petter wanted no publicity tied to the happen-stance of his marriage; nor did either of them want it for Pia.

Ingrid might look like a publicity-shy maiden, blinded by flash-bulbs, so embarrassed by intimate questions that her face flushed in mortification, but she was as canny as the most flamboyant star. In her free time she enjoyed harvesting the bounty of her publicity efforts, filling scrapbooks full of her clippings.

The articles about Ingrid manufactured in Hollywood had as little to do with journalism as professional wrestling has to do with competitive athletics. Ingrid was part of a creative collaboration between herself, the studios, and the press in creating the image of Ingrid Bergman: great star, great mother, great wife, great person. In January, when she saw what she considered two 'awful' interviews in the current *Silver Screen* and *Movies*, she knew that she was largely to blame. The Paramount publicity department had partially written the articles, and she had read and approved the final version. She could see now that she shouldn't have approved the publicist's having her talk about 'good' and 'bad' women, and about her family. She was even more worried about a forthcoming 'life story' in *Photoplay*. She wrote Selznick, asking him to try to do something. The Selznick office was able to see the copy before it appeared in print, a privilege for which they wired Macfadden Publications their 'deepest apprecia-tion'.

For the holidays Ingrid was back in Rochester, arriving two days before Christmas. On New Year's Eve, thinking how happy she was that she had come to America, she sat down and wrote Selznick a note. 'Dear Boss!' she began. 'I hope that 1943 is a good year and we stick together in spite of the big deals buzzing around us! . . . I'll promise, as I always do New Year's Eve, to be a very good girl.'

Midnight was drawing near. Ingrid and Petter opened a bottle of champagne, and heralded a new year that seemed to promise a bounty of success and happiness. Ingrid had so much to look forward to. The summer before, up in the Sierra Nevadas, she, Sam Wood, and Cooper had all read Edna Ferber's new best-selling novel, *Saratoga Trunk*. They had decided that they wanted to do the film together.

All over America people were talking about who should play the romantic leads. Cooper and Vivien Leigh had led a *Cosmopolitan* poll for the parts. At first, Selznick had not wanted Ingrid to play such an amoral character after the saintly Maria, but Ingrid convinced him, in part perhaps because she was suddenly one of the hottest properties in Hollywood and he wanted to cash in. Warners ended up paying Selznick $253,802.08 for Ingrid's services, while he paid her $69,562.30. As part of the deal he also received the services of

Olivia de Havilland from Warner Brothers for one film for $30,000; he quickly turned around and sold her to RKO for $130,000.

Selznick had been convinced that Cooper would turn down the smaller part of Clint Maroon, a role that would in no way do for his career what Clio might do for Ingrid's. It was, indeed, a measure of Ingrid's appeal for Cooper, that he was willing to take the part. 'Cooper wanted to do it,' remembers Hal Wallis, the producer. 'I think there was a romance with Bergman that had started on *Bell* that carried over on our picture, which didn't hurt the chemistry on our film. It was a two-picture deal.' Petter remembers meeting and talking with Mrs Rocky Cooper. 'Mrs Cooper talked about the two of them spending so much time together, and they're going to make another picture,' Petter says.

At the beginning of February, Ingrid left Rochester for the last time; Petter was coming west to take up his surgical internship at Stanford. On her way back to Hollywood she had agreed to make a side trip to Minnesota for the filming of a documentary film, *Swedes in America*, for the Office of War Information. Ingrid had at first appeared reluctant to make a week-long sojourn for which she would not be paid. Selznick had admonished her: 'I feel rather strongly that up to date you have been asked to do very little in the general and common effort and that we all have to put up with a certain amount of inconveniences.' Once it was made clear to her that her expenses would be paid, she was very willing to make the film.

Ingrid arrived the following evening in the winter-bound city of Minneapolis. Standing there waiting for her was Joseph Henry Steele, Selznick's new publicity director, a position that had the longevity of a front-line soldier in the battle of the Marne. Steele was a courtly, middle-aged gentleman. He had two crippling maladies for a movie publicist: too high principles and too big an ego. He was proud of the dignified image he had helped create for Ronald Colman, the British actor, before joining Selznick, but like most publicists, Steele had the feeling that his endeavours were not sufficiently appreciated.

Ingrid stepped off the train at Great Northern Station in a long mink, and a red-and-white-and-blue knitted hat. Behind her came the maid, carrying Pia in her arms. Steele was absolutely taken with Ingrid. He was amazed at her 'self-effacement', among the stern, gnarled Swedish-American farmers. He was struck by her 'energy and exuberance'. He loved her fresh beauty, which seemed almost eternal, beyond the craft of cosmetics. When she got ready for dinner with him in a mere fifteen minutes, he was astounded. 'It's not true,' he said as he helped her put on her mink. 'You're entirely fictitious.'

By the time they were back in Hollywood, Steele was probably in love with Ingrid. His was not a conventional love – Steele was seeking nothing so banal as a tryst in a hotel room – he was in love with Ingrid's golden image, with a Swedish goddess full of life and spirit.

From then on when he sat down to write articles for her or about her, when he advised her and trumpeted her praises, he did so with a passion, commitment, and concern that was rare among publicists. He believed in Ingrid, *his* Ingrid, and he wanted the world to know about her. Steele had been an occasional writer of fiction, and *his* Ingrid was a mixture of fact, fantasy, might-have-beens, conjecture. He saw in her glamour a transcendent beauty that he could touch by knowing her. He had the arrogance of a fan too, as if he knew and understood her better than she knew and understood herself. 'Sometimes I think she's the most beautiful woman I have ever met,' he wrote, in concluding one of many articles about Ingrid. 'If what I have told you is not beauty, then my forty years and more have been meaningless and I have learned nothing.'

By 2 March, when Ingrid went to work on *Saratoga Trunk*, the censors had already softened the portrait of a Clio Dulaine whose amorality is justified in the novel by little more than lust, revenge, greed, and ambition. The censors and the studios were partners in producing films that would not grievously offend American film-goers. The production code had created an organized hypocrisy whereby the studios adhered to the strictures yet did the films they wanted to do, largely the way they wanted to do them.

The censors were worried about a scene in which Clio, her black maid, Angelique, and her dwarf companion, Cupidon, were to be depicted in the famous New Orleans restaurant Beque. 'People of the Southern states may very strongly resent the inference that coloured people are permitted to comingle with white people in restaurants and public places,' Mr Obringer of the production code office wrote Jack Warner. And thus the scene was changed.

Ingrid had never appeared in such an elaborate film before. She had thirty-one costumes, but she didn't welcome fittings, telling Leah Rhodes, the designer, 'What's the use, they always fit properly.'

Ingrid looked sensational in the tightly bodiced outfits. When shooting began early in March, the chemistry between Ingrid and Cooper was still very much alive. In her dark wig and curious accent, Ingrid did not seem quite the French courtesan, but she exuded such wanton sensuality that it hardly mattered.

Ingrid and Cooper were full of high spirits. He called her 'Frenchie' and she called him 'Texas', as if they had become their characters. They were seen driving together down Sunset Boulevard, and there was considerable gossip about their relationship, gossip that may have reached the ears of Cooper's wife. But Ingrid was sacrosanct in the columns and movie magazines, and no conjecture about a romance appeared in print.

One day four-year-old Pia visited the set, the first time she had seen her mother at work. Ingrid was beautifully gowned for the ballroom scene. A score of elegantly dressed men and women swirled around the set while the camera focused on Ingrid and Cooper. 'I can be an actress,' Pia announced. 'I want to be an actress.'

Pia saw very little of her mother. Ingrid was off before Pia woke up in the mornings, and rarely back until late. Ingrid put in what the studio called 'a modern screen record', working sixty-two days in a row excluding Sundays. Then on 1 May she arrived at the studio with a voice so husky that it couldn't be recorded. She took to bed with what was called 'laryngitis and strained vocal cords', missing several full days of shooting before reporting back only two hours a day.

Saratoga Trunk was already weeks behind schedule, and Ingrid's illness was a serious handicap to the troubled production. A week later she was back on a regular schedule, but a month after that she was sick again. On 1 June a whole day's shooting had to be called off. 'Miss Bergman was not up in her lines', the production manager wrote in his notes for 12 June. Selznick blamed Ingrid's illness on Warners for 'having overworked her in your frantic haste to finish your picture . . . and not due to any ordinary incapacity on her part.'

Ingrid was under considerable emotional pressure as well. Petter had arrived on the West Coast to begin his surgical residency in San Francisco, only a short plane ride from Los Angeles. Up until now, she had had two lives; she needed them both – the freedom and adventure of her movie career, and the stability of her marriage.

When *Saratoga Trunk* was finished, Ingrid was scheduled to go up to San Francisco to spend five weeks with Petter. 'Ingrid Bergman, motion picture star, will bow out of existence,' the Warner Brothers publicity department announced, 'in favour of Mrs Peter Lindstrom, housewife.'

Ingrid's affair with Cooper was over. 'In my whole life I never had a woman so much in love with me as Ingrid was,' Cooper said years later. 'The day after the picture ended, I couldn't get her on the phone.'

Men often thought that Ingrid loved them with the very essence of her being. She seemed to be so completely with a man and then it was over, and he was left wondering what he had held in his arms, and who it was who had kissed and caressed him. The man didn't understand how Ingrid had played on his vanity, on his desire to possess her.

For Whom the Bell Tolls finally premiered on 16 August 1943, at Los Angeles's Cathay Circle Theater; it was the most star-studded opening since the beginning of the war. Ingrid arrived on the arm of Frank Freeman, vice-president of Paramount. She was on the cover of *Time* magazine as Maria ('Whatever Hollywood's bell tolled for, she rang it'), starring in what *Variety* called 'one of the most important pictures of all time'. Paramount had rolled out all the hoopla of publicity, and despite carping criticism in many papers, the film was, in *Variety*'s words, 'a boxoffice bellringer'.

The audience went to see the film, but *For Whom the Bell Tolls* was a great white whale of a movie, lying beached and lifeless. Up in the mountains Ingrid had been awed at Cooper's acting, but on celluloid his performance was so wooden that in kissing him it was a wonder that she hadn't ended up with a mouth full of splinters. Hemingway's novel was about people fighting for ideals, and about the victims of history, yet politics was boiled out of the movie so it was like a soup so watered down that one could see the bottom of the pot.

Ingrid had the best moments in the film, the exquisite vulnerability, poised between ecstasy and tears. Her attention to Cooper had paid off; as James Agee wrote in his review, 'his general support of Miss Bergman is nearly as good as the law will allow'. Ingrid was nominated for an Academy Award as best actress. Yet the film had not really worked, not even for her.

She wrote in her diary that she failed at playing Maria. She was too happy to portray a tragic figure.

Ingrid should have been extremely happy now; she was one of the biggest stars in Hollywood, who, as Agee wrote in his cover story in *Time*, 'hit the *Bell* such a valiant and far-sounding clang that there had been nothing like it since her great compatriot Greta Garbo enchanted half the world'. But unlike Garbo, Ingrid the person was being held up to the world as a beacon of light and virtue. 'Ingrid Bergman [is] without an enemy in the whole [Hollywood] community,' Agee wrote. 'The individual herself . . . happens to be an uncommonly well-balanced and charming one.'

While Ingrid was being eulogized, she was far from 'uncommonly well-balanced'. She was gorging herself again. Her face had broken out. Selznick set up a doctor's appointment, 'with a view to watching her diet, and seeing to it that she gets the proper rest at the same time'.

For her next film, Ingrid was scheduled to star in *Gaslight*, a remake of the British play and film. For several years she had wanted to play the part of Paula Alquist, a vulnerable, suggestible young woman whose husband, Gregory Anton, sets out to drive her mad. This was a new role for her, underneath its gothic veneer a tale of sexual subjugation. To do the film Ingrid was even willing to give top billing to Charles Boyer. Selznick was only too happy to loan Ingrid out to MGM, receiving $235,750 for her services as against the $75,156.25 that he eventually paid her. Selznick received even more money for the film, since he loaned out another of his stars, Joseph Cotten, to play Brian Cameron, the suave detective who saves Ingrid.

In playing Paula, Ingrid wouldn't be able to wear a wig as she had in *Saratoga Trunk*, fitting tightly over her still-short hair. For *Gaslight* she would have to be beautifully coiffed, her hair in cascading ringlets. That took time, as did her wardrobe. 'Ingrid was a large woman overall,' said Marion Keyes, the costume designer. 'She was just a big girl. In *Gaslight* she was corsetted. She didn't talk much. In those days people felt that Ingrid Bergman was rather remote.'

On weekends Ingrid flew up to San Francisco, where she and Petter stayed in a hotel. It was not like a marriage but like a weekend affair, hours of sightseeing, eating in restaurants, walking the hills.

For Ingrid's twenty-eighth birthday, on 29 August 1943, Petter flew down from San Francisco for a party at the Selznick's estate. Articles had appeared in magazines tallying up the money Selznick was making off her, and Ingrid had come to resent Selznick's hold over her. Yet the producer could be charming, and on an occasion such as this birthday celebration, Ingrid appeared admiring, even adoring, of David. In the evening, after Petter had departed, she sat alone wearing the pearls Selznick had given her, writing a thank you note. 'I am going home to empty a bottle of your champagne in exclusive splendour and gratitude for a perfectly happy birthday,' she wrote.

Ingrid and Selznick still had their moments of easy civility, but like partners in a doomed marriage, they maintained their relationship by avoiding discussing the unmentionable: the renewal of Ingrid's contract. They preferred discussing a happier topic: Ingrid's future roles for Selznick. Selznick still dreamed grand dreams, but he couldn't seem to get anything done any longer. Irene one day accused her husband of turning into a 'flesh-peddler', selling his contract artists to the highest bidder.

Finding a David O. Selznick film for Ingrid, indeed finding a group of films, was the producer's top priority. He sent his underlings scurrying around, working on a myriad of projects. What about Ingrid and Gary Cooper in Somerset Maugham's *The Razor's Edge*? Maybe they should resurrect *Joan of Arc* – and the Selznick people filled boxes of material on that one. *Mary Magdalene*: that was another possibility. *Magnificent Obsession*, the novel by Lloyd Douglas: what a great idea that was for Ingrid! Du Maurier's *Trilby*: another idea. Or what about *Sister Beatrice*? Ideas and ideas and ideas, yet nothing happened.

While Selznick spun out his golden dreams to Ingrid, he applied subtle pressure on her to renegotiate her contract. Irene Selznick took Ingrid around looking for a house lot in Beverly Hills. Selznick told Ingrid that he intended to buy it for her; privately he worried that she might think he was planning to buy not only the lot but the house to go on it. A few weeks later, after his intended largess had sunk in, Selznick wrote Petter about renegotiating Ingrid's contract, a letter Petter says he never received.

Steele was spending a good deal of time with Ingrid. By now, in Selznick's words, 'Miss Bergman mistrusted everybody in the Publicity Department except Joe Steele.' He was ready to guide Ingrid through all the shadowy labyrinths of Hollywood, seeking from her only a few scraps of attention; sometimes she treated him like just another Selznick hireling. There was a core of reserve, a mystery about her, that he could not get near. At 1.30 one morning he was driving through Beverly Hills in a drizzle, when he came upon Ingrid walking the streets alone, wearing a trench coat, flat-heeled shoes, and no hat. It was a strange spectacle, the woman whom *Reader's Digest* called 'The First Lady of Hollywood' walking alone in the middle of the night. Ingrid would not accept Steele's offer to drive her to her car, three blocks away, so the publicist walked with her through deserted streets.

At the end of 1943 Steele resigned as publicity director and learned the melancholy truth about his dear relationships with the Selznick stars. Nobody called to thank him, to say they were sorry, to ask about him – not even Ingrid.

When *Gaslight* finished, Petter urged Ingrid to go off on a month-long visit to American soldiers in Alaska. Petter says that he signed up for the US Army but was not called up because he was a physician. He says that he felt America had given him and Ingrid so much, and that while he worked long hours in the hospital she should also do something in return. It was, nonetheless, as if he and Ingrid were avoiding the day when they would truly be living together. She asked for only one day off before flying north on 18 December. She would be spending Christmas away from her husband and daughter, but she was full of excitement. Alaska was far from the front, but the frigid northland smelled of war: the wounded in the hospitals, the life of khaki-clad monotony, the thousands of lonely American soldiers looking at a living pinup. Ignorant of war up till now, she gained insights she had lacked before.

Ingrid wrote Selznick. 'The worst part . . . is going around the wards talking. We don't give the whole show but one girl sings and sometimes I sing, sometimes I tell a story. I started to cry the first time. I felt so lost for words.'

When she arrived, Ingrid had been taken in to meet a general, but she disliked him and decided to spend as much time as she could with the enlisted men. On Christmas Eve, she had not been at the officers' club but among the troops. 'Four hours without a pause I danced,' she wrote Selznick, as she flew high above the silvery landscape to yet another base. 'I wish you could have seen your reticent Swede in the middle of the room being taught to jitterbug by some nut with 500 boys standing around having the best time they ever had in Alaska.'

As a result of going from overheated huts to freezing temperatures outside, she got pneumonia and had to be hospitalized. She realized that she probably had not really recovered from her 'breakdown' during the filming of *Saratoga Trunk*. She found it curious that she, a sturdy Swede, should be the one to collapse first. She was not going to cut the tour short, however, and after a few days was up again.

Ingrid did meet at least one officer whose company she found appealing: Lieutenant General Simon Bolivar Buckner, Jr. 'Buck' was a Patton-like character who refused to wear an overcoat in the subzero weather. He became infatuated and visited her in California. She had always kept her love affairs well away from her home life; Buckner and Ingrid corresponded until he was killed on Okinawa on 28 June 1945.

CHAPTER 9

A HOLLYWOOD CAREER

From the moment their car turned onto the long ascending driveway, Ingrid and Petter knew that it would be their home. The chiselled stone and redwood one-storey house looked like a mountain lodge. It lay off Sunset Boulevard two miles up Benedict Canyon, protected by thick foliage in an area that was still largely rural. It had an enormous vaulted living-dining room that Ingrid called 'the barn'. There was a copper bar-grill, a kitchen, a master bedroom with separate bathrooms for Ingrid and Petter, and a bedroom for Pia that had been the servant's room. The unostentatious house felt a happy one; a further good omen early in 1944 was that Petter had finished his internship and had started his neurosurgical residence at Los Angeles County Hospital.

Ingrid and Petter had what only in Hollywood would be called a simple life. She was the number one actress in America, according to box office statistics. In the house there was a housekeeper, and a secretary. There was also a part-time secretary, Ellen Neuwald, and later a personal publicist.

Ingrid decided to give a housewarming party. She showed the list to Irene Selznick; it included producers, actors, cameramen, and writers. Irene told her that she couldn't invite such a disparate group. So Ingrid gave her party for the top list only. What she didn't comment on, and indeed didn't even think about, was that her original guest list was not so broad as to include anyone Petter might have enjoyed, doctors or medical people.

Until now Ingrid could maintain the illusion that her marriage mattered profoundly to her, but now that they were permanently together it would not be possible to hide the truth much longer. Petter did not view Ingrid as the rest of the world did. For instance Selznick was awed by Ingrid's lack of concern for her looks; indeed, she spent less time on her person and clothes than did practically any other star, but Petter thought his wife was full of vanity. He saw her spending half an hour in front of the mirror in the morning. 'Ingrid thought she would look more intelligent with a high forehead,' Petter says. 'So every morning she sat there and shaved one centimetre or so from her forehead. She didn't want anyone to know. Then she put on make-up, but did it in a way so it wouldn't look like make-up.' The reporters and columnists thought Ingrid didn't care much about publicity, and it was true that she did not exploit her family, as did many stars. But Petter watched her hover over her scrapbooks like a philatelist over his stamps. He thought she was consumed with publicity.

There were, nevertheless, good times in the house at 1220 Benedict Canyon Drive, when the guests sat in captain's chairs in front of the blazing hearth eating cheese and crackers, shrimp and lobster, when the house rang with laughter and fun. And Petter loved his new home, his wife, his child, and his position. He was broadly enough interested in the world outside medicine to make a few friends in the movie community. Two of their closest friends, Jean and Dido Renoir, lived up the road in a house on a hill visible from the Lindstroms'. Ingrid had been one of the first people the French director and his wife had met when they arrived in Hollywood in 1941, fleeing Nazi-occupied France. The friendship had deepened and now included Petter. Sometimes in the afternoons when Petter couldn't be at home he would send little Pia up to the Renoirs' house, its walls lined with paintings by Jean's father, Auguste.

Other close friends were George and Phyllis Seaton. George was a writer and director who won Academy Awards for *The Country Girl* and *Miracle on 34th Street*. Pia and Mary Seaton both went to Hawthorne elementary school, a public school. Often Pia came to play. Later, when the Lindstroms built a swimming pool, Mary learned to swim there. George Seaton was a good husband and a family man; he and Petter respected and admired each other.

The Selznicks didn't live far away either, and though Ingrid could not be her employer's true friend, she did become close to Irene Selznick. Irene advised Ingrid on the niceties of Hollywood. Irene and Petter were friendly too; indeed, later, Petter says that when the Selznick marriage was breaking up, Irene confided in him.

Ingrid took Petter along to a few Hollywood parties. She was no longer a foreigner to this world where professional and personal life have no boundaries, and deals are made as often on the tennis court or around the swimming pool as in the office. Ingrid had to go to fancy parties, seeing and being seen, receiving homage from producers and directors, discussing new deals, hearing the latest gossip.

When Ingrid talked with those who professionally courted and wooed and flattered her, Petter often talked to the wives. He could be a charming, gracious conversationalist who brought the same perceptions and insight to his social life as he did to counselling his patients. He enjoyed people as Ingrid often did not, in an undemanding way. More than anything, though, he liked to dance, and danced better than most people in Hollywood. Like many of his compatriots, Petter was usually sober, serious, self-controlled, but when he let go, he let go completely. If he knew there was going to be dancing, he carried an extra shirt to the party.

He did not particularly like dancing with Ingrid. 'She really was never a good dancer,' he says. 'She was a fair dancer, but she was terribly concerned with her appearance. She always had to look to see if others were watching.'

'Petter was a fanatical dancer,' remembers Gregory Peck. 'He hopped around like crazy, a lot of leaping around. I don't think Ingrid was terribly taken with that, and she would shake her head.'

As Petter whirled another actress, or the wife of a director or producer, around the floor, there were those who made fun of him. They thought that Petter was attempting to make Ingrid jealous, though he was only having a good time. Though Petter was a neurosurgeon, there were those who called him 'the dentist', an appellation that would be considered an insult only in America.

Petter was in superb physical condition; he loved challenging other men to arm-wrestling contests, particularly stars whose manly images he almost always deflated with a quick twist of the arm. At weekends he would take Pia on his back and run up the hillside towards Mulholland Drive, a habit that in the epoch before jogging seemed peculiar indeed. He spent more time with Pia than Ingrid did. According to him, Ingrid never visited her daughter's school. If his schedule permitted, he liked to call for Pia. 'I got out of school at two o'clock,' Pia remembers. 'I don't remember my mother picking me up.'

Some of Ingrid's friends considered Petter miserly and domineering. He was not in fact a selfish man. He shipped several hundred packages to their relatives in Sweden and Germany during the war; he was always helping people, be they relatives, poor patients or neighbours. To him simplicity was not merely a life-style but a moral value. As Ingrid and he grew wealthier his standards were put at risk.

There were those in the movie business who admired Petter but believed that he felt superior to Ingrid and her world. 'Lindstrom is an extraordinary doctor and humanitarian, but he had some old-fashioned European ideas,' said Lewis Milestone, the director. 'He had the attitude that he had bestowed his name on a poor orphan girl, and therefore she should be grateful to him for the rest of his life. He never let her forget it. But how long can you operate on gratitude?'

Visitors would be startled at Petter's domestic mastery. Probably only other Swedes could understand this aspect of the Lindstroms' relationship. 'Ingrid always wanted someone strong,' says Alf Kjellin, a Swedish actor and director, who had worked with Ingrid in her last Swedish film, *A Night in June*. 'That's why Petter Aron was so good for her. He was what she wanted a man to be.

'When I came up to their house in Beverly Hills, I was surprised at the way he talked at her and treated her. He was the man of the house. And he was the man. He probably had to suffer from being what she wanted him to be. Petter is the only *Peer Gynt* character I've met in my life, strong and vulnerable.

'As for Ingrid, she was like a character in Swedish folklore. There are men who work all night making coke in the forests. They see these visions of a beautiful woman with red hair peeking out of the trees. They seek to go after her and they find that her other side is only a hollow tree with a fox tail.

'Ingrid had that beautiful side and the other side too. She was a smart woman and had a coldness about her. She could fend for herself and still need a man. One side was completely open, and the other completely steel.'

In the first week of June 1944, Joe Steele drove up to the Lindstroms' new house in a chauffeur-driven limousine. A few days before, Ingrid had called Steele, talking to him with breezy familiarity, as if there had not been a half-year break in their relationship. She told him that she was going on a three-week war bond tour to nineteen cities, and she wanted him to go along as her personal publicist and companion. He readily agreed, beginning what he considered the most fulfilling part of his career.

'Isn't it wonderful!' Ingrid said as the limousine sped toward the railroad station to catch the Santa Fe *Chief*. 'How I like to keep going. I hate to sit still.'

And so Ingrid was off again, city after city, day after day, vignette after vignette. She seemed to personify goodness and nobility, and she sold thousands of dollars in bonds.

Back in Hollywood, Selznick was worried about *his* star. For the first time since *Intermezzo*, nearly five years before, he was going to star her in a David O. Selznick production. Shooting would begin soon after Ingrid returned, and he sent the script to her at the William Penn Hotel in Pittsburgh.

Spellbound would be a psychological thriller directed by Alfred Hitchcock and written by Ben Hecht. Selznick was in therapy himself, and perhaps that was why he was looking at Ingrid's emotional state in a different way. He knew her habit of 'getting herself three or four ice cream sodas by way of extra dessert'. He thought that his own analyst, Dr May E. Romm, 'might be helpful in getting a really good scientific dietician whose technique and psychology are such as to increase chances of whatever benefit can be secured being secured'. Ingrid was willing to try a new diet, and when Selznick talked to Petter, he reported that he 'accepted the idea although without enthusiasm'.

Ingrid began filming *Spellbound* only a few days after returning from the bond tour. In the film she played Dr Constance Peterson, a psychiatrist who falls in love with 'J.B.', an amnesiac doctor played by Selznick's newest star, Gregory Peck. J.B. is convinced that he has killed the new head of the clinic, whom he has been impersonating. Dr. Peterson helps J.B. to reach down into his psyche. By learning the truths of his childhood, he frees himself of the delusion. And by analysing one of J.B.'s dreams, she discovers the real killer.

Ingrid was not one to reflect on her own psyche. She could never understand why it was the rage in Hollywood to go through analysis. In most of America in the mid-forties, therapy for an adult was as unusual as braces on a child's teeth, and the film began with a self-conscious preface about the work of an analyst. The cast was told how to pronounce such esoteric terms as Freud ('Froyd') and therapy ('therr-ah-pee'). The script itself was full of pseudo Freudian jargon. The British-born Alfred Hitchcock was a brilliant director of psychological thrillers. He wore the same gilded shackles as Ingrid. He, too, had arrived in Hollywood to make a film for Selznick in 1939. He had nearly been assigned to direct *Intermezzo*; instead, he had directed the classic *Rebecca*. Since then, like Ingrid, he had been loaned out to other studios, for half a dozen other films.

On 10 July 1944, the first day of shooting, and the seventh anniversary of her wedding, Ingrid wrote a note to Selznick on stationery labelled 'The Green Manor', the name of the clinic in *Spellbound*. 'You are so nice to come home to!' she told him, and she was indeed glad to be back at work. For the first time she would be playing opposite a younger man, Gregory Peck.

Ingrid had at first wanted to turn down *Spellbound* because she 'didn't believe the love story'. Ingrid intended to have her say about how Dr Constance Peterson should be portrayed. In her first shot she was supposed to walk across a room, photographed by a camera on a crane above her. Ingrid wanted to say her lines standing in one spot, and she told Hitchcock so. But he would have none of her interference. During the shooting she thought he regarded 'us [actors] as intruders to his fantasy'.

Hitchcock was an obese man, who covered the director's chair like a shroud. Between scenes he often fell asleep, as if he could not be bothered with it all. He was full of as many private demons as any of the characters in *Spellbound*. As far back as 1941, he had had an idea for what Selznick considered a 'rather erotic story' starring Ingrid. That had not worked out, but there was an erotic undertone to *Spellbound*, as the straitlaced psychiatrist falls in love, a seemingly obsessive love. Ingrid, however, played the part as if she were the heroine of a romantic thriller. From the moment she looked lovingly at Gregory Peck for the first time, the audience knew that it was on familiar ground.

Even while *Spellbound* was shooting, Hitchcock was thinking about another film with Ingrid, in which the erotic, illicit quality would be to the fore, a film 'about a man who forces a woman to go to bed with another man because it's his professional duty'.

Hitchcock's quasi obsession with Ingrid was apparent on the set of *Spellbound*. 'He liked to kid Ingrid a lot,' Gregory Peck remembers. 'He was always flirting with double entendres. He'd say things that would verge on the obscene but in a dry way. He could make her laugh with his slightly obscene remarks about her bosoms or legs. She'd say, "Oh, Hitch, you're terrible."'

Humour was Hitchcock's defence, art his solace, film his voyeurism, and there was never any gossip about Hitch and Ingrid. The gossip had to do with Ingrid and Gregory Peck, particularly on the day that, according to another cast member, 'Ingrid and Peck came in later, all dishevelled, and there was a lot of speculation.' Peck says, 'That's not the kind of thing I talk about.'

In *Spellbound*, Ingrid played a psychiatrist who knows that the human psyche can be a dark magician, hiding away the truths of one's life, leading to endless obsessions and self-deceptions. Only through therapy or the most brutal shocks can the psychological sleight of hand be exposed, and the person enabled to live free. She might have asked herself, why was she compelled to fill every minute with activity? Why couldn't she spend some time at home with Petter and Pia? Why did Sunday seem such an endless, cursed day? Why once a film ended did she seek an excuse, any excuse, to be off somewhere, anywhere?

Ingrid did not ask herself such questions. Soon after production of *Spellbound* ended in mid-October, she was off on yet another lengthy journey, this time for a whole month, to sell bonds, to do a radio show, and to publicize her films. This took her to Canada and New

York City, as well as to Chicago and Minnesota. Few actresses would
have even contemplated Ingrid's schedule. She charmed her way
through a month measured out in teas, official luncheons, banquets,
cocktail parties, hospital visits, speeches, radio interviews, photography sessions with mayors and politicians.

In Toronto at the King Edward Hotel, she received from Selznick a
package of 'non-fattening foods and a pound of caviar'. She sent
Petter a wire that ended: 'AND JOE WON'T LET ME EAT.' She was like
a schoolgirl on her holiday. As soon as she arrived in New York,
where she was to appear on *The Kate Smith Show*, she went out to
Hamburger Heaven to eat, and then had a chocolate sundae at
Schrafft's. She was having so much fun that she wired Selznick for
permission to stay a few extra days.

Then she was off for Minnesota. Travelling with her, besides Joe
Steele, was Bob William, the Warner Brothers publicist who had
handled Bogart during *Casablanca*. William was a gregarious, unpre-
tentious sort. Steele was not terribly taken with the idea of having
another publicist along with *his* Ingrid; as for William, he found
Steele 'imperious, like a little Russian musical impresario, who was
really enamoured of her'. There was little glamour in this assignment,
sleeping in what William remembers as 'a crummy hotel, everything
a sickly green', travelling to outlying regions on 'a dinky train with
parlour cars'.

Then it was Thanksgiving Day – no rallies, no speeches, an
empty hotel room, an empty day. The phone rang in Ingrid's room.
William was calling with glad tidings. He had rounded up a
rental car, not an easy thing to do on a holiday in wartime
Minnesota.

'Thanks, Bobby, I was feeling sorry for myself,' Ingrid said. She
agreed to go with William and Steele for Thanksgiving dinner to the
Lowell Inn in Stillwater.

When Ingrid arrived down in the lobby, William handed her a
thermos with a red ribbon around it.

'There's martinis in here, Ingrid,' William said. 'And we're going
to have a toast at every stop sign on the way to the inn.'

The car, an ugly green 1938 Pontiac, stopped at twenty-six stop
signs on the road to the Lowell Inn. By the time the threesome pulled
up in the parking lot and toasted Winston Churchill and Franklin
Delano Roosevelt, they were smashed. The proprietors knew a star
when they saw one. They sat the party at a prime location, next to
the indoor stone fish pond.

'What's that for?' Ingrid asked, in a half-drunken voice.

'Oh, that's how we choose the fish for dinner,' the owner proudly told her.

'Oh,' Ingrid said, and stuck her arm into the water up to her elbow, getting her sleeve totally soaked.

A flash went off. A second flash went off in William's head. If that picture got into the papers he would be fired.

But it was Thanksgiving and such worries were forgotten. There was cream of mushroom soup with almonds, and turkey, and more good cheer. On the drive back, William told joke after joke. Ingrid laughed so hard that she slid down beneath the dashboard.

'Stop, stop,' she cried. 'My ribs are hurting.'

As soon as Ingrid got back to Beverly Hills, she and Selznick had to decide what her next picture would be. There were two possibilities: a Selznick film called *Daybreak*, which was still largely unwritten, or *The Bells of St Mary's*, with Bing Crosby, directed by Leo McCarey at Rainbow Productions, and distributed by RKO. The film was a sequel to the extremely popular *Going My Way*, with Crosby and Barry Fitzgerald.

At first, Selznick did not want Ingrid to do the McCarey film; he thought 'sequel' was synonymous with 'second best'. McCarey's films were extremely popular, but Selznick may have felt that a McCarey film was a little beneath a 'Selznick star'; after all, McCarey had a reputation for making films so gooey and sweet that one risked tooth decay watching them. According to Ingrid's recollections, she talked the reluctant producer into letting her play Sister Benedict. But the memo that Selznick dictated after their meeting states that 'Ingrid is in doubt as to which she prefers to do, "Daybreak" or the McCarey film . . . and I am reasonably sure that I can make her happy with whichever one I think she ought to do.'

Selznick tested McCarey's devotion to Ingrid by negotiating one of the most lucrative loan-out agreements in the history of Hollywood filmmaking. Selznick received $175,000 in cash, the rights to the services of Gregory Peck for one film, and the remake rights to *Little Women*. RKO also assumed Selznick's obligation for outside studio space. This was all worth about $425,000, many times what the producer paid Ingrid. Nonetheless, Selznick was unhappy that he had to pay Ingrid an extra $25,000 because the film commenced after the starting date stipulated in her contract.

McCarey was a handsome forty-five-year-old Hollywood veteran. Of Irish ancestry, he had made his way in Hollywood directing comedies such as the Marx Brothers' *Duck Soup*, *My Favourite Wife*,

and the Oscar-winning *The Awful Truth*. The director discovered a
rich vein of sentimentality and sheer good feeling that could be mined
not only for critical success but for a fortune. In *The Bells of St Mary's*,
McCarey was attempting to mine it again.

Bing Crosby played Father O'Malley, a good priest ready to break
into song at the hint of a sagging plot. Father O'Malley is assigned
to head a traditional parochial school, which is in trouble. Sister
Benedict, the school's mother superior, is an old-fashioned nun who
believes in the value of simple prayer. With the help of God, a slew
of child actors, and a miserly industrialist with a heart of gold, the
school is saved. In her nun's habit, Ingrid could eat her fill of sundaes
without worry. Her face was her fortune, and Ingrid almost levitated
with saintliness.

On the evening of the Academy Awards, Ingrid worked on the
set of *The Bells of St Mary's* until six o'clock. Then, before going
home to change for the awards ceremony, Ingrid, McCarey, and
Crosby wished one another luck. All had been nominated, McCarey
and Crosby for *Going My Way*, and Ingrid for *Gaslight*. Petter arrived
during intermission, and joined Ingrid and David Selznick in the
auditorium. As she awaited the announcement of the best actress
award, Ingrid held Petter's and Selznick's hands. McCarey had
already won. Crosby had won too, for best actor.

The nominees for best actress were announced: Ingrid Bergman.
Claudette Colbert. Bette Davis. Greer Garson. Barbara Stanwyck.

Ingrid couldn't hear.

'That's you, Ingrid!' Selznick shouted. 'You've won! You've won!'

Ingrid turned to Petter. 'Go get it,' he said gently, and kissed her.

The next morning Ingrid was back on the set, being toasted in
champagne and crying with happiness as she sat between McCarey
and Crosby. In the sheer exhilaration of the moment, she felt that
she would never reach such heights again; but it was a strange
happiness for all three of them. Here was Crosby playing good
priests, gregarious, selfless men whose character spilled over into the
public perception of Crosby himself. Yet he was a withdrawn,
emotionally miserly man whom Ingrid could not get to know at all.

Here was McCarey, the most celebrated popular director of the
day, lionized by the church, a man who would tell Louella Parsons
that he could 'never make a story that's in the least suggestive or
vulgar'. And this man was so deeply troubled that during the shooting
of *The Bells of St Mary's* he was arrested twice, once for creating a
disturbance while drunk, then for suspicion of drunkenness as he
drove out of control the wrong way down an incline to a highway.

And here was Ingrid, lauded across America as the perfect wife and mother. And as soon as the shooting was over she wanted to be off again, this time about as far from her house on Benedict Canyon as she could get, on a USO European tour. For years she pretended that she loved to cook, to play with Pia, but after a few days in the house she was climbing the walls. Petter was almost never bored. But Ingrid was bored with life as most people lived it . . . bored with wifedom and motherhood . . . bored.

'Goodbye, goodbye, goodbye . . .' Ingrid wrote Selznick 13 June 1945 as she sat in Compartment D on Car 182 of the Santa Fe *Chief*, heading eastward. 'I am so thrilled and can hardly believe I am on my way. Where I fell short in Alaska won't happen this tour. I can beat almost anyone with my jitterbug and I know samba, rumba, conga, swing, big apple and what have you!'

So much of the Europe Ingrid had known was gone. The Genoa from which she had sailed for America was now a city of the hungry and the maimed. Hamburg, her mother's city, was havoc, her once proud relatives dependent on the packages mailed by Petter from the States. And Berlin, where she had starred for UFA, was a city of hollow, burned-out buildings like the hollow, burned-out Berliners who haunted the ruins.

Ingrid arrived in Augsburg, an ancient city on the Lech River in Bavaria. The Americans had appropriated the best houses for their officers; Ingrid was driven to the USO quarters, in a large private house. In the living room she found an intense, wiry little man playing the piano; she had never heard the music before.

'That is such beautiful music. Whenever you play, I will come to listen.'

'It's just something I made up,' the pianist said, shrugging off Ingrid's compliments.

The pianist was Larry Adler, another member of the USO troupe and the most famous harmonica player in the world. That was an accomplishment that might seem on par with fame achieved by playing bongo drums, swallowing swords, or whistling, but only if one had not heard Adler play. He could do things on a harmonica that had not been done before; he was a virtuoso of the first rank. He was no homespun Tom Sawyer who pulled his mouth organ out of tattered jeans. Neurotic, fiercely opinionated, egocentric, and a political leftist, he was not the kind of man who attracted Ingrid. She loved to talk though, and Adler was a talker too; she delighted in his personal revelations and told him of her own life. She thought him a man of brilliance, and on the two-show-a-day circuit, she spent a great deal of time with him.

'Ingrid wasn't fascinating, but you were just dazzled by her beauty,' Adler says. 'You felt she'd never read a book. She had no interest in world affairs. The one thing I never got her to talk about was her filmmaking in Germany. I think if Ingrid could have made a good picture, she would have made it for the Nazis, for anybody. She was a very dedicated lady. She loved working. And I don't think any individual was as important as her work.

'I think she needed to show her power over men. She wasn't coquettish or a tease. Ingrid wasn't interested in sex all that much. She did it like a polite girl.'

On one of their first evenings in Germany, Ingrid and the others were invited by an officers club to a dinner party in the former hunting lodge of Fritz Thyssen, a wealthy German. After dinner the group moved into the music room, a hall of baroque splendour. At one end of the room there stood a grand piano, in front of it a white bearskin rug. Ingrid stood with Lieutenant Robert Orbach, who had fought his way across Europe with General Patton. A young pianist was introduced, a Hungarian refugee, one of the millions of nameless displaced persons who wandered the roads or huddled in camps behind barbed wire, the chattel of war.

The pianist had chosen a piece of great intricacy, and she played it magnificently. It was hard to believe that after all the ugliness and pain, such beauty could come from one who had suffered and lost so much. As the young woman finished, Ingrid swept across the room, dropped to her knees beside the piano. She thanked the woman in French, the only language they shared.

In the USO shows themselves, Ingrid's performance was rather limited. Ingrid did not have the humour of Jack Benny, the leader of the show; she couldn't sing like Martha Tilton, famous as Benny Goodman's vocalist; she couldn't play an instrument, like Adler; but she could play straight man to Jack Benny, recite something or other, and simply appear there, a beautiful image in front of the soldiers. She decided to recite from Maxwell Anderson's *Joan of Lorraine*, a new play that she hoped to do in America. The soldiers had not fought the war to make the world safe for Joan of Arc recitals; they were restless while Ingrid performed, waiting for more music, some jokes, or another broad. In Kassel, Ingrid plunged onward, ignoring their indifference; when she saw that some of the soldiers were waving GI-issue prophylactics in the air, she ran offstage in tears. Adler wasn't going to let such behaviour go unnoticed. 'What a pity you haven't a better use for those,' he told the GIs, a sentiment with which they surely agreed.

As Ingrid arrived at the Ritz Hotel in Paris, Marlene Dietrich was leaving: Dietrich had been a star in her native Germany and in Hollywood; during the war she sang before thousands of soldiers, and her famous 'Lili Marlene' was beamed on the radio not only to the GIs but to homesick German soldiers too.

Dietrich wasn't impressed. Now that the war was over, they were all coming: the actors and actresses, the singers and comedians, the politicians and businessmen, the rear-line officers in their front-line outfits, the columnists and reporters, decked out for war. The Ritz was full of them.

One afternoon Ingrid returned to her room and found a note under the door. Two men were asking her to dinner. They said that they didn't have money enough to send flowers and take her to dinner as well, and 'dinner won by a close margin'. Ingrid didn't usually do such things, and she had no idea who Bob Capa and Irwin Shaw might be. 'If we write much more we will have no conversation left, as our supply of charm is limited,' the note concluded.

There was something so appealing about their little message, why not? She wanted to see Paris, and if they turned out to be dreary bores she would simply dump them. When the phone rang in her room, Ingrid said that she would meet Capa and Shaw in the bar. She came downstairs at 6.30 wearing a red flower in her hair.

Capa and Shaw had fuelled their brashness on good liquor. Shaw had aspirations as a novelist; he would one day write *The Young Lions*, one of the best books about the war. Capa was the war's most celebrated photographer, but that didn't give one entrée to the likes of Ingrid Bergman. It was hard to believe that Bergman had actually come down to meet them. The two men greeted her. Capa saw the world through a camera's lens, a world of light and darkness, shadow and focus. Ingrid seemed to light up the dark room, 'like the lobby of the Music Hall'.

'You said you were going to take me to dinner,' Ingrid said, sounding to Capa like 'a school kid' taking a mischievous dare. 'I hope you have enough money, because I'm very hungry.'

They were off in a cab to Fouquet's, then on to Maxim's, and finally to Montmartre. They danced and laughed; no one wanted the night to end, and when Capa and Shaw ran out of money, Ingrid paid. When they said goodbye in the early morning, Ingrid and Capa knew that they would see each other again.

She was taken with the intense, darkly handsome photographer, who was two years her senior. In *For Whom the Bell Tolls*, Ingrid had made a film that was as much like war as glycerin is like a tear; Capa had been there during the Spanish Civil War. He had lost his lover,

Gerda Pohorylles, crushed under a tank, and he had shot the most famous photograph of the war: a Republican volunteer at the instant he was machine gunned to death. The photograph was a stark testament that transcended journalism to become art.

He had been born Endre Friedmann in Budapest, a Hungarian Jew. He lived like a citizen of nowhere. When he photographed happy families, babies, or buildings, he was a good photographer; but when he photographed war, he was the best there was and he knew it. It wasn't simply that he was brave; it was that he was always *there*; watching Italians surrendering at Palermo; riding an assault barge into Anzio; in Naples seeing the funeral of Italian children who had fought the Germans; wading in to Omaha Beach, D-day, the only photographer; riding with Spanish Republicans in to liberate Paris; during the Battle of the Bulge; in Leipzig at the end, standing in a room as a last soldier dies, and lies in a pool of blood.

Like Ingrid he was in some respects his own best creation. He treated life like a delicate portrait that had to be blown up into a gigantic poster of heroism. 'The fabrication of this legend was no longer simply a matter of entertaining his friends,' his biographer writes. 'It was also a matter of business.'

Capa didn't know where he was going now, and what was left that he wanted to photograph. In those first days, Ingrid had very little time with him; she had to be off again on the tour. The biggest event was the Fourth of July celebrations for the troops in Germany; when the USO troupe arrived in Berlin, Capa was there in the ravaged city.

Adler was there as well. In his own way he was as taken with Ingrid as Capa was; the threesome moved through the bombed-out streets of the city. In the middle of one street lay a bathtub, in which Capa photographed Ingrid and Adler. 'The next day we asked him for the pictures and he said the negatives didn't come out,' Adler says. 'He smiled and said, "I hate to take pictures of my friends."'

On the Fourth of July, Ingrid stood beside Adler on the balcony of Hitler's ruined Reich Chancellery. She recited the Gettysburg Address and Adler played the harmonica. That same day the troupe flew to Nuremberg and gave an Independence Day performance for the soldiers there.

Capa didn't go along on the whole lengthy tour, and Ingrid and Adler continued their relationship. One evening Adler and Ingrid saw *Saratoga Trunk* in a screening room in Nuremberg. She was especially interested in his opinion; although the film was being shown to GIs, it was still unreleased to general audiences in the States.

Adler considered subtlety a euphemism for lying. He told Ingrid that he had seen few examples of miscasting to compare with a healthy Swedish maiden playing a black-haired New Orleans courtesan. For several days she would have nothing to do with Larry Adler.

One day Ingrid and Adler were driving through the German countryside in a Mercedes. When the chauffeur ignored a sentry and drove on, the soldier fired a pistol shot at the retreating Mercedes. Adler felt the bullet hit him in the back. 'I'm shot! I'm shot!' he screamed as he fell to his knees. Ingrid held him to her bosom as he told her to bid adieu to his family.

The bullet had hit a spring in the seat, and the spring had hit the harmonica vituoso in the back.

Ingrid and the troupe returned to Paris in mid-August, in time to celebrate V-J day in the city of light. Paris had gone wild, the streets full of tens of thousands of celebrating Frenchmen united in joy and relief. She sat next to Capa in a jeep on the Champs Élysées. Ingrid watched girls bestowing kisses on random soldiers. And then the biggest star in America jumped out of the jeep and kissed a soldier on the mouth. And the soldier kissed Ingrid back.

When the USO troupe had first arrived in Paris, Ingrid, Adler, and Caper had been a merry trio, the three musketeers exploring the great city. 'One evening the three of us were in a nightclub at Montparnasse,' Adler remembers. 'Ingrid made it clear she wanted me to leave. The next morning she came into my room and said she was sorry. She felt she had let me down. I felt let down. After that, I felt a little different. But then Capa disappeared and I stayed with her in Paris.

'Ingrid, I think, feared going home at the end of the tour. She didn't want to go home. She suggested that we stay in Paris, and we did for a few days. But I was a coward. I knew that my wife and children would know that the tour was over, and Jack would be back. And I finally suggested that we go back. Ingrid didn't like that at all. She didn't want to go back to California. In New York she tried to get me to stay a few days. Then she wanted to take the slowest plane back to Los Angeles.'

CHAPTER 10

THE LONELINESS OF A BAD MARRIAGE

Ingrid's affairs were dangerous, not only to her marriage but to her image; but she was getting away with them, without a word in a column or a whisper among her fans. And among those who knew about them, no one seemed to think her the worse.

She often played roles in which her behaviour would have offended conventional morality but she made permissible. As Alicia Huberman in Hitchcock's *Notorious* her father has been convicted as a Nazi spy; she considered patriotism 'waving the flag with one hand and picking pockets with the other. She is a promiscuous alcoholic ('she's good at making friends with gentlemen'). In Miami she meets Devlin, a suave government agent, played by Cary Grant. Devlin asks her to go to Rio with him to help ferret out a Nazi group. Alicia agrees with a shrug of the shoulder, as if it hardly matters one way or another. In Rio, Alicia and Devlin fall in love. Devlin asks Alicia to meet an old admirer, Alexander Sebastian, played by Claude Rains. In the name of duty, and to avoid his own feelings towards Alicia, Devlin acts as a pimp, setting Alicia up with the Nazi. Alicia sleeps with Sebastian ('you can add Sebastian's name to my list of play-mates'). In order to learn the secrets of the group, Alicia agrees to marry Sebastian. She helps Devlin discover that the Nazis are mining uranium. When Sebastian and his mother discover Alicia's betrayal, they begin slowly to poison her. As Alicia lies dying, Devlin saves her and they escape together.

Alicia lives in a world where things never are what they seem to be. Devlin's kisses may only be meant to seduce her into counter-espionage. Her own passionate embrace of Devlin outside the wine cellar where the uranium is hidden is not a sign of love but a ruse to fool her husband. The coffee and tea that her husband brings to nurture her are laced with poison.

In her personal and professional life, Ingrid was playing a role not unlike Alicia's. She continued her relationship with Larry Adler. They were a curious duo, and a subject of considerable gossip.

'She was unhappy with Petter,' Adler says. 'He was a very hard man to like. I remember once at a dinner party at Ingrid's. Jean

Renoir and Alfred Hitchcock were there. Petter dominated the conversation and he didn't have much to say. Ingrid would say that she knew Petter was a difficult man. She said that he had done a lot for her. He had done a lot to make her grow up . . .

'The thing that prevented me from getting closer to her was that I knew goddamn well I would be Mr Ingrid Bergman, and I've got too much of an ego. I was serious about her, though, for a while. I was serious as long as she let me be serious. I thought I was in love with her, but I don't think she was ever in love with me. I think she was fond of me. She liked me.'

Ingrid liked Capa too. He had come to Hollywood presumably to write his war memoirs for a possible film, but in part to continue their relationship. They met at parties or surreptitiously for lovemaking at Irwin Shaw's home in Malibu.

When Ingrid arrived home from the studio, parties, or meetings with Adler or Capa, Petter's affection and solicitude were like a slow poison. 'I felt guilty for not being satisfied with all I had,' Ingrid said. 'Again and again I repeated to myself how fortunate I was, a faithful husband who loved me and did everything he could for me, a good child, a beautiful home. I had health and money and success in my work, but still I was a constant struggle inside, looking for something I couldn't put my fingers on. Petter understood my restlessness, maybe better than I did. We had long talks about our lives, and I felt a great relief in leaning on him and letting him make the decisions.'

Ingrid could not talk candidly to Petter about Capa and Adler and the others, but she could talk to him about her career. 'Ingrid said that Petter managed her career,' recalls Ellen Neuwald, her secretary. 'I think it was something that she gave to Petter so that he could be part of her life. I recall her saying, I have to discuss this with Petter. She really did defer to him.'

Ingrid's career was the primary thing in her life. And when Ingrid and Petter talked business, there was still the mutual interest and concern that they had seemed to have during their days of courtship so long ago. 'She said that she hated Selznick,' Petter says. 'She really didn't hate him, but she disliked Selznick for several reasons. He kept her out of work when she wanted to work. He wanted to prolong her contract against her will. He refused to let her appear on radio. When he sold her services to other studios, he never gave her an increase in salary, though even despite the wartime labour law, he could have found a way to give her more money. She had firmly decided never to make another contract with him.'

★   ★   ★

Almost nothing in Ingrid's life was what it seemed. Onscreen she and
Cary Grant had extraordinary chemistry, but the British-born star
had no sexual interest in her. One day Hitchcock filmed what would
become one of the most famous kissing scenes in film. For over two
and a half minutes Ingrid and Cary Grant nuzzled one another, kissing
on the lips, touching each other's neck and ears. 'Hitchcock said discuss
anything you want to discuss,' Grant remembers. 'We talked about
who is going to wash the dishes. It's a very cuddly-looking scene.
Noses are a difficult business in the kissing scene.'

It was not Grant who was infatuated with Ingrid, but the rotund,
almost grotesquely unattractive Alfred Hitchcock. In *Notorious*,
Hitchcock was directing his first true love story. He had lost close
to a hundred pounds, and looked positively wizened. He was full of
what his biographer Donald Spoto calls 'unrealized and misshapen,
adolescent romantic impulses of a lovesick middle-aged director
towards an unapproachable goddess'. Ingrid and Petter were good
friends of Alfred and Alma Hitchcock. Sometimes the Lindstroms
went to the Hitchcocks' home on Bellagio Road for dinner. One
evening, according to Hitchcock, Ingrid approached him in the
bedroom, insisting that he make love to her before they left. Hitchcock's biographer believes that the story was 'a fiction, fresh at the
time from the workshop of his [Hitchcock's] own fervid imagination'. Nonetheless Ingrid knew that Hitchcock adored her and was
in love with the performances he was getting out of her. She may
well have suggested an assignation, or teased Hitchcock, perhaps
knowing that he would never act upon it.

Her relationship with Selznick was another kind of unfulfilled love.
He saw himself as the true protector of *his* Ingrid. He felt that Ingrid
and Petter were profoundly ungrateful for all that he had done. He
loved Ingrid as if he had moulded her out of clay, breathed life into
her, and taught her everything. Instead of putting Ingrid on film
himself, Selznick had sold her again and again. To Ingrid, that was
a betrayal of their covenant. Such talk enraged Selznick; he would
not be dubbed a peddler of talent. He called the roll of Ingrid's hits;
he had chosen the parts with the same care as if he had been producing
the films himself, and he had often helped with the writing and
direction.

Ingrid's contract with Selznick was up at the end of 1945. She
already was signalling her intentions by negotiating a film on her
own for 1946, *Arch of Triumph*, based on the Erich Maria Remarque
novel. It was an exciting project, as good a choice for her new
beginning as she could have hoped for. It would be the first film by
a new company, Enterprise Pictures, and a potential blockbuster: a

big bestseller; a big-name novelist; a big co-star, Charles Boyer; a big director, Lewis Milestone, famous for *All Quiet on the Western Front*. And big money, for Ingrid alone $175,000 and 25 per cent of the net profits.

In November, Ingrid was on the cover of *Life*. 'BERGMAN'S YEAR' was the magazine's headline and Bergman's year it was. Already in 1945 *Saratoga Trunk* and *Spellbound* had opened to blockbuster business. In a few weeks *The Bells of St Mary's* would premiere as the Christmas attraction at Radio City Music Hall, and throughout America it would be viewed by more moviegoers than had seen *Gone With the Wind*. 'Guess what?' went a popular joke of the time. 'I just saw a movie without Ingrid Bergman.'

It was not Selznick's year. His life was in turmoil. He was leaving his wife, Irene, for Jennifer Jones, another 'Selznick star'. His production of films was down to practically nothing. He had touched Ingrid and turned her career to gold, but he was a Midas who did not dare touch anything any longer, for fear that he would turn objects not to gold but to dust. Ingrid was a symbol of Selznick's strength, his wisdom, his foresight. If she left him, his fear was probably not that she would fail but rise to even greater heights.

Ingrid always needed a strong man. When she arrived in America for good, Selznick was, on Hollywood's scale, the strongest man of all. She called him 'my father' and 'my second husband', listened to him, laughed at his jokes, teased him a little. He was never sure whether she was as spontaneous as she seemed. If she was a Delilah, she cut this Samson's hair not while he slept, but while he sat in the barber's chair approving the new style.

Selznick blamed Petter for the protracted negotiations; Ingrid always remained sweetly conciliatory to Selznick. She wanted to placate him enough so that he would not rush to make an extra, mediocre picture before the contract ran out. In the midst of *Notorious*, Selznick suggested that Ingrid's last film under their old contract be *To Each His Own*, at Paramount. Ingrid talked Selznick out of it. (The role went instead to Olivia de Havilland, who in 1946 won an Academy Award for it.)

Ingrid and Selznick had a lunch to discuss their future together. Now he wanted to do a film entitled *Katie for Congress*, as her last picture. He had purchased the property especially for her. She didn't like the script. Selznick agreed not to do the film, which would have starred her as a Swedish maid in Minnesota. (The picture became *The Farmer's Daughter*, for which Loretta Young received an Academy Award.) Instead, according to Selznick, Ingrid agreed to make another film for him under the old contract in 1946.

Soon afterwards, Petter wrote Ingrid's attorney a letter that suggested no such agreement had been made. Selznick was furious, accusing Petter of 'fantastic distortion', and having 'long been manoeuvring . . . to break up the exceptionally cordial and mutually beneficial partnership between Miss Bergman and ourselves'. Ingrid was perfectly aware of her own value and was not passively watching her future being decided. Her attorney told Selznick's negotiators that she 'was extremely sold on her own importance in the industry, and that this was affecting her thinking to a marked degree'.

In order to get another film under the current contract, Selznick had to begin production by 29 December 1945. In mid-November he frantically wired Jenia Reissar in London, trying to obtain the rights to George Bernard Shaw's *Candida*. But it was madness to attempt such a project in so short a time. Finally he realized that his only hope was to sign Ingrid to a new contract. As the remaining days of her contract dwindled to less than a month, he tried to pretend that he still might start a new film with her by 29 December. But she had procrastinated, albeit sweetly, in such a way that there was little likelihood of that.

Although he had given up trying to sign Ingrid to a new long-term contract, he at least wanted to sign her for one new picture. The money on the negotiating table now was enormous. He proposed to pay $150,000 plus 5 per cent of the gross for one picture in 1946. O'Shea cabled Selznick that Petter had turned down that proposal 'without moving an icicle of that frigid puss'. The rejection would seem to support Petter's assertion that Ingrid had no intention of signing with Selznick again. There still might have been an agreement, but Selznick had no film ready for Ingrid that she wanted to do and she was too expensive a property on which to gamble.

It was all over. If Ingrid had trepidations about a career on her own, she had the prospects of earning within a few years enough money to become immensely wealthy. To Selznick, it was as if he had lost a wife. He wrote Ingrid of his 'sorrow over our divorce after so many years together of happy marriage. You once said that you had "two husbands"; but Petter was the senior; and, of course, he knew all the time that his will would prevail . . . So long Ingrid! May the New Year, and all New Years beyond, bring you everything of which you dream.'

Selznick was not unwilling to seek a little revenge. He knew that for years Ingrid had been seeking to play Joan of Arc in a film. Selznick announced that he would be filming *Joan of Arc* himself in the summer and fall, starring Jennifer Jones.

★　　　★　　　★

Selznick was gone now, and Petter was the one strong man in Ingrid's everyday life. Now that Ingrid was on her own, it might seem that their marriage would have come together. If Petter had been a producer or director, perhaps it might have happened. But they were shadows passing across each other's lives.

Petter was the chief neurosurgical resident at Los Angeles County Hospital. With the wartime shortage of doctors, he was extraordinarily busy.

'We were both very much preoccupied with our professions,' Petter says. 'Looking back, it was a marriage that looked good at the beginning, but when you really considered it, the personalities and how our lives developed, it was not a marriage based on good foundations. She became so preoccupied with herself from the age of eight or twelve.'

Petter felt that he always did what Ingrid wanted him to do, always was what she wanted him to be. He continued to remind Ingrid about her slouching and overeating. And he spent long days at the hospital. There Petter was a creative surgeon who in his extensive charity work insisted on anonymity. To his colleagues he seemed to have everything: a brilliant career; a generous spirit; a lovely daughter; and as a wife, one of the most beautiful women in the world.

The fan magazines and movie columnists wrote that he had the perfect marriage. Once when Petter was driving home and thinking about his marriage, he became sick, and had to pull up by the roadside to throw up.

Late one night, Petter called Ruth Roberts's house and was told by Ruth that Ingrid was there. He drove to the house.

'I'd like to see her.'

'She's not here,' Ruth admitted finally.

'Where is she?'

'She has an appointment.'

'With a man?'

'Yes.'

'Where is she?'

'I don't know.'

She came back at three o'clock in the morning, according to Petter. 'That happened a second time. I went and she wasn't there. I didn't want to admit what was happening. I wanted to believe. That's how she got away with it.'

There is no loneliness like a bad marriage, and sometimes they talked about what was wrong. 'Why do we pretend that we have the perfect marriage, when you work all the time and I work all the time?' Petter remembers telling her once. At times she tried to show

more interest in Petter's work. Early one morning she and Joe Steele
visited the hospital to watch him remove a malignant brain tumour
from a nine-year-old black boy. As Petter probed into the open skull,
Ingrid appeared totally blasé, unaffected by the spectacle below.
Steele searched for an answer, and decided that all her life Ingrid had
hidden her emotions, releasing them only when alone in her bedroom.
And now, after all those years, this 'psychic subterfuge' had become
part of her personality.

Almost everywhere Ingrid went now, she was recognized. She
was comfortable among other celebrities, as if they were a species
apart. When she and Petter went skiing, it was not a weekend frolic
in the snow, but a great ski trip to Sun Valley even before the
resort was formally open, with Cooper and Gable and other stars.
Hemingway was up in Sun Valley too. He liked Ingrid, and she liked
him, and the Lindstroms saw him occasionally. One day on a spring
trip Petter went hunting with Cooper, Gable, and Hemingway. 'We
drove along the power lines in a jeep,' Petter recalls, 'and they shot
eagles off the power lines using telescopic sights and rifles resting on
tripods. Another day we went rabbit hunting. They engaged these
farmers to ride in trucks chasing the rabbits towards them. I didn't
shoot a single shot, either day. They killed maybe fifty rabbits.
Nobody wanted them.'

She hardly ever joined Petter on his jaunts with Pia up in the hills.
She sat at home working on her scrapbooks, going over her fan mail,
killing time. 'What do you do with yourself on Sundays?' Ingrid
asked the wife of a 20th Century-Fox executive. 'I hate Sunday, I
can't wait for Monday so I can go back to work again.' Now that
Notorious was finished, Monday was just another Sunday. She enjoyed
playing with Pia for a while, but that soon paled. She had to be off
again.

One day Petter, Pia, and Ingrid spent the day at Sam Wood's beach
house in Malibu. Ingrid walked into the water and began swimming.
She swam farther and farther out into the surf.

'Should we signal the lifeguard station?' asked Laurence Stallings,
a young writer who was working on a project with the director.

'Ingrid wouldn't like it,' said Wood. 'Someday Ingrid's going to
start swimming and never come back.'

'Why?' Stallings asked.

'I don't know,' Wood replied. 'But that's Ingrid.'

In the spring, before she began work on *Arch of Triumph*, Ingrid left
home for a visit to New York. There she spent a lot of time with
Cary Grant, whom she considered a charming companion, if only a

The transcendent beauty of Ingrid Bergman

Ingrid and her father

Ingrid as an extra.
Despite being placed in
the far left of the back
row, Ingrid made sure
her full face appeared

Ingrid (front left) studied
only a year at the
Swedish Royal Dramatic
School

Ingrid and Petter Lindstrom standing at the
altar at the Lutheran church in Stode,
Sweden

Ingrid and Petter as man and wife

Ingrid's first film role was in *The Count of the Monk's Bridge,* co-starring Edvin Adolphson

The Swedish *Intermezzo,* with Ingrid's idol, Gösta Ekman

A personal picture of Ingrid taken around 1937

A pregnant Ingrid making a film in Nazi Germany in 1938

Ingrid travelled to Nazi Germany to
make *The Four Companions*

Ingrid takes direction from Gregory
Ratoff in the American *Intermezzo*

Ingrid in Hollywood in 1939

One of the many unused Selznick
publicity shots taken in 1939

Ingrid and Leslie Howard in Selznick's *Intermezzo*

Ingrid and Burgess Meredith in *Liliom,* her American stage debut

Ingrid, Humphrey
Bogart, and Dooley
Wilson at Rick's Café in
Casablanca

Casablanca: The most
famous goodbye of all

Sam Wood directs Ingrid and Gary Cooper in the famous sleeping bag scene in *For Whom the Bell Tolls*

Cooper, Ruth Roberts, and Ingrid during the making of *For Whom the Bell Tolls*

Petter and Pia

Behind Alfred Hitchcock's back, Ingrid jokes for the camera

Ingrid, Cooper, and Clark Gable on
the ski slop

Gable proudly displays an eagle shot
off a Sun Valley power line while on
a trip with Ingrid and Petter

Ingrid and Pia in the living room of the house on Benedict Canyon

Ingrid and Petter's bedroom

Pia, Petter, and Ingrid

Ingrid, Leo McCarey, and Bing Crosby on the set of *The Bells of St Mary's* the day after they each received an Academy Award in 1945

A very rare publicity shot

On the clapperboard:
194
RE *Saratoga Trunk* 602
NGRID BERGMAN
TER "CLIO"
OBE #8 RIDE IN
NGE CARRIAGE
RN IN
S 100-101
ESTED 2-27-43
NGER
KS and S.E.
7-3-1
NG HAIR DRESS

A costume test for *Saratoga Trunk*

Ingrid reunited with Cooper in
Saratoga Trunk

Ingrid and Gregory Peck in *Spellbound*

Ingrid and Cary Grant in *Notorious*

companion. One evening they went to a cocktail party at the Sherry
Netherland Hotel. Neither of them enjoyed such parties very much,
but Grant had arranged for Ingrid to meet Howard Hughes, the
legendary multimillionaire owner of TWA, who collected stars and
starlets as if they were Boehm figurines.

It was raining which meant that Ingrid and Grant could walk
through the streets unobserved, moseying along Fifth Avenue in old
raincoats while New Yorkers scurried homeward. They looked in
the shop windows, knowing that any sweater, purse, or piece of
jewellery they coveted could be delivered to their hotel on approval.
Grant, always elegantly dressed, was properly attired to meet members of New York's social elite that evening; Ingrid wore a simple
skirt and blouse, among these superbly turned out ladies; people such
as these considered it the height of politeness to appear studiously
indifferent to the arrival of any mere celebrity, but when Ingrid and
Cary entered the room there was a momentary hush.

Hughes appeared and Grant made the introduction. For all his
reputation as a ladies' man, the handsome, ruggedly built Hughes
could be almost shy. While Ingrid talked to Hughes, one man after
another approached Grant to ask for an introduction to her. Later,
Ingrid, Grant, Hughes, and Irene Selznick went out dancing at El
Morocco. Hughes's associates kept calling Ingrid, trying to get her
to go out with him again. She remembered only that one evening
with Hughes, but Steele had vivid recollections of another evening,
at the Copacabana, where Hughes spent his time wooing not Ingrid
but Lana Turner, another star at the table.

Ingrid could have no complaints, however, about the number of
men who desired her. She felt comfortable in the warmth of masculine
attention. She didn't worry about what others might think of her
behaviour. She intended to live her life as she wanted to live it. In
New York this meant that she generally saved her evenings for Capa,
when he was in the city. One morning they were seen nestled together
at 4 a.m. in a Greenwich Village nightclub.

Ingrid kept her life in separate compartments. Joe Steele was a
lover of Ingrid's golden image, and the guardian of that image. In
New York she had to be free of Steele to live one of her lives. She
gave instructions that her phone calls at the Drake Hotel should go
directly to her, and not through Steele, but the publicist's self-esteem
depended on his being closer to Ingrid than the others.

One evening, he asked Ingrid if she had a date with Capa. She
became irritated and said that she was fed up with being watched
over. The next day, 26 May 1946, her schedule for the day appeared
under Steele's door. She was intending to view paintings and have a

drink with Grant, and go to the bathroom, and change her clothes for dinner. Then she would have 'Dinner (not with Cary)' and lastly, 'Home?' The question mark stood there like a taunt and a rebuke.

Soon it was time to return to Hollywood. Howard Hughes insisted on ferrying Ingrid back in his private plane, a Lockheed Lodestar; Hitchcock and Grant would also be on the plane. On the morning that they were to fly out of La Guardia Airport, the plane developed minor engine trouble. He decided to fly another craft. Ingrid promptly fell asleep in the one berth; she did not intend to pay for her trip by chatting charmingly with the magnate. Hughes, a famous flier, holder of several records, may have felt more comfortable piloting Ingrid than talking with her. Behind him flew another plane, in case this craft developed engine trouble. Touching down in Kansas City for refuelling, he was infuriated when a TWA Constellation revved up its engines: the noise might wake Ingrid. He ordered the engines shut down.

He flew the craft hundreds of miles out of the way so that Ingrid could watch dawn come up over the Grand Canyon. Steele shook Ingrid, who got up reluctantly and sat in the co-pilot's seat beside Hughes. She watched the Grand Canyon come alive, the pinks and browns and oranges sublime in the half light of dawn.

In *Arch of Triumph*, seemingly wanton, amoral Joan Madou loves an Austrian refugee and anti-Nazi underground leader, Dr Ravic (Charles Boyer), and in loving him becomes a character worthy of empathy if not emulation. That was an archetypal Ingrid Bergman role, but what followed was not. Joan's lover is deported from Paris, and she takes up with a ne'er-do-well playboy, Alex (Stephen Bekassy). Ravic kills the evil Nazi Haake (Charles Laughton) and seeks to renew his relationship with Joan. But Joan does not want to give up her new lover who, jealous nevertheless, kills Joan, as World War II begins.

A great movie could have been made about refugees in pre-war Paris, a motley breed carrying with them the truths about Nazism that most of the world was not yet ready to hear, but, as was painfully and expensively being learned, a great movie could not be made out of the Remarque novel. Irwin Shaw, who knew Paris so well, had tried to write the screenplay, but his pages were rejected. Then Harry Brown, a Hollywood screenwriter, wrote a version. His script was at least a beginning, and most nights during the shooting, more pages were written. Even Bertolt Brecht, the German émigré playwright, was called in to try a couple of scenes.

Ingrid wanted *her* Joan Madou to be the centre of the film. She and

Ruth Roberts had underlined her part in the novel, and God help Lewis Milestone if he deviated, or cut down Joan Madou's role.

'Ingrid loved the idea of playing the part,' remembers Norman Lloyd, who worked with the director on the film. 'She saw the chance of a great romantic part with Boyer. She wanted all the aspects protected. There's a scene when Ingrid and Boyer go off to the south of France for a holiday. When Brecht saw those shots he said that no one who saw them on the Riviera living so beautifully would believe it. The scene should be taken out or re-shot. Ingrid would have none of it because it was romantic and it showed her in a swimsuit. That's what the audience demanded, or so she thought. And the scene was kept.'

Ingrid's character in *Arch of Triumph* was hardly virginal, but she insisted on playing Joan Madou with the maximum of decorum. In one scene in Boyer's hotel room, Milestone showed Ingrid how she should undress, flashing her thigh as she undid her garter belt. 'I'm sure the women of that time didn't wear garters,' Ingrid said. 'I want simply to roll my stockings down.' And that was the way the scene was done.

When she was on the set, Ingrid lived her part. On *Arch of Triumph*, however, she often seemed to be somewhere else. Her next role would be as Joan of Arc on Broadway. Several days a week, she ran across the street to the Western Costume Company for the fittings of her armour. After *Joan of Lorraine*, over a year from now, she would star in a period movie, *Under Capricorn*, for Hitchcock. She and Ruth Roberts were already working on her costumes.

In the evening Ingrid often did not go home but joined other members of the cast in the office of David Lewis, the producer. There was good talk, food and drink, and it was usually late before Ingrid returned to Benedict Canyon. One morning she came on the set very disturbed. The night before, when she arrived home late, she had sat in front of the mirror taking off her make-up. Seven-year-old, golden-haired Pia had come into the room. 'Why aren't you home more?' Pia asked.

Her hairdresser saw an Ingrid who had not prepared her public face. 'She was a very unhappy woman most of the time,' Marcel Machu says. 'She would cry with no explanation. The subject she talked about most was her daughter. She was extremely proud of her daughter.'

Ingrid had told Larry Adler another story about her relationship with Pia. 'One day Ingrid told me that she was coming late from the studio and Pia came to meet her, rushed up to her to hug her and kiss her. And Ingrid slapped her. Ingrid said she was tired and she couldn't even say that she felt guilty about it. Ingrid was criticizing herself. She was saying, All I care about is my work and anybody who gets in my way, I take it out on them. She was ashamed of herself, but she never apologized, as far as I know.'

Pia's childhood was, if anything, better than that of many stars' children. She did not have a series of 'daddies' passing in and out of her mother's boudoir, and she was not shipped off to boarding school. She had not, however, spent her formative years in a family with mother and father both present day after day. She hungered for what, years later, she called a 'normal' life, though she had no idea what that might be. '"That's Ingrid Bergman's daughter", is the way I was inevitably introduced at school parties. Mama was a cinema queen, but I froze with shame whenever I saw gushing ladies beseeching her for autographs and making a fuss. She was so busy working that we had only minutes together from day to day. Visiting the movie sets, I was confused by the salaaming attention paid to Mama, the clutches of people chasing after her . . . In the middle of all this stood Mama, an island in a dark sea. I was separated from her – and from the world. I ached to be "normal" like everyone else.'

Ingrid was usually so involved in her professional life that she could shove personal problems aside, but now she was working on her first independent production, a film that she sensed would be a failure – and living at home within the failure of her married life. The tensions had begun to show. She started to smoke as part of her characterization in *Arch of Triumph*, and she soon started smoking heavily offscreen, a habit she would maintain for the rest of her life. She had always been a heavy drinker; now she seemed to drink even more, enough to have ruined the constitution of a lesser woman. 'She was so drunk one night that she fell and got a scar over her left eyebrow after the sutures came out,' Petter says. 'I was sleeping and I heard this fall. That was when I discovered a bottle under the bed.'

Ingrid's personal life suddenly risked coming apart like her film life. Capa was spending a great deal of time on the set. He stayed at the Garden of Allah and at least part of the time he lodged with Larry Adler. Capa had no real assignment from a newspaper or magazine, but he didn't seem to care. His expertise was photographing war, but he loved to take pictures of Ingrid, and he shot roll after roll. One day on the set, Ingrid sat on a stuffed chair, her head propped on her right hand. Nearby stood Lewis Milestone with a face that looked like a rumpled suit. The director gave the cue.

'I waited. Waited. And you never came,' Ingrid said, as Boyer stood over her. 'You've got to help me, Ravic!' As the cameras rolled on a poignant scene between Ingrid and Boyer, Capa shot his own still photos of what he called 'the greatest love scene ever filmed'.

Ingrid's life was like a Russian doll that opens up to disclose yet another doll, and inside that another. In the film Ingrid was making love to Boyer, but it was Capa with whom she felt she was in love, Capa who stood photographing her. And Capa was staying with Adler, with whom Ingrid was also having an affair. And then there was Milestone, her director, whose feelings for her, unrequited, bordered on infatuation.

Capa squired Ingrid around, taking her at least once to Ruth Roberts' home for a party; there even her own companion had no idea that they were involved with one another. Ingrid found time to see Adler as well.

In October, before she headed back to New York to begin rehearsals for *Joan of Lorraine*, she and Petter had a long discussion. According to Ingrid, she asked her husband for a divorce that evening in part because she was frightened of Petter, Petter's memories are different. He denies that Ingrid even hinted at a divorce; moreover, he finds it absurd that she might have been afraid of him.

Everywhere Petter went in Hollywood he met people who knew about Ingrid's affairs and talked behind his back. He felt betrayed. He was trying to hold on to his marriage, and on to his pride, and Ingrid may well have been afraid that one day he would let go.

CHAPTER 11

A SECULAR SAINT

Ingrid had read about Joan of Arc as a teenager in Sweden and been mesmerized by her story. For years, Ingrid had wanted to play the martyred French girl. Selznick's promised film had not worked out, in part because during the war he did not want to do a film that portrayed England as an invader of France.

There was always the possibility of doing Shaw's *Saint Joan*, but she was Shaw's Joan, 'a shrewd, plain pugnacious little girl, a sort of fifteenth century political agitator'. Ingrid wanted to play Joan as she knew she had been, an unassuming, uneducated lass touched by God, a maiden of simple beauty and beautiful simplicity, a beacon of purity. She wanted to *become* Joan, lighting up stage or film with her martyrdom and perfection.

Her image in the movie magazines and newspapers was Joan-like, a simple, noble Swedish lass, unspoiled and selfless. Ingrid could not be portrayed as a sacred virgin, but articles about her almost always mentioned the many months she spent away from her loyal, loving Petter, as if she were celibate for long periods. Joan of Arc was always alone. She was a woman among men, a peasant among nobles, a virgin among the knowing, a country woman among city dwellers, an illiterate among the literate. She was feminine but she was masculine. She was drawn to her martyrdom, and as the pyre was lit, her aloneness became transcendent, and in her aloneness she achieved sainthood, a woman unpossessed by anyone but God and her vision. Ingrid was not above rewriting her own past to conform to her image. She said that she had come to America as part of a sacred quest to play Joan. 'I knew I looked like Joan of Arc, who was a big peasant,' she said. 'I came here only because David Selznick said I could play Joan of Arc . . . and then he said, I can't do it now but someday I will, and so I waited and waited; and Ruth Roberts told me, have faith. And we read books about Joan and looked at paintings and statues and even wrote scripts ourselves. And soon I no longer thought of Joan as a role, I loved her so much . . . I love the real Joan so much I want to be true to her.'

Maxwell Anderson, a New York playwright, had sent her his new play, *Joan of Lorraine*. In his version, a group of actors are rehearsing a play about Joan of Arc. They have long discussions about such transcendent matters as 'Why do you believe what you believe?' The main character, Mary Grey, is to play Joan. The actress disagrees with the director about how Joan should be played. She believes that Joan would never compromise with evil. The director says that she would and did. When the actress plays Joan in a full rehearsal, she cries out: 'I know now! She will not compromise when her own soul is in question. She'd rather die!' For sheer intellectual pretension and longwindedness, Anderson's play made Shaw's *Saint Joan* seem like commedia dell'arte. But it was nonetheless Joan in the play within the play, and Ingrid decided to do it on Broadway.

Everyone was waiting for Ingrid on 5 October 1946, when she walked into the Alvin Theater with her familiar entourage of Joe Steele and Ruth Roberts. Ingrid's presence in *Joan of Lorraine* almost guaranteed success; tickets were already being sold for a twelve-week run. A group of fans waited outside to see Ingrid, and if they were lucky, to follow a few steps behind as she walked from the theatre to her suite at the Hampshire House on Fifty-ninth Street. Not only those on the outside were in awe of Ingrid. For the first few days of rehearsals, Sam Wanamaker, the young Broadway actor who played Jimmy Masters, the director, couldn't even talk to her; he was too taken by what he called her 'aura . . . partly her beauty, partly a spiritual quality, partly her dignity and reserve'.

Ingrid knew how to use that aura; she and Ruth had lunch with Maxwell Anderson almost every day. Anderson was no match for Ingrid. By the time she and Ruth were through with him, the play had become, by her estimate, 'seventy per cent Joan, and thirty per cent . . . talk . . . a complete reversal of how we started out'.

Joan of Lorraine was scheduled for three weeks' tryout at Lisner Auditorium in Washington, DC. Ingrid said later that when she arrived in the capital, she learned that the auditorium was segregated. She told Anderson, 'Shame on you, coming with this play to Washington. She then decided right before the opening to make a dramatic announcement. She would not return to play in Washington until black people and white people could sit together in theatres.

As Ingrid remembered the incident, her act had been Joan-like, a simple, profound moment of moral witnessing. Actually, she had not arrived suddenly on the scene in Washington to denounce so daringly the iniquity of segregation. For several weeks in New York there had been an organized campaign by the American Veterans

Committee, a liberal-leftist alternative to the American Legion, and the NAACP to end segregation in several important theatres across America. Several people worked on Ingrid to involve her in the effort, including Wanamaker and Steele.

Ingrid had never before expressed any great concern about racial injustice. When she stood up against segregated theatre, she did it as part of a major campaign, and she did it not so dramatically, the night before the opening, but the day she arrived in Washington. With Steele as orchestrator, Ingrid made a statement in the capital on 27 October. 'If I had known of discrimination before I signed I wouldn't have come,' she told a group of twenty-four reporters at the Carlton Hotel. 'I heard in the midst of rehearsals a few days ago that no Negro can come into the theatre. And in the capital city, too.'

Ingrid's energies were committed to *Joan of Lorraine*. The rehearsals were not going well. Two nights before the Washington opening, the cast worked until after midnight. Ingrid had had no rest for months. Steele sat in the darkened auditorium, looking at Ingrid's troubled countenance. He knew Ingrid well enough to read the signs of stress and emotional crisis.

Petter flew in the next day. He had been in New York overnight during rehearsals, on his way home from a short trip to Sweden. On that trip he had just missed catching Ingrid with Capa; the night before, they had been out late at Café Society in the Village. Capa sent a white rose to Ingrid in Washington. Ingrid cabled: 'My white rose is very near me.' Steele noted that Petter was not himself. He wondered if Lindstrom had heard an item broadcast by Sheilah Graham, a Hollywood columnist, that his marriage was about over. He wondered how much Petter knew about Capa.

Joan of Lorraine's first performance received a standing ovation. Afterwards, the cast and crew went to a big party at the 2400 Hotel. As the evening wore on, Kenneth Tobey, a young actor, shook Petter's hand in congratulation. Tobey found himself caught in the steely grip. In their tuxedos, the two men got down on the floor amid the dancers for a bout of Indian hand wrestling. They laughed and grunted, battling ferociously until Petter forced the actor's arm to the ground. Tobey demanded a re-match, and Petter beat him again.

The next morning Petter flew west to California. Soon afterwards Capa arrived, and as he sat in the first row, Ingrid gave what she considered 'her all'. The play still had problems. In the last week Sam Wanamaker took over as director in fact as well as playing the part. 'How do you feel?' Steele asked Ingrid, as she waited to make her entrance before the opening night audience at Broadway's Alvin

Theater on 18 November. 'If they don't raise that curtain pretty soon, I'll break into little pieces.'

Ingrid stood in the centre of the play like a beacon of light. Wolcott Gibbs of *The New Yorker* wrote that her performance 'may be incomparable in the theatre of the day'. To many of those present, Ingrid *was* Joan, a saintly figure. 'The cleanliness of her spirit is truly next to godliness,' wrote John Mason Brown in the *Saturday Review*, as if he were talking of a religious figure and not an actress. 'She contrives to make innocence exciting and virtue interesting.' Romney Brent, who played the Dauphin, said 'She had enormous charm and simplicity of manner . . . [is] genuine, self-effacing and considerate. Sometimes I think she really is Saint Joan.' And Maxwell Anderson wrote that she was so successful as Joan because she was 'so pure, so clean, so uncontaminated as a person'. A *New York Times* feature asserted that 'as Miss Bergman spoke she resembled more than ever the peasant maid from Domremy. One felt that faith had played a part in her success.'

Joan of Lorraine was the greatest hit in New York. After each performance crowds waited to see Ingrid. On matinée days, some hundred and fifty people would gather outside the theatre. Sometimes there were fans at Hampshire House too. One day a boy and a girl trailed Ingrid from the hotel for a dozen blocks.

Ingrid had a lovely suite on the twenty-sixth floor of the Hampshire House on Central Park South. She could look out the window and see all the way to the Brooklyn Bridge. What she loved best, however, was dusk, before she left for the theatre, and lights came on all over the city. Then she would usually be driven to the theatre, often a half hour or an hour before she had to be there for make-up. With hopes of getting Ingrid to extend the run, the Playwrights Company had knocked down two walls backstage to create a special oversize dressing room, with brightly coloured wallpaper trimmed in pink and blue. Ingrid had lined the walls with pictures of Joan of Arc. Here she met the celebrity theatregoers who came to offer tributes. She met Claude Bernheim, brother of Michael, the technical director. Claude was the head of Coty Perfumes in America, and a charming, sophisticated companion. Ingrid was often attracted to European men, and she started an affair with the Frenchman.

But Robert Capa was still her favourite. One evening she and Capa were walking arm in arm along Central Park South when they came upon Lewis Milestone and his associate, Norman Lloyd. Milestone had just finished editing *Arch of Triumph*. He was still infatuated with Ingrid. 'Bob, let's have a drink,' Milestone said, pulling Ingrid out of Capa's arms. Milestone appeared to Lloyd 'a picture of a man totally frustrated'.

Ingrid received more accolades for *Joan of Lorraine* than for any of her previous stage or film performances. She received at least twenty-one awards, including the Drama League citation for 'the most distinguished performance' of the year. Not only was Ingrid 'Queen of the Broadway Season', as *Newsweek* called her in a cover story, but she was the best paid, receiving 15 per cent of the grosses, or roughly $129,000 for the sold-out six-month run. Gallup certified her as the most popular actress in America. The Associated Press named her 'Woman of the Year' in movies.

Now she wanted to make a film of *Joan of Arc*. Selznick's grandiose plans for a *Joan of Arc* with Jennifer Jones had gone awry, and Ingrid had the field to herself. She was hoping to do it with Sam Briskin of Liberty Pictures, to be directed by William Wyler, whose credits included such classics as *Wuthering Heights* and *The Best Years of Our Lives*. Ingrid sought one third of the profits, but stood outside the negotiations, as if such matters were beneath her, while Petter attended at least one meeting with Briskin.

One evening Victor Fleming arrived backstage at the Alvin. The sixty-two-year-old director of *Dr Jekyll and Mr Hyde* had come to get Ingrid as star in his new film, to be produced independently by Walter Wanger. But as soon as he had seen Ingrid walk onto the stage he decided that his project was 'junk', and that the woman he was seeing now was a far different Ingrid, a great actress. The next day Ingrid, Fleming, and Steele had lunch at '21'. Steele could tell that he would do anything for Ingrid. The publicist suggested to Ingrid that Fleming direct a *Joan of Arc* produced by Walter Wanger.

Fleming became enormously excited by the project. He had had no major successes since *Gone With the Wind*. He was a near-alcoholic. A *Joan of Arc* was an extraordinary opportunity for him, an enormous film, a spectacle of war and peace, of blood and sacrifice, and at the centre the noble simple peasant lass, his Ingrid. For Fleming, it would be more than a mere film. He had fallen irresistibly in love with her. *Joan of Arc* would be an offering to his love, to art, to ambition, to history. It would be his greatest film, *his* in the way *Gone With the Wind* had not been. Ingrid had been attracted to Fleming once, but that was long ago, and she had gone on to other films, and other men. Listening to Fleming talk about *her* film rekindled the dead coals of infatuation. She had had affairs with directors before, but this relationship with

Fleming went beyond that. They were partners in a great and noble project.

For Christmas, Petter sent Pia ahead of him, with her maid. One day Ingrid and Pia went walking with Claude Bernheim's mother. Suddenly, Pia ran ahead.

'Come back, Pia,' Ingrid shouted.

Pia continued forging ahead.

'Pia, you shouldn't do that,'Mrs Bernheim reaffirmed more gently.

The child replied, 'I hate to walk with my mother with all those people looking at her.'

'It's not true that I didn't like to walk next to my mother,' Pia says now. 'It's that I was a small person, and it was difficult to be with her. I was shy in front of people staring at her. It made me feel conspicuous. I thought of her as my mother. I wanted not to be stared at. People always want to touch people who are well known. They put their hands on us. If you're smaller and you have to roll up the windows because they want to touch you, that's the thing that impressed.'

A few days later Petter arrived. 'A woman from the hotel came to me and said that Pia and the maid had been on a different floor until the day I arrived, the same day Fleming left,' Petter recalls. 'She said that Fleming had been in the room adjoining Ingrid's. I asked Ingrid, "Why do you have two rooms?" She said, 'I can afford two rooms.'''

In those last days of the old year, Ingrid became sick. She lost her voice. Then her eye became swollen, and when that got better, she came down with a bad cold. Petter left and Ingrid revived, but she still had complications beyond complications in her life. Capa was in Europe. He wrote Ingrid regularly, sometimes almost daily. He wrote of the '850 bottles of wine' left over from the previous time that he did not 'want to drink with anyone else'. 'I will write you a gay New Year letter, if I ever hear from you again,' he wrote from Paris. On New Year's Eve he wrote again: 'Pop, why is it so difficult to think, to write simply and say the things which cross my head in moments of . . . drunkenness.' The next day he wrote her of his hangover. Then from Istanbul: 'There is no champagne in Turkey . . . I hope you can hurry up your Joan film project . . . *Please* listen to my voices.'

Ingrid read Capa's letters and put them away. She talked to Petter regularly too. They chatted with the intimate camaraderie of a happily married couple. He advised her and undertook many little tasks. She told him of her plans to do *Joan of Arc* with Fleming and Wanger and asked him to extricate her from negotiations with Liberty Pictures. He wrote to William Wyler saying that Briskin had called the deal off because Ingrid wanted too much money, concluding the letter: 'I would like to add that in no way is Ingrid responsible for the outcome of our negotiations.'

'Lindstrom really was the patsy,' said Wanger. 'She was always going off half-cocked, making crazy financial commitments, and he was the one who had to extricate her. She had bum judgments, phony enthusiasm.'

Fleming took a seventy-five-dollar-a-day suite at a reduced rate at the Hampshire House and preparations began in earnest for *Joan of Arc*. Ingrid would be not merely a paid employee on the film but a partner in a production company that included Fleming and Wanger. Richard Day was named art director and joined the group at the hotel. Noel Howard, a young artist, was hired to go up to the medieval Cloisters in New York and make sketches.

A feeling of artistic fellowship prevailed. It wasn't all talk of *Joan of Arc* either. John Steinbeck visited Fleming's suite. So did Boyer, Remarque, and other friends and acquaintances. They talked and drank and gambled into the morning hours.

To set up the film, Fleming made regular trips back to Hollywood. Ingrid was upset by the endless business matters Fleming had to attend to, with 'everyone trying to find out where and how to get the last dollar out of the picture'. And yet she was negotiating a contract that paid her $175,000 plus 5 per cent of the gross revenues once they equalled 2.6 times the negative costs.

Fleming could not stand being away from Ingrid for even a few days. Wherever he was – a compartment on the *Super Chief*, a studio office, a hotel room – he wrote her passionate letters, frightening in their intensity.

'Tears are just as wet and salty in my bed as in your own – and night is just as dark,' he wrote, in mirthless reflection on their past affair. 'For what I've lost is lost for ever . . . I love you.'

Soon he was back at the Hampshire House. One evening Petter arrived unannounced. Ingrid was not in her suite and he waited in the hotel lobby. Early in the morning hours, Ingrid arrived from '21' on Fleming's arm and went upstairs. Petter took the elevator to Ingrid's suite, but she was not there. He telephoned Fleming's suite. Ingrid said that she would be right down.

The next morning at around eight o'clock Fleming rang Steele's room, and told the publicist that the episode had been 'damn embarrassing' and 'pretty rough'. That afternoon Petter came to see Steele, and didn't even mention the incident. He hurried off to catch a late afternoon plane to Los Angeles.

There have been many cuckolded husbands too preoccupied or too vain to note the signs of their wives' affairs. Petter, however, had been confronted with the reality of Ingrid's relationship with Fleming. He had even seen the director's love letters in Ingrid's suite. But on one level he still refused to see and understand. He still hoped. It was an act of monumental will to hold in his anger and feelings of betrayal. Ingrid was glad to see him go. He was a messenger bearing tidings that she did not want to acknowledge. Those days in New York, whenever he visited her she seemed to become sick, and when he left, the frenetic pace of her life picked up again. She didn't want Petter around, interrupting her career and her affairs.

As the last weeks of her run in *Joan of Lorraine* approached she experienced a bewildering array of emotions. She felt that her performances weren't so good any longer; she could barely get to the theatre each morning. As the most lauded actress in New York, she was sought after for every benefit and gathering imaginable. For her new film Ingrid had responsibilities that she had never had before. Capa told her one thing; someone else had other suggestions to make about the script. She didn't know whom to believe, what to do. Maxwell Anderson had been hired to write the movie script, but he couldn't catch on to Ingrid's idea of Joan's simplicity. Ingrid was exhausted; she was drinking too much, eating too much, having too many late nights.

She would soon be home with Petter, who had written her that 'the boy that made sure you had flowers at Oscar's Theater – he is still longing for you'. She told Steele, 'Petter is so lonesome.' Yet, as she wrote to Ruth, she dreaded to return to the atmosphere of the early years of her marriage.

That was the horror of it. The very things that Petter had to offer she didn't want any more, at least not from him, and perhaps she didn't want them at all. Fleming was working indefatigably on the project, but his love was a burden of time and emotion too. She wrote to Roberts that she shouldn't think that Ingrid had control over Fleming. She said that she would attempt to speak like an angel, but have the strength of a god. 'Now starts the battle for Joan!'

Fleming left the Hampshire House for the last time, to return to Hollywood and begin production of *Joan of Arc*. The *Super Chief* streaked westward, and he wrote Ingrid that he couldn't sleep or eat. When he arrived at the station in Los Angeles, he was crying, saying, 'There's no fool like an old fool.'

Petter arrived in New York a few days before the final performance of *Joan of Lorraine*. Ingrid developed a cold serious enough to force cancellation of the last Wednesday matinée, but by Saturday, 10 May, she was well. After the last matinée, about three hundred people were waiting outside the Alvin to see her emerge. She had decided not to leave the theatre for dinner. She asked if the throng might be allowed inside, so that she could address them. Her fans trooped in. As the word passed along Broadway, more and more people came, filling the orchestra. Ingrid stood onstage in a wine-coloured dressing gown, thanking them.

In the evening, the formally dressed audience was far different from the motley fans who had crowded into the theatre a few hours before. For the final curtain, fifteen or so of her most fervent fans entered the theatre and trooped down the centre aisle. One of them, thirteen-year-old Frank Edwards, worked part-time in a florist's in the Bronx. He had brought an armful of daffodils, and as Ingrid stood before the curtain in Joan's simple robe, Frank and his friends threw the flowers at her feet.

The next day Ingrid and Petter flew to Los Angeles. At the airport Petter pushed aside the fans who had come to say goodbye to Ingrid. As the skyscrapers of Manhattan disappeared into the haze, Petter sat reading *Time* magazine. Beside him, Ingrid put her head on his shoulder and closed her eyes.

Ingrid had had great roles before, but never had she starred in a film in which she was so much the centre as *Joan of Arc*. Never had she spent so long on one project. Although she began work on the movie as soon as she got back to Los Angeles, *Joan of Arc* didn't begin filming until 17 September 1948, continuing for ninety-two shooting days, with major filming completed by Christmas.

The Joan of Arc that Ingrid wanted to portray was not the historic figure playing out her life in the blood-drenched, morally ambiguous world of fifteenth-century Europe. It was not a Joan who made of humility a circular virtue, carrying it to the point where it became high arrogance. Ingrid wanted to play the mythic Joan, the Joan of her school chapbook. Her challenge was to embody that spiritual miracle, to make Joan's sainthood believable, to make the audience feel that they, too, were burning, that innocence and goodness were burning.

Ingrid was *serious* about playing Joan of Arc, and everyone in Hollywood knew it. Charades were all the rage at Hollywood parties in the early postwar years. At one gathering, the guests agreed that they would have her act out Joan of Arc and pretend not to understand whom she was playing. Ingrid opened the slip of paper. She got down on her knees and began praying. She led imaginary armies against the battlements of Orléans. She grimaced as if she were burning at the stake. No matter what she did, all that greeted her were blank, bewildered stares. Finally, when she had tried everything except setting herself on fire, she was told of the joke. Everyone laughed, everyone but Ingrid.

The company for *Joan of Arc* set up business at the old Hal Roach studios in Culver City. Ingrid's four-room bungalow was refurbished into a modern suite and dressing room at a cost of $5000. Ingrid felt at home. 'That little studio was full of friendship, and when the work was over, we laughed together. I was very hungry for laughter in those days.'

Ingrid was possessed of special cunning in her relationship with Petter. He never knew for sure about Adler, Capa, or Fleming, in part because Ingrid gave no better performance than when she and Petter met one of her lovers socially. 'Ingrid was supposed to go up to San Francisco for some kind of promotion and she wanted me to come with her and afterwards to Honolulu,' Adler says. 'This was the only time my analyst took an active part. He said, As long as you're a patient and still married, I think it would be disastrous for you to do something as dramatic as that. I don't know whether he was right or not, but considering that the romance with Capa was in full bloom at the time, I could never figure it out: why would she do that?'

Ingrid's contradictions remained unexamined, as did her failing marriage with Petter. Neither of them wanted a confrontation. Ingrid's way was always to avoid the unpleasant. As for Petter, that man of strong principle, it was unthinkable that he would be married to an adulterous woman, a woman whom he still loved.

Now that Ingrid was no longer a Selznick star, many people thought that Petter was the man to see if you wanted to sign her. One of those who sought Petter out was Howard Hughes. Hughes had taken more than a casual fancy to Ingrid. At Steele's urging, she had set up a meeting with him at her bungalow. Shortly before the four o'clock meeting, she told Steele that Petter insisted she cancel the appointment.

Hughes told Ingrid that he would make her the great star of RKO Pictures, his newest acquisition. He wanted to take her on a three-month 'promotional' tour of South America. Ingrid told Petter that Steele was behind the idea and would be the chaperon. Petter says that Steele told him years later that he had had nothing to do with the proposed trip.

'Ingrid wanted to go,' Petter remembers. 'Five times Hughes came out to see me, driving his worn-out little Dodge car. He always checked that nobody was in the house. I enjoyed talking to this very strange man. He was trying to buy me. He offered me some money if I cooperated. He couldn't understand me, why I gave him a flat no.'

Everything possible had been done in preparing the $4.6 million *Joan of Arc*. Researchers had documented the smallest detail for historical accuracy. When the king drank wine, a servant would hold a saucer under his chin, as it had been done in the European courts. The music he listened to would be authentic fifteenth-century music played on instruments copied from museum originals. Draft horses were brought from Iowa and trained by cowboys wearing armour. A craftsman prepared Ingrid's armour of exquisitely wrought, light-weight aluminium, shining silver bright.

Everything was ready, except the story. There is nothing in art quite so complicated as simplicity, there is nothing more difficult to portray on film than the spiritual. Fleming was the least spiritual of directors. When he had begun to work on *Gone With the Wind* he had told Selznick, 'David, your fucking script is no fucking good.' This time the original script was no good either, but Fleming didn't know what to do about it, and he didn't have a Selznick to work out the problems. There was a sheer silliness about part of the script; that was true even in the final version. In one scene the Dauphin greets the saintly peasant maid with the immortal line: 'My dear Joan, you look radiant.'

Fleming tried everything he knew to get hold of the true picture; he repeatedly screened *Gone With the Wind* searching for guidance. One evening he, Ingrid, and Laurence Stallings sat watching *Great Expectations*. In the film, a small boy is shown walking up a staircase and along the hall of an English mansion. Ingrid and Fleming knew how the scene helped set the whole tone for the film. They knew, too, that the shot had required a crane and was very expensive. Stallings compared it to the famous scene on Rhett Butler's stairway in *Gone With the Wind*. 'But the cost,' Ingrid complained, no longer simply an actress but a co-producer, a financial partner. 'Think of the cost.'

'Vic Fleming wore himself out on the picture,' Ingrid said years later. 'I think the pressures got to [him]. He was so anxious to make this a great success because he knew I was in love with Joan and her story.'

Unable to get a hold on the story, Fleming poured his energy into the sheer spectacle of the film. There was no burning of Atlanta in *Joan of Arc*, but there was the battle of Orléans, a dinner at the palace of the Dauphin, the coronation, and the burning of Joan. So much money had already been spent, however, that the great battle scene had to be filmed on a sound stage. Sierra Films had taken what was then considered to be the largest bank loan ever on a film, $3,500,000. Nonetheless, to complete the film Fleming deferred payment on $120,000 of his $175,000 salary. Wanger not only deferred payment on his entire $50,000 salary but invested an additional $100,000. Ingrid, whose idea the film had been, took her full $175,000 salary. She did, however, defer about $70,000 in overtime payments.

Fleming wanted Ingrid to be the radiant centre of the film. For the battle scene at Orléans, he wanted her to raise her arm and, holding her sword high, lead the charge. Alas, it was impossible in fifteenth-century armour – or even a lightweight replica – to raise an arm above one's head. Fleming was so upset that, in Howard's words, he went 'berserk'. The armour was modified with rubber so that Ingrid could do the scene the way Fleming insisted it be done. The director watched over the tiniest detail. He helped Ingrid to adjust her armour, and daubed her countenance with mineral oil, to resemble perspiration.

'I remember that in one scene Ingrid had to be out of breath,' recalls José Ferrer, who played the Dauphin. 'And she started running, and running. For a stage actor that was funny.'

Despite the high-minded aspirations, at some moments Ingrid seemed to be playing not *Joan of Arc* but the tin man in *The Wizard of Oz*. She spent hours resting against a tilted board in full armour. A special-effects crew of four or five men was devoted to her armour. When she signalled, they would oil her joints, or help lift her onto her worthy steed.

The horse was another problem. Ingrid had had directors and co-stars attracted to her, but this was the first time she had to deal with an infatuated horse. Whenever the horse saw Ingrid, he greeted her with an enormous erection. For their big scene together, the horse was sedated with tranquillizers and Ingrid got up on a wooden platform and attempted to mount. The horse started walking away. As Ingrid fell to earth Howard caught her, one hand around her shoulder, the other hand firmly grasping her crotch. The photographer who caught this unsaintly scene had his film confiscated and destroyed.

While Fleming watched *Gone With the Wind* in his office, Ingrid screened Carl Dreyer's 1927 *Joan of Arc* in hers. The silent film classic dealt with the trial and burning. Watching it, Ingrid sought new inspiration. She had little sense that things were not going right, and adored every moment of the filming. She asked friends and colleagues to come onto the set to see her as Joan. She invited Pia once as well. She had scores of pictures taken for her own use. 'Every actress wants to play Joan of Arc,' says Ferrer. 'Actors identify with a noble character and they feel they have a real deep handle on it. Their professional lives are full of corruption, and yet they're idealized beyond their contribution. I think that Ingrid began to believe her own mythology. She was a strange woman.'

The greatest moment in *Joan of Arc*, and what boded to be the most transcendent moment of Ingrid's film career thus far was Joan's burning at the stake. The crew referred to the scene as 'the barbecue', but Ingrid was not so irreverent. Indeed, for Christmas she distributed to crew members and helpers, replicas of the simple robes that Joan wore for the burning, a gift that the recipients found extremely bizarre.

On the day of the burning, the set was full of spectators. Ingrid stood on the pile of fagots, tied to the stake. Soon she was led down, and a double took her place. Ingrid took her own photographs of the spectacular scene as the stand-in stood on the burning pyre. As the flames leaped upward, the double left, to be replaced by a dummy. Within minutes the flames had engulfed the stake, and there was nothing left but fire and smoke, and an actor dressed as a priest holding a cross above the inferno.

Soon after Ingrid finished filming *Joan of Arc*, she and Petter went off skiing to Mount Rose and Heavenly Valley ski resorts near Reno, Nevada. Always before, vacations had been Petter's time, days of skiing and outdoor activity. Maybe there would be stars and Holly-wood people around, but it was still a good time for Petter. But now Ingrid seemed not to want to be alone with her husband. Capa had travelled to the resort to be with Ingrid. What act of will did it take for Petter to pretend that Ingrid was still his loyal and loving wife? What could she think of this man, her husband, to taunt him with her infidelity? Or did she want Petter to confront her? Did she hope that now he would make the final break? Did she want Petter to act as she could not act? Or did she not know what she wanted Petter to do?

There was still a childlike quality in Petter that was one of the most endearing things about him. He was proud of his physical prowess, and when Capa offered to teach him to ski, Petter found the proposal amusing. Capa fancied himself as a skier, but when they got on the slopes it was clear that Petter was far superior. Petter took his skiing seriously, and he was a joy to watch, schussing down the powdery slopes, cutting back and forth with geometric precision. He fancied himself a rational man, a man of science, and he knew that he was better than Capa, a better skier, a more disciplined man. While Ingrid, who had twisted her ankle, stayed in the lodge, Petter skied and skied some more.

One evening Capa went down to the casino to gamble. The photographer gambled the way he did everything else, as if he were wagering his life itself. It was his night, and after a while he brought his chips up to show Ingrid, as if they symbolized his luck in life and love. Later, Petter went down to the gaming room. He knew the odds, and was not a gambler. He watched Capa's luck change. Petter took no pleasure in watching a man throwing his money away. He went upstairs to tell Ingrid what was happening.

Ingrid hobbled down to the gaming tables, but she could not stop him. The next morning she saw Capa. One look at his face and she knew he had lost everything.

'Capa was gambling and wanted her to be there,' Petter remembers. 'During the ski trip I saw them staying up and drinking together. I went skiing and they went together. Then just one day to the next I said we're going to go home, we're not going to stay here.'

Ingrid said later that if Capa had asked to marry her, she probably would have assented. But Capa didn't ask, in part probably because, in Adler's words, 'Bob Capa couldn't take being Mr Ingrid Bergman.'

Running off with Capa was a notion better to contemplate than to act upon. He was a marvellous man with whom to spend a few evenings, an interlude. His constant wanderings, his drinking, his gambling, all were wonderfully romantic, if one didn't have to clean up after his life. Despite her own wanderings, her ceaseless affairs, Ingrid demanded a certain order in her life. If she had run off with Capa the results almost certainly would have been disastrous.

Soon after the ski trip, one of the most extraordinary evenings in their married life took place, according to Petter. 'Both Adler and Capa had come to the house before, but rarely together,' he recalls. 'When one was there, the other wasn't. Both were friendly with me. Capa had wanted to teach me to ski. Adler gave me a harmonica.

'Then each one came to tell me about their affair with Ingrid and to complain about the affair the other one was having. They were sure that I knew about it. It was obvious to me that they thought I had a kind of marriage where that sort of thing was acceptable. They said it can't go on like this. It was as if they wanted me to select between them.

'Ingrid admitted it. I told her that I was going to get a divorce. I said get the hell out of my house, though I didn't have a right to say that. Then she started to put on a show and started to cry. She said I was the only one she loved. She put on such a show the next weeks that I gradually believed her. I dropped the idea.'

Ingrid never talked about this incident, but she was what might charitably be called reticent in talking about her love affairs. She would admit to one affair during her married life, but not to more, and not, certainly, to two or three at a time.

Larry Adler, however, who is anything but a reticent man, asserts that he never talked to Petter about Capa. 'I would not have betrayed in any way,' Adler says. He points out that in 1949, at the beginning of the blacklist period, he left the United States instead of betraying political friends. He does say, however, that his relationship with Ingrid continued at a diminished pace until he left for Europe.

Petter remains just as strong in his recollections. It seems impossible to know absolutely what happened, but soon after the time that Petter says Ingrid promised to reform, she wrote a letter to Ruth Roberts about Capa. 'We are drinking our last bottles of champagne. I am tearing a very dear piece away from my life, but we are learning and also making a clean operation so that both patients will live happily ever after.'

CHAPTER 12

'TI AMO'

Ingrid loved to tell the story of the evening in the spring of 1948 when she and Petter went to a theatre on La Cienega Boulevard in Los Angeles to see Roberto Rossellini's *Open City*. When Hollywood made movies about Nazism, they were usually like *Casablanca*: romantic adventures. This was different. The searing documentary-like film told the story of a group of Romans in the last days of the Nazi occupation. To Ingrid, this neorealistic Italian film was a lens opened upon life itself.

A few months later Ingrid was in New York to do a radio programme. She said that she was taking a stroll when on a marquee on Broadway she saw Rossellini's name again, over *Paisan*. She bought a ticket, and once again was stunned by Rossellini's art. She told Irene Selznick that evening that she was tired of Hollywood films; she wanted to be in a film like *Paisan*. According to Ingrid, her friend's first reaction was to tell her that Rossellini would 'misunderstand', but that perhaps Ingrid was 'the only one who can write the sort of letter which will *not* be misunderstood'.

And so Ingrid wrote a short note to Rossellini. And many lives were changed.

Ingrid's story of first seeing Rossellini's films is a scene out of a romantic novel, the great star mesmerized by the art of a great director, while her husband sits beside her. In her account of writing to Rossellini, there is all the purity of impulsiveness. She has acted with noble intent, on her own, not for sordid careerism but for the nobility of art. The truth, however, is far more complicated. Ingrid did not see *Open City* in the spring of 1948 with Petter. The film was not even showing in Los Angeles then. She saw it two years before, when it opened in the United States at the World Theater on Forty-ninth Street in New York. She saw it that spring of 1946 not with Petter but with Steele. She was impressed with *Open City*, but she did not think about the film until two years later when she saw *Paisan* in New York, and was worried about her career.

It was not Ingrid but Irene Selznick who suggested that she write

to the Italian director. Indeed, Irene says that Rossellini was only one
of five directors whose work intrigued Ingrid. 'She told me she
didn't care about money,' Irene Selznick remembers. 'She wanted
opportunity. She was prepared to take a real cut for the chance to
work with any one of five directors; she named William Wyler, Billy
Wilder, George Stevens, Roberto Rossellini, and I believe, John
Huston. She wondered what to do about it. I came up with a plan
that was as simple and direct as Ingrid herself. The thing to do was
to write each one, in her own charming style, asking him to bear her
in mind in case the right story came along.'

In some ways it was extraordinary that Ingrid should have even
considered seeking work. Her three films released in 1946 had grossed
$17,500,000, an enormous sum, as much as that grossed by some
studios in a year, and she had been the number one female star in
America, the biggest box office draw of them all. However, no
Ingrid Bergman films had been released for over a year, and there
were rumours that the forthcoming *Arch of Triumph* was a disaster.

Ingrid had plenty of offers, nonetheless, and she could have contacted the American directors by picking up the phone. As for
Rossellini, the letter itself may have seemed like one of the madly
impulsive gestures of which she was capable; but it was equally the
result of calculation and forethought, a scheme generated by Irene
Selznick, who understood Ingrid very well.

Ingrid wrote: 'If you need a Swedish actress . . . who, in Italian
knows only "*ti amo*" I am ready to come and make a film with you.'

By writing '*ti amo*' – I love you – Ingrid was not trying to entice
Rossellini into thinking that his rewards from employing her would
be more than professional. Ingrid had learned the two Italian words
from her role in *Arch of Triumph*; the year before, she had even signed
a letter to Lewis Milestone '*ti amo*'.

She mailed the Rossellini letter to Minerva Films in Rome. It was
found when the studio was burning old correspondence. Mr Potsius
of Minerva Films, the man who had bought the rights to *Open City*
for a pittance, opened Ingrid's letter by mistake, and made the not
astounding deduction that Roberto was being handed a 'beautiful
present'. According to Ingrid, when Roberto read the letter, he
remembered that he had first seen Ingrid in the American *Intermezzo*
three times during a bombing raid.

And so on 8 May he cabled Ingrid:

> I JUST RECEIVED WITH GREAT EMOTION YOUR LETTER WHICH HAPPENS
> TO ARRIVE ON THE ANNIVERSARY OF MY BIRTHDAY AS THE MOST
> PRECIOUS GIFT. IT IS ABSOLUTELY TRUE THAT I DREAMED TO MAKE A
> FILM WITH YOU . . .

He promised to send her a long letter, with his ideas for a movie spelled out in detail.

His telegram was the opening aria in his relationship with Ingrid. Roberto conceived life as an opera, of which he was the composer and conductor. He did not let the banalities of facts distort the grand themes of his life. He had in fact received Ingrid's letter not with 'great emotion' but with the zeal of an entrepreneur onto a good thing. He hadn't considered the letter 'the most precious gift'; it was not 'absolutely true' that he had been dreaming of making a film with Ingrid. It might be romantic to think of Roberto watching *Intermezzo* three times during what must have been one of the longest raids in history. It was not so romantic to think that his sister Marcella was the one who had first mentioned Ingrid's name, after seeing *The Bells of St Mary's*. As Marcella remembers it, Roberto had shrugged his shoulders and said, Who cares?

Roberto was the least punctilious of men, but soon after his telegram, a letter came. He told Ingrid that he had been journeying by car north of Rome when he saw a high barbed-wire fence enclosing a field full of refugee women. Roberto stopped his car, and although the guards called him off, he walked up to the fence. There he saw a Latvian woman who grabbed his arm. Haunted by the woman's image, Roberto returned to the camp, to find that she had run off with a soldier.

'Shall we go together and look for her?' Rossellini asked rhetorically. Should they go together to the island of Stromboli where the soldier had taken the woman? Could they give life to a film that would show this woman attaining real happiness, a life of simplicity, devoid of selfishness?

Ingrid had never received a film idea anything like this. Roberto was not asking Ingrid to come to Europe to make something so banal as a movie; he was asking her to join him in a glorious journey, inviting her to share with him in an artistic quest. She was full of ideas about her roles, but always before she'd had to insinuate them with her directors. Now from the outset she would be a partner in the making of a noble film.

It would be wrong to think that she immediately saw in Roberto an antidote for all that was wrong with her life in Hollywood, but she did see promise in the project. She knew that she needed to do something new, something dramatic. After all, she was thirty-two years old, an age when an actress knows that her days as a young romantic lead are numbered. She was on her own now, without the security and judgment and public relations savvy that Selznick and his organization had provided. She had made her first two independent films, and she was aware that they were both potential failures. She was flattered by Roberto's long letter, struck by his passionate commitment to art.

She would have been less enthusiastic about him if she had known what he was up to in Rome. For while he was sending his impassioned letter to her, he was professionally courting Jennifer Jones, soon to be Selznick's wife and Ingrid's rival for the part of Joan of Arc. Indeed, Roberto was supposed to be signing a contract with Selznick, with whom Ingrid was hardly on speaking terms. The very week that he received his letter from Ingrid, he had dinner with Jenia Reissar to discuss his contract with Selznick. He pulled out the letter from Ingrid, and asked her to translate it into French. 'From the time I read the letter, the whole dinner was spent talking and asking about Ingrid Bergman,' recalls Reissar. 'He knew about her. He was like a child with it. He kept asking questions about it. He kept taking the letter out.' It never occurred to Reissar that Roberto already knew the contents of the letter, and was using Ingrid's note as a negotiating ploy.

As Roberto was penning his effusive reply to Ingrid, he was also writing one to Selznick about Jennifer Jones. He said that he was particularly thrilled with the prospect of making a film with her. This time the master was once again driving through northern Italy, among the lakes. 'I was thinking about Miss Jones, and I immediately felt it to be the ideal setting for her character and qualities.' He sketched a story of an unhealthy, selfish American businessman and his wife. Jones would be 'a symbol of redeeming love . . . the message that all are waiting for'.

Selznick was all for making Jennifer Jones the symbol of 'redeeming love'. He thought that he had a contract with Rossellini and that Jennifer would make the film early in 1948, and possibly make two films. Rossellini kept changing conditions, though, and Selznick was afraid that he would lose him. 'This danger is aggravated by the fact that Ingrid Bergman and others who are after Rossellini may talk him into changing his mind,' Selznick wrote Reissar. 'However, Bergman knows that Rossellini is tied exclusively to us.' This was not true, but Ingrid did know now that she had competition for Rossellini's services from her former employer.

Ingrid had even greater interest in working with Rossellini after *Arch of Triumph* proved a commercial disaster. The four-million-dollar film lost most of its money, reputedly the largest loss in Hollywood history. The film was not the noble beginning but the ignominious end of Enterprise Pictures. Ingrid was to have shared

25 per cent of the profits of the film, and she felt this failure as she had never felt one before. The reviews too were outside her experience. 'How that role cried for Dietrich and the quality she would have brought to it!' wrote one critic – an odious comparison for a star of Ingrid's stature. 'Too much of a good thing – even of Bergman and Boyer – is too much,' wrote Bosley Crowther in the *New York Times*.

Ingrid had little time to contemplate her losses. In June she flew to England to make a film directed by Alfred Hitchcock, produced by Sidney Bernstein for their new Transatlantic Pictures. 'Ingrid was upset that Hitchcock was getting 30 per cent of the profits and she was getting only 25 per cent,' Petter remembers. 'She said, "I have a bigger name than his. You must go and tell them and say what you want." I went to Bernstein. He said he'd talk to Hitchcock. He came back and said they'd both have 30 per cent.'

The production costs were so large that the fledgling company had to borrow $2.5 million to make the film. For her third time in a row, Ingrid was starring in an expensive film produced by a new company, with a director who was infatuated with her.

Hitchcock had chosen a project that was not a natural for him, but one that he thought would appeal to her. In *Under Capricorn* Ingrid would play the withdrawn, tragic figure of Lady Henrietta Considine, an alcoholic English lady married to the baseborn Sam Flusky, played by Joseph Cotten. Ingrid saw the film as a chance to get away from the enclosed sound stages and routines of Hollywood. During her first weeks in London, Ingrid wrote letters to friends in the States about visiting nightclubs and having a great time. Despite her promises to Petter, one of those Ingrid saw in London as well as in Paris for weekends was Capa. Their affair had decidedly cooled, but she still enjoyed Capa's company. Yet she was restless and seemed not to know what she wanted. She might laugh and joke with Capa, or sit in a nightclub with other friends, but then she would go back to the hotel and write a letter to Petter. She said later that her marriage was already dead, but there was still part of her that needed Petter, as long as she could manipulate him. She wrote asking him to write her every day. Petter himself later suggested that his love for Ingrid was dying, but here he was writing so often to her that in two days she received five letters from him and three from Pia.

'What a wonderful family,' Ingrid wrote on the evening of 19 July, after the first day of shooting. She thanked him for sending pictures, asked for more, and then discussed Petter and Pia's trip to England. She wanted him to come by ship so that Pia would experience a transatlantic crossing. 'You don't have to bother with her. You can find some little girl, like Mrs Lindstrom ten years ago on her trip back. You can dance and read.'

Petter still had faith in marriage, and he prepared for his European trip with anticipation.

In getting away from the stifling world of the Hollywood studios, Ingrid discovered that she had given up more than she had intended. The crew was unbelievably slow. Then there was the problem with Hitchcock. The director had decided to experiment with long takes, some of them six or eight minutes in duration. To Ingrid it was a child's game. Given the way *Under Capricorn* was proceeding, it might have seemed that Ingrid would have been counting the days until Petter and Pia arrived.

She was counting the days, but with mounting dread. She wrote further that she had gained ten pounds, and was chain smoking.

More than anything she was looking forward to seeing Rossellini. To arrange their meeting in Paris, she sent a telegram to Amalfi where the director was working on *The Machine That Kills Bad People*.

Roberto was known as not only a great filmmaker but a great lover. No casting director, not even the most fervent believer in neorealism, would ever have chosen Roberto for the role of lover. Here was this plump Italian burgher with tiny feet and hands, narrow mouth, beaked nose, and thinning black hair, smelling of perfume and talc; yet to some women he was a man of almost infinite seductiveness, enveloping them in such attention, such romantic fantasy, such drama, that for a while they forgot everything.

'He creates a dream atmosphere about him,' said his sometime friend and collaborator, Sergio Amidei. 'The women around him live in a dream world. He is very tender but at the same time can be brutal and vulgar. He is the true man of today. The rest of us are silly romanticists with foolish notions about how gently women should be treated.' In his attitude towards women, Roberto was not unlike many Romans of his time, only he was more successful, and his charms were not nearly as appreciated by women of his own country as by foreigners.

His life was in constant turmoil, juggling with so many women that he was like a short-order cook with a dozen differing orders frying and steaming away. There was Marcella de Marchis, his wife, the mother of his young son, Renzo; she was a compassionate, rather simple woman, of good blood and infinite understanding. He had left her years before, but they remained good friends, and he kept Marcella on a back burner, bubbling peacefully along, to be stirred only occasionally. Then there was Miss America of 1946, whom he met on one of his jaunts to Paris and brought back to Amalfi, where he wrote her into a movie. She was a choice delicacy, to be eaten and forgotten. There were others, but at the centre of his life was an enormous boiling cauldron: Anna Magnani.

Anna and Ingrid were as different from each other as it was possible to be. Men fell in love with Ingrid for her beauty, her vulnerability. No one fell in love with Anna for her beauty, nor did anyone want to protect her. She and Roberto had a relationship that Father Antonio Lisandrini, their close friend, calls 'a phenomenon of nature, incredible in love and anger'. Anna tried to seal off Roberto from other women, but it was hopeless.

One day Roberto and Anna were sitting in an outdoor café in Amalfi with Bill Tubbs, an American actor, and his wife, Helen. Near them sat a young Italian beauty in a bare midriff. The girl had aspirations to a movie career, or at least to a matinée performance with the master himself. In her hand she held a glass with a frothy pink concoction that she was using not to quell her thirst but to increase Roberto's. She stroked the glass, running her fingers up and down, occasionally glancing over at the director. Anna tried to ignore this, but suddenly she exploded. 'I was a whore before you were born,' she screamed, a statement with which no one saw fit to quarrel, and that effectively quashed the performance at the next table.

Roberto had learned that he must go to extraordinary lengths to avoid Anna's jealousy. He was worried that Anna would learn about Ingrid and the fact that he was suggesting for her a film he had originally intended for Anna. At the Albergo Luna Convento in Amalfi, where he and Anna were staying, he had given orders that foreign mail should be delivered to him discreetly. The head porter considered Anna to be practically family. He brought Ingrid's telegram to their luncheon table.

If Anna was one of the greatest actresses in the world, at that moment Roberto was trying to be the greatest actor. With a languid, disinterested air, he stuffed the unopened telegram in his pocket. Anna continued mixing a plate of spaghetti.

As she swirled the spaghetti in the bowl, she asked Roberto if he liked the way she was mixing the dish. It was terrifying to know a person the way Anna knew Roberto. She could smell the truth.

Roberto said that it was fine.

'Good.'

She picked up the serving bowl and threw the spaghetti in Roberto's face.

If all Roberto's machinations had been known, Anna might not have been the only one to want to crown him with spaghetti. As he was setting up his meeting with Ingrid, he was cabling Jennifer Jones, whose film *Duel in the Sun* had recently been released, congratulating her on her 'wonderful performance' and hoping to do a film with her in the near future. Selznick didn't know what to make of the cable. He thought his negotiations had fallen apart for good. Selznick was still ready to go ahead, though, and Roberto agreed to meet Reissar in Paris between 23 and 27 September to sign the contract. On Thursday, 23 September, Selznick's representative called the Hotel Raphaël, to be told that Rossellini had already left, leaving no address. Reissar called again on Friday, but there was still no message. 'Personally, I don't believe any penalties, however severe, would make any difference to Rossellini,' Reissar wrote to Selznick. 'He is temperamental and irresponsible.'

While Reissar fumed in London, Rossellini was preparing for his Sunday meeting with Ingrid at the Georges V Hotel. Ingrid was met by the director, Rudolph Solmsen, a producer and his European representative, and Ilya Lopert, a foreign film distributor in the United States. Roberto kissed her hand and then talked about the film he and Ingrid would make together. He didn't care what language she spoke in the film, or what clothes she wore. None of that mattered, only the reality of the story, of the art they would create together. Ingrid listened to this story of love on the barren island of Stromboli, and was impressed. Petter has no recollection of meeting Rossellini in Paris, only of sitting with three Italians who chatted with Ingrid while he listened. No contract was signed that day, but it was agreed to go ahead once Roberto sent Ingrid a full synopsis of the story. Back in Rome, Roberto could not restrain himself from commenting on his impressions of Petter. 'Swedish women are the easiest in the world to impress because they have such cold husbands,' he said. 'The love they get is an analgesic balm instead of a tonic.'

In November, Ingrid finally received a letter from Rossellini. The story he outlined promised her anything but an analgesic balm. He wrote of those who loved so passionately that there was no room for pity.

He didn't have a script for her. He didn't work that way. He was infusing into Ingrid's film life a whole new level of danger, of risk.

For years, she had sought danger in her personal life, risking exposure; reading Roberto's letter, she wanted more than ever to make their film on Stromboli. Before she signed any contract, however, she would have to wait until early in 1949, when Roberto was coming to California.

Another reason for Ingrid's excitement was the failure of *Joan of Arc* which opened that month in New York. No role had meant more to her than this one, no film ever monitored by Gallup's polls had ever been so anticipated; three hundred thousand dollars had been spent on magazine advertising alone; there was a paperback book in drugstores, with Ingrid's picture on the cover; she was on the cover of *Life* in armour, riding a horse; high above Times Square stood an eight-storey-high figure of her in white plastic armour, which had cost $75,000; a few blocks north, the Victoria Theater had been remodelled, the walls sheathed in aluminium mail. The premier was a glorious opening, but Ingrid had never received such mixed reviews. Some critics ridiculed her whole persona, the glorious image that had taken a decade to grow to its present eminence. 'Possibly Ingrid Bergman may be partly held to blame for this lack of the deeper human feelings and comprehensions in this film,' wrote Bosley Crowther in the *New York Times*, 'for Miss Bergman, while hand-some to look on, has no great spiritual quality.' C. A. Lejune in London's *Observer* wrote, 'Miss Bergman, in fact, makes an important principal boy, and Hollywood's Joan of Arc . . . is a triumph of matter over mind and spirit.'

Joan of Arc was a disaster of the magnitude of *Arch of Triumph*. The film took in only a little over two million dollars. Nothing was left of Sierra Films except endless legal squabbles. Fleming was suddenly an old man. On 6 January 1949, he died of a heart attack, brought on, many people felt, by his work on *Joan of Arc*. Joe Valentine, the cameraman, and Casey Roberts, the set decorator, also died soon afterwards, just as unexpectedly.

Although Ingrid continued to see Capa in Europe, she was taking an interest in her family unlike any she had ever shown. She was thirty-three years old, and with the failure of two pictures in a row, she might have settled down into a slowly declining career and the blessings of family life. But instead she embarked upon a fantasy. She decided to have a son – not simply a child, but a son, whom she would call Pelle – as if she and Petter had that much control over their destiny. She began to renovate their house, putting in a nursery and a maid's room. She worked with the architect, and according to Petter told him that these were the happiest days of their married life. But she didn't become pregnant. 'I was reluctant to have another child since our marriage seemed so shaky,' Petter says.

Nothing seemed to be working out right for her – neither her plans for a new baby, nor her career. 'She was obsessed by her failures,' Petter remembers. 'She kept saying, "I have to get out of Hollywood. I hate Hollywood."' He worried about her heavy drinking but was in no condition to help her. He had suffered a serious case of food poisoning over the Christmas holidays. For the first time in their marriage, Petter was sick, and he had the feeling that Ingrid didn't care.

She seemed to be clearing away the debris of her professional life. Even years later Steele could remember every detail of the day in January that Petter called him and told him that he was fired. Steele insisted on a meeting, and at three o'clock in the afternoon arrived at the Benedict Canyon home. He found Ingrid and Petter seated in the grass next to the pool. Ingrid didn't even greet him. Petter explained that Ingrid would no longer be needing his services. Ingrid sat silently, eyes down, as her longtime aide and confidant defended his efforts to Petter.

Petter claims that he was only doing what Ingrid had asked him to do.' She said, "I want to get rid of Joe because he knows too much about me and is checking up on everything I do."' Once again, Petter's public image of strength was found wanting when it came to Ingrid, whereas her seeming reticence was a mask for her strength. Steele should have remembered that when he had left Selznick, his beloved Ingrid had acted no better than any of the other Selznick stars. She hadn't even called him until months later, when she needed him. But he forgot things like that because he wanted to forget them. And he blamed Petter solely and absolutely, and hated him with a passion almost as great as his love for Ingrid.

In 1946 she had gone out on her own sure that her fortunes would prosper as never before. *Arch of Triumph* and *Joan of Arc* had started as glorious projects and had ended as two of the biggest debacles in Hollywood history. She could not know how *Under Capricorn* would fare, but there had been major problems on the set, harbingers of more doom and failure. 'Ingrid was desperate,' Petter says. 'She said, "In Hollywood, you're never any better than your last picture. I have to do an artistic feature in Europe."'

Going to Italy did not signify a jettisoning of her Hollywood future. Rather, in one daring move she was hoping to achieve an unprecedented position in world cinema. Roberto would bring to Ingrid a level of art almost unknown in Hollywood. If their collaboration succeeded, if they produced a film on the level of *Open*

City and *Paisan*, then Ingrid would have a success undreamed of even in Hollywood.

It was perfect. Not only did Roberto make art out of everyday life, he made life into art. He was everything Petter was not – romantic, adventurous, a creative genius.

Ingrid thought that she and Roberto were kindred spirits. Alas, like her, he was egocentric, a man of impulse who expected those around him to serve him. Her primary interest in him was her career, but he wasn't contemplating world success standing together with Ingrid at the heights; he thought about himself and Ingrid together in quite another position. 'I'm going to put the horns on Mr Bergman,' he announced to his friends. There was nothing lyrical in Roberto's desires. But first, he had to divest himself of Anna. One evening at the Excelsior Hotel in Rome, where he and Anna stayed, he told her that he was going to walk the dog. He left the animal with the concierge and took off for America. Anna spent the evening accompanied by Bill Tubbs, going from restaurant to restaurant trying to find him.

In New York, Roberto accepted the New York Film Critics award for *Paisan* as best foreign film of the year. The smell of an affair was already in the air. While Roberto rode the train westward to Los Angeles, Walter Winchell, the radio gossip columnist, announced: 'Ingrid Bergman's one and only love is coming to Hollywood to see her!'

Roberto would think of staying nowhere but the exclusive Beverly Hills Hotel (the bill paid by Ilya Lopert, the producer). Soon after arriving, Roberto visited the Lindstroms' house in Benedict Canyon. Ingrid had prepared for this momentous event by laying down a thirty-foot runner of red carpeting into the house. Roberto had had some curious greetings, but never one quite like this, a welcome as befitted a king of cinema. 'I was uncontrollably nervous,' Ingrid remembered. 'When he walked in, I couldn't talk. I tried to light a cigarette, but my hand trembled so much that the flame died out.'

Ingrid did not remain nervous long. Roberto told her about his childhood and life in Rome. Although she complained later that Petter had been too old for her, Roberto was nearly a year older than her first husband. He was born on 8 May 1906, the eldest son of a wealthy architect. Roberto had been brought up in a great Roman house in the best part of the city, with nannies and tutors and indulgence. Money was for spending, and he had squandered his inheritance disdainfully, as if he thought the notes might dirty his hands. He had not bothered with a university education, but had got into film work for the fascists. In Los Angeles, he had plenty of time to discuss art and life and love with Ingrid in French, time to meet with Hollywood producers and moneymen, discussing films and ideas in terms that made no sense to the Americans.

They approached Sam Goldwyn. The legendary producer was famed for his cynical wit. He spoke fractured English, but he was a shrewd, observant man. He saw possibility in this union of America's great star and Europe's great director. At a dinner party, Goldwyn screened Rossellini's *Germany Year Zero*, filmed in bombed-out, ravaged Berlin. The film was not a facile attack on Nazism but the bleak account of a Germany where the spiritual rubble lay deeper than the physical. When the lights went up in Goldwyn's screening room, there was an uneasy silence.

Ingrid got up, walked over to Roberto, threw an arm around him, and kissed him on the cheek. She meant her embrace to symbolize artistic camaraderie. The other guests read more personal meanings into her gesture.

Ingrid and Roberto were the centre of the evening. Petter stood to the side, confiding to Hedy Lamarr that 'he went to these functions with his wife because he knew it was good for her career'.

'As time wore on, Ingrid was standing with Roberto in a corner, twisting a button on his brocade vest and looking into his eyes with a tiny, inviting smile,' Lamarr remembered. 'She was beautiful and it was clear her charm was being appreciated. When I saw Ingrid and Roberto, hand in hand, stroll over to Petter, who was still standing alone trying to look happy, I was drawn closer, to hear what would be said. A dramatic moment was definitely coming.

'Ingrid very coolly said to Petter (while Roberto looked on smiling), "Mr Rossellini is going to take me home. May I have the key, please?"'

'I could see Petter was terribly embarrassed yet reluctant to make a scene. Hesitantly he brought out his key chain, opened it and slid a key off. Without one word he handed her the key and she didn't say one word in return. Then Ingrid and Roberto walked out.'

The next day Goldwyn discussed with his son Sam junior his decision to turn down the project. 'I can't understand a guy who says, "I want to make up the scenes when I see the actors,"' Goldwyn said. 'I'm crazy about Ingrid. Everyone in town is offering her scripts. Why does she want to get into a story without a script? There's got to be something else going on. They're either having an affair or about to have one.'

*   *   *

Roberto insisted on living in high style and he could not be bothered with such petty concerns as chequebooks, contracts, deal memos. Goldwyn backed out of the deal. Lopert felt that Roberto had doublecrossed him by seeking another producer, and he stopped paying Rossellini's bills. According to Petter, Roberto didn't give a second thought to borrowing two thousand dollars from him, as well as money from Ingrid's agent and her insurance salesman. When Roberto didn't have enough money to remain at the Beverly Hills Hotel, Ingrid invited him to stay in their guesthouse. Petter greeted the director and went to his office.

Ingrid and Roberto went off too. They experienced Los Angeles in a way that, in all her years in the city, Ingrid had never experienced it. They drove up the coast, and into the mountains. They lunched at the Farmer's Market and Don the Beachcomber's, where Ingrid had first dined when she arrived in Hollywood. They went to drive-ins. They had dinner with Billy Wilder, the director and writer. They had meetings and lunches with many other leading Hollywood people. They went everywhere together, talking in Ingrid's poor French or Roberto's fledgling English.

'Roberto was so warm and outgoing,' Ingrid said of those first days. 'When I was with him, I didn't feel shy or awkward or lonely – perhaps for the first time in my life. He was easy to talk to and interesting to listen to. Most of all, he was alive, and he made me feel alive.'

Roberto brought to their relationship a vitality that he seemed certain to bring to their film life together. Only two months before, Ingrid had wanted a new child and a re-modelled house, but now she could not stand the idea.

She took Roberto to Howard Hughes, who agreed to finance their film for RKO, his new studio. Here she did not let her adulation of Roberto stand in the way of business. She would receive $175,000, the same basic salary she had earned on *Arch of Triumph* and *Joan of Arc*. She also would receive 40 per cent of the net profits, and Roberto would receive a salary and 20 per cent of the net profits. As an American star making a film in Italy, Ingrid would also receive a subsidy from the Italian government worth at least $50,000. Rarely has idealism paid so well. For her adventure into the world of Italian neorealism, Ingrid would earn far more than she had ever earned. If the film was a major success, she would have wealth beyond anything she had yet known.

Ingrid and Roberto went out to a nightclub on the Sunset Strip to celebrate. Petter made a belated appearance and spoke to his wife in Swedish. Soon afterwards, a Hollywood column retailed gossip about a certain famous star's public spar with her doctor husband.

One evening Celeste Holm invited Ingrid and Petter to a party, in part to celebrate Ingrid's forthcoming movie in Italy. The two of them arrived and found all their friends. Petter danced with abandon, changing his shirt at least once. Ingrid was more interested in talking about the film she and Roberto would be making on Stromboli.

'Oh, it's going to be so marvellous to get out of this predictable society!' Ingrid said emphatically.

'Is it a good script?' asked George Seaton.

'Oh, there's no script,' Ingrid said, as if she had to instruct these novices about the new cinema. 'We get there to a place and we do it.'

'I always thought a good script is a good idea,' said Charlie Brackett, the actor, with wry understatement.

When the time came for Roberto to leave, he wanted to buy a gift for his son, Renzo. In the toy store he bought cowboy boots, a cowboy hat, and an Indian headdress. Then Roberto spied an enormous stuffed cow, wearing an apron. It was about as big as a real calf and cost seventy-five dollars. Roberto charged the cow to Petter's account and took it home to a delighted Pia. On 27 February 1949, the evening before he left, he and Petter sat down for a long talk. Roberto remembered Petter telling him that 'Ingrid is easily enthusiastic, sensible but not intelligent, and that she has a temperament that makes her thoughtless'. Petter denies talking about Ingrid. He says that Roberto said that he cared for him 'as his own brother'. He was a man Petter could trust with his wife. He would take care of Ingrid in Italy, protecting her from gossip. He would introduce Ingrid to Anna. Also, according to Petter, Roberto promised that he and Ingrid would take separate boats to Stromboli, a tacit admission of the rumours.

The next day Roberto left for Italy, and Petter and Ingrid went to Aspen, Colorado, for a skiing vacation. Ingrid was supposed to begin work in Italy on 1 April, but she couldn't wait to be with Roberto. She told Petter that Roberto had promised to take her to Capri, Amalfi, and Messina before beginning the film. Petter did not like the idea of his wife travelling around Italy with Roberto and he told her so.

Ingrid wrote Roberto from Aspen that though she would like to be with him, she was afraid Petter would hurt her physically. Her letters were childlike in their trust, as if she and Roberto were in a conspiracy against the world. She wasn't worried about complications; she didn't think about bad publicity; she didn't give Pia a mention. She simply wanted to be with Roberto, and she wanted desperately to work.

On 9 March, she said goodbye to the household help and to Pia as she had said goodbye so many times before. She looked back and waved at Pia. At the airport, seeing Petter standing there, 'so lonely and silent', she felt 'sentimental'. She had had other affairs but she had always returned to Petter, and Petter had always been there. He represented her past, her country, her language, the soil from which she had sprung. What a burden of yearning and caring, memory and remorse, their marriage carried. So much had not been said; so much could not be said. There had been so many times when their marriage had torn apart, to be sutured up again, leaving new scars. If she abandoned Petter, she would in a sense be abandoning herself, her history, her memories. Ingrid was not one to weigh alternatives, to think of consequences. She didn't imagine that this time she might be headed for an affair that she could not control.

Petter returned to the half-empty house in Benedict Canyon, with its new nursery. His strategy had been to wait; until the arrival of Roberto, his plan had worked. He went into Ingrid's dressing room, adjoining their bedroom; standing there, he knew that this time was different. Ingrid had cleaned out many of her possessions. Gone were two fur coats, two fur jackets, many of her dresses, and all the jewellery that she kept in the house. Gone were her clipping books, personal letters, and photo albums. Gone, too, were Ingrid's promises, their years together. Everything was gone.

CHAPTER 13

THE PRINCE OF DISORDER

For the whole week in New York, Ingrid had been frantic with excitement. As soon as she had arrived, Roberto telephoned her at the Hampshire House. She could have talked to him ten times a day, but she was worried about the gossip.

There was only a week to wait anyway. She went to see several plays. Visiting with José Ferrer, who was starring in *The Silver Whistle*, she sat in his dressing room until the morning hours, drinking Scotch and talking about Roberto and movies. On her last evening in America, she went to see Irene Selznick in her new apartment at the Pierre. Irene's divorce had become final three months before. Ingrid didn't want to talk about Irene and her new life as a Broadway producer. She wanted to talk about herself. Listening to Ingrid's endless monologue, Irene thought that she 'was not so much exhilarated as fevered'.

Irene, who lived life as if discretion were the highest virtue, didn't want to know about Roberto. She undressed for bed, but even that didn't stop her guest. Finally Ingrid picked up the phone and called Roberto in Rome. It was so late now that Ingrid didn't want to go back to the Hampshire House alone. She asked Irene if she might stay and sleep next to her. For hours Ingrid had been drinking and smoking and talking. As she walked to the bathroom, she slipped and struck her head on the side of the air conditioner. 'She fell so heavily I thought she was a goner,' Irene remembered. 'An eighth of an inch in a different direction and she wouldn't have gone to Rome.'

In the week that Ingrid had been on the East Coast, she had not called Petter or Pia. If she had called, and if Petter had been candid with her, he would have told her that he'd had a visit from Lopert, the disgruntled producer. 'Lopert didn't get any share from Rossellini and RKO,' Petter recalls. 'He said to me, "Rossellini is a liar and a cheater and now he has fooled me again. There is one thing I want you to know. Before we arrived in Los Angeles, he said to me, "I will have Bergman in bed within two weeks."''

As the plane droned eastward, Ingrid was fairly relaxed. At Rome's Ciampino airport a great welcoming crowd started to gather well before the scheduled arrival of the plane at midnight on Sunday, 20 March. In the years before World War II, Hollywood had captured the hearts of Italians; in early 1939 the most popular film in Italy was *Snow White and the Seven Dwarfs*. Now the American films were back, capturing over 70 per cent of the audiences. The American presence was everywhere, even in several of the best neorealistic films themselves, like Vittorio De Sica's *Bicycle Thieves*, where Papa has his bicycle stolen while working at pasting up posters for a Rita Hayworth movie. The Italians didn't want to see a mirror held to the scars left by the war; they wanted to see, in the magical mirror of Hollywood, a life that was bigger and more beautiful, if only for an hour or two.

'Italy had just come out of the war,' says Federico Fellini the great Italian director who was then working with Rossellini. 'The people were starved. There were disasters. The figure of Ingrid was like an ambassadress of well being. She was very familiar, like all the myths of Hollywood, like Clark Gable, like Gary Cooper, like Mickey Mouse. 'You could expect anything from her. She gave this feeling of being a fairy queen who could make little miracles. She was more like a Walt Disney character. This was the fascination. For Italians, who are so deeply touched by the Catholic Church and the figure of the Virgin Mary, she was someone who reminded you of an American saint.'

The Italians *believed* in Ingrid, in this pure, transcendent being who was blessing them and their land with her presence. And she was not coming merely to use Italy as a setting for a Hollywood film. She would be starring in a film directed by the master of the modern Italian cinema.

Searchlights played on the plane as it touched down. All the other passengers filed out. As Roberto entered the plane with an enormous bouquet of long-stemmed roses, Ingrid kissed him and whispered, '*Je t'aime*.' Then in her fur coat, and holding the flowers in her arms, she stepped out into the cool Roman air. Spread out below was a great crowd, welcoming her, she said later, as if 'it was a queen arriving'.

Roberto thrust a way for them through the crowd. Ingrid had pushed her way through adoring fans before, but there was a celebratory fury here unlike anything she had ever experienced. Roberto merrily grabbed one photographer, ripping his coat down the back. Then he rammed his way to the door. The crowd pursued him, but Roberto finally pushed Ingrid into his red Cisitalia sports car, and accelerated off into the night.

In front of the elegant Excelsior Hotel on Via Veneto, another crowd stood waiting to catch a glimpse of Ingrid. Roberto led her through the throng into the grand lobby. Roberto had a permanent room at the Excelsior; he liked always to make *la bella figura*. Few people realized that it was a tiny, dark, inside room, more appropriate for pails and mops than for love affairs. For Ingrid, though, Roberto had taken a suite, to be paid for by RKO.

Roberto planned the mise-en-scène of his love affairs with a precision and concern for detail that he didn't always bring to his films. Although it was nearly three o'clock in the morning, his friends were waiting to greet Ingrid. There was champagne and little gifts and what Ingrid considered Roberto's wondrous, magical presence. Everything went well until Roberto introduced Ingrid to Helen Tubbs whose husband was acting in Roberto's films.

'Here is the correspondent from *Variety*,' Roberto said. Ingrid looked at Tubbs with eyes that the American reporter thought full of terror.

'Don't worry,' Roberto said.

'I'm not writing gossip,' said Mrs Tubbs. 'I won't put in what you don't want.' Ingrid looked relieved.

Roberto had planned this moment, even to the extent of making sure that Anna Magnani would be out of the country. Anna still loved Roberto, and she understood him as well as she loved him. From London she called her friend Suso Cecchi d'Amico, a prominent screenwriter.

'Did Ingrid arrive?' she asked.

'Yes.'

'Did Roberto go to the airport?'

'Yes.'

'At the airport, which road did they take?'

D'Amico thought a moment. Two roads led to Rome. The new modern highway, a direct swath cut through the countryside; that was the road everyone took. Then there was the Via Appia Antica, the ancient route, tree-lined, meandering, romantic, a road that had been there since the Romans. This was the road on which Roberto had often driven Anna, mesmerizing her with his tales of ancient Rome.

'I think the old road.'

Anna hung up.

On Ingrid's first day in Rome, Roberto scheduled a press conference in one of the mirrored salons of the Excelsior. A crowd of about three hundred reporters, photographers, publicists, and hangers-on were jammed into the room. Roberto pushed his way to the front of the room, pulling Ingrid along with him. Some of the pressmen were not going to settle down to the mundane business of asking questions, when Ingrid's autograph could be captured. Scores of people pushed forward while the photographers took hundreds of pictures. Ingrid tried to smile, but she'd never been in anything like this; she was afraid. 'Give her air!' Roberto shouted. He had had enough. 'Let's go,' he shouted, and tried to force his way out of the room. The crowd would not let Ingrid out. Roberto gave no quarter. He and Ingrid finally popped out of the room. '*Maleducati!*' he screamed, as he and Ingrid made for the elevator. Afterwards Ingrid was blasé about it. 'I always knew Italians were very passionate people,' she said, 'but I didn't know they were that passionate.'

Ingrid was totally mesmerized by Roberto and Roberto's Rome. He had told her about his family's home at Ladispoli, just north of Rome on the coast. In broad strokes he had sketched an image of an idyllic retreat, something out of Chekhov, and Ingrid insisted on driving out to see it. Vittorio De Sica and Sergo Amidei joined them.

Whatever the town had been before the war, it was now little more than a wart on the land. But as Ingrid and Roberto walked hand in hand through the cluttered, dirty streets, Ingrid was in ecstasy. She saw only the glorious images Roberto had created for her. De Sica returned to Rome to tell his friends, 'Ingrid's completely crazy. It's a bidonville and she was enchanted.' He coined a new term to describe Ingrid: '*la grande ignora.*'

Like other visitors, particularly when in love, Ingrid was enchanted by the sundrenched land. The Frenchman may fancy that he speaks the language of civilization, and that if God does not speak only French it is because he saves the language for state occasions. The Italian feels that his is the language of life, and better to speak it poorly than not at all. He believes that if God lives in heaven, he takes his vacations in Tuscany. Roberto was the most Italian of Italians. He was just as proud as Petter, but whereas Petter's was a moral pride, Roberto's was proud of knowing how to live, how to feel, how to love.

He was charming, but even his sister admits that 'people would say he was charming like a snake, like a snake with little birds'. Love has no rules, at least as Roberto played the game; he wanted to make Ingrid irrevocably his. To win her, he first wanted to show her his Italy on their journey to the island of Stromboli. So after a few days in Rome, Roberto and Ingrid took the Appian Way out of Rome. The red Cisitalia convertible sped southward, the wind blowing Ingrid's hair.

To Ingrid, each twist in the road, each new village, each new town, brought more moments with neither past nor future. Roberto knew his Italy, and as they sped onward, he spun his web of anecdotes and history. Roberto led Ingrid to Capri, but he neglected to tell her about his personal romantic history on that most romantic of islands. Indeed, one of his previous lovers, Roswita Schmidt, a German actress, was still living there. At Amalfi, they stayed at the Albergo Luna Convento. The former Capuchin monastery was a favourite stopping place for Roberto. It was here that Anna Magnani had thrown a plateful of spaghetti in Roberto's face. And it was here that Ingrid sat down to write a letter to Petter, asking for a divorce.

Petter had been writing. Though he knew that Ingrid and Roberto were lovers, his letters were resolutely innocent, full of advice and goodwill, as if even now he could not face the reality of his life without her. Sitting in her hotel room before a blank paper emblazoned with the hotel's name, Ingrid could no longer forget Petter and her past. She tried several times, before she said what she wanted to say.

Petter lilla [little] –
It will be very difficult for you to read this letter and it is difficult for me to write it. But I believe it is the only way. I would like to explain everything from the beginning, but you already know enough. And I would like to ask forgiveness, but that seems ridiculous.

It is not altogether my fault, and how can you forgive that I want I stay with Roberto?

It was not my intention to fall in love and go to Italy forever. After all our plans and dreams, you know that is true. But how can I help it or change it? You saw in Hollywood how my enthusiasm for Roberto grew and how much alike we are, with the same desire for the same kind of work and the same understanding of life.

I thought maybe I could conquer the feeling I had for him when I saw him in his own milieu, so different from mine. But it turned out just the opposite. The people, the life, the country is not strange. It is what I always wanted. I had not the courage to talk more about him at home than I did with you as it all seemed so incredible, like an adventure, and at the time I didn't realize the depth of his feelings.

Min [my] Petter, I know how this letter falls like a bomb on our house, our Pelle,* our future, our past so filled with sacrifice and help on your part.

And now you stand alone in the ruins and I am unable to help

* Years later, in her autobiography, Pelle was changed to Pia.

you. Stackars lilla pappa men also stackars lilla mama [Poor little papa, but also poor little mama].

Mama

Ingrid believed that it was Petter who stood 'alone in the ruins' while she had moved on. She would suffer her moments of sadness, but nothing of the burden that her husband carried. With Roberto she might outface fate. For ten days they journeyed south, unaware of the tidal wave of turmoil that pursued them. In Rome, Roberto's friends and relatives were already worried that the affair might engulf him. He had had his affairs before, but they had always been subordinate to his work. His relationship with Ingrid, however, risked becoming a circus that would dominate his life. 'I was worried about what Ingrid would mean to my brother's life,' his sister Marcella remembers. 'I worried because Ingrid's coming here would bring all these awful things – not her, of course – the paparazzi, all of that, so we couldn't live any more.' Roberto's cousin Renzo Avanzo felt much the same. 'Sure, we disapproved,' he said, 'but not from a moral point of view. Nobody gave a damn about that. We disapproved because we knew that, with her, he was through making the kind of pictures he should be making. She came out of a proper, serious, commercial world of filmmaking. He didn't fit in with that. They were enamoured with the idea of what they could do together artificially – and it was a lousy idea.'

Roberto was under the same illusion as Ingrid: that he had control over his life. To Ingrid he was this god of the cinema who created greatness out of nothing. He needed no script; the dialogue and scenes would spring full-blown out of his genius. He needed no professional actors; he would anoint his cast, plucking them off the street, choosing a face, a figure. On the beach at Salerno, he told Ingrid, he would find her leading man. Twenty minutes later he returned to tell her that he had found two men, and one of them, Mario Vitale, a handsome twenty-one-year-old fisherman, became the romantic lead for the munificent pay of seventy-five dollars a week.

The farther south they travelled, the poorer the land became. They sped along narrow roads bordered by windowless huts where peasants worked the soil with spades and sweat. In this forgotten land, movies were the main, and sometimes only, contact with the urban world. Ingrid appeared almost as well known here in southern Italy as in Dayton or Des Moines. In the town of Catanzaro, the main street was lined with well-wishers. Ingrid and Roberto had the finest room in the hotel, but even that had no private toilet. When Ingrid had to go to the bathroom, the local dignitaries were still standing in the hallway; she was applauded in and out, though her audience allowed her to perform her ablutions in silence. For their bed at the hotel, the mayor of Catanzaro donated his silk wedding sheets, asking that they kindly sign them in the morning. He would keep them like a relic of the church.

By the terms of their contract, Ingrid and Roberto were supposed to begin work on the film 1 April 1949, but it was already 4 April before they sailed from Messina. Since the only regular passage to Stromboli was a weekly mail boat from Naples for the filming of *Stromboli*, as the movie was eventually titled, an old forty-foot fishing schooner had been leased. The *San Lorenzo* was hardly the luxury cruiser that a Hollywood star might have expected; there wasn't even an awning to protect the passengers from the unyielding Mediterranean sun and it stank of dead fish, but she smelled only the fresh sea. Ingrid hadn't complained of the hardships during the filming of *For Whom the Bell Tolls*, and she did not complain now as the boat lumbered along, the motor coughing and spitting. On their way they spied the island where Anna Magnani was having her artistic revenge, making a film entitled *Volcano*.

For four hours the boat chugged towards Stromboli, the most northerly and remote of the Lipari Islands. Suddenly, there rising out of the ocean stood the great steaming three-thousand-foot-high cone of the volcano, then the black bulk of the mountain, and finally the island itself, little more than a pedestal for the volcano, one of the most active in the world. Only recently it had erupted, spewing forth a mass of lava and smoke and flames, the lava spilling down its side to the sea; some days the smoke blotted out the very sun. Anyone who lived on this island could have few illusions about man's control over his destiny.

The boat nosed around the farther side to the tiny village. Above the black sands stood a group of whitewashed Moorish-style cottages huddled together. Once there had been five thousand people living there, but now there were only about five hundred; the young had gone, leaving Stromboli to the old, the lame and the inert, an island shrouded in the black of widows, and in the grey of the volcano.

The arrival of Ingrid and Roberto was the greatest event in the history of Stromboli, and the entire village stood on the black sands, waiting. As Ingrid looked on the island for the first time, she thought that it was 'a spectacular setting for a movie'. She did not think that it would be difficult to make a film here that would capture the world's imagination.

Unquestionably, Stromboli was a spectacular setting for a love affair. For the first week or so, that was Roberto's main concern, even if it was on RKO's time and money. Roberto was an expert diver and spearfisherman; the waters around the island are rich with fish, and time and again he dived into the sea, surfacing seconds later, with a fish to deposit at Ingrid's feet. They lived in the schoolmaster's home, the best house on the island. Each had a bedroom. The island had no running water; for Ingrid a bathroom was specially built onto the end of the house. It included a makeshift shower, consisting of an old oil drum on the roof that the maid filled with water heated on the stove. There was a little courtyard where Ingrid and Roberto could at least not be overheard. 'I have seen her sit on a low wall outside the house – the Love House as it came to be called – for hours on end without saying a word,' said Michael Wilson, the British public relations man assigned by RKO to the film. 'Just nodding her head, while Rossellini talked.'

On 7 April Roberto began filming in his languid, desultory way. Filmmaking is the most collegial of arts, combining a dozen abilities and crafts; with Roberto, Ingrid thought she would share in the artistic process. Roberto, however, was a man of monumental hubris, along with an insecurity that he masked with bravado. He was unwilling to share the creative process. He was the screenwriter, but he had no screenplay to be picked over and criticized by producers, actors, and others. He had only his ideas, and by writing the dialogue and the scenes almost as he filmed them, he controlled the daily production of the film.

Ingrid had a grandiose conception of her life as an actress with Roberto. Here finally she would begin exploring roles with all the depth and subtlety of a Magnani. But Roberto had cast *Stromboli* with the islanders not simply because they looked authentic, but because he didn't want 'actors'. He treated them as little more than puppets who mouthed whatever words he told them; on *Stromboli*, he even tied string to their big toes which he pulled when he wanted an 'actor' to speak.

Ingrid had no string, and she tried to act with depth and subtlety in a part she didn't understand, in a plot that hardly existed. In the evenings, while, if she was lucky, Ingrid had some lines to memorize, Ellen Neuwald worked as a dialogue coach with the other cast members. 'The actors could hardly speak Italian, only their dialect Italian,' Neuwald says. 'At night I had to hammer the Italian words into them. Rossellini said, "Don't you dare tell them what the lines mean. Just drill the lines into them. I'll supply the meaning."' Ingrid tried to pretend that all was well. Finally she exploded.

Roberto listened in silence, but he did not change. In Ingrid, as in most of Roberto's women, there was a vein of masochism, which he mined with great skill. He had Ingrid doubly under his sway. As her lover and as her director, he dominated her, forcing her to do his bidding, at times almost humiliating her.

There was a puritanical strain in Ingrid; she had never posed for revealing pictures. In one scene Roberto asked her to raise her skirt. She pulled it up a few inches.

'A little higher, *carissima mia*,' Roberto said. 'A little higher.'

Ingrid pulled her skirt up slightly above her knees.

'No,' Roberto said, as he walked over to her. 'Not like that – like this.'

Roberto yanked her skirt so that her white thighs appeared naked before the camera.

If Ingrid had reflected on all that she knew about Hollywood and publicity, about men and love and marriage, she would have realized that her idyllic moments could not last much longer. But she treated her life as if it were a series of films, of episodes and characters, that one lived and then forgot, or relegated to a few snapshots of memory.

On 9 and 12 April Petter cabled Ingrid asking her to telephone him. He had no idea that the island had no telephone. Pia was anticipating her mother's call, and she spent all Easter Sunday inside a bungalow in Palm Springs, waiting for it. On 13 April an item appeared in Cholly Knickerbocker's column in the New York *Journal American* about 'rumours' of a romance between Ingrid and Roberto. 'I had to be pretty careful,' remembers Igor Cassini, who wrote the column. 'I had to be pretty sure. I knew that the story was going to break. I wrote it very carefully. You had to be more careful because scandal in a person's personal life was taboo. I knew that she was in love with that man.' Within days of the New York column, the story was appearing almost everywhere. The most sensational evidence of Ingrid's new love was a picture in *Life* of her and Roberto holding hands.

After writing her letter to Petter in Amalfi, Ingrid apparently had been afraid to take the irreconcilable step of mailing it. Roberto, infuriated, had taken it from her. Before mailing the letter he displayed it to his friends like a Sicilian bridegroom hanging out bloody wedding sheets. And thus the news found its way into Italian and American newspapers.

All his life, Petter had tried to avoid publicity; now he found himself hounded. He had wanted Pia to be brought up like any other little girl, but now even her name was bandied about in the columns. He sent her off to stay with Lydia Vernon, the wife of their business manager. When summer came, she went to Minnesota to live with friends on a farm.

In his reply to Ingrid's letter he did not attempt to win her back to him ('a wife that does not want to stay with me is no good to me'). He focused on the morality of the situation. He clearly thought of Roberto as a Latin Svengali. He could rarely bring himself to write Roberto's name, referring to him as 'your Italian'. He pointed out that Roberto was married, living in a Catholic country. Ingrid would end up as merely his mistress. This man to whom Petter had taken breakfast in the mornings, to whom he had loaned money, was betraying not only his wife but Petter. He swore on his mother's memory that when 'the Italian' left Hollywood he had promised he would take care of Ingrid. This was not the kind of man, the kind of relationship, for a woman who was 'originally good and fair'. He told Ingrid it was 'about time you grew up'. He called up the litany of all that he had done for her, all his sacrifices. Job-like, he called out in anguish and disbelief that this woman, his wife, would drag their years together into the filth of publicity. If she wanted a divorce, he insisted that she not hide away in Italy but return to America and get it there. Ingrid cried when she read the letter.

'I think probably Ingrid felt like Charlie Chaplin, with one eye laughing, the other crying,' said Ellen Neuwald. 'We were both thirty-three years old, a good age for a woman to be. And I suppose when you aren't that happy in your life, it can be a wonderful thing to be in love. And I think the combination that they could work together, and the liberation that she felt, was all positive. And at the same time it was a very hard period. I said, Whatever you do now is going to be incredibly painful for you, and I think especially for Pia. She cared for Petter and couldn't understand.

'After the first week or so the whole thing broke. We spent half our time answering cables. It could only be done at certain times. Suddenly the whole world had converged on Stromboli. It was the most important thing.'

At first Roberto thought that he could keep the journalists away. When the first two American reporters descended on Messina, he generously offered them the use of the *San Lorenzo*, to bring them to Stromboli. Alas, the boat developed mysterious 'engine trouble'. Several days later, when the journalists rented their own vessel, they found themselves under house arrest, accused of the nefarious crime of seeking to interview a Sicilian bandit. 'Sometime afterward, I learned that it was Rossellini, with a fine Machiavellian touch, who had tipped off the police,' wrote Michael Stern, one of the reporters.

Even Roberto could not hold back the tide of reporters and

photographers. Soon the tiny harbour of Stromboli was full of boats. The whole western world seemed to have an insatiable appetite for news of the scandal. Editors printed column after column of speculative stories.

One day a larger ship anchored offshore. Several hundred excited, gesticulating Italians from Naples descended on the island. The tourists had signed up for a one-day excursion, and they bounded merrily up to Ingrid and Roberto's house. Roberto was outraged, but he had the good priest of Stromboli hold the crowd back while he and Ingrid ascended to the balcony of the priest's house. Here they stood while the visitors took snapshots and appraised Italy's newest tourist attraction.

If there was an element of amusement in the tourists' arrival, there was none in the message brought by another series of emissaries. Ingrid's affair had begun to affect a commodity that the world takes more seriously than love: money. In Los Angeles and New York lived moguls, moneymen, agents, columnists, and publicists who felt betrayed by this new Ingrid.

RKO had the most to lose or gain from the film. Ed Killy, the corporate production manager, was on Stromboli when the filming began, to push the film along. He had never seen such a haphazard approach to filmmaking as Roberto's; not only time but RKO's money was being squandered. Killy could do little to speed Roberto up, and he lasted scarcely a month before being replaced.

RKO was not spending hundreds of thousands of dollars to finance a romance. Killy's replacement was Harold Lewis, a six-foot-four-inch-tall movie 'troubleshooter'. Lewis was paid, not to care about art and nuance, but to get films finished quickly and cheaply.

Even if the film went way over budget, *Stromboli* had received so much free publicity that it was bound to be a great *succès de scandale*. It was doubtful, however, if audiences were going to line up to see Ingrid play a virgin saint in *Joan of Arc*. Walter Wanger cabled Ingrid to accuse her of 'endangering my future and that of my family . . . if you do not behave in a way which will disprove these ugly rumours . . . Do not fool yourself by thinking that what you're doing is of such courageous proportions or so artistic to excuse what ordinary people believe.'

The industry that had brought Ingrid wealth and celebrity was now in deep trouble. Television was not yet major competition, but the studio system of long-term contracts was beginning to end. The House Un-American Activities Committee had begun its investigations into communist and leftist influence in Hollywood. Actors, writers, directors, and others were being blacklisted. Larry Adler was among those who left the country; Robert Capa felt threatened as well.

Hollywood stood accused of cultural as well as political betrayal. Newspaper columns were full of scandalous tales, but nothing to equal the sensation of the liaison between Rossellini and the star who played Sister Benedict and Joan of Arc. Joseph Breen, director of the Production Code Administration, was ready to censor not only Ingrid's films but her very life.

Like almost everyone who had known Ingrid in America, Kay Brown had a vested interest in the 'old' Ingrid. Kay's career had been based in part on her only partially deserved reputation for having discovered Ingrid. She was now an agent at MCA, the giant entertainment company; her biggest coup had been signing Ingrid as a client. Kay's concern, however, was not simply the 10 per cent that Ingrid represented to MCA; she knew Ingrid; she knew Petter and Pia. She understood Ingrid's impulsiveness, her impressionability and where they might lead her.

Kay was soon flying over to Italy, as MCA's representative. She arrived on Stromboli at six one morning in a fishing boat, attired in a mink coat and high heels; she was carried ashore on a sailor's back. Roberto was waiting on the beach to greet her, but he was not happy to see her. Even if she had been on another mission Roberto would not have liked her. He had no use for agents; he considered them parasites sucking the blood of creators. Moreover, her personality grated on him, as it did on his sister Marcella, now in residence on Stromboli. Marcella expressed the family sentiment succinctly: 'Kay is so American. It's terrible.'

Ingrid might have been expected to express some pleasure at finally seeing an old, trusted friend, but that was not so. Kay warned Ingrid that she would lose everything: Petter, Pia, her career. Ingrid said that was true, but she seemed unable to act.

Kay remembered: 'At Stromboli Ingrid looked shell shocked, defeated.'

Ingrid's life of glorious romance had lasted no more than three weeks. Now she stood at the centre of intrigue, suspicion, and calculation. Wherever she looked, someone was pulling at her. Roberto and Petter were both capable of emotional cunning; Petter was six thousand miles away, but his letter had been a cry in the night. For a husband who felt that he had given his wife so much, his demands were deceptively small: he asked only that Ingrid stop behaving so scandalously, and return to the United States to discuss a divorce.

Roberto would have nothing of it. God's little joke on the devious is that they are forever doomed to imagine that others may be just as untrustworthy as they are. Roberto didn't trust Ingrid to go off to California alone to settle things with Petter. He certainly didn't trust Petter alone with Ingrid; he swore to Ingrid that if she left him and returned to Petter he would blow his brains out with a revolver.

A marriage does not die overnight, and beyond the legal questions, Ingrid and Petter had much to say to one another. Petter was not willing to sail blithely into the adulterous lair of Stromboli; he wanted Ingrid to fly to London or somewhere else in Europe. Roberto would not allow that. And so it was decided that the meeting would take place the first day in May in Messina, the Sicilian city from which less than a month ago Ingrid had embarked so excitedly. Petter agreed with only one stipulation – that Roberto not be present.

A century earlier, Messina had had a famous architectural seafront, lined with palaces whose balconies were protected by exquisite wrought iron. Only remnants of that remained now; it was a bustling provincial city, whose chief hotel, the Albergo Reale, had a splendid entrance, and a grand and elegant double staircase leading to a series of dark, nondescript little rooms. Ingrid arrived with the entourage of a prima donna. Of course there was Roberto, who would not think of allowing Ingrid to meet alone a husband whom he feared might manipulate her. Then there was Kay Brown; Art Cohn, a writer working on the English-language version of *Stromboli*, and his wife, Marta; and others of Roberto's entourage, including an attorney.

Unknown to Petter, Roberto was the grand maestro of the occasion, shuffling the others in and out of their rooms, displaying a talent for secretiveness worthy of a Medici courtier. Outside in the streets there was a great May Day parade, the streets awash in red flags, the communist slogans reverberating down ancient streets, a scene that to the Americans looked like a harbinger of revolution.

Petter wanted to meet his wife alone, to discuss matters in a way that he could not among these jabbering strangers, gesticulating and arguing in Italian and English. In the evening Kay was led through a labyrinth of back alleys and corridors until finally she stood before Ingrid's door. She took Ingrid to Petter's room, and left the two of them alone. Petter locked the door.

As soon as Roberto learned that Ingrid and Petter were together, he flew into a rage. Ingrid was *his* now, and she was locked up with a man whom Roberto considered an icy tyrant, who might once again lay his steely grasp on Ingrid's body and soul. He probably had another worry. On Stromboli he could see that Ingrid was no longer full of joy. He may have been trying to make Ingrid inexorably his by impregnating her, and may have feared that if Ingrid did have his child, Petter would claim it as his own.

Roberto called the police. The police decided that the dreadful crime taking place was that a man and his wife were together in a hotel room. If the police would not do their sovereign duty, then Roberto would have to act on his own. He stationed three of his worthy underlings at the entrances to the Albergo Reale so that Petter would not be able to spirit Ingrid out of the hotel. Then he jumped into his sports car and began racing around the hotel.

Later Ingrid called the evening a nightmare. She remembered that Petter had talked all night long.

Petter insisted that Ingrid tell Pia herself. She must return, meet Pia, and tell her of the wreckage of their marriage; only thus could she feel and see what she had done, whom she had hurt. And only in Ingrid's act of contrition could he win moral vindication, and go on with his life, alone with Pia. Until that time, Petter asked only that Ingrid act with a modicum of discretion, and not stir up further publicity.

Ingrid talked later of the five or ten hours 'of insults that were hurled at me by Dr Lindstrom in the room where he had locked himself with me'.

'I didn't insult her,' Petter says. 'There was no argument and no car running. I decided on a divorce. After our talk she promised to see Pia in London if I waited a couple of weeks. She said she would cooperate in a final, simple divorce. We didn't stay together all night either. She went out.'

Before everyone left Messina, Petter met with Ingrid and her advisers. 'Kay Brown sat there,' Petter remembers, 'and this writer [Art Cohn] and the writer's wife. I stood up and made a little speech. I said, I'm going to arrange for a divorce no matter what happens. I insisted that Ingrid talk to Pia before the divorce. I said I'd bring Pia to London or Ingrid could come to the United States. I said she should tell the child. That was the end for me.'

Petter made his position clear, but there were more meetings and discussions among the others. To Kay Brown, the whole event seemed like 'an Italian farce'. The others agreed that on Stromboli Ingrid and Roberto would live separately and make no public appearances together except those involving the film. In Rome or on location they would live apart and not socialize publicly together.

Ingrid's advisers decided that some kind of statement had to be issued. Ingrid said later that she wanted to announce the divorce, but that the others were far more concerned about completing the picture, and maintaining her reputation, than they were about either the truth or her happiness. The group argued over the language, producing a document that even diplomats might consider a classic in obstructiveness. 'I have met my husband here and have clarified our situation,' the statement said. 'I am returning to Stromboli . . . to continue work on my picture. On its conclusion I will leave Italy and meet my husband either in Sweden or the United States.'

Messina had shown no more interest in the proceedings than in a fisherman and his wife squabbling in the street. Roberto was sure that that would not last and that by now the reporters and photographers would be onto them, and that when the group left the hotel the streets would be full of autograph seekers and photographers. To avoid all this, he had planted a series of white paper flags to guide his party from their rooms, down lengthy corridors, and out a back door of the hotel. Petter insisted that he walk out the front door of the hotel. Roberto had no choice but to signal his co-conspirators that the cars should be brought around front, but when Ingrid marched out of the Albergo Reale the only person to greet her was a young boy with a Leica camera.

Roberto and Ingrid jumped into his sports car, and he accelerated madly. Kay and the Italian lawyer followed in a tiny Fiat. A mile down the road, Roberto's car broke down. Roberto and Ingrid piled into the Fiat and the solicitor drove on.

The two women said goodbye in Messina, and Ingrid and Roberto sailed back to Stromboli. A crowd was waiting there to greet them. 'She looked tired and haggard,' said a photographer who was there that day. 'Roberto practically danced off the boat, hugging everyone who was close to him. She stood there white-faced for a moment, and then she said sharply, "Roberto, come on!" He followed immediately. You could tell he had won and she was still in a great quandary.'

Petter was supposed to fly from Rome to Paris on 4 May but he did not show up until 6 May. Nevertheless the French reporters were waiting for him. Until now his mere refusal to give interviews had been enough to make the press leave him alone, but now his comings and goings were chronicled for the public. 'I am very tired and all I want is to be left alone,' he said.

Petter remained in Paris a few days and then flew to London to wait for *Stromboli* to finish shooting, in what he had been told would be two weeks. Then Ingrid was supposed to fly to him and they would have the talk he so desperately desired. He stayed in Kent with Sidney Bernstein, the producer of *Under Capricorn*, then took private accommodations.

Petter had been suffering from gastritis. His stomach pain

worsened. He lay in bed for some days. He had nothing but time on his hands to stir the dying coals of his marriage. Days passed, and then weeks, and still the filming continued, and Ingrid's promise to see him seemed more distant still.

He appeared to some to be living in a tomb of memory. He wrote Ingrid that he was writing on the anniversary of their engagement, a date that now meant nothing to her. He apologized that for some weeks he had not been able to help her. Clinging to the last vestiges of their life together, he said that whatever happened they must remain friends.

'Petter called me like someone drowning,' recalls Britt Engstrom, Ingrid's Swedish cousin. 'I left my baby and I went to London. He was quite sick. Petter said I was the only person, the last chance. He knew if I begged Ingrid, she would do as I said. He wanted to see her again, to talk to her. I think he thought she would come back to him.'

Britt had seen and known Petter as an attractive young man in Stockholm; she had seen him go off to America and succeed in his way, as Ingrid had succeeded in hers; she had known his pride, his generosity, his hope for the future. The man she saw in London was someone else. 'I've never seen anything like that,' Britt says. 'He was like a little boy.' According to Petter, he had had no contact with Britt for years. He says that she had refused to see him on three visits to Sweden and that he had not asked her to come to London. He says that he was in no way emotionally sick.

Britt made the journey down to Stromboli. She told Ingrid that Petter had lost much weight and seemed like a broken man. 'Ingrid didn't want to see Petter, but I convinced her,' Britt says. 'Roberto didn't want her to see him. He thought Petter would kidnap her. Roberto said he would commit suicide if she went.'

Ingrid acted as if she had fled from a tyrant who had controlled her every moment and built a great moat around her emotional life; she didn't see that she was the one who had largely manipulated each of her relationships. Now, however, she was with a man who played these games of love with weapons that she had not thought existed. She had always fled from emotional strife. She was no match for a man who threatened to kill himself. Roberto was more feminine in his guile than Ingrid, however masculine in his ego; he played upon her emotions as upon a fine instrument. She had dreamed of a life of artistic and emotional freedom. And here she was trapped, chained down. She had left Beverly Hills to soar free and here she was trapped. On some deep level she couldn't think about what had happened to her; she couldn't fight any more.

She decided to renege on her agreement to see Petter before going ahead with the divorce. She wrote him that she was sending a lawyer to London to seek a legal separation. She said that she was afraid of going mad.

Petter, that tenacious man, was tried beyond endurance. 'I was waiting in London for the film to finish,' says Petter. 'She was going to take the plane to London. Two months was a long time to wait. Every week I thought she'd come. She didn't come. She said, I'm sending an attorney. She never sent an attorney.'

Petter might have given up now, but he wrote Ingrid another letter from England on 23 June, saying that he wanted to see her once again, 'alone and at peace and then leave you as a friend', without 'hard words or reproaches', but with his memory of Ingrid 'as the little girl in the grey collar'.

Ingrid told Petter that he should go ahead and tell Pia that her parents were getting a divorce and that her mother would not be returning immediately from Italy. She sent an emissary to meet him in Paris.

'My mission was to ask him to please give Miss Bergman a divorce,' Marta Cohn testified later. 'He was very tense and angry at first, but he had consented to meet me, so I pressed the issue. I told him the divorce matter was important and urgent and that Miss Bergman was going to marry Mr Rossellini as soon as she could get a divorce.

'Dr Lindstrom laughed. He said it was entirely out of the question. He said he would not give her a divorce . . . Dr Lindstrom wanted Ingrid to tell Pia herself . . . I also told him that Ingrid loved him sincerely and loved Pia . . . He said, "By the time I get through with Ingrid, she will never be able to see Pia again and I will blacken her name."'

Petter denies threatening to destroy Ingrid's reputation, and says that he asked only that Pia's mother be the one to tell the child about the divorce. 'I said I'd meet Ingrid anywhere, except Russia, of course,' Petter testified two years later. 'She [Mrs Cohn] said he [Rossellini] was threatening to shoot himself if Ingrid ever saw me again. And she said she had to take the revolver away from him. I told her, "This sounds like nonsense. If he would wave a pistol and let a woman take it away from him, there is not much substance to the man."'

Finally, Petter returned to the States.

When they returned from Messina, Roberto honoured the verbal agreement by moving out of the house he had shared with Ingrid

and Marcella; for a while he and Ingrid pretended that their relationship was strictly professional. Roberto, however, was the prince of
disorder; both his art and his life demanded turmoil. It was time,
Roberto decided, for his entourage to leave the languid clime of
Stromboli for Rome.

Hollywood directors do not whimsically drop their cameras and
crews in the middle of a production; the day-to-day costs are simply
too great. Roberto didn't care about those who had accountants'
souls. Nor did he concern himself with the humdrum, tedious
demands of public relations. On the boat from Stromboli to Messina,
Michael Wilson, the RKO public relations man, tried to talk Roberto
into turning back. 'Ingrid took no part in the discussions, though
they became pretty violent,' Wilson wrote later. 'She just lay quite
still on an old grey canvas sail. I don't think she moved once on the
whole of the eight hours' journey. It was impossible even to guess
at her thoughts. Through a pair of dark sunglasses her eyes gave
nothing away.'

Ingrid was now penned up within her fate, impotent to act. The
emotional logic of her life had always been to avoid pain and conflict
for herself. Now whichever direction she took brought recriminations and threats. In Rome only two months before she had been
at the centre of a glorious romance and adventure; now Roberto
shuttled her off to a small apartment with his sister. Here she sat
away from reporters and observers, while for much of the week
Roberto moved freely around the city.

When they returned to Stromboli Ingrid had no one on the island
in whom she could confide. She felt that she needed someone who
cared and thought indisputably for and about her. When Joe Steele
wrote she responded quickly. The last time she had seen the publicist
was the day Petter told him he was fired. She didn't mention that
day. Nor did she come right out and try to hire Steele, but simply
asked what his plans were at the end of June.

Steele left for Italy, not even thinking about a contract or expense
money. He was a man of great decency, a professional failing that
was now catching up with him. He believed that doing what was
morally correct on Stromboli would be correct public relations as
well. He thought that it was morally right for Ingrid to see Petter
again, as she had promised. He told Ingrid, and once again Roberto
threatened to kill himself.

Roberto was like a child with a cherished doll that he would not
let out of his sight, night or day. He didn't even care if the film was
partially sacrificed on the altar of his jealousy. In *Stromboli*, Ingrid
was supposed to be married to her co-star, Mario Vitale. Roberto,

however, wouldn't let Ingrid kiss the fisherman; their scenes together had as much excitement as the mating of insects.

In Hollywood, Steele had spent days alone with Ingrid; on Stromboli, he saw her primarily over meals, where the air reeked of paranoia. Ingrid and the other English-speakers spoke *their* language and had *their* conversations. One day Steele found Ingrid alone for a few seconds. He told her that things couldn't go on the way they were, that she would have to see Petter another time. Ingrid did not disagree, but said that Roberto had threatened to kill himself if she went.

As soon as Roberto saw Ingrid talking to Steele, he came over and asked what they were discussing. Ingrid told him that both she and Steele agreed: she had to see Petter.

'Okay,' Roberto said, and turned away. He had weapons other than bombast and suicide threats. He walked to the dock and took the *San Lorenzo* to Messina. When he returned the subject was dead, at least for a few days.

Sometime later in May or early in June, an event occurred on Stromboli that made the discussions about meeting Petter totally moot. Ingrid revealed that she was pregnant. She must have known for several weeks that she was carrying Roberto's child, that whatever had passed as a scandal before was a minor irritation compared to the wrath and condemnation that would fall on her now.

She never talked about when she first suspected she was pregnant, or how she told Roberto; but he told his story of the day he learned to Father Antonio Lisandrini, as a friend, not in the secrecy of the confessional.

'When they began work on their first film they had an intimate relationship,' says Father Lisandrini. 'Ingrid came into the room and told Roberto, "Roberto, I feel I am pregnant."

'A moment of silence. "Ingrid, this is a very important moment. I know what will happen when the public learns. You are Jeanne D'Arc. You can imagine. Ingrid, do as you like."

'Ingrid stood up. "You don't mean this thing. This is my child. Even if the whole world should fall down upon me, I don't care. This is my child, and I want him."'

Roberto's version of Ingrid's reaction to her pregnancy has all the marks of a great director's mise-en-scène. Later in the year she wrote a letter to Steele about her pregnancy that almost certainly comes closer to the truth. 'In the beginning I did not have the courage to go through with it, to face worse scandal, more insults, more dirty talk, more stones thrown,' she wrote. 'But slowly, through Roberto,

I gained the strength and the courage . . . It would have been possible, when I had regained my health after Stromboli, to do something about it. But, after all, what a poor, miserable way out.'

Ingrid, then, had contemplated getting an abortion as soon as she left Stromboli, and Roberto apparently talked her out of it. Roberto was not a practising Catholic, but he would not have made the films he did if he had not had a profound sense of the sanctity of life. He had lost one of his two sons, and he wanted more children.

There were other reasons. What greater sign of his possession of Ingrid could there be than her bearing his child? He wouldn't have to worry about Petter any longer, or about Ingrid leaving him even for a day. He cared little for her career or her fame, except as a symbol of his high conquest. Her ambition, her celebrity, could drop from her now, like scales before her eyes. He thought little enough of actors and actresses. He wanted Ingrid to give up her career, to be his wife, the mother of his children.

Roberto almost certainly knew that Ingrid was pregnant when he filmed the last scenes of *Stromboli* wherein the husband is so jealous that he nails up the windows and doors of the house, imprisoning his wife. When she discovers that she is pregnant, she escapes up to the volcano. There, in Roberto's words, 'in the midst of hostile nature, broken by fatigue, bowed down by a primitive terror, in animal despair, she unconsciously calls upon God'.

On the morning that they began shooting up on the volcano, a team of eight mules stopped in front of Ingrid's door. There had never been any mules on the island before the filmmakers arrived. It was only 3.30 a.m. She was wearing pants and boots. She looked haggard and worn, as if she belonged on the island now. She got on one mule, and she and Roberto and the film crew set off for the volcano. The mules struggled upward, jumping across the smaller gullies, scratching for a foothold on the black gravelly surface.

Roberto had the cameras set up near the cone of the volcano. For her scene walking up to the volcano, Ingrid wore thin sandals, scant protection against the black lava sands, as hot as a tar roof on a summer afternoon. Ingrid was never one to complain about the rigours of filming; she began her walk under the unyielding sun. Roberto was usually in favour of quick takes, but he rehearsed this scene over and over. Repeatedly Ingrid struggled upward, through the fumes and the stench of sulphur. She was soaked with sweat. Michael Wilson noticed that Ingrid 'was trembling. From time to time her mouth twitched in painful spasms'.

When Ingrid and the others returned to the village at noon, they were on foot. To save time, they had slid two thousand feet down the mountain on their behinds. Their faces were black and sweat-streaked. They looked as if they had suffered a terrible defeat up on the volcano. Steele waited for them. He thought she looked like newsreels of rescued coalminers after a disaster.

Ingrid and the others returned to the volcano again and again. One day Lodovici Muratori, a production executive, was overcome by the fumes and died of a heart attack. The shooting continued.

In Hollywood, RKO did not know about the rigours of the shooting; the studio knew only that the film was supposed to be shot in six weeks and the crew had been on Stromboli over twice that long. Ingrid was paid $17,500 a week, and financially, at least, she was onto a good thing.

On Stromboli, Harold Lewis issued Roberto an ultimatum: either finish filming immediately or RKO would take drastic action, possibly even shutting the production down. Roberto, Steele, and a few others wrote a cable to be sent by Ingrid to her lawyer, Mendel Silverberg protesting against Lewis's action. By now Steele was as much a part of this Italian melodrama as anyone else, and the cable was excessive not only in length but in hyperbole. Ingrid, Roberto, and the others were involved not in anything so routine as a mere movie but in a dangerous, dramatic artistic quest.

'NO ONE REALIZES WHAT SACRIFICES WE MADE EXCEPT THOSE WHO HAVE HAD TO LIVE ON THIS ISLAND.' (Alas, it was equally true that no one except those on the island knew about the weeks Roberto had run off to Rome, or Sicily, or merely to go spearfishing.) 'ONE OF OUR MEN DIED OF SULPHUR FUMES ON VOLCANO. ROSSELLINI SUFFERED SEVERE INJURIES IN FALL AT CRATER AND IS NOW WORKING DESPITE DOCTOR'S ORDERS TO REST FOR TEN DAYS.' (Muratori had, indeed, died on the volcano, as much a victim of Roberto's penchant for 'realism' as of his own weakened heart. Roberto had not fallen on the crater and been injured and there was no doctor on the island.) 'THIS IS THE MOST IMPORTANT PICTURE I HAVE EVER MADE.' (For all that Ingrid had gone through, all the professional and personal sacrifices she had made, that had better be the truth.)

Silverberg cabled back that Roberto could have a few more days to complete *Stromboli*. Even during the last days of shooting, the question of Ingrid and Roberto's future had to be faced. Roberto's attorney, Signor Verdozzi, arrived from Rome. He said that Roberto's request for an annulment rested in the Italian court, and advised that both legally and strategically, Ingrid should make a last visit to Petter.

The attorney did not know that he was involved in an elaborate charade; his client had told him everything about the situation except for the one essential fact: Ingrid was now two and a half months pregnant. Ingrid told Steele nothing about the pregnancy either. Ingrid and Roberto had a double reason to be quiet. As long as there was a possibility that Ingrid might seek an abortion, they could afford to tell no one. Public knowledge that Ingrid had ended her pregnancy would wreak such havoc on their personal and professional lives that what had come already would seem as nothing. In many ways Steele was the saddest of all those deceived. He saw himself as the impresario of Ingrid's image. He had come to her as soon as she had called. And now he was engaged in a frantic, foolish, misguided, misinformed attempt to salvage Ingrid's reputation.

Steele stayed up much of the night of 27 July writing a letter to Ingrid and Roberto. He did not think of this as a story of love and lust, of jealousy and ambition, but as a grand historical drama starring a woman who despite her threats to give up her career would soon desire to rescue the career that God had intended for her, and a man who like Ingrid lived in a world full of duties and tasks that he could not deny. Steele argued that Ingrid should see Petter again because it was morally wrong to deny him. He feared that Petter might issue a statement full of bitterness and hate. The publicist was not merely proffering advice. He was writing a scenario. He dreamt of the very day that they would meet. Ingrid would cry and that would be the end.

Ingrid and Roberto said nothing to Steele about his interminable letter. Instead, under the supervision of Roberto's lawyer, Steele was instructed to prepare a dramatic statement to be released a few days later in Rome.

CHAPTER 14

THE EDGE OF A VOLCANO

On 2 August, Ingrid and Roberto left Stromboli for good. On their way back to Rome, they stopped in Amalfi for two days. Here, four months before, she had come flush with romance, excited by the prospect of making a great film. She remembered so well the day they had taken a walk together, a day of unfettered happiness. She remembered how the photographers had photographed them walking hand in hand in the ruins of an ancient house. The photograph was published in *Life*, and helped to set off the whole furore.

So much had changed. What Ingrid had lost was bad enough, but now Roberto and his advisers were asking her to make the ultimate sacrifice – to end her career in films. Steele was the one person left in Italy to whom she could turn. Although she was still deceiving the publicist about her pregnancy, she asked him to come to Amalfi from Rome to advise her. She told him that she would not consider retiring; he pointed out that if she announced her retirement, *Stromboli* was less likely to be boycotted. Moreover, she could always resume her career later.

The following day, 5 August, Steele issued a press release in Ingrid's name to reporters in Rome:

> It was not my desire to make any statement until the conclusion of the picture I am now making. But persistent malicious gossip that has even reached the point where I am made to appear as a prisoner has obliged me to break my silence and demonstrate my free will. I have instructed my lawyer to start divorce proceedings immediately. Also, with the conclusion of the picture it is my intention to retire into private life.

The day after Ingrid's announcement, the news of Ingrid's pregnancy was splashed across a page of *Corriere Della Sera*. Ingrid had decided to have the child, but she and Roberto needed time before announcing her pregnancy. If the story got out now it would create a new controversy, probably causing the banning of *Stromboli* in the United States, and complicating the divorce proceedings still further. Their concern over *Stromboli* was far from one of mere artistic vanity.

Roberto was in his usual financial straits; *Stromboli* was the way out. Between them Ingrid and Roberto would get 60 per cent of *Stromboli*'s net profits; they could expect to earn more than a million dollars, a figure few stars and directors achieved.

Ingrid saw Steele as her best weapon in killing the story. The publicist was outraged at such sordid lies and wanted Roberto to file a libel suit. He saw the arrival of Hedda Hopper in Rome on 9 August as fortuitous. Roberto and Ingrid were not so sanguine; the famous Hollywood columnist could not be trusted to shape the story to fit his demands.

Hopper was a great arbiter of power in the film business. There was a beautiful simplicity to her use of power. For her column she wanted news. If you were a star and you or your publicist gave her news, then you were generally written about positively; if you did not, then you were ignored. And this stately lady in flowered hats was a fierce moralist who raged against what she considered the moral decay of the new Hollywood. Scandals threatened her professionally, for she told her millions of readers that there was a different Hollywood, Hedda's Hollywood, a studio upon a hill where stars like Ingrid lived good American lives, raised their families, and went to church.

Ingrid understood the workings of publicity as well as Steele did. In agreeing to see Hopper she knew she was playing a dangerous game; the truth would not stay hidden forever, and when it came out, the columnist's reputation for accuracy would be as sullied as Ingrid's image. For now, though, Ingrid would have to give a great performance.

Steele escorted Hopper to the interview in Roberto's chauffeur-driven car. Hopper usually set the time and circumstances of her interviews. Now she was in the midst of an Italian melodrama, being escorted to a secret rendezvous. The car stopped in a residential area where Enrico Donati, Marcella's lover, waited to lead Hopper to his apartment. There Ingrid sat waiting for her.

She rushed forward to greet Hedda as if she were her oldest friend. As they chatted, Hopper cast a practised eye over Ingrid, looking for telltale signs of pregnancy. Ingrid had dressed with particular flair that day, all in red, from her dotted blouse, and her skirt, to red slippers. Alas for Hedda, if ever a woman's body had ever been constructed to hide a pregnancy, Ingrid's was. Not only was she tall and big-boned, but she was often ten or fifteen pounds overweight, as plump as a Swiss milkmaid. If she looked pregnant, then every robust, healthy-looking woman in the world looked pregnant.

Hopper questioned her for an hour or so. Ingrid frequently punctuated her conversation with the word 'hell', a profanity that had previously never passed her pristine lips in Hopper's presence. She spoke like a woman who had been cooped up with people to whom she could not easily talk. She shed her usual professional modesty and talked to Hopper with a pride that was bound to rankle the columnist's readers. 'I took a beating on the island of Stromboli,' she said. 'I am sure no other actress could have stood physically the things I did willingly because I felt we were getting a great picture . . . I would like to see another actress work on the edge of a volcano with sulphur fumes choking her almost to death and the wind trying to blow her into the crater. Well, I did it . . .

'People don't seem to understand. Never before in my life had I been tired, but on Stromboli I have been so tired I cried from exhaustion, and when I realized that I was a prisoner – I never received my mail, my messages – I cried from rage . . . I have been the victim of a lot of lies . . . Now I just want to go away and hide.'

'But, Ingrid,' Hopper countered, 'there is no place in the world you can hide. You can rest for three or four months and then the longing for work will return and you will be right back in harness.'

Finally Hopper asked the one question she had come to ask.

'Was Ingrid pregnant?' she asked.

'Oh, my goodness, Hedda, do I look it?' Ingrid laughed.

'That's all I wanted to know,' said the columnist, content that virtue and her column had been served. Ingrid, however, had the actor's vice of always wanting strong exit lines. She went on to give Hopper the impression that she was about to sue *Corriere Della Sera* for their disgusting, dishonest story.

Hopper left to write her column. 'A more bewildered girl I never talked with,' she wrote, hardly the impression that Ingrid had tried to convey. The columnist thumbed her nose at the rumours of pregnancy by relegating that part of the story to the last paragraph. 'Ingrid declares she will bring a suit against the Italian papers which said she was going to have a baby.

'I don't blame her; there is not a word of truth in it.'

Ingrid did not have the sort of bohemian spirit that considers a child born out of wedlock a child of love. One of the paradoxes of her life is why, once she decided to have Roberto's child, she didn't immediately pursue a divorce, if not in the United States, then in Sweden. The partial explanation must be that she and Roberto feared, if her pregnancy became known, *Stromboli* would be banned in the United States and they would lose a fortune.

According to Steele, Ingrid tried to file for a Swedish divorce, but the technical difficulties made it impossible; all the same, it is doubtful that Ingrid went as far as she might have in exploring a Swedish divorce. As with many actors and actresses, there was in Ingrid a core of passivity. She waited for roles to fill her up. When she could not flee from unpleasantness, she waited for something to happen to her.

Roberto was a man for the great occasion, and 29 August 1949 should have been a memorable day, the celebration of a triumphant romance as much as Ingrid's thirty-fourth birthday. Roberto did his best, giving Ingrid a diamond scorpion brooch. Ingrid, however, was full of bourgeois strictures about buying only what you can afford. She could not have been unaware that Roberto was as pursued by creditors as by reporters, and that in marrying him she was marrying his debts as well. Roberto did his best to make the evening lighthearted, but gaiety fell like a dull thud. He had been feuding with RKO, seeking to cut, edit, and score *Stromboli* in Rome, not Hollywood. For a while he had even refused to give up the last shots of *Stromboli* to the studio.

Ingrid was trapped in their rented apartment on Via Antonelli, unable to go out by herself. At times she thought the unthinkable: if only she could be back in Beverly Hills, if only she could have Petter and Pia back. On 3 September, she wrote to Petter's sister, Anna-Britta, in Stöde:

> You know, if I woke up tomorrow and found that I was in Beverly Hills, California, and I had dreamed this, all these months of soul agony, tears, scandal, etc., I would probably be satisfied and continue my life as before. I am always thinking of Petter and Pia, but at the same time I tell myself that it is impossible to go back. Petter is a settled, good man, I really know that, and I am *flyttfågel* [bird of passage]. I have always, ever since I was a little girl, looked for something new, new. I had longed for the big adventure, as much as I had, saw and lived through, it was never enough. I tried to get through the daily tristesse and find happiness and satisfaction. But I didn't know what gave me happiness and peace.
>
> How do I know, dear Anna-Britta, if this is the real happiness? I understand well that I have taken the big step. But who knows the end?

Ingrid may have had her doubts, but being pregnant, she had little choice but to pursue the divorce. There were many Rossellini family discussions, some of them overheard by Roberto's cousin, ten-year-old Franco Rossellini. 'From what I heard, a lot was based on the fact that she had made a lot of money in America,' Franco remembers. 'A lot of things were based on feelings but also on cash, cash and carry.'

Roberto's attorney, Signor Verdozzi, hired forty-year-old Monroe E. MacDonald, an American lawyer living in Rome. He went to New York and Los Angeles as Ingrid's emissary, to find legal representation on the West Coast, and to push the proceedings along.

MacDonald carried to the States Ingrid's account of her years with Petter. The confidential document had none of the heartfelt perception of her letter to Anna-Britta, but was a tough, one-sided legal brief. It would be a useful weapon as her case was prepared, as well as an explosive missile if it ever found its way into the newspapers.

As soon as MacDonald landed in New York, he met with the columnist Igor Cassini – 'Cholly Knickerbocker'. The next day, 21 September, the first-page banner headline in the New York *Journal American* read: 'NOW FOR THE FIRST TIME: INGRID'S REAL LOVE STORY.' Cassini's article was a devastating attack on Petter, based on both MacDonald's and Ingrid's statements, and full of errors:

> Since her marriage . . . Ingrid has been a faithful and devoted wife. The doctor dominated her completely. Eleven years her senior, he had complete ascendency over her, and never let her make a decision by herself. Every contract Ingrid has ever signed always had to be first okayed by Petter. He controlled all the money . . . Although they had a splendid home and lived luxuriously, Ingrid never owned a single piece of jewellery except her wedding ring since they were married. When she left for Europe last March he gave her $300, and that's all she has received from home since.

Sooner or later all the pettiness, the ancient grievances, the endless recriminations, surface in a divorce, like maggots from the earth. They do not, however, usually find their way to the front page of newspapers. Even if Cassini had written the full truth, it served no one – not Petter, not Ingrid, not Pia – to have the stories told in the press. It demeaned Petter, but it demeaned Ingrid too, and demeaned the years of their marriage together. Moreover, the story had appeared the day after Pia's eleventh birthday, a curious gift indeed. Ingrid expressed herself as appalled that MacDonald should have handed out her statement to a gossip columnist. It is unlikely, however, that the attorney would so brazenly have violated his mandate. He could have been disbarred or censured for violating his pledge of confidentiality.

In Rome, MacDonald had talked not only with Ingrid but with

Roberto and other members of the Rossellini family. Indeed, Cassini reported in his article that MacDonald had come to America with full power of attorney 'to negotiate with Dr Lindstrom for Ingrid's freedom and *to present before the American public the real facts behind the great love story*'. Cassini was of Italian descent. He had 'friends in Italy and was the best informed columnist on Europe'. He says that he does not remember how MacDonald contacted him, but it may well have been through Rossellini's intrusion, either directly or by means of intermediaries. That possibility is reinforced by the fact that Steele found Rossellini strangely unaffected by the turmoil over the disclosures. Roberto had taken a profound dislike to Petter. He would have enjoyed making a public spectacle of him.

In Los Angeles, MacDonald hired Gregson Bautzer as Ingrid's attorney. She had met the lawyer when he had come to Rome on Howard Hughes's behalf to try to buy her and Roberto's rights to the profits of *Stromboli* for a lump sum. In Hollywood, Bautzer was as well known for his techniques in the boudoir as in the courtroom. He was involved with Joan Crawford, Lana Turner, and other stars and starlets, but he was also a tough, ambitious attorney. He immediately let it be known that he was offering Petter a queen's ransom for Ingrid's freedom.

'INGRID OFFERING FORTUNE TO GAIN MARITAL LIBERTY', read the banner headline in the *Los Angeles Examiner* on 23 September. The story, by Louella Parsons, said that Ingrid was 'prepared to offer Dr Peter Lindstrom half of their community property – the remaining half to be put in trust for the use and benefit of their daughter, Pia. Miss Bergman will ask for part-time custody of their daughter. All she wants from Dr Lindstrom is an oil painting of her little girl.' Bautzer was an old hand at playing the press, and he had struck a dramatic opening note. Ingrid appeared a generous free spirit willing to give up everything for love, while Petter seemed a miserly soul hoarding the gold of Ingrid's earnings.

Until now, Petter had maintained a semblance of a relationship with Ingrid. He had even talked to her recently on the phone. But in the face of this new onslaught of publicity, he lost whatever residue of goodwill he had left. Nevertheless he still refused to talk to reporters. In Hollywood, silence is fool's gold, and George Seaton wanted to set up a press conference where his friend could tell his side of the story. Ake Sandler, another friend and a fellow Swede, wrote an article for *Collier's*, but Petter decided not to have it published. He did not want to create even more scandal which would affect Pia.

All the same, two days after the Cholly Knickerbocker column, Petter's rebuttal found its way into the newspapers. John Vernon, Ingrid's former business manager, issued a lengthy statement in which he was described as a 'spokesman for Dr Petter Lindstrom'. It was Vernon and his wife who had looked after Pia during Petter's lengthy sojourn in Europe, and Mrs Vernon who had taken her to Minnesota.

The most interesting part of Vernon's statement dealt with financial matters. Vernon said that Ingrid 'did not go to Europe with $300' but with an unnamed larger sum. He said, moreover, that Ingrid had 'always had full access to all of her funds' and had 'transferred to Italy quite a few thousand dollars and could have more for the asking'. He added that aside from their home, their joint assets were nominal.

Petter was so upset by the publicity that he wrote Ingrid to complain. Ingrid wrote back that people probably thought her a fool for giving up all her assets in America to Petter and Pia.

Ingrid was anything but a fool. California has a community property law that divides assets equally between husband and wife. Ingrid and Petter's joint assets in the United States was surprisingly small, given the over half-million dollars she had earned on her last three films, as well as Petter's income as a surgeon.

Tangible assets consisted of the house in Benedict Canyon, valued at around $70,000, savings accounts of approximately $30,000, savings bonds worth about $19,690 in cash, substantial life and health insurance policies, three automobiles (a 1947 Chrysler Windsor, a 1948 Pontiac convertible coupe, and a 1949 Chevrolet), a small farm in Sweden worth a few thousand dollars, plus jewellery, furs, household furnishings, and personal effects. These assets were worth over $200,000, her share being half of that, or something over $100,000.

Ingrid's own assets in Italy were already larger than the total assets in America. For her earnings on *Stromboli* Ingrid had received $205,000 from RKO, paid in a country where avoiding taxation is considered one of the creative arts. That did not include the large Italian subsidy or anticipated profits on the film. As Steele learned later from Bautzer, Howard Hughes had offered Ingrid and Roberto $600,000 for their share of the American and European rights; that was an enormous sum, but Ingrid and Roberto rejected it in anticipation of even larger earnings.

If Ingrid and Petter's total assets were equally divided, she would have had to pay a share of her *Stromboli* earnings to him. That may have been unfair, particularly when Petter was at the beginning of a lucrative medical career and Ingrid's future earnings were so uncertain; but that was the law. Petter says that he never sought nor would have accepted what he considered the tainted money of *Stromboli*. According to Ingrid, however, Petter asked for 50 per cent of the film money, first for himself, then for Pia, while offering her only a third of their assets in the United States, presumably with Petter and Pia dividing the rest.

Whatever the truth, the divorce negotiations were a nasty business, fought not over right and wrong, love and emotion, but over money and property.

Petter saw no reason to hurry the divorce along, especially when Ingrid's minions pilloried him in the press. He felt that he had acted well and asked for little – only a meeting between Ingrid and Pia – and had been abused and tricked. He sought what his supporters called 'justice' and his foes deemed 'revenge'. He had no truck with those who tried to be 'objective' or 'philosophical' and wished to discuss 'Ingrid's side of the story', as well. If you were Petter's friend you were *his* friend.

Petter had a hard time knowing just whom he could trust. During his years with Ingrid, the men who had clasped his hands most fervently had often been Ingrid's lovers. The hospitality and friendship in the film community had been for Ingrid, and not really friendship at all. He found it impossible to maintain relationships with people who thought they could be Ingrid's friends as well.

In Rome, Ingrid heard almost nothing but bad news. *Under Capricorn* had opened in Radio Music Hall, the great theatre where so many of her movies had been spectacularly successful. But not this one. The movie was Ingrid's third bomb in a row, the third that destroyed a new film company. The exhibitors in Chicago exploited Ingrid's current plight in their newspaper ads: 'STRANGE THINGS KEEP HAPPENING TO INGRID BERGMAN. YOU'LL SEE THE HEIGHTS – AND THE DEPTHS TO WHICH A WOMAN CAN GO.' Even that didn't help.

The bird of passage was now a caged bird, incarcerated in the apartment on Via Antonelli. Roberto bought her furs and jewels, the money conjured out of somewhere – a distributor, a banker, probably Ingrid's own accounts. When, rarely, Ingrid went out, her shoulders were graced with mink and her fingers sparkled with diamonds, but her eyes were red and raw. Her only friend in Rome was Joe Steele. He kept trying to talk to her, but Roberto put him off. Finally Steele decided that it was time he returned to America. Full of sorrow, he came to tell Ingrid that he was planning to go. Roberto sat beside her touching her, stroking her cheek, whispering to her. Steele thought that all the blue of Ingrid's eyes appeared washed out. Her cheeks sagged. Her voice was a whisper. She appeared sick and alone.

On the evening of Steele's departure, he came again, to say goodbye to her over dinner. She had thought they would be alone, but Roberto had invited other guests. After dinner, Ingrid motioned Steele to another room. Roberto entered, and told her to get back to her guests. Later, she went with Steele to the front door. Her lips quivered. She hugged Steele, and they cried, and then the publicist left, without saying goodbye.

Soon afterwards Ingrid took sick, suffering from a serious cough that she attributed to her sadness. She had no sense of place any longer, and in the midst of her new illness she was rooted up once again and moved into a new apartment at 49 Via Bruno Buozzi, in the suburb of Rome known as Parioli.

The apartment was large and decorated with antiques, but to Ingrid these were cold lodgings indeed, barren of the homely touches that had made the house on Benedict Canyon Drive so friendly and inviting. She had never been a woman who cried often but she kept sobbing. Roberto was used to a woman like Anna, who cried in great cathartic outbursts, thunderous torrents of tears that lasted no longer than a summer storm. Ingrid's tears came from somewhere deeper inside. Roberto, appearing helpless, sat in the poorly heated apartment playing solitaire.

Ingrid kept trying to call Pia. Finally, she reached her daughter in Los Angeles. Pia asked when the picture would be finished and Ingrid would come home. For a good while she had been planning to tell Pia that she had left her father for good but she never could quite say it. When she had first written Petter that he was 'alone in the ruins', she seemed to believe that it was Petter who would have to reassemble the broken shards of their life together. Petter, in trying to force Ingrid to be the one to tell Pia about the divorce, was meting out his own exquisite revenge, forcing her to act with what he considered responsibility.

Pia had read about her mother and Roberto, and probably had heard about them from schoolmates or others. 'The experience of having my mother go from being a saint to a tramp in a few days was traumatic,' Pia says. 'Both my father and I suffered a tremendous sense of loss. The publicity was monstrous. It happened to be my mother. She happened just a week before to be my mother. I think she went through the rest of her life carrying a profound guilt.' Pia wrote Ingrid that she refused to look at the map in her schoolroom because she couldn't stand seeing Italy. She asked her mother why she hadn't come to Hollywood for the dubbing of *Stromboli*. She said that none of her mother's pictures had ever gone on so long.

Ingrid suspected that the fine hand of Petter stood behind Pia's letter. Inevitably, though, Pia's initial sympathies were for a father who was there, not for a mother who had rarely been there and one day departed, leaving her with a father and memories. Like many children of separation and divorce, Pia had spun a cocoon around her emotions, seeking to protect herself from news she did not want to hear. Pia was only eleven years old, but she was mature for her age, even by Hollywood standards, a pubescent child–woman who sat at the head of the table, playing the mistress of the house. Finally, as the Christmas season drew near, Ingrid wrote to her, telling her of the divorce.

Sitting alone in the apartment, Ingrid wrote many letters. On 26 November she composed a long, gossipy letter to Steele that sounded like the old Ingrid. She wanted the publicist to know that no matter what he read, she loved Roberto and Roberto loved her. The next day, before she sealed the envelope, Ingrid added a second message: 'There is only one thing I have to warn you about . . . if again somebody prints that I am pregnant, don't sue them, because you will be sure to lose your case . . . that's all in a nutshell.'

Steele was stunned. He believed that he understood Ingrid better than anyone, and was sure she trusted him in ways that she could not trust Roberto. He needed to believe that, or what was he but a poorly paid retainer, a flunky whose integrity was for sale by the hour? He might have raged against an Ingrid who had dropped him once with no more ceremony than if she were returning an overdue library book, then picked him up again, and rewarded his loyalty by having him unknowingly spread the seeds of falsehood. But he still loved Ingrid. He considered her life a great epic in which he wanted to play a part. He wrote back the next day, offering not recriminations but advice. He told her, 'Don't trust anyone', and he warned her that if the newspapers learned the truth, it would finish *Stromboli* in the United States, a threat of which she and Roberto were only too aware.

Steele had hold of the greatest secret in American popular culture, and he wanted to tell someone, wanted to help. He decided to tell Howard Hughes, and to ask him to release *Stromboli* immediately, a move that would benefit not only Ingrid and Roberto but the coffers of RKO as well.

He went to see Hughes on 11 December. When Ingrid had first known Hughes he had been debonair, handsome, and adventurous enough to have won his share of stars and starlets even without his immense wealth, but already he was showing signs of the quirkiness that would lead to a pathetic, hermetic decline. Greeting Steele in sloppy, unpressed trousers and a white shirt, Hughes beckoned him to sit down on a sofa. Steele said that his comments had to remain confidential. Hughes nodded his assent.

'Ingrid is going to have a baby.'

'What did you say?'

'Ingrid is pregnant.'

Hughes did not appear excited about the dramatic news. He listened sympathetically as Steele outlined his plan to book *Stromboli* immediately in as many as five hundred theatres. Before the two men parted, Hughes gave Steele the impression that he would go along with the plan.

The next morning, the *Los Angeles Examiner* headlined:

INGRID BERGMAN BABY DUE
IN THREE MONTHS AT ROME

Louella Parsons's story played on front pages across America. She made some remarkable historical comparisons. 'Few women in history, or men either, have made the sacrifice the Swedish star has made for love,' she wrote. 'Mary Queen of Scots gave up her throne because of her love for the Earl of Bothwell. Lady Hamilton, beautiful English queen of society, gave up her position in the London social world to bear a child out of wedlock to Lord Nelson. King Edward VIII . . . renounced his throne to marry the woman he loved.'

Parsons did not have to beat her little drum any louder. The story had a stunning impact across America, driving such matters as President Truman's announcement of the development of the hydrogen bomb off the front page. It touched a raw nerve end, creating a great, dramatic controversy.

The United States of the late 1940s was the strongest power in the world but had the sexual maturity of an adolescent. Teenagers were told that masturbation leads to insanity, a statement that, if true, would have created a generation of lunatics. It was a land so consumed by sexual questions that if a person asked, 'What are your morals?' he meant primarily, 'What are your sexual attitudes?' Sexuality was kept well hidden. Roosevelt had had mistresses; for years there was a whorehouse a few blocks from the Capitol, which some lawmakers frequented with the same regularity that they went to church or gave speeches about the sanctity of marriage and the family. All this was *understood* and nobody minded so long as it was not openly flaunted.

Hollywood was much the same. As Gregory Peck points out, the film community was not surprised by Ingrid's affair with Rossellini because Hollywood knew about Ingrid's affairs. Hedda Hopper, Louella Parsons, and the other movie reporters were as certain to know about Ingrid's relationships as White House reporters were to know about Roosevelt's affairs. In Hollywood, there was plenty of wenching and whoring, adultery and abortions, though perhaps not any more than in Detroit or New Orleans. Almost anything was permissible as long as it didn't get in the papers, and there were battalions of highly paid publicists to see that such news didn't make the press.

Ingrid had left her daughter and husband to run off to Italy with a married man. It was an act that most people would find morally objectionable, but that did not account for the enormity of the scandal. It was Ingrid Bergman who had done this, not Rita Hayworth, or Lana Turner. Ingrid had refused to be what America thought she was and, indeed, she had wanted America to think her to be. She had flaunted her relationship with Roberto, had thumbed her nose at the mores of the country that had made her a great star, and a symbol of the moral system that she was so thoroughly violating. Worse still, she was committing her sin at the very moment that America's system of sexual mores was beginning to crack at its hypocritical foundations.

The psyche of fundamentalist America feared Europe as the home of communism and free love. Communism was seen as a seductive mechanism that could enslave the minds of good Americans. A man like Roberto was viewed as an enslaver of the minds and wills of women, a dark Don Juan against whom God-fearing American men could hardly compete, a man who, in the words of Senator C. Johnson, was 'vile and unspeakable'.

As soon as the news reached Rome, the reporters began their watch in front of Ingrid's home. Inside, the phones rang; members of the family ran in and out; Roberto added his own level of melodrama to the events. Ingrid was the one island of calm. She could even be dispassionate enough to find Roberto funny, as he ran around, hair on end, his clothes dishevelled, screaming, 'I beg you, take something for your nerves. You are driving me crazy. I can't stand to see you hysterical. Do you hear what I'm telling you?' Finally he fell asleep, only to wake up and chase around the apartment in his bathrobe. Then he dropped back in bed, to be served his food on a tray as if he, not Ingrid, were seven months pregnant.

He finally got up and dressed and decided that he and Ingrid should give their only press interview to Camille M. Cianfarra, of the *New York Times*. Roberto dominated the discussion. The scholarly reporter usually covered the Vatican – an appropriate background for deciphering the meaning of Roberto's comments.

'Whether she is or is not [pregnant] is nobody's affair,' Roberto said. 'I think that report deserves neither denial nor confirmation because it is an attempt to pry into the private life of a woman who, to assert her right to her own life, has given up her career – which is what an artist regards as the most important thing in life. Isn't that enough?' Of the meeting in Messina, Roberto told the reporter: 'Our situation was fully discussed. And I want to make clear at that time the relationship between Ingrid and myself was absolutely correct.' If Roberto were telling the truth, Ingrid had been impregnated by immaculate conception – the greatest story a Vatican reporter could want!

Ingrid was denied the tranquillity and rest needed by any woman in the last weeks of pregnancy. She hardly dared to leave the apartment. The best she could do was to sit on the terrace, in wry moments spitting over the railing, aiming at the photographers keeping their watch on the street. Over the holidays a story appeared that Ingrid had had a nervous breakdown. Early in January, Roberto told the Rome *Daily American* that he had 'planted' the story so that 'we could be left in peace over the Christmas and New Year holidays'.

On 22 January 1950, a sunny day, Ingrid decided to leave the apartment for the first time in a month, and go for a drive with Roberto. She went downstairs in a long fur coat and ankle-high boots, looking decidedly pregnant. As she stood waiting for Roberto to pick her up, a photographer jumped out of nowhere. Ingrid hurried for the protection of a newspaper kiosk. By now she should have known some choice Italian expletives, but she relied on her English: 'Stop it, you devil.' The photographer ran around the other side of the kiosk and got another full shot as Ingrid burst into tears.

If Ingrid and Roberto had merely let the photographers get their pictures, they would have been left alone, and the drama would have been partially dissipated. But they were all part of this gigantic melodrama and Ingrid, who had been photographed thousands of times, considered the photo a violation.

Ingrid and Roberto felt under siege. RKO had taken away the final editing of the American version of *Stromboli*. Not a man to sit moping about the past, however, Roberto was already off in the mountains outside Rome, shooting *Francis, Jester of God*. For Roberto that was decidedly healthier than worrying over *Stromboli*, but it meant that Ingrid was alone with servants much of the time.

The good news was that Roberto was awarded an Austrian annulment of his first marriage. On 23 January he registered the document. Only Ingrid's delayed divorce now prevented a marriage that would allow the baby to be born in wedlock.

Ingrid's attorneys decided that the only way to obtain an immediate divorce was to get one in Mexico. She was waiting for the final decree from Mexico when at noon on 2 February 1950 the telephone rang. It was Lydia Vernon, and Ingrid at first feared that Pia might be hurt or sick. She was disturbed that Mrs Vernon had her number, because that meant that Petter had it too.

Having read that Ingrid was going to Mexico to get a divorce, Mrs Vernon was willing to escort Pia there to see her mother. She told Ingrid that Pia cried because of the bad things she read about her father in the newspaper.

Ingrid promised to see Pia soon. As she set down the phone, she felt the first contractions. She knew that she had a good while to wait before she would have to go to the hospital. She would have time, she thought, to write a letter to Pia.

It was so much like Ingrid to hide away unpleasantness until forced to face it. She told Pia that she was 'expecting another baby' and that she 'couldn't come home and have the baby' but would stay in Italy, where Pia would come and Ingrid would visit her. This difficult news would not be received by Pia until well after the baby was born.

In the early letters from Italy, the words seemed to have flowed from Ingrid's heart without forethought or calculation. There is, nonetheless, a mannered quality to many of her supposedly candid letters, more so as time went on. This letter to Pia, which Ingrid thought might be the last, spends more time trying to elicit Pia's sympathy than commenting on the child's difficulties. She tells Pia of her problems with the press, how newspapers printed things that were only negative, and that she was not able to travel freely ('I have not left the apartment for five weeks'). She gives her daughter a little of her own philosophy – to forget the past, to hide it away, and to go on.

By the time Ingrid finished the two-and-a-half-page typewritten letter, the birth contractions were coming less than every three minutes. It was already after three o'clock. She called Dr Pier Luigi Guidotti, who arrived at the apartment on Via Bruno Buozzi at four o'clock to take Ingrid to the exclusive Villa Margherita Clinic on Via di Villa Massimo. As she left the doctor's small car, there were no photographers or reporters outside. That evening, at seven o'clock, Ingrid gave birth to seven-pound-fourteen-ounce Robertino.

Ingrid rarely talked about her labour or the joy of her first son. She spoke of the publicity, the circus of her life. 'The guards at the gates directed the crowds like a Hollywood premiere,' she wrote Steele later.

Robertino's 'premiere' had in fact ruined the premiere of Anna Magnani's *Volcano*. When Magnani learned that Ingrid had chosen *her* moment to give birth, the actress reportedly said that this was Roberto's ultimate sabotage. It was indeed a bad night for Magnani. During the middle of the showing at the Fiamma Cinema, the projector bulb broke. That was perhaps God's grace, for the film was terrible. The reporters and photographers, learning that Ingrid had given birth, took off to witness a different melodrama.

Over thirty American reporters and photographers were in Rome, and scores of Italian and European correspondents. For the next few days it seemed that all of them congregated in front of the newly locked iron gates of the clinic. The photographers salivated at the thought of what an exclusive picture of the new baby might bring: five million lire was offered – roughly eight thousand dollars. The reporters knew that an interview with the new mother would bring accolades and bonuses galore. As Roberto rushed into the hospital, he viewed the press with disdain. It was a cold night and the journalists built a fire, snapping off branches from stately old oak trees. In her suite Ingrid could hear the raucous clamour as the media representatives pounded on the gates, tried to climb over the wall.

By the following afternoon the reporters and photographers were a more mannerly bunch, their good behaviour fostered no doubt by the timely arrival of the Celere, the Roman riot police. Civility is often a journalist's last subterfuge, and several of the reporters convinced the director of the clinic to let them inside to inspect the new reception room. Once within, the photographers, who had hidden their cameras under their coats, took off down the corridors in search of their five-million-lire prize. The reporters ran after them, pursued by nuns into the kitchens and the sickrooms. A photographer for *Life* scurried up a back stairway and made it all the way to the locked door of Ingrid's suite before he was accosted. Then, with the help of the *carabinieri*, the clinic was cleansed of the scourge.

The inventiveness of the press was endless. Photographers shimmied up rainpipes, danced along the tops of the clinic walls, and tried to bribe a nun to open Ingrid's door. A photographer fell off the wall and broke his arm. One reporter had the good luck to have a pregnant wife, whom he enlisted in the cause. She took a room in the clinic. When the good nuns who opened the woman's valise found that she intended to garb her new child in a collection of cameras, she was asked to leave.

Alas, Ingrid gave no interviews and permitted no photographs. Neither did Roberto, though he kept his impeccable reputation with the press by punching an American photographer in the stomach. All they had had to do was invite the journalists in for a few minutes, and they would have been free. But this was a contest that took two teams of players, and if all the journalists succeeded then none of them did, and the story became little better than a press release. Roberto had a small moment of revenge when after twelve days Ingrid and Robertino left the clinic; he planned the getaway with the detail and surprise of a bank heist.

'Let's go,' he said dramatically at 4 a.m. Ingrid grabbed Robertino and hurried after Roberto. Patients weren't allowed to go running off in the middle of the night, and nuns pursued the fleeing couple. Ingrid jumped with the baby into Roberto's car. He accelerated away, followed by a friend in a second car and by the now wide-awake photographers and reporters.

The press cars might have caught up and photographed Ingrid and the baby as they entered the apartment, but Roberto had planned a parting gesture. Suddenly, his friend spun his car around in the road, blocking off the press cars from further pursuit.

CHAPTER 15

A CHILD OF LOVE

1950

Ingrid was happy with her new baby, but her emotions were nothing compared to Roberto's. He was a proud Italian father, ready to show off his son to his friends if not to the world. They wanted Renato Roberto Giusto Rossellini, to be considered legitimate. Unfortunately, by 9 February 1950, when Ingrid's Mexican divorce was granted, it was too late and according to Italian law Ingrid could not be called the child's legal mother. The child was registered 'mother unknown.'

Unsurprisingly, Robertino's birth augmented the criticism. Monsignor Dino Staffa of the Vatican's Supreme Tribunal accused Ingrid and Roberto of 'living publicly in adultery' if they went ahead with a civil marriage. In the United States, *The Pilot*, the Boston Catholic paper, was hardly more welcoming to the infant, saying that 'while thousands of pious people milled about the Eternal City with the glow of holy pilgrimage in their eyes, a simpering Swedish actress and an Italian director become the parents of a little boy. And the whole world is informed of the progress of illicit love.' *Variety* announced the results of a survey of movie owners asked whether they would show *Stromboli*. The theatre proprietors took a position of rare moral subtlety: they would ban *Stromboli* if after its first days' showing it did not make money. In Indianapolis, the owner of a group of theatres called for a boycott of Ingrid's movies. In Annapolis, a legislator tried unsuccessfully to push through the Maryland state assembly a resolution condemning *Stromboli*.

On 14 March, Senator Edwin C. Johnson of Colorado took to the US Senate floor to denounce Ingrid and Roberto. Speaking in the Senate, the Honourable Mr Johnson did not have to worry about suits accusing him of slander or defamation of character. He savaged Ingrid and Roberto without subtlety or grace: 'Mr President, even in this modern age of surprise it is upsetting to have our most popular but pregnant Hollywood movie queen, her condition the result of an illicit affair, play the part of a cheap chiselling female to add spice to a silly story which lacks appeal on its own . . . The disgusting publicity campaign . . . the nauseating commercial opportunism . . . the vile and unspeakable Rossellini who sets an all-time low in

shameless exploitation and disregard for good public morals . . .'
The senator went on to call Ingrid 'one of the most powerful women
on earth today – I regret to say, a powerful influence for evil'.

To counteract this 'evil', Johnson was going to introduce a bill that
'demands the licensing of actresses, producers and films by a division
of the Department of Commerce'. The law would have been nothing
but veiled censorship. It was a mark of the moral climate of America
in 1950 that a senator could make such a speech and not be condemned
for it. Johnson was adept at the craft of publicity and he reaped his
own rich bounty of attention. Indeed, thirty years later, his attack
on Ingrid Bergman was the best-remembered action of his political
career.

The marketplace condemned Ingrid and Roberto and their film
Stromboli with a finality beyond even Senator Johnson's words. The
American version of the film opened 15 February 1950, in 300 theatres
across the country, including 102 in the New York City area. 'This
is it!' the handbills and advertisements screamed. One might have
expected to see nuns and priests and ministers picketing the theatres
while outraged mothers pulled their impressionable daughters away
from the lines in front of the box offices. However, on Broadway
that first morning there were only ten people in line, fewer moviegoers than reporters and photographers. The film was a commercial
disaster both in America and Europe. Ingrid and Roberto would
make no more money from *Stromboli*.

Although the film received several awards in Europe, it was
generally considered, as Bosley Crowther wrote in the *New York
Times*, 'incredibly feeble, inarticulate, uninspiring and painfully
banal'. Roberto raged against the desecration of his work, condemning the brutal editing and the American narration, which suggested
a happy reconciliation at the end. He renounced his American earnings
on the film, a gesture that would have been more noble if it had come
before the film's disastrous opening. In the communist weekly *Vie
Nuove*, he attacked the 'low level of culture and intelligence of
Hollywood. The setting had been redone and I have discovered at
my expense what the brutal and uncivilized methods of Hollywood
are.'

In Rome, Ingrid was leading the most private, the most restricted of
lives, yet she was as deeply fascinated by her publicity as she had
ever been. When Janet Flanner, a writer for *The New Yorker*, visited
her she reported that 'in the vast, rather empty salon of her apartment,
her clippings . . . form a sort of cheap, extra upholstery laid out over
the divans and chairs'.

In the past months Ingrid had received thousands of letters from all over the world: congratulation cards from America, whose uplifting sentimental messages hardly fit the case of a married woman giving birth to another man's child. Sacred medals which their senders hoped might drive away the criticism. Congratulatory notes from Italian-Americans, as if Roberto had impregnated Ingrid in the name of all Italians. Letters condemning Italians, one of which included a picture of Roberto over which two pithy words had been scrawled: 'Wop wolf.' Letters and cables in support from Cary Grant, Ernest Hemingway, Helen Hayes, Georges Simenon, John Steinbeck, and other celebrities. Letters that mentioned Hawthorne's *The Scarlet Letter* and condemned not Ingrid but puritanism. Letters savagely rebuking her for leaving her husband and child. A letter in French from '*Un homme nordique*' in Alsace, who threatened to kill her.

Always before, Ingrid had been appalled by negative publicity. Now, as much as she disliked the criticism, she appreciated the sheer volume of attention. Slowly, though, the world began to look elsewhere for its drama. By the end of March Ingrid could look out of the windows in the apartment on Via Bruno Buozzi and see no reporters.

In Stöde fourteen years before, Ingrid had wed Petter in a ceremony of such beauty and elegance that it seemed their marriage would last forever. Now she would marry Roberto in a ceremony that was elegant only in its manipulation of the law. Steele had implored Ingrid to come to Mexico to be wed and to see Pia there, but she could not face that. Instead, she and Roberto decided to marry by proxy. Roberto's friend and attorney, Marcello Girosi, flew to Mexico City to represent Ingrid, while a Mexican attorney represented Roberto.

Ingrid considered her marriage to Roberto not a mere formality but a sanctification of their relationship in the eyes of God and society. Many is the unhappy bride who looks back on her wedding day and reads omens there that she once pretended did not exist. Ingrid wanted her wedding to be more than a rude legal formality. On 24 May 1950, at 10.30 a.m., while the vows were being said by attorneys in Mexico City, Ingrid planned to exchange her own sacred vows with Roberto in Rome. It would be early evening in Rome, and Ingrid picked out a lovely little church for the ceremony. She dressed in a blue and white silk dress with white cuffs and collars. Then she waited for her husband-to-be to return from his day of filming. And she waited. And she became almost hysterical.

When Roberto finally arrived home, the church had already shut its doors for the night. Ingrid could not be angry at Roberto, on this of all days. Roberto found another church, the Chiesa della Novicella, near the Colosseum. There they knelt and held hands and repeated their vows. Afterwards a dozen of their friends saluted them in Roberto's champagne, and Ingrid displayed his wedding gift: a gold charm bracelet with a tiny police whistle.

Roberto had promised Ingrid that they would go to Paris for their honeymoon and stay at the Raphaël, his favourite hotel. Ingrid had bought a new wardrobe for the trip. Just before they left, Roberto told her that Anna Magnani was planning to be at the Raphaël at the same time, and had asked that the newlyweds stay elsewhere. Another bride would have suggested that her husband's ex-lover take herself elsewhere, but Ingrid said nothing. Roberto was so upset that the Paris trip was called off.

They went to Capri instead where Roberto went spearfishing, swam too deep, became temporarily deaf and lost his equilibrium, so they were forced to return to Rome.

Ingrid tried to settle into the life of a Roman matron. She was infinitely more comfortable as the mistress of a hotel room or a dressing room, where she could ring for food and drink, laundry and sundry services. 'Most of the time I stare out the window, and smoke and smoke and smoke,' she wrote Steele. She might complain, but she did not lead the housebound life of most new mothers. For the summer, Robertino had been sent up to Fiuggi with his nurse and grandmother. After their return from Capri, Ingrid and Roberto drove to the mountain resort to see their son. They did not stay very long, however, and they were soon off to Florence, Pisa, and Portofino.

Roberto was everything to Ingrid now, and much of her life was spent waiting on him, or waiting for him. In Rome she planned a dinner party, with Artur Rubinstein and his wife as the honoured guests; the Rubinsteins had been Ingrid's next-door neighbours in Beverly Hills. They arrived to find that their host was still working. Ingrid called the studio, but Roberto didn't care that one of the world's greatest pianists was sitting in his living room nursing his third drink; he was busy cutting his film. As the party sat down to dinner, Ingrid called again; Roberto was still busy. After dinner, Ingrid found Roberto had come home and was in bed with a 'head-ache'. Ingrid dutifully went back to the living room where she proceeded to make her limp excuses.

'Maestro!'

The double doors to the living room burst open. There stood Roberto, his arms outstretched. The two men embraced and talked until well into the morning hours.

Roberto had infinite charm, which he drew on at will, buying his way out of almost any problem or unpleasantness by the sheer force of his personality. He was, however, a magician with only so many tricks, and there was a distressing similarity to his performances. On another occasion David Lean and his wife-to-be, Ann Todd, were dinner guests. Lean was already a prominent figure in films and Roberto might have been expected to want to meet him, or at least to show up for dinner, but that evening he was in bed asleep. Ingrid did her best to be a considerate hostess over dinner, and afterwards keep the conversation moving along.

'David!'

Suddenly, there in the doorway stood Roberto, in his pyjamas. The two men embraced . . .

He was hospitable enough with friends, visiting his house on *his* terms. He was most comfortable with Italians, and at their parties and gatherings Ingrid was usually the only foreigner in attendance. 'I saw her the first time in their house,' remembers Federico Fellini, the director, who was working for Roberto then. 'She was the way she always was in films, a queen, serene and pacific and saintly.'

Ingrid was indeed like a fairy queen who did not quite understand the world around her. 'She had this necessity of always trying to understand,' says Fellini. 'She couldn't understand why we were laughing sometimes. When we were at the table once, someone compared a woman to a monkey and said that she was cute. Ingrid couldn't understand why we would call her cute. I remember Ingrid's innocence. She was very naive. For those of us who knew Roberto well, it was amazing to see them together, always surprising.'

She had a good ear and picked up Italian rapidly, albeit with grammatical errors which the Rossellini family joyfully mimicked. Even when she understood the conversations, though, there was a dullness about her, an inability to grasp the nuances and subtleties of the Italian mind. 'Ingrid's reaction was always late,' recalls Giulietta Masina, Fellini's wife, who would gain international fame as the waif in her husband's film *La Strada*. 'She would always discover things with a delay. It wasn't only language.'

In later years, when Roberto wanted to put Ingrid down he would say that she was 'a Swede'. Roberto had no particular quarrel with Scandinavians, but Ingrid was not one of those who are born with the music of Italy sounding in their ears. That did not mean that Ingrid did not love Italy, for she surely did; but she was distanced from the Italians.

Ingrid's most trusted friend and confidante during those early years in Italy was Fiorella Mariani, the teenage daughter of Roberto's sister, Marcella. She was doubly sensitive, possessing an artistic temperament and being a child of a broken marriage. Ingrid first became close to Fiorella in August 1950. She taught Fiorella English and talked to her for hours about Pia. Fiorella was a young woman of fierce loyalty. One day when photographers tried to take pictures of Ingrid, Fiorella threw stones at them.

'We were like sisters,' Fiorella says. 'We called each other sister. I was sixteen but I was like twenty-one because sorrow brings you maturity. She was childish in a way, and the difference between us was completely gone. I had suffered because of my mother and father, and maybe I was a help to Ingrid to understand Pia's feelings. I was always severe about that. She never understood why Pia was so angry. I said, You went away. There is no excuse for a child. She was always very upset when I was telling her that. I said what my experience was. I had suffered and I said there was no reason why Pia shouldn't have suffered.

'I became Ingrid's best friend. With my uncle it was not so easy because he had this intellectual life that was a hole between them. She was not a cultivated woman. If he was reading about something that had nothing to do with Ingrid, they could not talk. She was not the kind of woman who could help him intellectually. She realized that but she didn't care.

'You could never see what she really felt. She could be bursting with laughter and holding a tragedy within. She was afraid of suffering. She was afraid of evil. She couldn't stand discussion of it. She was afraid of violence, of things that maybe she couldn't say.'

Already in the late spring of 1950, when Robertino was only three months old, Ingrid had begun to think seriously about ending her 'retirement'. David Selznick visited her in Rome and found her, as he wrote Jenia Reissar, 'with a very definite nostalgia for her contractual past with us . . . completely finished with Rossellini type of pictures'. Selznick had heard rumours that Ingrid was already talking with Sam Goldwyn, who was very interested in signing her to a new contract.

Ingrid expressed a certain bitterness at the way her professional life had been handled. 'Kay Brown has apparently lost all of her influence with Ingrid as a consequence of some advice she gave to Ingrid which Ingrid thought very bad, at a critical moment,' Selznick reported. 'She is thoroughly aware that Joe Steele and all the others, with whom she surrounded herself, helped to do her in, not of course deliberately but through bad judgment.'

Ingrid might rail against Steele to Selznick, but she continued to write the publicist long, chatty letters. She admitted to Steele that she had in fact had discussions about new pictures with 'several people'. She said that she hardly ever saw Roberto, and that it seemed foolish that she should sit at home while he carried 'the enormous load'.

Even epic romances do not maintain themselves at a fever pitch; already Ingrid was complaining that she hardly ever saw her husband. She was incapable of perceiving the irony of her plight. In the States, she had been the one to fly off for filming, bond tours, assignations, and meetings. Roberto had not remained the adoring loyal husband for very long. One night he was walking down the street when he spied an old friend, a prominent director who had once worked with Rossellini. 'Let's go to a bordello,' Roberto said. The man was aghast. Roman gentlemen didn't go to brothels the way many of them had before the war. 'You are living with one of the most beautiful women in the world,' the director reminded him. 'Ah, yes,' Roberto said, 'but she doesn't do the things that a whore does.'

Roberto, like many men, saw oral sex as a mark of submission. Ingrid had refused him, but Roberto subjected her to an even greater humiliation, though one that she was almost certainly unaware of. He told his friends about her sexual inadequacies. 'If you someday want to get married, don't get married to an actress,' he told one of them, 'because they're actresses also in bed.' Years later he confided to his assistant Francesca Rodolfi that Ingrid was 'a woman without passion'.

Though Roberto may have found his new love passionless, Ingrid felt differently. 'While she was not a good woman for him, he was a good man for her,' said Father Lisandrini. 'One time she told me confidentially, "Father Lisandrini, I am happy. This man of Rome has gotten me upside down, turned my world upside down. I know what's love in Rome. This man has been unbelievably beautiful."'

Ingrid might have been happy for a while had she lived a pampered existence, savouring the pleasures of Roman life and her hours alone with Roberto; but she couldn't even do that, for she was confronted with severe money problems. Roberto owed the banks, the shop-keepers, his friends, and other creditors. In his films and in conversation, Roberto criticized the spiritual emptiness of the Italian bourgeoisie, their acquisitiveness and showing off; but he understood that world so well because he was part of it. He was capable of grand gestures when he had money, but he was a prisoner of his life-style, sacrificing if not his artistic freedom, then at least his tranquillity on that altar. Even since Ingrid had come to Italy, he had spent a small fortune. It wasn't just the furs and jewellery for Ingrid, or the costs of lawyers and transatlantic telephone calls; nor the parties, the dinners, the vacations: these were just the beginning. He had purchased a summer home on the Mediterranean at Santa Marinella, fifty-nine kilometres from Rome; the seven-acre estate consisted of an eight-room house, a caretaker's cottage, and another large, dilapidated two-storey house.

And he could not be the *grande signore* without a retinue of household retainers; in the garage there was a retinue of automobiles – his new red racing Ferrari, an Alfa-Romeo sedan, a Fiat coupé, a Fiat station wagon, and later a Rolls-Royce.

Roberto parted company with the bourgeoisie when it came to paying for his acquisitions. He had learned one of the great secrets of modern finance: if you owe enough money, if your debts are positively horrendous, there is very little your creditors can do except give you more money or wait helplessly. It is a system that requires charm and audacity, both of which Roberto had in ample supply. He could go in to talk to a banker who was determined to call in a loan, and walk out with twice as much money for a new project. He was forever selling this piece of movie or dreaming up some future project that somehow never became a reality. He was the most democratic of borrowers, taking from both the biggest banks and the smallest neighbourhood storekeepers, from his friends and his enemies.

Ingrid came from a land where historically people survived by hoarding food and supplies for the long dark months. She had never been comfortable with extravagance; she was far from comfortable with Roberto's debts; after all, they were now her debts too. She had come to enjoy Roberto's luxurious life-style, and she was perfectly willing to help pay for it. Working was a joy to her, and she wanted to help Roberto 'carry the enormous load'. Indeed, if she worked for Selznick, Goldwyn, or another American producer, she would earn far more than her husband; nevertheless, as she wrote Steele, she 'would not do anything without Roberto'.

The truth was that he would not let her work with any other director. His friends see this as a mark of Roberto's virtue: despite all his debts he was unwilling to hire his wife out. In fact, Roberto was unwilling to let his wife out of his sight, and unable to face the fact that she was still a bigger international success than he was.

Ingrid's other problem was Pia and the American divorce. Petter could not entertain the idea of his young daughter going to Italy; he was not, however, trying to shut off Ingrid from Pia totally. In the early part of 1950, he arranged to have Phyllis Seaton take Pia to see her mother. According to Mrs Seaton's sworn deposition, she telephoned Ingrid to 'express to her my hope that she would allow

me to bring Pia to her, either in England or in any other place of her
choosing except Italy . . . Miss Bergman appeared to be pleased that
I called but she declined my offer to arrange such a meeting between
her and Pia.'

Ingrid believed, as she said later, that one of the keys to happiness
is a bad memory. She did not want to feel bad inside, to feel guilt,
remorse, and pain. Pia was a witness, who wrought with her all the
memories, and much of the pain.

She wanted to see her daughter, but she was seemingly unwilling
to risk the unpleasantness of a trip, or other discomfort. She had the
forlorn hope that in the summer, when Petter journeyed to Sweden,
he would leave Pia with her for a visit. She didn't understand that
Petter thought of Roberto as a moral cancer that at all costs must be
prevented from infecting his daughter; he thought that Roberto might
in fact kidnap Pia.

In Los Angeles, Petter was proving a remarkably tenacious op-
ponent in the settlement proceedings. Ingrid was hardly an easy
mark. She was no longer offering Petter and Pia all her property in
America while seeking to hold on to the rights of *Stromboli*; the
film rights were almost worthless. Now Ingrid asked for *all* the
community property, including the house, cars, and furniture, on
the grounds that she was the one who had earned the money to pay
for their life-style; $154,000 that she claimed Petter was holding from
Stromboli; plus complete custody of Pia.

The negotiations over a property settlement were complicated even
more when John Vernon mysteriously disappeared, carrying some
of the pertinent documents with him. Several days later Ingrid's
former business manager was discovered suffering from amnesia,
unable to talk coherently. The accountant was found to have em-
bezzled some of the money. Ingrid's attorney, Greg Bautzer, reported
finding $80,000 in Vernon's name in a Los Angeles bank, plus a
cashier's cheque made out to Petter for $10,000. According to Petter,
Vernon had actually stolen about $15,000. On 26 October 1951,
Vernon died by swallowing an overdose of sleeping pills. His suicide
note concluded: 'I no longer blame Ingrid and Petter for my breakdown. Lydia must take the responsibility . . .'

By late April, the attorneys had largely worked out the property
and divorce settlements. On 19 April 1950, Petter signed a property
settlement that supports his assertion that he had never received any
money from *Stromboli*. The agreement makes no mention of Petter
having the money, but gives him the house and furniture in Benedict
Canyon, plus one half of their savings bonds, his life insurance
policies, one half of their savings, their three automobiles, and **their**

Swedish property. Ingrid received the other half of the savings and savings bonds, her life insurance policies, plus all interest and money from *Stromboli*, *Under Capricorn*, and *Joan of Arc*.

Two years later, in court proceedings, Petter's attorney, Isaac Pacht, detailed the moneys he said Ingrid actually received from the property settlement. Pacht told the court that Ingrid had received over $140,000. This included $15,000 in savings, $19,690 in cash from savings bonds, $43,000 in cash from life insurance policies, a $30,000 tax refund, a $50,000 Italian government subsidy for *Stromboli*, her furs and jewellery. That did not include the film money from *Stromboli*, which brought in close to $200,000 more.

Ingrid gave up seeking complete custody of Pia, a point that was largely a negotiating ploy; she settled for seeing her daughter during vacation, but the question was where and how. Because she was living outside the United States, she resigned as co-guardian of Pia's estate. The estate had been started with $10,000 that during the war Ingrid and Petter had contributed to a bank account in Los Angeles. Ingrid agreed to pay $10,000 more into Pia's estate, a fund to be drawn upon each year to help pay her living expenses.

On 17 August, Petter's attorney wrote to Bautzer responding to his letter 'of 9 August 1950, requesting that $10,000 be paid to Mrs Lindstrom out of the guardianship of their daughter Pia'. Ingrid may have felt that she had done enough. Petter was financially in excellent condition, while she was already in the midst of severe money problems. Moreover, she apparently felt that the money would go to Petter. This $10,000 was nevertheless her one direct contribution to Pia's day-to-day upbringing.

The exchanges between Ingrid and Petter were now only barely civil. He had agreed to send Pia to Europe chaperoned by Phyllis Seaton, but Ingrid had turned that down. Petter felt that he had taken full responsibility for their daughter, and Ingrid had even foresworn her minimal financial obligation, giving nothing for Pia's upbringing and education. Ingrid wanted Pia to visit her in Italy, but more than ever, Petter felt that he had to protect her.

Ingrid did not understand Petter's intransigence.

On 1 November 1950, the proceedings finally reached Judge Thurmond Clarke at Los Angeles Superior Court. Petter had been coached by his attorney, Isaac Pacht. His testimony was full of the same sort of disingenuousness of which he often accused Ingrid. Contrary to his statements later, he claimed that he had gone to Messina to dissuade Ingrid from staying in Italy with Rossellini. 'She said she would have to change, that she would stop,' Petter said, as his attorney gently nudged him along. 'She also promised that she would discontinue the relationship she had started – that she would have nothing more to do with the Italian director outside their professional relations . . .'

'Do you have any bitterness in your heart as far as Mrs Lindstrom is concerned?'

'No, I have no bitterness,' Petter said calmly. 'I feel sorry for the awkward predicament she has placed herself in. I think she has many good qualities besides being very beautiful.'

Ingrid's attorney wanted Petter to agree to allow Pia to visit her mother. Petter pointed out that boats sailed both ways across the Atlantic and nothing prevented Ingrid from visiting her daughter. 'I would be glad to take Pia to see her mother,' he said. 'But I have no intention of taking my daughter to Italy.'

Ingrid did not contest the proceedings, and after an hour Judge Clarke granted the divorce. He did not specify the grounds, 'to avoid legal difficulties later'. He gave Ingrid and Petter joint legal custody of Pia. Petter was to have physical custody, but Ingrid could have Pia during one half of her school vacation in the United States. Ingrid's attorney filed a stipulation for Petter to take Pia to Europe to visit Ingrid within a year, barring any restrictions on travel or their daughter's illness.

On 10 November, nine days after the divorce, twelve-year-old Pia appeared at Federal Court in Los Angeles to become an American citizen. She wore a checkered jumper and had ribbons in her hair, and looked very grown up as she stood with 250 others. On this day she changed not only her nationality but her name. She had come to hate the name Pia; her schoolmates had made fun of her. She had hated the way the name was supposed to be derived from Petter and Ingrid and Aron, as if she were a hybrid creature. Now she would be Jenny Ann, a name of her own choosing. For once Petter was cooperative with the press, taking Pia to another room for pictures. He, too, was seeking a new life, selling the house and moving on. A few days later he received a letter from his attorney in New York, Lawrence E. Brinn, that reinforced his intention to keep Pia away from Italy. 'Mr Borre from my Italian office was in New York recently and he stated that you should not take the child to Italy,' Binn wrote.

Ingrid tried to keep up contact with Pia, but it was haphazard and unsatisfactory – a telephone call, a gift, a letter. 'If I didn't telephone now and then, I wouldn't know if they were still alive,' she wrote Steele. Ingrid sent money to Steele to buy 'a big toy monkey and a couple of new children's books'. Petter wrote Ingrid that one of the

books Pia – or Jenny, as she was now known – received was entitled
Jenny, or The Abandoned. He told her that when no Christmas gift
for Pia arrived, he gave their daughter two dolls 'from Ingrid'.

Ingrid finally gave up hope that Petter would bring Pia to Italy.
Indeed, on 20 March 1951 Petter wrote that she would be able to see
Pia in England in the fourth week of July. Ingrid had agreed not to
publicize any mention of the impending visit. Petter warned her
that 'you and your spokesmen have repeatedly . . . discussed the
probability of Pia's . . . meeting with you and under such circumstances I must inform you that if that is repeated I might without
further notice cancel all plans of taking Pia to England where she
could visit with you.' Court permission had to be obtained for Pia
to go to Europe, and to have $2000 of her $22,084 estate used for the
trip. Superior Judge Newcomb Condee only allowed the trip after
he was assured that Pia 'would be certain to return to Los Angeles' and
that Petter would take 'special precautions . . . to prevent anything
happening'.

As the summer approached, Ingrid and Petter had several telephone
conversations. They still knew how to probe each other's vulnerabili-
ties. Ingrid was not going to allow Petter to dominate *her* visit with
Pia. She insisted that she had the right to take Pia wherever she
wanted in Europe. Not only did Petter disagree with that, but he
now suggested that Ingrid see Pia in Sweden. When Ingrid became
more conciliatory, Petter wrote: 'I have decided that the best place
for Pia to meet you and where she would be the least exposed to
complications and planned publicity, would be in Stöde, Sweden.'

Petter felt that Pia would be safe in Stöde. That was true, but he
would be forcing Ingrid to return to the scene of her first wedding,
in a village among Petter's people. Petter's attorney announced on
10 July that Ingrid would see Pia in Sweden for 'an extended visit'
under conditions 'where she would not be involved in any contact
with Roberto Rossellini'.

Petter finally relented and agreed to let Ingrid see Pia in London.
Late in July, Ingrid set out for London, where Petter and Pia were
staying with Sidney Bernstein, who was Ingrid's friend as well as
Petter's.

Petter suspected that Ingrid would make a publicity spectacle of
her first visit with her daughter in a year and a half, but she wanted
nothing of that. She remembered how she travelled by train from
Italy to France and on a ship across the English Channel, all that time
managing not to attract the attention of reporters and photographers.
Fiorella Mariani travelled with her to begin school in England. She
remembers Roberto accompanying them as far as the Italian border.

Petter was fearful that Roberto would come to England to be with Ingrid. 'I had requested that Ingrid come to London without Rossellini,' he said. 'However, the day that Ingrid arrived in London, Sidney Bernstein informed me that he – that same day – had paid for Rossellini's transportation from Calais to Dover. Rossellini had gotten as far as Calais with his expensive sports car but did not have the money to get over the Channel. Amazingly, Ingrid told me that she did not know anything about Rossellini's travelling to London at the same time. Due to his presence in London, I became more concerned about the protection of Pia.'

Roberto did, indeed, arrive in London, at least in time to pick Ingrid up. Petter took precautions to protect his daughter. He and Pia met Ingrid at the home of David Lean and Ann Todd. Here Ingrid and Pia were to spend their first night together. Ingrid was highly emotional when she first saw her – her daughter was cold and withdrawn. Ingrid later claimed that this was due to the fact that 'her father had given her a sleeping pill, just before she came. This Pia told me herself', a statement that Petter denies. Petter stayed in the house for several hours. Lean said in an affidavit given the following year that Petter feared he might be locked out of the house. According to Lean he gave Petter a key and early the next morning found him inside the house.

'I had a lovely bedroom suite in that house,' Ann Todd remembers. 'Ingrid had permission for Pia to stay in our house. Petter arrived and he stayed that night. Ingrid cried. It was the only time she cried.'

Petter denies that he had a key to Lean's house and says that he arrived at nine o'clock in the morning to take Pia to Bernstein's estate, where she spent about five days with her mother. 'She kept repeating in front of the child that she had a right to take the child wherever she wished,' Petter said in an affidavit. Ingrid 'insisted on bringing up our past in front of the child and in berating me. She unfairly reprimanded me in front of the child saying "Why did you save money and why did you buy all that insurance? We could have spent the money and had fun with it." I found it necessary to answer her that we had lived well and that she had never been denied anything she wanted. She retorted "we live much better on debts. We [Ingrid and Roberto] have more cars and servants than you and I ever had but we have nothing but debts."'

Ingrid's memory of those days is totally different – Petter threatening to take Pia away to Sweden, condemning her within earshot of Pia, and harassing her emotionally. 'I recall when Dr Lindstrom grabbed me by my arms and stared into my eyes, swearing that he didn't love me any more and that he wouldn't want to have me back, even if I tried,' Ingrid said in a sworn deposition the following year. 'At another moment, he told me he was delighted to see me cry and suffer, as it would make me understand how much he had suffered in turn . . .

'As I happened to mention the name Pietro, Pia asked who he was. I said our chauffeur . . . "Oh, you have a chauffeur," she said with her eyes sparkling. Dr Lindstrom saw this and saw that after all his blackpainting of Italy and my life there, I might have *something* that attracted a twelve-year-old girl, were it only a chauffeur. So he said immediately: "Sure they have a chauffeur, lots of sevants, lots of cars and lots of debts . . ."

'Once and only once, it was I who spoke in front of Pia . . . of my right to have the girl with me. It was at the Bernsteins' country place, the very last morning . . . I sorted out, in front of both, my lawyer's letters reporting the text of the Court's order . . . All I wanted was Pia to realize that her father was exaggerating, especially in his accusations that I was not to be trusted and I would try to steal her. I was happy that Pia herself smiled during those silly kidnapping stories.'

'We both suffered tremendously,' Pia says. 'I want to correct the impression that there is someone to blame. He was mother and father to me. He tried as much as he could to make up for the loss. Everyone tried to do the best they could. There has been a great deal of suffering through the years.'

On their way back to Los Angeles, Petter and Pia stopped in New York. An Associated Press reporter asked him if he had any romantic interests. Petter smiled and looked at Pia. 'Yes, this is the one,' he said.

As much as Pia cared for her father, she was learning to hide her emotions. Petter saw only a smiling, happy child, but others saw a different Pia. 'I remember going on a six-hour auto trip with Pia in 1951,' said David Lewis, the producer. 'She talked all the way, almost as if the wind would tear her words away and no one would hear them. She told me how much she missed her mother, but that she didn't want to hurt her father.'

In Rome Ingrid and Roberto went out frequently. Sometimes they went to a small fish restaurant near Santa Marinella for dinner with Fellini and Giulietta Masina; sometimes it was one of Roberto's favourite restaurants in Rome. Roberto was usually well groomed and perfumed, and Ingrid had begun to dress with greater flair.

Roberto always wanted the best table in the house. One evening in June 1951, the best table was in full view of the avenue. A passerby noticed Ingrid and soon a crowd gathered. It was the hottest night of the year, and Ingrid was wearing a low-cut dress, provocation enough for the young boulevardiers. They began shouting comments; Roberto took offence. He marched boldly out on the street and asked the revellers to disperse. This brought on more comments, boos and shouting, drawing even more spectators. Before long the crowd's amusement turned to anger, and it took riot police to disperse the large group.

For Ingrid, life had meant her work, but now when she did work it was only for Roberto, a mere prop for his vision. Her life was a succession of small dramas; she and Roberto lived like kings and fled from their creditors like gypsies. She had few real friends; she was at peace, if boredom is peace; but she didn't think about the irony of fate; she had blocked it all off.

In the fall she began work on her second film with Roberto, *Europa '51*. Roberto's screenplay told the story of Irene Girard, a self-satisfied, self-absorbed, self-indulgent Roman lady, not unlike some of those in the circle in which Ingrid and Roberto often moved. Her life is without focus, full of a terrible busyness. Irene, played by Ingrid, is shocked into awareness of the world around her when her young son, the same age as Pia, commits suicide. In the wake of tragedy, Irene travels into the bowels of society seeking to do good work, and to meet others doing good work. She befriends a prostitute, and an unmarried mother (played brilliantly by Masina). She is disillusioned everywhere, as much by the Communist organizer who purports to exalt the poor, as by the disenfranchized themselves, dumb to their plight, and irresponsible. She says, 'If I thought I had great spiritual powers, I would be insane. My love for them is born out of hate, hate for myself.' She is a 'fool of God', and when she helps a young man escape the police, she is institutionalized in a mental hospital.

Ingrid tried her best to play the part, but she simply couldn't understand how a woman of that class and background would make such a journey. Even if she had better understood the role, working with Roberto was for her an endless exercise in frustration. Shooting was supposed to begin at 1 p.m., but that was Italian time, Rossellini time. The crew and cast began arriving at 2, and work wasn't finished until 8 or 10 at night.

Although Ingrid talked warmly about her husband in public, there were already rumours that their marriage was failing. 'Ingrid was like the sun, clear like light,' says Masina. 'She was cut in a direct manner. Roberto was completely different, from his education, to his temperament, to his tradition. It was very difficult to reconcile

these two manners of living. I liked Roberto very much as a friend,
but I wouldn't want to have a life with him. It was impossible to
have confidence in him. He gave a lot and then he was off somewhere.
He was unstable in a way. He was a man who spoke well, who liked
to listen to you, and to talk, an extrovert. But he was a man who
was born to be alone.'

Roberto was not a man but a mosaic of men. He was an intuitive
genius; he was a fraud; he was a soothsayer; he was a charmer; he
was a liar; he was an adventurer; he was a crook; he was a man of
saintly generosity; he was a cheat; he loved humanity, he manipulated
human beings; he was an egomaniac; he reeked of insecurity.

One day on the set of *Europa '51*, Roberto talked to an interviewer
from *Bianco e Nero*:

> The world is more and more divided in two, between those who
> want to kill fantasy and those who want to save it, those who want
> to die and those who want to live. This is the problem I confront
> in *Europa '51* . . . The ability to see both sides of man, to look at
> him charitably, seems to me to be a supremely Latin and Italian
> attitude. It results from a degree of civility which has been our
> custom from very ancient times – the habit of seeing every side of
> man. For me it is very important to have been born into such a
> civilization. I believe that what saved us . . . was this view of life
> we have, which is unmistakably Catholic. Christianity does not
> pretend that everything is good and perfect: it recognizes sin and
> error, but it also admits the possibility of salvation . . . The only
> possibility I see for getting nearer to the truth is to try to understand
> sin and be tolerant of it.

Roberto's film was a miserable commercial failure both in Italy and
in the United States. In the *New York Times*, Bosley Crowther called
Europa '51 'dismal and dolorous', an opinion shared by most of the
critics. His themes of alienation and loneliness and isolation are now
such clichés that the great originality and daring of *Europa '51* is
almost as lost now as it was in 1952. Roberto had not strayed as
much from neorealism as his critics charged. He had filmed the rubble
and blood of the war in Italy, and the devastation of Berlin. Now
his camera turned to the spiritual ruins of Europe, to the psychological
devastation. It wasn't easy to make what Roberto called 'a cinema of
the Reconstruction', and he admitted later that he perhaps 'wasn't
capable of producing it'. Nonetheless, *Europa '51* made Roberto a
hero and a mentor to a generation of filmmakers, including Antonioni
and Godard.

In her role, Ingrid, in the words of Bosley Crowther, 'does what she's asked to do fitly, with a maximum of confusion and dismay revealed in her lovely eyes and features as she represents her thwarted woman's grief'. If Roberto had tried to help Ingrid understand her part better, the film might have been better. That was not his way, however; and even if he had tried, Ingrid might not have understood.

During the filming of *Europa '51* Ingrid was pregnant again, this time with twins. She became so enormous, and the pregnancy was so difficult that on 28 May 1952, she entered Salvatore Mundi nursing home. There, during the last weeks of her pregnancy, Ingrid would lumber back and forth on the roof, and try to relax, while accustoming herself to intravenous feeding. She worried not only about the two children she was carrying but about her firstborn.

In those June days a sad, dramatic spectacle was playing out in a Los Angeles courtroom. In April, Ingrid had filed suit in superior court asking that Pia be permitted to visit her in Italy in the summer, accompanied by an escort other than Petter. He had already lost one professional opportunity because of the notoriety over the divorce, yet he still felt so strongly that he was willing to fight Ingrid in public battle. This time, however, it was Pia who was the one and only focus. Petter did not want his daughter to testify. Nonetheless, his claim that she did not wish to go to Italy in the summer was the centre of his case, along with his assertion that Pia should not be in Rossellini's presence. In retrospect, it is unlikely that a US court would order a father, an American citizen, to send his daughter, also a citizen, overseas to visit a mother who was not a citizen. But Petter was so determined to win that he put in evidence the letter that Ingrid had written him from Amalfi telling him of her love for Roberto. Bautzer had the unenviable task of making a case with a client unwilling to testify in person. Since the divorce, Bautzer had visited Rome. 'I don't think I've ever seen a woman as ravaged with feelings of guilt, love, and remorse,' Bautzer says. 'Ingrid was a tremendous woman. But who knows what happens to a woman hopelessly in love. Rossellini was a Svengali. She was like a prisoner. I pleaded with her and Rossellini to come back. I said, You're condemned. You've got to come back. Rossellini wouldn't let her go. He was afraid that Petter would prevent her from returning. He was the most jealous man that I've ever known.'

During the first days in court, character witnesses attested to Ingrid's and Roberto's virtues, while Pacht, Petter's attorney, slashed away at their reputations. He read from Senator Johnson's attack on Roberto, calling him a 'narcotics addict', as well as immoral, and a wartime Nazi collaborator. 'I don't want the child to be exposed to

Mr Rossellini,' Petter told the court. 'He has a bad reputation in this country and abroad. He ran away with the mother of this child. He has a reputation as a drug addict and a habit of living with mistresses who are married to other men.'

When Roberto learned of Petter's charges he vowed to fly to Los Angeles to defend his reputation. He cabled Bautzer, asking that he be 'afforded time and the opportunity to make myself heard'. Judge Mildred D. Lillie was unwilling to postpone or unduly delay the trial. Roberto ended up sending the judge a long, impassioned letter that years later she still had in her files.

The crucial person in the trial was neither Petter or Roberto. It was Pia. A few months before, during her Easter vacation at Squaw Valley, Pia had written an autobiography, as was done by all graduating students at the Hawthorne School. Pia was an excellent student, and the essay was well written. Extraordinarily, in all the pages Pia did not once mention Ingrid.

Before having her testify about her mother, Judge Lillie wanted to speak to Pia privately. As Phyllis Seaton drove Pia to the judge's house, the girl asked, 'Will the judge talk about my mother?'

'I'm sure she will, dear, but I don't know,' Mrs Seaton replied. 'It's not appropriate to ask a judge what she's going to say.'

'If she asks me, what shall I tell?' Pia asked.

'Pia, you and I must not even talk about this. When the judge talks to you it will be private. And when she asks you, tell the truth.'

Judge Lillie was a sympathetic figure, and young enough to be Pia's mother. After talking to the girl, she decided to allow Bautzer to question Pia in chambers. On 13 June, Pia, on her father's arm, walked into chambers. She wore a blue, high-collared dress and looked as if she had dressed with great care for the occasion, brushing her shoulder-length blonde hair until it glowed. From certain angles she resembled Ingrid amazingly.

'Friday the thirteenth!' Pia exclaimed. 'This is supposed to be an unlucky day.'

'Some of my luckiest days have been the thirteenth,' Petter reassured her.

In chambers the questioning began.

'Have you ever written your mother letters in which you told her that you loved her?' Bautzer asked.

'I always sign them "Love Pia."'

'And does that express the way you feel about her?'

'No, it's just the way I end the letter.'

'Now I take it when you signed your letter "Love Pia" you didn't actually love her?'

'I don't love my mother. I like her.'

'And you don't miss her?'

'No.'

'And you don't have any desire to see her?'

'No. I would rather live with my father.'

'Do you feel that your mother doesn't care about you now?' Judge Lillie asked.

'Well, I don't think she cares about me too much.'

'Why do you say that?'

'Well, she didn't seem very interested in me when she left. It was only after she left and got married and had children that she suddenly decided she wanted me.'

Bautzer seemed determined not to give up until Pia showed some sign of deep affection for Ingrid. 'Miss Lindstrom, whether or not you know your mother very well or whether you will have the opportunity in the future to know her well, do you love your mother?' he asked.

'No, not very much,' Pia answered in a thin, emotionless voice. 'I mean I have seen her enough, and I know I have met her, but I haven't seen her enough to really love her. My father has mostly been taking care of me. I lived with my father mostly.'

For Petter, it was a pure moment of vindication, spoiled for him only when others suggested that he had coached Pia. To Bautzer, Pia's repudiation of her mother would always be 'one of the most extraordinary moments of my career'. He had the unpleasant duty to call Ingrid and Roberto and tell them of Pia's testimony. For Ingrid, there was a dual shame: the public humiliation of a public figure and a mother's private humiliation. As she sat in her hospital room sobbing over Pia's words, she did not blame her daughter. She blamed Petter. She conjectured that 'perhaps she had to say things like that because she is living with her father'. She remembered how just a few weeks before she had talked to Pia on the phone and her daughter had said, 'Oh, are the twins coming soon? You must cable me as soon as they arrive.' It did not occur to Ingrid that Pia might be able to be different things to different people.

Ingrid's babies were overdue, and in the heat of Rome, the wait was agonizing. On 18 June, her doctor induced the birth of two hefty baby girls, Isabella Fiorella Elettra Giovanna, weighing seven pounds three ounces, and Isotta Ingrid Frieda Giuliana, weighing eight pounds five ounces. Roberto was doubly delighted. The healthy, wailing fraternal twins seemed testimony to the father's manhood and the mother's maternal gifts.

The superior court in Los Angeles had a different verdict on Ingrid's maternal gifts. For a week Judge Lillie had listened to charges and counter-charges. Although Ingrid was not paying child support, Bautzer had argued that she had 'bargained for and bought' the right to have Pia, as if she were a puppy or a vacation home.

On 24 June, Judge Lillie ruled that it was not in Pia's interest that she go off to Italy. Pia was not a chattel to be 'passed back and forth between parents to satisfy their pride, convenience and desires'. The judge said that 'whether Miss Bergman wishes to admit it or not, the responsibility rests with her'.

Judge Lillie did not blame only Ingrid for the fact that Ingrid and Petter's love for Pia had led them to this pathetic end. The judge criticized both father and mother, as being 'more interested in what each deserved or was entitled to under the law than what would be to the best interest of the child'. She warned that 'unless both of you put aside pride and selfishness, this child will never have the normal affection and love she is entitled to from both parents'.

By the time Judge Lillie gave her verdict, Ingrid's catharsis of grief was over, and her emotions had frozen into hard anger. She was not going to accept the verdict passively, but would appeal, this time attacking Petter without reserve. Bautzer had failed her, and she asked him to contact Jerry Giesler, a prominent celebrity attorney whose involvement would mean publicity and more publicity.

She then called reporters into her hospital room, and raged against Petter and the verdict. In her blue dressing gown, Ingrid looked positively maternal, but she was full of anger pledging no longer to 'hold back from saying things that would hurt my ex-husband', and 'now I will have to let my hair down'. Her one solace was Roberto, the 'best and kindest man I ever met . . . I punished myself plenty for falling in love with this man'.

Ingrid vowed she would come to the United States to 'fight like a tigress' for custody of Pia, even though she was 'practically broke'. Ingrid raged against Petter. '[I] kept up our home with my salary, but I don't regret it,' she said. 'However, I am bitter against him . . . I gave up most of my financial substance . . . just to have Pia with me during the summer,' she claimed. 'You can say that I am practically broke and my husband is providing for me.' If that was true, in less than three years Roberto and Ingrid had spent over $300,000 of Ingrid's money, expenditures that she could not justly blame on her former husband; but Petter had become the great symbol of all Ingrid's frustrations, and there was little wrong in her life that she didn't trace back to him.

Even when Ingrid wrote to Pia telling her of the birth of the twins, her anger spilled out on the page. She wrote that Judge Lillie couldn't possibly hurt her; she was right and she would fight endlessly for her daughter.

Soon after the court verdict, Petter and Pia moved to Pittsburgh, where he became head of the Department of Neurosurgery at Aspin-wall Veterans Hospital as well as director of a research project on brain disorders at the University of Pittsburgh's Addison H. Gibson Laboratory. Three years later he married Dr Agnes Rovnanek, a lovely twenty-six-year-old paediatrician, twenty years his junior. They began a family of their own, and Petter tried to forget Ingrid. The scandal was so notorious that he subsequently lost positions offered at two prominent universities before being hired as Chairman and Professor of neurosurgery at the University of Utah and head of neurosurgery at the Veterans Administration Hospital in Salt Lake City.

CHAPTER 16

THE DONNA OF SANTA MARINELLA

On a grand summer day, Ingrid and Fiorella drove out to Santa Marinella. Ingrid was just as happy driving her little Fiat, and not being chauffeured in the Rolls. She cherished moments like this one, away from the servants and the telephones, the money problems and the guests, away from the constant melodrama of life with Roberto. Suddenly, in the rearview mirror, she saw the familiar red of Roberto's racing Ferrari zooming up behind. Roberto manoeuvred alongside Ingrid's car, waved gaily, and pulled in behind. Ingrid laughed. It was boring always driving the same stretch. Roberto wanted to liven things up by having a little race.

Ingrid floored the accelerator. The Fiat shot ahead. Roberto let Ingrid lead for a while. Then he moved up beside her again, the Ferrari roaring like an enraged lion. He waved again and eventually dropped back behind. She sped onward, occasionally watching Roberto in the mirror. Once again Roberto moved to pass Ingrid. Once again he waved and dropped back. Ingrid sped onward, noticing that the Ferrari had dropped out of sight.

When Ingrid and Fiorella arrived at Santa Marinella, they were still laughing about their little race. Fifteen minutes went by and Roberto didn't arrive. Then a half hour. Ingrid began to worry. She jumped into the Fiat and drove back towards Rome. A few miles down the road, Ingrid found Roberto on the shoulder. He had run out of gas. 'Don't laugh,' he cried out. 'Don't laugh. It's not funny.'

Ingrid had many wonderful moments with Roberto, and in the scrapbook of her mind those were what she remembered. She had painful times too, and these memories she tried to turn into benign anecdotes, commentaries on Roberto's idiosyncrasies.

He had a violent temper. Ralph Serpe, a producer long associated with Dino De Laurentiis, remembers 'how Roberto mistreated her. I was once walking behind them on Via Veneto when he slapped her. His reputation was hurt by the way he treated Ingrid.'

Their fights were so dramatic that when they began they would send their dog, Stromboli, upstairs to Roberto's sister's apartment. For a while Ingrid tried the same approach, simply disappearing, but that didn't work. She decided that she would have to do something about Roberto's rages. Roberto suggested that the next time he exploded, she boldly rush up to him and embrace him. Ingrid did not have to wait very long. As Roberto spouted and fumed, she threw her arms around him. Roberto broke her grasp, hurling her from him. Ingrid made a joke of the incident.

It sometimes seemed to her that Roberto didn't even let her share fully in the parenting of their three children. He treated his children the way he did his lovers, showering them with affection and concern, and then rushing off. 'Father would say he was the big pig and we were the piglets,' Isabella remembers. 'He was always in bed, and we would get in bed with him. He said the thing he regretted most in life was not being able to nurse us. I remember him telling a reporter once why it was so important being a father. He said he was like a Jewish mother.'

One evening when the twins were beginning to talk, Ingrid and Roberto gave a small dinner party. 'Children, it's late,' Ingrid said at eight o'clock, clapping her hands. 'Go to bed.' 'Oh, no, my children,' Roberto said, drawing them to him. 'Oh, stay a little longer with your father, my good children whom I love so much.' When the children finally went to bed, Ingrid turned to Roberto. 'You rob my children of my heart,' she said coldly. 'You take away my children from my heart.'

Ingrid was always present for Roberto's friends and gatherings, but he was often not there for hers. For visiting stars from Hollywood and celebrities from all over, Ingrid's home became almost as much a stopping place as Sistine Chapel or the Colosseum. Roberto didn't like Ingrid's friends partly because he feared that they were trying to talk Ingrid into going back to Hollywood films. And they did, indeed, consider her return, often in films they would either star in or direct. Despite the debacle of *Stromboli*, it was remarkable how much interest Hollywood still had in Ingrid. The producer Sam Spiegel had flown to Rome in June to discuss a film also to star Marlon Brando. Walter Wanger was sending her scripts. Graham Greene thought Ingrid the perfect choice to star in the film of his novel *The End of the Affair*. Even Howard Hughes, who had lost hundreds of thousands of dollars on *Stromboli*, had not given up on Ingrid. 'I was in Hollywood with Howard Hughes,' remembers Gina Lollobrigida. 'He was mad at Rossellini because he had succeeded in taking away Ingrid from him. He really wanted to get her back. I never saw a person so angry.'

Ingrid was not yet ready to step out artistically on her own. She was more interested in putting on a show of domestic bliss than in other sorts of public performances. Hers was indeed a peculiar fate, to be ensconced at Santa Marinella, with Roberto often off somewhere, or arriving home in the middle of the night, the throbbing motor of the Ferrari signalling his arrival. A railway line ran past the villa, and when the train went by, the passengers looked out the window, waving at Italy's newest national monument, the *donna* of Santa Marinella. When Ingrid was in the right mood she waved back.

Evenings were often the best times now when Roberto wasn't there, and it was Ingrid and Fiorella, and perhaps Roberto's son Renzo. 'We'd talk on and on until four o'clock in the morning,' Fiorella remembers. When we started talking about God, that meant that we had drunk too much. Oh, the *bel vino*. In Roberto's films God is always the solution.'

Renzo recalls, 'She told wonderful stories in her moments of loneliness . . . some love stories, very open, all in great detail.' Ingrid was like an old lady recounting her life. She usually started talking to Renzo after dinner, telling him that it would only be for a drink or two. Soon it would be midnight, and then, of course, they would have to wait until 1 so they could see the mouse that every night at that hour raced across the railing of the terrace on its way to bed. Ah, but after the mouse made its nightly dash, it was close to 2, and they might as well wait to see the fishermen in their boats. And by now it was dawn, and the sun was rising up out of the sea.'

Ingrid was getting offers from Hollywood, but Roberto would have nothing of it; his wife would work with him or she would not work at all. It did not matter that so far their collaboration seemed to have benefited neither of them. He would try again. Ingrid did what he wanted her to do; she did not like the films that they were making, but it was as if she had no energy left to throw off the artistic yoke that Roberto had placed over her.

In the summer of 1952 Roberto directed Ingrid in *The Chicken*, a short humorous film, one of five segments in *We, the Women*. Her next major role was in *Journey to Italy*, the most autobiographical of Roberto's films. *Journey to Italy* does not exploit the drama of Roberto and Ingrid's life together, but traces much of Roberto's spiritual journey with Ingrid, through the story of a wealthy British couple, Alexander and Katherine Joyce. After ten years of marriage, they travel to Italy to visit a house they have inherited, and to get away from the mind rot and boredom of their deteriorating marriage. In the vapid, tedious exchanges between the couple, there is all the existential horror of a love gone bad, of courtesies and routines that have no meaning, except to hide the truth. There is a stench of death in *Journey to Italy*, not of the skulls and ruins that the couple visit in Pompeii, but of lives that are entombed. Alexander seeks out a prostitute and travels by himself to Capri. Slowly, though, in the warmth and depth of Italy, Alexander and Katherine discover themselves and their feelings. During a religious festival, a small miracle takes place: the resurrection of Alexander and Katherine's own love. The film ends with the couple determined to try again.

Roberto's reputation had reached the point where in order to raise money, he needed an international star to play opposite Ingrid. He chose George Sanders, whom Ingrid had worked with years before in *Rage in Heaven*. Sanders had made a career out of playing charming men of questionable character. A dour, self-absorbed, melancholic man, he was an actor of large, if unappreciated, skills, who needed a director who directed, a script that was a script, and a working day full of order and discipline. He needed anyone but Roberto Rossellini.

Sanders arrived in Italy convinced of Roberto's greatness. Before long he had decided that Roberto had every attribute of a genius except genius. By the time the film began shooting in Naples, Sanders wanted out. One day he started crying in front of Ingrid: 'I can't go on, I can't do this *commedia dell'arte* and invent and get the lines at the last minute.' He began calling his psychiatrist in Hollywood, worried only about his very sanity.

Roberto's film was *his* spiritual autobiography, not Ingrid's nor Sanders's. The actor could have told the character he was playing a thing or two about bad marriages. Sanders had the not uncommon honour of being married to Zsa Zsa Gabor; it was about over. His wife was having an affair with Don Porfirio Rubirosa, the Dominican ambassador to the Republic of France. When Zsa Zsa visited her husband, Sanders took her with him when the film went on location in Ravello. A Hollywood film was also shooting there: *Beat the Devil*, directed by John Huston, starring Humphrey Bogart, Jennifer Jones, and Gina Lollobrigida. The whole group was sitting on the hotel terrace when Ingrid sauntered up.

'I want to meet George's wife,' Ingrid said, stretching out her hand to Zsa Zsa in greeting.

'And I also would like to meet Mrs Rossellini,' replied Zsa Zsa.

Zsa Zsa appraised Ingrid's clothes like a jeweller looking over a handful of glass baubles. She felt that Ingrid left almost immediately because 'she did not want to appear as she appeared completely without make-up, in a shapeless sweater and slacks'. Whether or not Ingrid was so easily put off, she probably realized that *she* could have been the one starring with Bogart, and not Jennifer Jones, sitting there demurely in her tailored black slacks and white blouse. It could not have been easy, moreover, to have Bogart, her co-star in *Casablanca*, tell her bluntly that he disliked 'everything Roberto does – even without looking at it'. Still, Ingrid enjoyed being with these Hollywood people. There she heard laughter, for, as she wrote Steele, there was not much laughter on her film.

More and more, whatever joy and gaiety Ingrid had in her life was lived offscreen from her marriage with Roberto. She was once again practising the gentle arts of subterfuge; a craft she had practised so well on Petter. It wasn't new lovers she was looking for, but life, moments of laughter and fun and flirtations.

Helen Tubbs was doing public relations for the film, a job she had taken on after her husband died. Ingrid noticed Helen drinking with some American naval officers in the bar. One evening Tubbs telephoned Ingrid in her suite at the Continentale, telling her that the officers were calling. 'Go down to them,' Ingrid said quietly. 'Then call me and say I must go down. Make a reason.'

Another evening Roberto called Tubbs to tell her that he had to drive to Rome. He wanted her to keep Ingrid company by having dinner in their suite. When Tubbs arrived she found herself in the midst of a typical Rossellini melodrama.

'Ah, the children have a fever,' Roberto moaned, as if it were time to call a priest for the last rites. 'I don't want to leave.'

'Oh, come on, all children have fevers,' Ingrid said, in exasperation.

'Oh, all right,' Roberto replied uncertainly, running to hug and kiss the children once again. '*Cari miei, cari miei.*'

Ingrid waved goodbye to him from the balcony and then turned back into the suite. 'Now for martinis,' Ingrid said, suddenly alive. 'I'm the great Bergman, so you mix the first one for me.'

Tubbs mixed her finest martini. 'It's fine,' Ingrid said, as she emptied her glass. 'But I'll do better.'

The two women proceeded with their competition. After a while Ingrid started to do imitations, mimicking one celebrity after another.

Suddenly, the door was flung open. There stood an incredulous Roberto. 'I leave my poor children with you and look!'

'I looked in.' Ingrid shrugged.

'I've come back to take their temperatures and you're in an alcoholic stupor!'

The telephone rang and Tubbs answered. 'It's Captain Hal,' she said brightly.

'Oh, I was supposed to have dinner with him,' Ingrid said.

'You're not going anywhere at all.'

Roberto took the children's temperatures, tucked them in, and set off once again for Rome. Ingrid waved him adieu. As soon as he was out of sight, she and Tubbs started drinking again.

During the filming of *Journey to Italy*, Ingrid announced that she was 'through with films' and would work onstage 'only if I could be near my husband'. Her 'retirement' from films may have been providential; she wrote Steele that she didn't think her new film was very good. When it opened in Italy it was clear that Roberto had contrived another commercial failure. It was however viewed by the critics with respect. In 1958 *Cahiers du Cinéma* named it one of the twelve greatest films of all time. In 1964 Bernardo Bertolucci, who would one day win notoriety for *Last Tango in Paris*, paid homage to Roberto in *Before the Revolution*, in which a character says: 'I saw *Journey to Italy* fifteen times . . . Remember you cannot live without Rossellini.' The tragedy of Ingrid's professional life with Roberto wasn't that they made bad films together. It was that although Ingrid knew that some people still admired Roberto's work, she didn't have any sense what it was they admired. She didn't understand her husband's artistic sentiment and daring – the best thing about Rossellini.

In late April, after the film was finished, the family moved into a large modern apartment at 62 Via Bruno Buozzi. In the fall Roberto would direct the Paul Claudel-Arthur Honegger oratorio *Joan at the Stake*, with Ingrid playing the one speaking part, but that was months off. Meanwhile he had time to take part in a hundred-mile road race. Halfway through, his car broke down, but he took pride in the fact that he had been averaging one hundred miles an hour, and his assistant had passed out beside him.

Roberto did not limit his road racing to scheduled events. In June he and Ingrid drove to Stockholm to attend a Saturday evening party in her honour. For Roberto, the great unfairness of most races was that if you did not arrive on time, you could not compete. Driving to Stockholm was different, and Roberto was not ready to leave Rome until Friday morning for the more than fifteen-hundred-mile journey. Ingrid sat beside him as he sped northward, stopping only for gas. He drove a day and a night to the Hamburg dock; he had made extraordinary time but missed the Denmark ferry by a few minutes. Ingrid began to cry. 'This is part of the fun of travelling,' Roberto laughed, ever the philosopher. They finally reached Stockholm at 3 a.m. on Sunday morning. The party was still going on.

In December, Roberto staged *Joan at the Stake* at the Teatro San Carlo in Naples. Ingrid wore her by now familiar sackcloth and spoke her lines firmly. The performance received generally good reviews.

Roberto took the oratorio on to La Scala in Milan. One evening Ernest Hemingway and his friend A. E. Hotchner came to visit Ingrid in her hotel suite. Ingrid hugged the novelist and took him into the living room full of red roses an admirer had sent.

'How do things go?' Hemingway asked. 'How do they really go?'

'Oh, when I think how it was a few years ago and how it is now! If only in a crisis one could learn to have patience, everything would be fine.'

Hotchner asked if she had any movie roles in the offing.

'No, none,' she said. 'But I really don't care. The way things are now I could just concentrate on being a housewife and be perfectly happy, because I have a husband who is in the theatre and talks movies, and artists are around all the time.'

'Listen, daughter,' Hemingway said. 'I have looked into Dr Hemingstein's crystal ball, and a housewife is one thing you ain't gonna be. When they are starved enough for your talent, they will come to get you. In the meantime anything I can do with my chequebook or my sixteen-gauge Winchester or maybe just to cream a couple of characters who need creaming, you have only to say the word.'

Roberto insisted on filming the oratorio, though there was no real audience for such a film. He was having no easy time finding backers for his film ventures, and he and Ingrid needed money. So they took the oratorio to Barcelona, Paris, London, and finally Stockholm.

Roberto was proud that he had refused to replicate his early success, never seeking to make another *Open City*. Here he was, though, travelling through Europe with his wife and three children, the nanny, and the Rolls-Royce, endlessly repeating himself. Before Rossellini, Ingrid would never have gone on tour, yet now she was being burned at the stake nightly, in five different countries.

Ingrid and Roberto were a spectacle that transcended any drama on the stage. When they arrived in Stockholm the streets were lined with the curious. If there were those who thought that Ingrid was a blot on the Swedish flag, there were many others who admired her immensely. The opening of *Joan at the Stake* on 17 February 1955, was one of the events of the season at the Stockholm Opera House. The list of dignitaries was headed by the prime minister himself, and included most of the leading social and theatrical figures in Sweden. The next morning the *Swedish Daily*'s critic wrote that 'the Joan of Ingrid Bergman seems comparatively vague and cool, basically lack-

ing the right charisma. What's all right in this interpretation is the
actress's clear voice that carried the text clearly and steadily through
the play and is never artificial.'

The reviews were far from the best Ingrid had ever received, but
not the worst. What stung her more than anything ever written about
her was a piece by Stig Ahlgren in the *Weekly Journal*. In person
Ahlgren was a mild man, but he wrote satirical columns full of spite
and bitterness. He might have been ignored if he had not been so
amusing, and often just enough on target to raise welts on his victims.

> The criticism both here and abroad has been acid against Ingrid
> Bergman. Her register is too narrow. Her tone of voice is too
> trivial. She doesn't know what passion is, etc. What she earned
> when she acted as Joan of Arc was not small change . . . Ingrid
> Bergman is not an actress in the usual meaning. Her career has been
> on a completely different level. To compare her with professional
> actresses is both mean and unjust. She travels around and is shown
> for money. The promoter is Roberto Rossellini, with whom she
> has three children and one Rolls-Royce. With art this travelling
> company has nothing to do . . . But why criticize? . . . Ingrid
> Bergman is not an actress but a clever businesswoman. Coolly and
> soberly she has assessed the chances of making money out of her
> special attraction . . . Ingrid Bergman is a commodity, so far a
> desirable commodity which is offered in the free market. She is
> paid according to the same pricing mechanism that is valid for
> herring and pig iron.

It was at this time, Ingrid said, that a reporter and a photographer
'tried to break into my hotel suite early one morning to take pictures
of Roberto and me in our bedroom . . . they went from door to
door listening for the sound of children's voices. When they heard
Robertino playing with Little Isabella and Ingrid, they forced their
way in and began snapping pictures of the children. It was only
because the nurse threw herself in front of our door that they did not
burst into our bedroom.' Roberto called the police and sued the
reporter, but Ingrid decided to mount her own attack against her
detractors. In her years in Italy she had become inured to criticism
in the press, but Sweden was different; she felt that her native land
was a small country full of small-minded people who attacked anyone
who went abroad and became successful.

On Sunday evening she was supposed to make a few remarks at a
charity benefit for the Swedish polio fund. 'I summoned all my
courage and got up and told them of the attempt to break into my
hotel room,' she said. 'I said, "The entire Swedish press emphasizes

lies and insults. This is my only chance to fight back, and that's why
I'm doing it, because they cannot say anything worse about me than
they have." The lights went on, and I could see men and women
crying. They kept calling me back to the stage. When I finally left,
I was weeping, too.'

The truth was that though she was not greeted by the critics in
Stockholm as if she were bestowing a great gift on her native land,
the opera house was filled to overflowing every night. She raged
against the press, but Stig Ahlgren had been the only writer to make
a personal attack, and he even poked fun at King Gustaf. And Sussie
Bjuvstedt, the reporter who dared to violate the inner sanctum in
Ingrid's family life, paid a fifteen-dollar fine and suffered rebuke in
the press. Her story was different from Ingrid's:

> My editor understood there was to be a press conference the
> morning after the opera opened, and a photographer and I went
> to the Grand Hotel, where the Rossellinis were staying. It was 10
> a.m., not early in the morning . . . The desk clerk said he wasn't
> aware of any press conference. Since I knew the number of the
> suite, we went up and knocked on the door. A nurse opened the
> door. She spoke only Italian. I gestured toward our camera to
> signify we wanted to take pictures. She called another nurse, who
> asked us, in French, to come in. The photographer took one picture
> of the boy and one of the three children together. The nurse helped
> and even wrote down the names of the children and the way they
> were standing. The whole thing took about five minutes. As
> the photographs show, everyone was friendly and smiling and
> pleasant.

If it was indeed 10 a.m. when Bjuvstedt and her photographer
arrived, Ingrid would have had time to read the reviews of *Joan at
the Stake*. She would not have been in a particularly gracious mood.

Ingrid had played Joan of Arc so many times, in so many ways, that
people thought she was like the Maid of Orléans. One evening at
Santa Marinella, she was sitting out on the terrace with Masina,
Fiorella, and Father Apra, a friend of Roberto's.

'When you did Joan of Arc, you felt you had to do such a saint?'
the priest asked.

'No,' Ingrid replied. 'I loved to do the role and I thought I could
understand it.'

'And you, Giulietta?' the father asked. Masina had just had a
brilliant success starring in Fellini's *La Strada*.

'I was really inside the character,' the actress said. 'I felt I was part of her.'

'I was not,' Ingrid said. 'I was Joan of Arc like a shoemaker doing his shoe.'

It was Ingrid's inability to reach deep within herself that limited her as an actress. And now the shoemaker was working on a splintered last, producing shoes that no one wanted to wear. She and Roberto had made yet another movie together, *Fear*, filmed in Germany. She played a bored wealthy housewife who is blackmailed when she takes a lover. The film received the now familiar complement of bad reviews that often had a few kind, if slightly patronizing, words about Ingrid's performance. Ingrid could ignore most of the criticism, but one review, by Angelo Solmi in *Oggi*, had the deadly resonance of truth:

> [Miss Bergman and Mr Rossellini] will either have to change their style of work radically – or retire into dignified silence. The abyss into which Bergman and Rossellini have plunged can be measured by *Fear*. This is not because this film is any worse than their other recent motion pictures together, but because after half a dozen tries with negative results it proves the inability of the couple to create anything accepted by the public or the critics. Once the world's unquestioned number one star and successor to Greto Garbo, Miss Bergman in her latest pictures has been only a shadow of herself.

'If a good picture comes up, it might be better to do that so as to buy the children new shoes,' Ingrid wrote to Steele. Even Roberto realized now that things could not go on as they had been. He decided that he would allow Ingrid to work with another director – not just with anyone, but with Jean Renoir, the great French director of *La Grande Illusion*.

For years Ingrid had dreamed of working with her friend from her early days in Beverly Hills. In Paris, Roberto and Ingrid went to the building where Renoir was working, and waited for him outside. Ingrid became tired and sat on the kerb. Suddenly, the rotund, cherubic Renoir appeared, accompanied by Mrs Renoir. 'I give you Ingrid,' said Roberto dramatically, 'she is very unhappy.'

In June, Ingrid announced from Santa Marinella that she and Roberto were 'splitting artistically' and that she would be making a film with Renoir in Paris. Three weeks later Ingrid sent the Rolls-Royce to bring Hedda Hopper out to the villa for an interview. The last time Ingrid had seen Hedda was in Rome, when she had led the columnist to believe that she was not pregnant; if she was going to renew her film career, she needed Hedda on her side. But as soon as

Roberto saw the ageing columnist, he took a profound dislike to her. He sat over the lobster, squash, figs and loquats, fruit and cheese, eating in disdainful silence. Ingrid and Hedda talked about Ingrid's future movie and stage projects. There was the Renoir film. Then there was the stage play of the American hit *Tea and Sympathy* that she was planning to do in Paris. And Hedda mentioned that she had heard about a possible role in *Anastasia*, a 20th Century-Fox film.

The conversation could have taken place ten years before in Hollywood. Looking at Ingrid, it was hard to believe that in two months she would be forty years old, an age when most actresses are playing mothers and middle-aged wives, not romantic leads. Hedda had 'never seen her looking better'. There was a definition to her face, a depth that she had not had before. This was a face that had known joy and pain, a face that might grace a woman who would play great parts in great plays and great movies.

Ingrid was still a star, and as she laughed and charmed Hedda, it was as if Roberto weren't there. She talked about Selznick and Kay Brown, and other Hollywood personalities. She talked about everything but her husband. Who could blame Roberto for not listening. He was the grand cuckold now, cheated not by another man but by the seductions of a career. He was the one left in the ruins, unable to get backing for his own films, left with debts and with movies that few people wanted to watch.

Hedda was not going to be fooled by Ingrid again. As she left she thought to herself that Ingrid's 'love idyll is over'. She wrote in her column, 'how sad careerwise it's become'.

Ingrid waved goodbye as the Rolls glided onto the highway. Then she began to berate Roberto. Roberto said that he didn't care what Hedda thought.

There was so much about Ingrid that Roberto didn't care about any longer. He didn't care enough even to pretend. Ingrid didn't care that much either, but she had had enough of scandal and controversy. She would do her own work now, pretending to the world that her life with Roberto was the same as always, though the heart of their marriage was dead.

'From the beginning Ingrid's union with Rossellini seemed a bit strange,' Fellini said. 'But it seemed like the same kind of relationship that Pinocchio had with the blue-haired fairy. Through Ingrid, Rossellini could be transformed into a good boy, though perhaps it was the blue-haired fairy who risked becoming a female Pinocchio. But before Pinocchio could become a good boy, the fairy left. The miracle never happened.'

CHAPTER 17

'WELCOME HOME, MISS BERGMAN'

The Parisian winter of 1955–6 was the coldest in decades, but as Albert, her French chauffeur, drove back and forth from the film studio, she insisted that the car windows be rolled down and the heat be turned off. She rode with her beaver coat open, without a hat, either napping contentedly or chatting amiably to her shivering companions.

Ingrid did not have the finest dressing room, and her co-star, Mel Ferrer, was concerned about her. 'Why are you sitting here with a shawl around you in a dressing room with no heat, waiting to be called to go on a picture that probably will never be released in the United States?' he asked her one day. 'I mean, it's not a great picture. Jean is failing now. It's not great Renoir. Why are you sitting here freezing to death?'

'Mel, I work because I like to work,' Ingrid said. 'I'll work until I'm an old lady and I'll play grandma parts.'

Ingrid was doing the one thing in life that fulfilled her. In Jean Renoir's comedy *Paris Does Strange Things*, Ingrid played Elena, a poor Polish princess, who uses her considerable charm to enchant and then dismiss various suitors, including General Rolan (Jean Marais) and Count Henri (Ferrer). It was filmed simultaneously in French and English, a double burden. Ingrid was so enthralled with acting in a fully-fledged, professionally scripted movie that even when she wasn't working in a scene, she occasionally showed up at the studio in Joinville, outside Paris, to watch. On Sunday, when the studio was closed, she haunted the movie houses of Paris, watching two or three films in a day. She frequented not simply the great first-run theatres, but the dank, musty art theatres of Montmartre. There she sat among the students and the movie buffs, watching *Carnet du Bal*, *Les Enfants du Paradis*, and other classics.

Now every knock on the door seemed to bring her good tidings. For months Kay Brown had been looking for a suitable film to reintroduce Ingrid to the American public. Kay was now an agent for ICM, a prominent entertainment company, and Ingrid was her biggest client. She decided that Ingrid should star in *Anastasia*, a

20th Century-Fox film about the woman who claimed to be Grand
Duchess Anastasia, the youngest daughter of Czar Nicholas II, and
the only member of the royal family not to have been murdered.
Kay saw *Anastasia* as a way for Ingrid to enter what she considered
the 'real' movie world.

But Ingrid was still a controversial figure in the United States and
Fox decided to poll theatre owners before offering her the part. The
results were decidedly mixed, and both Spyros P. Skouras, the
president, and the sales force preferred Jennifer Jones; but Darryl F.
Zanuck, the executive producer, and Anatole Litvak, the director,
insisted so strongly on Ingrid that she was offered the part for a
reported $200,000, alongside Helen Hayes, as the grand duchess,
and Yul Bryner, as Bounine, a White Russian general and her
Svengali.

Her career had begun again. Roberto was upset and said that he
was going to kill himself. Ingrid barely cared. She was tired of
Roberto, tired of his histrionics, tired of his excesses, tired of their
failed films, but she cared about the image she and her husband
presented. His position in Paris was intolerable. Everywhere he
looked he saw signs of Ingrid's success, and his own failure. He was
supposed to direct a play about Judas at the Theatre de Paris, but he
had his ideas and the cast had theirs and he was fired. Then he was
hired by Skouras to go to Jamaica to direct *Sea Wife*, starring Richard
Burton and Joan Collins. Five years before he would have laughed
at the idea of directing a commercial Hollywood film. Now not only
was he accepting the job, but he was being given it by Skouras as a
favour to Ingrid, a kind of artistic alms. Roberto flew to Jamaica, but
he had his ideas and the producers had theirs and he soon left the
film.

In January, Roberto had stormed out of the Raphaël, telling Ingrid
that he would never come back; their life together was now full of
ugly scenes. He wore her down until she signed a letter of separation,
stating that the children could live only in Italy or France.

Since September 1955, Roberto had talked about travelling over-
land to India to make a documentary film. He had been saying it so
long and had put the trip off so many times that 'Roberto's India
trip' had become a standing joke in the family, but now he was
planning it seriously.

It was a mark of her renewed ambition that for the first time since
marrying Roberto, Ingrid was not living in the same house as her
three children. She had shipped them to Santa Marinella for the
summer and well into the fall. In the summer of 1956, when she was
working in *Anastasia*, Roberto came to see her only once at the Savoy

Hotel in London. A film set is a fraternity that has little time for outsiders, and it was just as well that Roberto stayed away.

Ingrid threw herself into the part as she could not in a Rossellini film. Often she sat in her dressing room reading a book about Anastasia given her by Felix Aylmer, who played the cynical old court chamberlain. Ingrid tried to understand the nuances of the character. She had decided to wear her hair in a bun in the early scenes, then in a swept-back style similar to her own coiffure. Looking at the pictures in the book, she saw that instinctively she had chosen hairstyles like those of the character whom she was playing.

Anastasia is a grand romantic saga, unlike anything Ingrid had attempted since *Saratoga Trunk*. The name Anastasia is derived from a Greek word meaning 'of the resurrection'. In the film Ingrid's character goes through a stunning resurrection, changing from a mousy, frightened, half-starved refugee into a regal princess, glowing with beauty. If in the early scenes Ingrid looked too well-fed and radiant, the fault lay as much in her forty-one-year-old beauty as in the relentless glamourizing of Hollywood.

Helen Hayes had no trouble looking the aged duchess. When she lost her teenage daughter to polio, her main solace was not her career but her strong marriage to the playwright Charles MacArthur. But now he had died too. She had not even wanted to take the role, but to stay at home alone with her grief and her memories. 'I think that Ingrid was at home only in one place in the world: working,' Hayes says. 'As for me, I was always a shadow in my professional life, yearning for my personal life.'

Ingrid had never before acted in a movie where she played her greatest scene with the other female lead – the dramatic meeting where the grand duchess must decide whether Anastasia is an impostor.

'We had a fierce experience together doing that scene,' Hayes remembers. 'We played that confrontation scene for nearly two weeks with all the different cuts and takes. She had been working with Rossellini and she said, "I don't understand these takes." He didn't do any of that, and she couldn't get herself back. It was a nightmare. Keeping the emotion low and then at the end they said we had to loop it. So each of us in turn had to go into a darkened room speaking out lines of high emotion. That was just slow death. I think in my heart it finished my career in pictures.'

For Ingrid, however, *Anastasia* was part of a professional resurrection. Already in September, with the opening of *Paris Does Strange Things* in Paris (with the French title *Elena et les Hommes*), that resurrection had begun. The queues outside the theatre on the Champs Elysées were yards long.

Even while she was shooting *Anastasia*, Ingrid was busy at the weekends studying her role in *Tea and Sympathy*. At one point Roberto had been asked to direct the play, but he took a violent dislike to it, pronouncing it 'trash'. *Tea and Sympathy* is a very American play of the 1950s, with a subject matter and sensibility that might seem totally alien to a sophisticated European audience. It is the story of a boarding school boy who is thought to be homosexual. He is teased by his classmates because of such clearly deviant behaviour as playing tennis and enjoying poetry. Ingrid, as the headmaster's wife, grows close to the young man. In the climactic scene, she makes the ultimate sacrifice, initiating the young man into the wonders of sex. In the Broadway play, Deborah Kerr merely unbuttoned the top button of her blouse. But this was Paris, after all, and Ingrid stripped down to her bra, a black one at that.

By the time the play had its first Parisian opening, on 1 December 1956, Ingrid had been preparing the role for over a year. And for over a year Roberto had been mocking her, denigrating the play. He was sure that after opening night, Ingrid would be the one needing tea and sympathy. But by now *Elena et les Hommes* was a great hit in Paris, and there was every indication that *Tea and Sympathy* would be even bigger. On the opening night the theatre was full of Parisians eager to see Ingrid Bergman and to hear her speak French.

Roberto was still planning to leave for India, but he was there in the dressing room at the Théâtre de Paris. He had lived among actors and actresses, and he knew that these last moments before the curtain opened were sacrosanct. It was particularly difficult for Ingrid, who was recovering from an appendectomy and was going to have to go onstage speaking a language she still only half understood. Roberto knew all this and yet he chatted with her in Italian. She remembered him saying that after the first act half the audience would leave.

They did not walk out and when the play ended they applauded until their hands were red; the cast received fifteen curtain calls. As the great waves of applause rolled over Ingrid, Roberto stood offstage. One of the other actresses, Simone Paris, saw him standing there: 'his face was red with fury.'

Ingrid saw him too, as the audience continued its applause. When Ingrid took her solo bow, she saw Roberto standing in the wings. And when she looked into his eyes, she knew her marriage was finished.

The next day Roberto packed his bags. Ingrid went with him to the railway station to see him off. He was finally leaving for India.

Tea and Sympathy was a smash hit. The French consider the mispronunciation of their language practically a felony, but no one seemed to mind that Ingrid spoke French as if she had put it through a blender. The crowds were coming to the Théâtre de Paris to see Ingrid, not to hear the language of Racine.

In Paris a play has a public opening and a critics' opening. For the second opening, two weeks later, Ingrid had a special guest, Robert Anderson, the author. Anderson's wife, Phyllis, a literary agent and producer, had died a few days before, after a five-year struggle with cancer. The playwright was buried in grief, hardly able to perform the basic rituals of daily living, much less attempt writing again.

Anderson was tall and handsome enough to have been a leading man. Much like his youthful hero in *Tea and Sympathy*, he was so open to emotions that his more macho brethren wondered why he had such a way with the ladies. His best friends were almost always women; he was the archetypal 'sensitive' man that in the age of women's liberation would become an emotional cliché.

Anderson remembers: 'Phyllis and I had met Ingrid in Rome, when she said she liked the play and wanted to do it. Then I came to Paris. I wouldn't dare write the story. It's so corny that nobody would believe it. Ingrid had been writing me, saying, You have to come over for the opening. I told her Phyllis was ill and I said I don't think I'll be able to make it. Ingrid would get quite angry at me. She would say it will be a great opening. And then Phyllis died and I just wanted to die too.

'Ingrid said, You belong here. I packed up all these letters of condolence, a thousand, Phyllis was so popular, and Kay Brown took me out to the airport. It was winter and the plane was delayed and over Boston we lost a propeller. Then we couldn't come down in Paris.

'When I finally walked into her suite, Ingrid said, "You should be older." I said, "I'm sorry I'm not." She was extraordinary. She really took me in hand and I think I took her in hand. It was one of those weird times when people need each other. At the theatre I would be in a little stage box, and she would occasionally look up when I was there. We'd either go out for drinks or supper, or go back to her place. She lived right across the hall. She was marvellous.

'She had such energy. She never wanted to go to bed. She was drinking a great deal. She would polish off a big bottle of champagne or Scotch, and it would mean nothing to her. She'd want to stay up and talk and chatter.

'She was self-centred. Sometimes it would drive you crazy. It would seem that all she could talk about was herself. But she was very caring. She nurtured me for weeks and this was a very selfless act. Of course, she needed me too. She didn't have patience for people who were sad too long. She said, "If you had children you'd have to shape up sooner than this."

'She took me everyplace. She didn't accept an invitation without including me. In the morning I would sit over the letters, crying, thanking people for all the wonderful things they said about Phyllis, and in the evening I'd go out with Ingrid. She was the toast of Paris.'

Ingrid was courting scandal with Anderson, but Roberto was gone now and she wanted to get on with her career and her life. It was no simple matter to say when Ingrid and Roberto's marriage died. For a long time the heart and brain of their marriage had been dead, kept alive by such mechanical rationales as routine and convenience. Did it begin to die when Ingrid and Roberto came to know each other properly? Did it die when Ingrid became pregnant and found she was no longer free? Did it die when their films died and there was no money? Or did the missiles of the press wound it mortally? Perhaps it finally expired on that opening night of *Tea and Sympathy*. Or perhaps it had never been a great love but fostered on illusion. Ingrid herself saw the truth variously, according to the mood of the moment, but one thing was certain: she had been through enough controversy for five lifetimes and had no intention of ending her marriage to Roberto in scandal and a struggle over the children.

As it was the children had been shunted in and out of her life. Robertino didn't come home to find that his mother had prepared a glass of milk and a sandwich for his lunch; more often than not he would go to an expensive restaurant to meet her for their midday meal. To him and the twins food was something that arrived on linen tablecloths, and all you had to do was dial a phone. As a mother, Ingrid was a woman for the great occasion. For Robertino's seventh birthday she hired two clowns and a large private room for the party. The children loved such events but they didn't grow up seeing life as it was for most people.

'When I look back on my childhood, it's very difficult because of the confusion over real remembrances and film, whether it's something I saw on film or something that happened,' says Robertino. 'Mother was filming from the time I was born, and we saw the film all the time. It's a little bit of confusion. We were moving so much and

changing apartments because we were going around Europe. Even
when they were married, my parents weren't living together that
much. I remember living with my sisters. We were used to being
very much alone. I don't remember the typical family home. For me
our life was normality. It's still like that. I think that people living
very quietly are not normal.'

Soon after the opening of *Tea and Sympathy* in Paris, *Anastasia* opened
in the United States. Ingrid's professional resurrection was complete.
The movie was her first international hit in a decade, and a critical
success as well. In the *New York Times*, Bosley Crowther called her
'nothing short of superb . . . a beautifully moulded performance
worthy of an Academy Award'. At the end of the year the New
York Film Critics voted Ingrid the best actress of the year, and invited
her there to accept the award.

The previous July, Ed Sullivan had announced on his popular
variety show that he was considering showing a film clip of Ingrid
and Helen Hayes in *Anastasia*. 'Now I know that she's a controversial
figure, so it's entirely up to you,' the dour columnist said. 'If you
want her on our show, I wish you'd drop me a note and let me know
. . . and if you don't . . . you also let me know that too because it's
your decision.' In the world's greatest democracy, the citizenry voted
on such transcendent matters as all-star baseball teams and favourite
movie stars, but never before had they voted on the moral propriety
of allowing a soiled movie star to appear live in homes across America.
Sullivan usually took such matters into his own hands; with Elvis
Presley, the scandalous new rock-and-roll singer, he had made the
Solomonic decision of showing the gyrating singer from the waist
up, a video castration that made him morally tolerable. The results
after a week were hardly gratifying to Ingrid: 6433 respondents
didn't want to see her, while 5826 did. No matter what the
figures, Ingrid had no intention of being exploited on *The Ed
Sullivan Show*, and neither did 20th Century-Fox. What Sullivan
accomplished, however, was to generate sympathy for Ingrid,
and editorials in her favour, while underscoring the fact that
almost eight years after she left America she was still a figure of
controversy.

So that Ingrid could go to New York to receive the Film Critics
Award, Fox bought up three performances of *Tea and Sympathy*. Her
arrival would be nearly as dramatic a moment as her arrival in Rome,
and Ingrid prepared for her two-day visit with apprehension and care.
She knew that she must arrive alone, without entourage, without
spokesman, without protectors. As the day approached, she decided

that she would not have the time to see Pia, who was a freshman at the University of Colorado.

Ingrid remembered seeing her eldest daughter only once since leaving the United States in 1951. Petter, however, says that he took Pia to Europe not only in 1951 but in 1953 and 1955 as well, and on all these occasions Ingrid met Pia in England. For her part, Pia says that she remembers going to Europe twice, and recalls visiting Ingrid in London in 1951 and 1953; but there is a vagueness about Pia's recollections that seems a devastating comment on the relationship with her mother. Pia does, however, vividly remember her mother's trip to New York. 'I was very sad that she would make a trip to the United States and she wouldn't see me,' Pia says. 'I offered to come to New York and she said, "Don't do it." She had her own reasons.' The truth was that Ingrid was not going to clutter up her return to America with the emotional baggage that came with Pia. She looked at the bright side of it, anticipating calling Pia from New York. She wrote Steele that she looked forward to talking to her daughter by phone. 'Then we'll have no trouble hearing each other and we can have a nice, long, quiet talk,' she continued. 'It'll be wonderful to hear her real voice and not that awful sound that comes over the radiophone.'

Saturday morning, 19 January 1957, was cold and overcast, and the TWA plane from Paris was already a good two hours late. Some of the journalists awaiting Ingrid's arrival at Idlewild Airport were cynical about the whole thing, particularly about a motley group of 'fans' camped out in the arrivals lounge, carrying signs of welcome ('DEAR INGRID: THANK YOU FOR RETURNING – THE ALVIN GANG'; 'WEL-COME HOME, MISS BERGMAN – THE ALVIN GANG'). The reporters were connoisseurs of publicity stunts; they would have bet a lukewarm cup of coffee that the whole bunch had been hired by 20th Century-Fox. One of the reporters was intrepid enough to go up to the 'fans' and ask them some impertinent questions, hoping to add a sardonic paragraph or two to his story.

The 'fans' were indeed fans and they viewed the reporters as out to assassinate Ingrid anew; they included four members of the group that a decade before had stood outside the Alvin Theater when she played in *Joan of Lorraine*. Warren Thomas was the most loyal of the loyal, who saw in the woman he called 'my lady' a moral and spiritual perfection rarely found on this earth. He loved her with a fidelity and concern that none of Ingrid's lovers had ever shown her. He was sixteen when all Ingrid's public trouble had begun; he had written her in Italy but received no reply. He tried to pass messages on through columnists and others flying to Rome, but that hadn't worked either. He had joined the army in the hope of being assigned to Europe; he was sent to Korea instead. To welcome Ingrid back, Warren with Adaire and Frank of the old Alvin Gang and a few other friends had come out to the airport in the middle of the night. On the subway they had pulled down advertising placards and on the back written some more welcoming messages in lipstick. When the reporter accused the group of being mere hirelings, Warren exploded.

The plane finally glided down and taxied towards the terminal. The passengers quickly descended, everyone except for Ingrid. Five minutes. Ten minutes. Still, no Ingrid. Finally she appeared, standing there in a full-length mink and a white kerchief, waving at the hundred or so photographers, reporters and fans. The photographers and cameramen surged forward. Whatever doubts the journalists might have had about Ingrid were all over now. There was no other star in America with such a radiant glow, a light that shone in good movies and bad movies alike.

'Miss Bergman, do you have any criticisms of the way the press in general handled the story of your life?' one reporter asked.

'Oh, sure I had some criticism,' Ingrid said, half smiling. 'I think a person has to have a private life. But I also know that if you choose being an actress, you have to take both sides of the coin. So there it is.' She seemed both a sophisticated European woman and a wistful child.

'Looking back on it, do you have any regrets about anything that you've done in the last few years, Miss Bergman?' a reporter asked.

'No, I have no regrets at all,' she said, suddenly serious. 'I regret the things I didn't do, not what I did.' Ingrid threw her head back and laughed. 'No, I think my life has been wonderful,' she continued, speaking with the intensity she often showed when talking of her past. 'I have done what I felt like. I was given courage and I was given adventure and that has carried me along. And then also a sense of humour and a little bit of common sense. It has been a very rich life.'

She was driven to the Pierre Hotel, where she was to stay with Irene Selznick. She had scarcely time to chat a little with Irene and change before she was off to the exclusive Colony Restaurant for lunch with Buddy Adler, the 20th Century-Fox production chief. This was supposed to be a private luncheon, but Adler reported that within minutes there were 'at least fifty photographers from every wire service, syndicate and magazine surrounding us. She posed for their pictures throughout lunch.' Adler could smell the fragrance of adulation once again blooming around Ingrid. He was willing to take full credit for signing her to do *Anastasia*. Now he was attempting to sign her to a long-term contract.

It was not just the producers and publicists and photographers and other professional admirers who hovered around Ingrid; as she left the Colony a crowd of perhaps a thousand fans stood in the street. With the help of eight policemen, Adler led Ingrid to her next stop: a matinée performance of *My Fair Lady*, the biggest hit in New York. Saturday matinées on Broadway are as glamorous as jars of cold cream, but as soon as the audience saw Ingrid slip silently into her orchestra seat, there was a tremor of excitement. As the musical ended, Ingrid applauded like everyone else and then left to go backstage. The audience gave her a standing ovation as great as the one they had given Rex Harrison, Julie Andrews, and the rest of the cast.

Wherever Ingrid went that day there were crowds to greet her. Two thousand fans waited in the street when she stopped at the Roxy Theater, where *Anastasia* was playing with such success. There were crowds in the evening outside '21' when she arrived for dinner, and crowds when she left. There were crowds outside Sardi's, where she went to appear on television's *Steve Allen Show* and then to receive the New York Critics Award. And there were crowds when she left.

Ingrid had won not only the fans but New York's proudly cynical journalists, whose stories *Newsweek* called 'well-nigh rhapsodic'. She could have spent much of Sunday merely reading the press accounts. Instead, she went off to see Robert Anderson, who had returned to the United States on 5 January. It was a visit that could have embroiled her in a new romantic controversy.

'I had given her a big gold bracelet,' Anderson remembers. 'She said that at the airport the bracelet created a big stir. "Who gave it to you?" they asked. She wouldn't say. The next day she came over to my apartment and was well chaperoned by Irene Selznick. She was taking a big risk as it was. I thought it was pretty brave of her to have the car drive up in front of my place. I said to Ingrid, "When I come back and take a place on the Left Bank, may I see you?" And she was always a little hesitant. She said, "Come, but don't come now." I think she felt the relationship had gone its course.'

Ingrid had found time on Saturday to call Hedda Hopper in Hollywood, ensuring that she would be the subject of Hopper's Sunday column. She did not find time to call Pia until Sunday, before she left.

Pia tried to live her own life, but she was haunted by Ingrid's legacy. She told reporters that she had had a 'nice' conversation, but her attempt at diplomacy was not completely successful; she said that she could not remember the previous occasion on which she had talked to her mother.

As the plane took off, Ingrid wrote to Anderson on pages in a small notebook:

> Dear Bob,
> . . . I cried. I turned my face out the window, so no one would see it. I am so tired, Bob, but I was also moved by all the people that were there . . . I was just on the verge of breaking down and cry in front of them . . .

On Monday evening Ingrid was back once again on the stage of the Théâtre de Paris, back alone at the Raphaël, half a world away from her husband. In many respects she had the best life she had known in years. She was the star of one of the biggest hits in Paris, and she was being wooed by producers and studios again.

She was up for the Academy Award as well. The night of the award ceremony, 27 March 1957, she took a sleeping pill so that she would not toss and turn all night; in Hollywood, Cary Grant had agreed to accept the award for her, if she won. 'I seldom went to the ceremony unless I had been nominated, and even then reluctantly,' Grant remembers. 'But I turned up that night so that no other person could get up and say, "Dear Ingrid, we forgive you". All that crap. I didn't want to risk anyone else getting up.'

When Ingrid's name was called, Grant stepped forward: 'Dear Ingrid, wherever you are in the world, we, your friends, want to congratulate you, and I have your Oscar here for your marvellous performance, and may you be as happy as we are for you.' Ingrid was sitting in the bathtub when the 20th Century-Fox publicist called to tell her that she had won.

Late in April, Anderson visited Ingrid, to spend his fortieth birthday with her. Like so many men before him, Anderson sought to break through to her, to share a profound intimacy with her. They had come together in a moment of mutual need and pain. For Ingrid, though, what was past was past. When the playwright returned in June from the Congo, where he was working on *The Nun's Story*, Ingrid had a new suitor, introduced to her by Kay Brown. The agent had come to Paris to discuss a new movie deal. She had another client to see as well, Lars Schmidt, a theatrical producer, also living at the Raphaël. Kay didn't consider matchmaking her metier, but she thought two Swedes working in Paris – indeed, living in the same hotel – should meet.

Lars took Ingrid to the Coq d'Or for dinner. Ingrid stared at her

Swedish compatriot and told him how bizarre it was that they had never met. Lars said that they had met, the evening Ingrid attended Lars' production of *Cat on a Hot Tin Roof*.

But she didn't remember the elegant gentleman who had poured her champagne between acts. She thought he was the head-waiter.

Lars did, indeed, have the manner of a headwaiter. He carried simple matters of eating, drinking, socializing, to such perfection that it seemed a livelihood on its own.

The next time Lars called Ingrid, to invite her to lunch, Anderson was back in town. She declined with a white lie, Lars caught her out, and their friendship was launched.

Ingrid's marital life might have developed in the predictable pattern of so many professional marriages. She would have her affairs, and Roberto would have his, and they would meet at the accountant's and at family gatherings, and have occasional interludes of cohabitation. But that was not Roberto's way. On 17 May 1957, at 3.27 a.m., Ingrid was wakened by a half-hysterical husband. He said that she must not believe anything she heard, that it was all nothing but blackmail.

Roberto was having a torrid affair with a very wellborn, and very married, Indian woman. Indian women simply did not have affairs, and certainly not with married Italian directors. Much as he had in Beverly Hills, Roberto had befriended the husband, Hari Das Gupta. Das Gupta loaned and eventually sold Roberto his American station wagon, invited him to dinner, and introduced him to his beautiful twenty-seven-year-old wife, Sonali, the mother of their two small children. Roberto was almost immediately infatuated with the doe-eyed, silken beauty.

Sonali was not the only Indian woman to whom he was attracted. Later, an Indian film starlet told reporters that she had dated Roberto soon after his arrival in Bombay. She had gone to his room at the Taj Mahal Hotel in Bombay to discuss movie projects but had left when he took off his shoes and 'the atmosphere was too intimate'. His cameraman Aldo Tonti, says, 'There was another woman he tried with too. She also was married. But Rossellini loved Sonali . . . With women Rossellini was an enchanter. He talked and talked and talked.'

Sonali was not only a great beauty but a woman of strong intellectual interests; he could talk to her the way he could not talk to Ingrid. By the time Roberto called Ingrid, however, there was little time for intellectual discussions. The story of his latest romance was about to break and Sonali was ensconced in the Taj Mahal Hotel, in a suite adjoining Roberto's, protected by hotel guards from her husband and his relatives. Sonali came from a prominent Indian family, and when Prime Minister Nehru learned of the love nest he reportedly called Roberto a 'scoundrel'.

'My wife and I have much understanding,' Roberto told a reporter in his less than impeccable English. The reporter said that if he hurt Ingrid, the women of the world would consider him a Dracula. 'Tell the women of the world they have nothing to worry about,' Roberto replied nobly. 'I know my wife. She is a strong woman, stronger than I in many ways. She is very independent. Believe me, I know what I have done to her life, how she has suffered. But remember, she did what she wanted to. I did not kidnap her, and we have had a good life together. What else about me worries the women of the world?'

Roberto was told that the women of the world were interested in knowing why he was such a success with their sex.

'I don't know the secret of my influence over women,' Roberto said. 'But I'll say women are very human, easily touched by a humble, simple, honest man, and I do pride myself on being absolutely honest about my work and myself.'

'And your women?'

'And my women.'

On 29 May the Italian embassy announced that Roberto had promised to stay away from Sonali, a promise that would have sounded familiar to anyone who had been in Messina in early May 1949. Within a few weeks Roberto was in deepest trouble again. He was planning to leave India, but because of tax and other legalities he was not being allowed to take his film with him. He had another problem: Sonali was pregnant.

In Paris, Ingrid gave some of her most skilful performances. 'There were tears,' said Simone Paris, her fellow actress in *Tea and Sympathy*. 'When she heard about Roberto and that Indian girl, she sobbed hysterically backstage. She said, "How am I going to play?" But somehow, at the last minute, she pulled herself together and did it.' She knew that her saintly image had long been superseded by that of a passionate woman who sacrificed everything for love. What did it say about *that* Ingrid if Roberto could debase their marriage in open scandal? She wrote Steele that it was all false, created by a reporter upset with Roberto.

Roberto and Sonali were indeed in great trouble in a land where the traditional wives' manual states: 'Be her husband deformed, aged, infirm, offensive . . . debauched, immoral . . . a wife should always look upon him as her god.' Sonali had been denied a passport to leave India, but that was resolved. Now Roberto's most immediate problem was to get his film out.

Early in July, he called Paris once again in the middle of the night. According to Ingrid, he told her that it was all lies. Nonetheless the one person who could extricate Roberto was Nehru, the Prime Minister of India. Ingrid called her friend Ann Todd to try to help Roberto. Ingrid knew that Ann and her husband, David Lean, were friendly with Vijaya Lakshi Pandit, the Indian ambassador in London, and Nehru's sister.

Todd set up a dinner for the following evening, 5 July; *Tea and Sympathy* was in summer recess, and the children had already been sent to Italy. At the ambassador's residence, Ingrid met Nehru, who was in London for the Commonwealth Conference. Nehru made no promises, but Roberto's problems in India ended almost immediately.

Ingrid flew back to Paris and on to Rome, where five-year-old Isabella had undergone an emergency appendectomy. Isabella was fine, but Ingrid's life was still in crisis; the papers were full of stories of Roberto's new romance. While, in India, Roberto publicly denied that he was coming back to spend the summer with his wife, Ingrid told reporters: 'We will spend the summer together at our Santa Marinella villa as we always have since our marriage.'

Then Pia's arrival in Paris to spend the summer with her, so Ingrid had to turn around and fly back to Paris. The press was chronicling Pia's journey as if it were a historic event. On 5 July, the *Los Angeles Times* had a front-page photo of Petter and Pia at the airport. On 6 July the papers noted that Pia was in Stockholm, on her way to see Ingrid.

Pia was now a nineteen-year-old college student. Her hair was blonde, her eyes deep blue. She was pretty, tall, and slightly plump, appearing not voluptuous but as if she were still carrying baby fat. She was charming but some observers felt a coldness in her, a mistrustfulness. Her arrival at Le Bourget on 8 July 1957, was the most dramatic moment in her life since she had told Judge Lillie that she did not love Ingrid. Some seventy-five reporters and photographers waited, about the same number that had covered Queen Elizabeth's recent state visit to France. The other passengers left the plane first. Then Ingrid entered to see Pia in private before running the gauntlet of reporters. As mother and daughter stood before one another, with a look as much wary as loving, a flashbulb illuminated their first greeting. The photographer who had been hiding on the plane, had the exclusive photo for which *Paris Match* was paying him.

Later that day Ingrid and Pia left the Hotel Raphaël to dine in a café in Montmartre. 'Mama ordered a bottle of champagne,' Pia remembers. 'We drank to our meeting again, to happiness and the best of days.' Pia spent over a month with her mother, travelling to Rome, Santa Marinella, and Capri, visiting Robertino, Isabella, Isotta, and other Rossellinis. She had never been to Italy before, and her mother, the *paparazzi*, the daily drama of Ingrid's life, all blended together in a cacophony of images and memories.

'That summer I fell in love with Italy,' Pia said later. 'The family camaraderie in Italy, the buoyant expression of feeling, the loving care and consideration for others – all this provided an armour against loneliness.'

Pia says now that the trip was a 'media circus'. It was indeed that, but much of the time Ingrid was the ringmaster. She was the one who invited a photographer into her suite at the Raphaël to take intimate 'candid' shots of mother and daughter. She seemed always to understand what the journalists wanted. She complained frequently about the press, but it was thrilling to have photographers and reporters constantly about, especially for Pia.

Who could blame Pia if she found life with Ingrid more exciting than her life in America? And who could blame Ingrid if for a few weeks she found solace with her daughter.

On 18 August, Ingrid and Pia flew from Rome to Copenhagen. Ingrid said goodbye to Pia, who immediately got on another plane to join her father in Stockholm. The photographers noticed that whereas Ingrid always smiled for them, today she looked downcast.

Roberto flew into Paris on 21 October, after an absence of ten months. As soon as he got off the plane, he was deluged by reporters and photographers asking about Sonali, who was rumoured to be in Paris already. 'It is rubbish – how you say rubbish,' Roberto said emphatically. 'This girl means nothing to me. I love my wife.' In the midst of this, Ingrid appeared, running towards Roberto across the crowded arrivals lounge. She hugged her husband, and they kissed on the cheeks in the Italian manner. 'I am very happy,' she said, her eyes glistening with tears. It was a touching scene. And at the request of the photographers, she kissed Roberto a few more times. As a director, Roberto believed in one take, but he kissed Ingrid back. 'That's enough,' Ingrid said finally, and she and Roberto left in a waiting car.

In the privacy of her hotel suite, Ingrid vented her anger. They both knew that it was all over. They discussed terms of divorce. According to Ingrid, Roberto agreed that she should have the children, but asked that they never go to the United States, a demand that echoed Petter's feeling about Pia and Italy. He also asked that

Ingrid never remarry, a demand that brought a smile to Ingrid's face.

Tea and Sympathy had finally closed. Early in November, Ingrid returned to Rome to finalize the divorce and end her life in Italy. On 7 November 1957, she and Roberto appeared secretly before Rome Civil Court President Mario Elia to sign a separation agreement. As they had agreed in Paris, Ingrid was given custody of the three children; they would be educated in Europe in the Italian language. Roberto agreed to pay $976 a month for their support.

On the day they signed the agreement, they went to the apartment on Bruno Buozzi. And there in the bathroom was the dog they had named Stromboli and taken to the island back in the summer of 1949. The dog was dead. As the time for Ingrid's departure approached, she finished packing the last few things she would take from the apartment that she and Roberto had shared. Roberto watched her, as she methodically and neatly put things into her suitcase. The apartment was bare now of almost everything but memories. There was only one painting left on the wall, a painting that Ingrid had never liked.

'Ingrid, take also that painting,' Roberto said.

'It's not good,' Ingrid said firmly. 'I don't like it.'

'But it's a very important painting,' Roberto said.

'Who is the painter?' Ingrid asked, suddenly curious.

'It's a Guttuso,' Roberto said, naming a prominent contemporary Italian artist.

'How much does it cost?'

'Oh, very much.'

'Then I'll take it away.'

Ingrid got up on a chair and took down the painting by Renato Guttuso. Soon afterwards, she was gone, leaving Roberto sitting in the empty apartment, alone with Father Lisandrini. The priest kept thinking about Ingrid taking the painting down. 'You have no money,' he scolded. 'You could have sold it to somebody and made enough to live on for a month.'

Roberto looked at the priest, full of rage. 'You . . . you . . . you Franciscan father!' Roberto shouted. 'You son of St Francis of the Poor. You! You tell me this thing.'

CHAPTER 18

A MAN OF PERFECT MANNERS

Ingrid flew out of Rome like a star, with a sable coat, fifteen pieces of baggage, and no children. When the plane landed in London, where she was to begin work on *Indiscreet*, Grant and Donen were waiting for her. So were the photographers and reporters.

Ingrid tried to sound as upbeat as possible, saying that the first thing she was going to do was to find 'a home big enough for all my children'. The reporters were not as interested in her immediate future as in her immediate past. 'Why don't you leave me alone?' she implored wearily. 'I will say no more.'

'Come on, boys,' Grant said finally, gently shepherding Ingrid towards his waiting silver-and-white Rolls Royce. 'You've had enough.'

Like Grant, Ingrid was as bankable as a pound note. She was a modern, independent Hollywood star now, a creature as much of commerce as of art. Indeed, the most creative aspect of *Indiscreet* was not what would appear on the screen but the deal itself. The primary owners of the film were not a studio but Cary Grant and Stanley Donen's corporations. Grant's deal even included the Rolls Royce, which would be used in the film and then become his property. Ingrid's deal included 2,327,000 francs for her wardrobe, $75,000 as an 'employment contract', plus 10 per cent of the gross above $4,000,000 and the payment of any excess taxes because the picture was shot outside Italy.

This was a great deal of money. But when Ingrid arrived at the Connaught Hotel she had nothing. 'Mother had to borrow a hundred dollars from the hotel,' says her daughter Isotta. Steele wrote, concerned about Ingrid's financial situation. She reassured him: 'I am finally planning to get rich . . . By the time I have finished these pictures, we will have "champagne and caviar" every day.' She approached her renewed film activity with a gambler's eternal optimism, as if it were a bet on a horse race, or a pull on a slot machine. Only, with this kind of gambling, if you were the star, and the contract was right, the game was indeed a sure thing.

Indiscreet represented a coming out for Ingrid as a romantic comedienne and as a sophisticated, elegant lady of the screen. In this endeavour, Grant was a perfect partner. He may have been fifty-five years old, but he was still a role model for many young men, as well as the romantic ideal of women half his age. Since the days when he and Ingrid had worked together on *Notorious*, Grant had developed a persona of lighthearted sophistication; he was a man who showed his feelings to about the same degree that he showed his cuffs.

The publicist promoted the film as if it had three stars: Ingrid, Grant, and Ingrid's wardrobe. That was just as well, for *Indiscreet* had an anorexic plot. The story was little more than a device that allowed Ingrid and Cary to be relentlessly amusing and gay, wear elegant clothes and go to elegant places. The story, such as it was, concerned Ann Kalman, a wealthy, world-weary actress, with just enough similarities to Ingrid to allow the audience to think that they were watching life itself, if only they could get there. She meets a NATO official, Philip Adams, a confirmed bachelor who tells Ann that he is married to a woman who refuses to grant him a divorce. In the end, he admits the truth and proposes marriage. *Indiscreet* was an hour and a half of pleasant diversion provided by two actors who enjoyed the sheer craft of making a film. 'She was so good on camera because she had a completely rooted quality,' Donen says. 'She was completely at ease. She never seized up while acting. Her concentration was complete. She was in her element.'

Ingrid was glad to be out of the daily realities of her second marriage, and talked often of the sheer magic of filmmaking, in an 'atmosphere of makebelieve. The people who work in them are like children creating an illusion.' 'We had a wonderful time making the film,' Grant recalls. 'I found her a joy to be with. One day she said, "Do you realize the two of us make a hundred years together?"'

Ingrid was off by a couple of years, but *Indiscreet* seemed to prove that romance is wasted on the young. So did Ingrid's personal life. Anderson wrote saying that he was coming to London to live, and asking if he still had his toe in the door. Ingrid answered that although he might still have a toe in, Lars Schmidt had his whole foot inside.

Since their meeting in Paris, Ingrid's romance with her compatriot had blossomed. Lars looked very Swedish, so much so that he could have been Petter's brother. He was tall and blond and handsome, and wore horn-rimmed glasses that gave him a vaguely intellectual look. A man of perfect manners and grace, he had certain similarities to Cary Grant's character in *Indiscreet*. Not only did he intend to remain single, but at his best he was full of gracious repartee that could have been lifted from the film's dialogue. He was a producer, not a wildly romantic, irresponsible director, nor an ambitious surgeon. He was a man who could advise Ingrid on matters large and small, a man who listened for hours as she talked about movies, the theatre, and herself.

Ingrid's life in London was all so wonderfully civilized. She had planned to bring the children here, but finally decided against it. Roberto was proving difficult; the London winter was dreary and cold, and she preferred to leave the children a bit longer in Rome, with the nanny and Marcella, her former sister-in-law. She would bring them back with her after Christmas. As the holidays approached, however, she decided that that wouldn't do either. She was indeed involved in a legal dispute over final custody, but appeared more interested in her film career than in her children. Moreover, in February she would be off to Formosa on location for her new film, *The Inn of the Sixth Happiness*. Even during the periods when she could have spent more time with her children, she did not. She flew to Rome on 23 December 1957, and spent only a week with them before they were sent to Switzerland for a long vacation.

She was back in London in time to spend New Year's Eve with Lars; they greeted the new year in front of Big Ben, toasting each other with champagne, then they went off to the Milroy Club for Donen's party, and danced and drank till dawn.

Ingrid had not wanted to become seriously involved again so soon, but she was not a woman who could get along without a man for very long. There were still aspects of life that she felt incapable of dealing with on her own; and she hated solitude. Lars took care of her the way no man ever had. He was willing to organize her life, to be everything for her from banker to valet, publicist to lover. He had a producer's ego, revelling not in publicity but in creating publicity. He enjoyed not applause for himself but knowing that without him there would be no applause.

He had been born into a wealthy shipping family in Göteborg. As a young man he travelled to Wales to learn firsthand about the shipping business. He spent part of the Second World War in New York, where he was introduced to Broadway theatre life. He bought the foreign rights to the hit *Arsenic and Old Lace*, and began a lucrative career, primarily taking Broadway plays and producing them in Scandinavia and elsewhere in Europe.

Lars was a man who was always seeking ultimates. He sought them not in religion or in art but in the details of life. He could not write plays himself, but watched over every facet of their production, meticulous and demanding to a fault. In his personal life, every meal had to be right, every towel in place, every flower arrangement exquisite, every ashtray clean. Life is full of dirty ashtrays, and hardly a day went by when Lars didn't experience endless petty frustrations, demands not met or half fulfilled, and people who did not measure up. The great sadness of his life was not the failure of his first marriage but the death of his son, electrocuted when he put his fingers in a power socket. It was not something that he talked about, but he had been as much affected by it as Roberto had been by the death of *his* son.

There was a spiritual aspect to Lars, and in March Ingrid travelled with him to Sweden to see that part of the man whom she was considering marrying. The area on the southwest coast of Sweden where Lars was taking Ingrid could have been in Japan; the Swedes are, in fact, in certain ways like the Japanese. They are both people of almost rigid decorum, who suddenly explode in reverie, or drunkenness, in excessive joy or sadness. They have a similar aesthetic sense too, seeing beauty in simple things.

The fishing boat from the village of Fjällbacka cut its way through the ice towards the island that Lars had recently purchased. As the boat approached, Ingrid could see that Danholmen was little more than a rock in the water: a hectare of land, and two large, plain wooden houses. The ice age had smoothed the rocky surface until it was like glass. There was nothing there; no electricity, no telephone, no neighbours – nothing but the sea and the sky and the rocks and the two wooden houses.

'The house was upside down,' Lars remembers. 'It became her place as much as mine.'

Ingrid was not willing quite yet to say publicly that she would marry Lars, but when they returned to his large family estate in Göteborg, the reporters asked Lars about a marriage. 'We can neither deny nor confirm that,' Lars said. 'That says a lot, doesn't it?'

They were both in their early forties, entering a graceful middle age; they were in the same profession. If it was not a mad passion, so what; Ingrid knew where mad, impulsive gestures led.

'Ingrid said, "You want to get married to me and I want to get married to you,"' Lars remembers. 'She said, "But no man will ever be able to play the second fiddle." Ingrid knew her strength. She knew a man would always blame her for being first. I said, "You have a big ego. And I may have a big ego too. I'm fairly successful and you're successful too."'

Ingrid was almost devoid of insight into the kind of man she needed, nor was she perceptive about her future husband. She believed that Lars was not only extremely honest but highly uncomplicated, though he was an immensely complicated man, capable of deviousness. She believed, as she wrote to Steele, that for the first time in her life she had a lover without a large ego.

Ingrid could not get a divorce in Catholic Italy; before she and Lars could get married, her marriage to Roberto had to be annulled. This was done by arguing that their Mexican marriage had not been legal in the first place. In June 1958 the courts voided the eight-year marriage, creating considerable controversy. A high Vatican official told UPI: 'We reach this enormity – two persons first go through all legal strategy and tactics to justify their concubinage, and when the experience is over they themselves admit that the so-called marriage was null and void.' The annulment was scandalous enough to Italian conservatives that in August the Roman prosecutor filed an appeal, preventing Ingrid from marrying legally for a number of months.

Because of problems with the Chinese Nationalists, *The Inn of the Sixth Happiness* was filmed not in Taiwan but in Wales. Ingrid played Gladys Aylward, a British servant who decides to go to China to do missionary work, converting the Chinese to Christianity. In *Europe '51*, she had played a bourgeois Roman lady who sets out to help the poor, and discovers that in the modern world there are few things as difficult as truly to help another person.

In Hollywood of the 1950s everything was possible, however, everything except casting Chinese as Chinese. Better, by far, to have a dying Robert Donat play the cynical mandarin, with a cynical mandarin's beard and eyebrows, and to have Curt Jurgens play the Nationalist general – after all, a German was exotic enough. The movie reeked of goodness, as good Gladys leads a hundred singing orphans over the mountain, the screen awash in Technicolor. *Time* said that the film contained 'more sheer treacle than anybody has seen since the Great Boston Molasses Flood . . . the woman's simple story comes to seem rather like a Cecil B. DeMille version of "Now I Lay Me Down to Sleep."'

Isotta and Isabella came to visit their mother in Wales. They travelled like rich gypsies, from place to place, from parent to parent. UPI noted: 'The children have divided their time between father and mother in Rome, Paris, London, Wales and the resort coast of central Italy.' In Wales, Ingrid decided that it was time to tell the six-year-old twins that their mother was planning to remarry.

Isotta and Isabella lived in their own world, above such traumas as divorce or remarriage. Robertino was not as enthusiastic about Ingrid's remarrying, but even he tolerated the idea of his mother living with Lars. 'I was maybe a little jealous,' Robertino says. 'My father was so furious. Maybe he pushed us a little.'

Lars drove Ingrid and her children to Choisel, an hour outside Paris. Here he had purchased an estate, where he hoped they would make their home.

Roberto was spending much time in Paris, where Sonali was hidden away. He was bitterly disdainful of Lars. He did not want Ingrid to remarry, but it was doubly painful that it would be a man like the Swedish producer, a businessman of the arts. He was suspicious of a man who would buy an estate with his future wife, and yet have the papers in his name only. Ingrid said that this was done simply to hide the matter from the press, but it was the beginning of Lars's careful management of Ingrid's finances. Almost the entire Rossellini family thought that Ingrid was making a terrible mistake. 'Some of them felt that Lars was not a creative person and was after Ingrid for the prestige of her name and for her money,' says Franco Rossellini, Roberto's cousin.

Roberto was a man of overweening pride. He might complain and condemn Lars until eternity, but one fact remained: in a failed marriage, the best revenge is no revenge at all, to go on and love again, and to forget the pains of the past. Ingrid had done just that, leaving Roberto mired in his problems.

The children served as human antidepressants, pulling him up out of his despair. It didn't matter that it would be hard for him to give the children the home they needed. He wanted them, and more than that, he needed them.

In October, Ingrid went to a railway station in Paris to pick up her children and the maid. Roberto was at the station as well, for after he put them on the train in Rome, he had flown to Paris. Roberto insisted that the children come with him to stay at his hotel. In the end Roberto put Robertino in his car and Ingrid drove off with the twins.

One of those present that day to witness Ingrid's anger was Joe Steele. He was living through hard times. Ingrid had been the greatest thing in his life, and he had nothing to show for it but clippings and letters and memories. He had saved no money, and in Hollywood he was reduced to taking piecemeal jobs as the unit publicist on quickie, ten-day pictures. Another man might have figured that Ingrid owed him something, not Steele. Instead, he decided that he would write a book about her. Steele was in his early sixties; he had lived a peripatetic publicist's life; he had never experienced the solitary confinement of writing a book. For months he sat over the typewriter that Ingrid had given him fifteen years before, not taking a full day off for close to two years, going ever deeper into debt.

It was a work of love. He filled the pages with Ingrid's letters and private conversations, and thoughts. He knew that he would have to get Ingrid's permission, and when he was finished, he borrowed five hundred dollars and flew to Paris. Ingrid read the manuscript and said that it was fine and true, and eventually *Ingrid Bergman: An Intimate Portrait* was published. Steele made some money, though not nearly as much as he had hoped, and while Ingrid stayed friendly with him, privately she condemned her old publicist for making money out of her life.

Ingrid wanted to rid herself of Roberto and his problems. She wished to formalize her marriage as soon as it was finally feasible. In Rome, however, the appeal dragged on and on, and Lars took action. 'I met an English barrister,' Lars says. 'He said, "Do you want to get married or not?" He said that we shouldn't worry about the legal situation. Ingrid can never be a bigamist. And so we decided to go ahead. This was at a time when we were followed everywhere. *Paris Match* said they'd be at our wedding. I said let's make a bet.'

Lars managed the wedding with the same meticulousness that he gave to his theatrical productions. The ceremony took place at 11.15 a.m., 21 December 1958, at Caxton Hall which is a favourite wedding spot for celebrities, but not on a Sunday morning, when the building is empty except for watchmen, and the street outside bare of traffic and onlookers. To ensure privacy, Lars had told practically no one except the guests: Lars's old friends Göran and Marianne von Essen, his attorney Ambrose Appelbe, and the Sidney Bernsteins. After a champagne luncheon at the Connaught, the newlyweds flew to Paris with the von Essens. By the time the group reached Choisel, Bernstein had announced the wedding on Granada Television, and they were soon under siege. Reporters pushed and jostled outside the gates, climbed up on the walls, and tried to force their way into the house.

Lars was not going to be held hostage inside his house, and he called the police. French gendarmes are not usually called out to shoo away photographers; they could not understand why Lars and Ingrid didn't simply let the journalists get their pictures and go back to Paris. Lars was not going to face photographers and reporters on his wedding day; it was not until the next morning that pictures were taken of the smiling, happy couple.

Ingrid was sure that this time her marriage would last. Lars might look a little like Petter, but he was tolerant and understanding in a way that Ingrid felt her first husband was not. Lars wasn't like Roberto either, burdening her with his melodrama, his debts, and his artistic dreams. This time, Ingrid had thought the thing through. She was settling for something realistic; she was sure that she would obtain it.

At first glance, Choisel seemed very much Ingrid's home. Lars had filled the rooms with souvenirs of Ingrid's career and life. On the walls were two paintings by Ingrid's father: a self-portrait and an oil of her mother. There was a three-foot painting of Ingrid in *Joan of Arc* that once had been a lobby display, and a bronze of her as Joan from her days in *Joan of Lorraine*. On a desk there was yet another souvenir of her career as Joan: autographed photographs of Arthur Honegger and Paul Claudel, the composer and librettist of *Joan at the Stake*. There were also autographed photographs of Ernest Hemingway and Maurice Chevalier.

Despite Ingrid's mementos throughout the house, Choisel represented Lars's taste far more than it did Ingrid's. He was the master of Choisel. Ingrid thought that she cared about neatness and cleanliness as much as anyone, but she was practically slovenly compared to Lars.

For a while Ingrid enjoyed playing the mistress of Choisel and having Lars totally managing her investments and business. Indeed, if one symbol of their marriage was Choisel, the other was a small, seventh-floor walk-up apartment in Geneva that allowed Ingrid Swiss tax status.

Once, Dora Jane Hamblin, a writer for *Life*, spent the weekend at Choisel. 'My sense was that it was clearly an adult love affair,' she remembers. 'If they were put in separate beds for the night, they wouldn't have been upset. They weren't demonstrative in their affection, but they amused one another. The children were there too, and Lars was dealing with the kids. She treated the children as if they were adults, very cool, while he was indulgent.' Lars was the grand host, offering 'a tour of Scandinavia by aquavit', serving glasses of the fiery Scandinavian liquor, to the occasional accompaniment of a Swedish drinking song. Then it was time for another Scandinavian custom, a nude jump in the sauna.

Though their marriage began well enough, Lars and Ingrid were not the kindred spirits that they appeared to be. As her two previous husbands had discovered, there was an impenetrable quality to Ingrid, and large aspects of life in which she had absolutely no interest. Lars was a man of deep intelligence, and though Ingrid was highly perceptive about the plays Lars produced, there were many things that she could not talk about. He was not beyond putting her down, even in the presence of guests. Though he found having Ingrid as a wife helpful professionally, he was far from comfortable with all the publicity.

'We were too much in the limelight, but I think Ingrid liked publicity in a way,' Lars says. She could never admit that; she always played the coy maiden startled by the burst of attention. Sometimes the press was an irritant, but it was no more a problem to Ingrid than a rough sea is to a sailor. Even her children, particularly Robertino and Isabella, were slowly learning to regard them as a natural part of life. 'I may be more honest than the others, but I think Mother and Father both hated and enjoyed the publicity,' Isabella says. 'I sensed that myself. When they are not there it's frightening. You lose your social status. All of a sudden you get frightened to go to a restaurant. You sort of fear that now you're not going to be spoiled any more. And it's a very frightening feeling. And I think that all the family had that.'

At Choisel, Ingrid was too far from the bustle of photographers, the happy nods of recognition, the life of streets and people, the laughter and energy of the boulevard. Choisel was boring. Lars treated her like a precious objet d'art that he had accumulated on his travels, to be appraised, catalogued, and set down in its appropriate place. He was often off on trips. 'Separation is not good,' Lars says. 'She had that enormous personality to handle with her private and public life. At Choisel she'd come back after a picture and say, "I've been sitting here for ten days. I can't sit out here." I had a lot to do. I should have been there more. She should have been there.'

Ingrid enjoyed their forays to Paris, to attend the opera, theatrical openings, dinner parties. Unfortunately, though Choisel was only an hour from Paris, it was a world away from the excitements and energy of the city. Ingrid could not walk here, as she loved to walk, strolling along the pavements looking into shopwindows, gazing into the anonymous faces. She had no friends with whom she could on a moment's notice go out for lunch. As much as she enjoyed Choisel for short intervals, she enjoyed setting off from it even more. And slowly, very slowly, she became a wife of the special occasion, as she was already a mother of the special occasion.

She would have been better off living in Paris for other reasons as well. In January 1959 she won a provisional ruling by a French court, giving her custody of the three children. The court ruled, however, that they must attend an Italian school in Paris. The court ruled also that their father could have access at weekends. To ensure that the children did not leave France, their passports were surrendered to the judge.

The dilemma facing Ingrid was common enough among divorced parents. Roberto made things difficult. He could hardly bring himself to mention Lars's name. He couldn't stand the fact that the children were with Lars. In a letter to Ingrid, he wrote that when the children were in Rome, 'they don't see this stranger and they are happier and they are always more comfortable with me'. It was inevitable that Roberto would be jealous of Lars, and worried that he might steal the children's affection. What was striking, however, was how petty and vindictive he was. Nothing delighted him more than hearing the children tell him of some little trick they had played on Lars, or some argument they had had.

Ingrid fought for legal custody of her children, but she was not willing to make emotional and professional sacrifices. The children could not possibly live at Choisel and commute an hour and a half to the Italian school. Another mother would have insisted that her new husband move with her to Paris so that the family could live together; instead, Ingrid took a suite for the children at the Raphaël, where they lived with Elena, the maid. Since Roberto frequently visited the children on weekends, and they were in school all day, Ingrid saw relatively little of them. But they did not feel that they were suffering. 'We lived in an hotel and we changed rooms sometimes to a cheaper hotel,' Isabella remembers. 'I looked forward to visiting Choisel. We could go to the farm next door and play with the cows. I would come home smelling like shit. Mother wouldn't say no. She would just wash us. It wasn't an emotionally difficult time. I thought that Father was coming every weekend just to visit us. But Father also had Sonali in Paris. Sonali was pregnant and hiding in Paris. Father didn't say right away that he had another relationship. I think that he and Mother were in an emotional stress. The only time I sensed that was when Father had to tell us that he had another woman and family. I really got frightened, because I didn't know what he was going to tell us. He was trembling, looking for words. Father had a much more difficult time expressing himself than Mother. Mother could control herself. I don't think she felt guilty marrying Lars. Maybe my father did feel guilty.'

Roberto's guilt did not reach such heights that he felt he should make his child-support payments. He continued a legal fight for full custody and confined his largess to extravagant presents. One weekend he arrived with a little monkey for his daughters. The management of the Raphaël was running a hotel, not a menagerie, and the monkey was shipped out to Choisel, where Lars had the task of caring for Roberto's gift. On another visit Roberto arrived with a live kangaroo. This was too much even for Choisel, and the animal was shipped by rail to a zoo in Rome. The children had no idea that their father's gifts were wildly impractical. They knew only that they they had a father, a magician who brought joy and excitement, and left as suddenly as he appeared. Of course they didn't realize how much he was struggling in his professional life.

In April 1959 Ingrid and Lars flew to Hollywood to attend the Academy Award ceremonies and several parties. With the worldwide success of *Anastasia* and now *The Inn of the Sixth Happiness*, Ingrid was once again a box office attraction of the first magnitude. There were a hundred reporters and photographers waiting to greet her as she arrived, on 3 April, almost exactly ten years from the day she left Hollywood. That times had changed was signalized by the big news the reporters were after: was she pregnant? Ingrid said that she hoped to have the child that Lars wanted, but 'that's something between God, my husband and myself. And anyway, I don't think I should tell the newspapers before I tell my husband.'

Pia flew down from Mills College in northern California, where she was completing her education. When she saw her mother it seemed always to be at moments of drama and special attention. Pia was a stunning blonde now, so grown up that her mother's representative didn't recognize her when he met her at the airport. He took Pia to Ingrid and Lars's cottage at the Beverly Hills Hotel. 'We will be going to parties, parties,' Ingrid said, 'and Jenny will be with us.' Pia insisted that everyone call her Jenny. She attended the Academy Awards ceremony, where Ingrid presented the award for the best movie of 1958 to Arthur Freed, producer of *Gigi*. 'It is so heart-warming to receive such a welcome,' Ingrid said as the applause for her finally ebbed. 'I feel that I am home. I am so deeply grateful.'

There was a party afterwards and a splendid dinner for two hundred in Ingrid's honour given by Buddy Adler of 20th Century-Fox. And then Ingrid and Lars were off, and Pia was back at school. She spent her holidays with her father's family in their new home in San Francisco, where Petter was chief of neurosurgery at both Presbyterian Medical Center and Children's and Adult Medical Center, with an international reputation for his work with ultrasonic surgery.

Back in Paris, Ingrid continued her struggle with Roberto over the children. In April she petitioned the Italian court to make Roberto pay 9,000,000 lire ($14,500) in back child support and start regularly making the 600,000-lire (about $1000) monthly payments. In September she flew to Rome, where the children were spending the summer with their father at Santa Marinella. There outside the civil court she saw Roberto for the first time since her third marriage. 'Why can't we be friends as we always were?' Roberto asked, as they stepped into the courtroom. Ingrid smiled slightly, and put out her hand.

Inside, Roberto told the judge that Ingrid was a 'bigamist' for having remarried while her annulment was still in question. When Ingrid left the courtroom two hours later, her eyes were red from weeping. She walked down the long corridor alone, and could not even find her way out without the help of a policeman. She had won, turning back Roberto's attempt to win full custody, but at the price of confrontation and pain.

Soon after winning the case, Ingrid flew out of Rome, on her way to New York with Lars to appear in her first television production, Henry James's *The Turn of the Screw*; she was playing the governess. She worked hard with John Frankenheimer, the director, but she loved her free time in Manhattan. She went up and down Broadway, searching for joke gifts for the children: fake flies, wind-up teeth, fake horns that stick on one's forehead. The production was taped one long frustrating evening that lasted well into the morning hours. 'It's no good!' Ingrid shouted after the fourth take. When it was shown on NBC, the critics thought otherwise, and Ingrid would win an Emmy for the year's best dramatic performance by an actress.

By the second week in October, Ingrid was back in Rome, to take the children to Paris. When she called to make the final arrangements, she learned that Roberto had spirited the children away from Santa Marinella and was refusing to give them up. It might seem that the children would suffer profoundly from being used as emotional chattel; but they had grown up in the hot light of publicity and seemed to take it in their stride.

'I don't see why I should be forced to return my children to Ingrid, who is living with a man they cannot stand,' Roberto told a reporter. Nonetheless, under a court order he was told to give up the children by 5.00 p.m. on 15 October. At 4.55 he called Ingrid and gave her an address on Bruno Buozzi, across the street from the apartment where she had once lived. While a UPI photographer with a telephoto lens recorded the exchange, and their mutual attorneys observed, Roberto handed the children back to their mother.

Roberto was not quite ready to give up. He sent a telegram to the police, objecting to the fact that Robertino's passport had been handed over to Ingrid. This was improper, he complained, because Ingrid's name was not mentioned on the boy's birth certificate as his mother. This final gesture was one of extraordinary disdain for a woman who had borne him a son out of wedlock. Roberto was not able to separate his son from his daughters, however, and Ingrid and the three children flew out of Rome on 16 October 1959.

Roberto continued his court fight. Ingrid fought back, matching Roberto revelation by revelation, accusing him of being the father of Sonali's two-year-old daughter. Her attorneys submitted to the court a letter that Roberto had written from India admitting his relationship with Sonali. In June 1960, as the struggle for final custody continued, the court formally annulled the Rossellini marriage.

During the summer Ingrid and Lars took the children to their island for the first time. At first, it was hard for Ingrid to go back to Sweden. Ingrid was bitter as one can be only toward a blood relative. Her memory of her reception in Stockholm during the *Joan of Arc* oratorio was still painful, exaggerated into a time of brutal rejection and stunning impoliteness; but the longer she lived with Lars, and the more often she came to Danholmen, the more she made peace with her native land.

Roberto had filled the children's minds with tales of the bizarre rites of the Swedes, and as much as they enjoyed having their own island, they were wary of them. 'Everyone swam naked,' Isabella remembers. 'But Lars went behind a rock to take off his trunks. I crept up and watched. The next time I saw my father, in order to please him I told him that Lars had a penis like a pig's tail. He laughed and laughed and every time guests would come he would make me tell the story again.'

When the children told Roberto of Lars's new boat, he decided to buy *his* own. But it was a sad old boat, and when he took his children out on the water, it sputtered and coughed and broke down.

Although Ingrid had legal custody of the children, in the fall she sent them back to Italy to live with their father. In Paris she was at work again, on the film version of Françoise Sagan's *Aimez-vous Brahms?* 'I would have little time with them since we start at noon, work until 7, then look at rushes,' she told Hedda Hopper.

That was true enough, but it was clear that Ingrid was more interested in custody of the children as a symbol than as a nurturing day after day obligation.

In *Goodbye Again*, as it was called in America, Ingrid played Paula Tessier, a middle-aged interior decorator. Her love life centres on Roger Demarest, an ageing roué played by Yves Montand. She takes up with Philip Van der Besh, fifteen years her junior. Left without either man, she ends up staring at her ageing, lonely face in the mirror.

Yves Montand was famous in France as a singer, but he was struggling with English and acting. Anthony Perkins would later become a major star in films such as *Friendly Persuasion* and *Psycho*, but he was already considered one of the most promising young stage and screen actors in America. Ingrid was an astute judge of actors and she knew that Perkins was so strong that 'he could steal it'. As for Perkins, although he called Ingrid his 'idol', he went into the picture like a boxer going into the ring with a champion. 'I wanted to remain on my feet,' he said. Soon after completing the film, he told a reporter that when he arrived in Paris, Ingrid had said, 'So you're Tony Perkins. I hear you're pretty good. I guess maybe I better watch out for you.'

Perkins remembers that 'Ingrid started talking about how as an actor she always kept her ego out of it. She said how she'd done a play and she went up to someone and said, "I understand you can be very hard to work with and are very competitive and I don't work that way." I was grateful to her for her frankness and having the first salvo – how wonderfully air-clearing.'

Ingrid's story was possibly apocryphal, but it ensured that the success of *Aimez-vous Brahms?* would be as much due to Ingrid as to Perkins. Soon afterwards, before their first kissing scene in the film, Ingrid called him into her dressing room. 'It'll take time, the kissing,' she said in her most professional voice. 'We'll get it wrong. Let's practise kissing.'

Years later, in a lengthy interview with a reporter from *People*, Perkins remembered how Ingrid had attempted to seduce him. 'She would have welcomed an affair,' he was quoted as saying. 'Every day she invited me to her dressing room to practise a love scene. I insisted on standing near the door, which I kept open.' Perkins now, however, asserts that the quotation was 'a presumably undeliberate distortion of me'.

One day Anatole Litvak, the director, stopped work to wait for evening, to shoot an outdoor scene on the streets of Paris. Ingrid and Perkins went to a small bistro for dinner. Afterwards they walked slowly back towards the shooting. Turning the corner, they could see the cameras and the crew and the lights up the street. In the dark it was like a glowing hearth in the distance.

Ingrid started walking quickly towards the set.

'What's the matter?' Perkins asked urgently.

'Look at that,' she said, pointing towards the scene. 'This is all for me.'

The film was as big a success in Europe as it was a failure in the United States. For every reviewer who talked of Ingrid's 'indestruc-

tible inner grace' or 'compassion and dignity', there was another
reviewer who spoke glowingly of Perkins. 'No one, of course, can
completely cast Miss Bergman into shadow,' noted the *Saturday
Review*, 'and she pulls out a few organ stops of her own (always in
a minor key, though) in an attempt to compete with the astonishing
Mr Perkins.'

Ingrid and Lars were both extremely busy. Lars had won the European rights to *My Fair Lady*, as good a source of wealth as an oil well
in Kuwait. He had time, however, to be the executive producer of
Ingrid's second American television production, *Twenty-four Hours
in a Woman's Life*. Ingrid played Clare, a grandmother, recounting
her sad amorous past.

If *Twenty-four Hours in a Woman's Life* was a fair indication, Lars
was far better at refurbishing American musicals than at producing
projects for his wife. The hour-long drama received almost univer-
sally dreadful reviews. *Variety* reported the rumour that close to half
a million dollars had been squandered on the project. But as boring
as the drama was, the audience realized that it was watching something that was supposed to be serious. Indeed, Ingrid's career in
America had reached the elevated status where her name no longer
meant 'scandal' but 'culture'. She signed an agreement with American
and British television to do plays produced by Lars and David
Susskind.

Under this agreement Ingrid's first role was Ibsen's *Hedda Gabler*.
The production was shown first on the BBC in England and then on
CBS in the United States. Ingrid starred in the drama with a brilliant
British cast including Michael Redgrave, Ralph Richardson, and
Trevor Howard. She also played the role in 1962 at the Théâtre
Montparnasse in Paris, with a cast of equally outstanding French
actors (Claude Dauphin, Jean Servais, and Jacques Dacomine).

Ingrid had never been attracted to the dark plays of Ibsen and
Strindberg. But *Hedda Gabler* is one of the great female roles in
modern theatre. Hedda Gabler is a contemporary Lady Macbeth
trapped in a wifely role. In her manipulations she seeks not great
kingdoms but only to alleviate her boredom and ennui. To have been
a great Hedda, Ingrid would have had to open the trapdoor into
herself, grasping among the shadows for self-knowledge; but she
was incapable of that and her Hedda was light and unbelievable,
lacking energy, daring, and depth. A French critic wrote that she
was 'too obviously a nice person to play a wicked woman'. And Jack
Gould asked rhetorically in the *New York Times*: 'But what of Hedda,
the embodiment of evil and destruction, who generates an ascending

tension that should be almost unbearable? On television Hedda was too much the suffering heroine of the cinema and not enough the Ibsen animal of cold cunning and temperament who savours her evil acts.'

Ingrid was reaching an age when many actresses go through a professional menopause. She was a great movie star, after all, not a dramatic actress with years of training, apprenticeship, and performance in the theatre behind her. Audiences were used to seeing her in romantic roles, looking stunningly youthful and beautiful. She became more aware of her appearance than before, and John O'Gorman, a talented make-up artist, eventually became an indispensable part of her artistic entourage.

It was Anthony Quinn who came to Ingrid with her next role. She had known Quinn since the old Hollywood days. Then, when he was a struggling actor, she had met him one day when she was having a malted milk at a drugstore. They had seen more of each other in Rome when Quinn had such a brilliant success in *La Strada* opposite Ingrid's other old friend, Giulietta Masina. Now he was a big star. He still admired Ingrid immensely, though he knew that she was at an age and a stage in her career when she was not getting many choice film roles. He was delighted when, after several years of negotiation and discussion over the script, Ingrid agreed to star with him in *The Visit*, based on the play by Friedrich Duerrenmatt. It was a role that any middle-aged actress would die for. Ingrid would play Karla Zachanassian, a role that offered almost as much potential as *Hedda Gabler*.

In the stage version Lynn Fontanne had had a stunning success, creating a memorable portrait of evil and vengeance. Seduced and pushed into prostitution by a youthful rake, Karla returns to her small town seeking vengeance. Her seducer, Serge Miller, is the town's leading merchant, and Karla is one of the wealthiest women in the world. 'The world made me into a whore,' she declares. 'Now I will turn the world into a brothel.' She agrees to give the townspeople a fortune if they will prosecute Serge, legally condemn him to death, and execute him. As Duerrenmatt sees it, prostitution, legal or otherwise, is a matter of price, and the people condemn the town's leading citizen to death. *The Visit* could have made a stunning movie; unfortunately, by the time Ingrid was through with Quinn, *The Visit* was not *The Visit* any longer.

'Ingrid begged me not to make her an old lady,' Quinn remembers. 'But I thought that this most beautiful woman playing the most ugly woman in the world would be a credit to her as an actress. I said,

"Beauty is not only face. A woman can be very beautiful and be very ugly because the ugliness comes out of the soul." But she chose to play the part sympathetically and I would have done anything to do the picture with her. So we did the picture and it wasn't the play any more. It was something else.'

Ingrid used the same technique on Quinn that she had used on many co-stars and directors. She became romantically involved with him. And soon Anthony Quinn wasn't Anthony Quinn. That was the higher irony: here was the actor who seemed to personify animal vitality and rude energy, a man that no woman could ever push around – until Bergman.

'When you like someone too much, it's like a horse riding you, and you not riding the horse,' says Quinn. 'I like Ingrid Bergman so much that I seemed to lose my identity. I wasn't fighting for my identity. She was so dominant. She was too strong for the average man. She was even too strong for Mr Lars Schmidt.

'I don't think Ingrid wanted to dominate, but she was such an enormous personality that she dominated everything around her. The only people that survived working with her were people where you know there can't be any romance. They could dominate because they didn't care. Anybody that cared, she took over. I would say that falling in love with Ingrid Bergman would have been a tragedy of my life, because not being able to control a woman, or at least not having equal dominance, is an impossible situation.'

During the making of *The Visit* at Cinecittà on the edge of Rome, others on the set noticed the romantic chemistry between the two stars. 'Somehow in the course of the film, when the love scene comes they went out and had dinner and one gathers they spent a lot of time together,' says Mark Nichols, the publicist who went on location with the film. 'It was more like method acting, building up to the scene.'

With *The Visit* Ingrid had what might have been a classic part; instead, she had one of the worst failures of her career. 'At the Cannes film festival the critics criticized her performance and the audience shuddered over the film,' wrote Leonard Mosley in the *Daily Express*. 'Can the once-golden name of Bergman touch filmgoers once more? Or is this the moment of truth for her too – as it once was for Greta Garbo, Joan Crawford, Bette Davis? They lost the Midas touch and got out – Garbo for good, Crawford and Davis until they found new roles as ageing horror-film actresses. I can hardly see Bergman as a murderous old lady, can you?'

Even before the release of *The Visit* Ingrid was in London making another film, *The Yellow Rolls-Royce*. The film consisted of three episodes, each with different stars. Ingrid was in the final segment, playing a lovely American widow who meets up with a Yugoslavian partisan (Omar Sharif) in early 1941. Ingrid still looked delectable on screen, and it did not seem entirely ludicrous that the youthful guerrilla would forget the Germans long enough to wage a struggle to bed down the widow in the back seat of the Rolls.

As the *Sunday Telegraph* critic noted, *The Yellow Rolls-Royce* 'looked less like a film than an investment, laden with everything that money can buy'. In the marketplace, Ingrid was still top of the line, earning $275,000. That was more than was received by Jeanne Moreau ($67,660.23), George C. Scott ($75,000), Rex Harrison ($240,000), Omar Sharif ($75,000), or Alain Delon ($99,000). It was the newest star, Shirley MacLaine, who earned $560,500, more than double Ingrid's salary. Ingrid magnanimously agreed that the billing for the female stars should be alphabetical, 'but on the understanding that she will actually be in top position on that column'. She might have asked that her name be buried, for the film was a complete failure, 'terrible' in the words of *The New Yorker*. The producers had made an expensive commercial film. They had paid Ingrid $275,000 for a month's work. It would be a while before anyone would pay her that kind of money again.

When she returned to Choisel, it was to an empty house. Back in May 1961, Ingrid and Roberto had ended their lengthy custody fight. The decision gave the children to each parent a year at a time, starting with Roberto during 1961–2. Of her own volition, however, Ingrid gave over complete custody, limiting herself to visits such as during the making of *The Visit*, vacations, and other trips. In interviews, Ingrid always pictured her action as a generous one, ending three years of unpleasantness. In private, she was more candid. 'She said to me that she was not as good a parent as her former husband because she was more interested in having actress written on her tombstone than wife or mother,' said Mark Nichols, remembering a discussion during the making of *The Visit*. 'She saw the children when she could, but her devotion to the children wasn't as good as Rossellini's.'

For all Roberto's struggle over his 'Italian' children, he didn't even live with them in Rome. He had his own new family with Sonali. Robertino, Isabella, and Isotta lived in a separate apartment with their new housekeeper, Argenide, and a governess. Roberto would come rushing in, kissing and hugging them, telling them of his work, and then, when the whole house seemed ready to burst with his personality, he would be off somewhere else. 'My uncle would call

many times a day, but the children were not listening to him because
he was not following their everyday life,' says Fiorella. 'That's why
it was so difficult. I remember saying to them, "You can't pretend
that you want them, because you are not living with them." You
can't be severe with someone you are not with. Ingrid was in Paris
or London. They went to her with their little problems. For their
big problems they took care of themselves.'

Roberto continued to outdistance his creditors, though the rich
brocade of his life had grown threadbare. Isabella remembers the
times their furniture was repossessed, and friends bought it back at
auction. For Sonali there are memories not only of bare rooms but
of bare cupboards, of the days she wondered where she would get
the money to put dinner on the table.

'Roberto was a spoiled child,' she says. 'He was a child who
couldn't choose between the cake and the lollipop. But he always
gave. There was no selfishness. People came to him to take, to take
not only tangible things. It was such fun to be with him. But after
they left they were full and he was empty. I told him once, "You
have no friends." He said, "Don't I know it."

'I don't know if it was possible to be his friend. He needed converts.
Whether he made a confusion between that and friendship, I don't
know. Whether in a difficult dramatic moment and without com-
plexity at two in the morning he could call a friend and say, "I need
you", I don't know.

'I happened to live the difficult years, but he was still so full of
enthusiasm. We were always studying. He'd wake me up at two
o'clock in the morning. He was always in bed reading. He used to
say this is a sign of great civilization. It only looks like laziness.'

The remarkable thing about Ingrid's visits to Rome now was that
she could see her entire family. Amazingly Pia had moved to Italy
and was living with Robertino, Isabella, and Isotta.

Life had meted out some harsh lessons to Ingrid's eldest daughter.
In 1960 she ran off to Nevada and married twenty-eight-year-old
Fuller E. Callaway III, a divorcé, the heir to a Georgia fortune. Her
marriage received wide publicity, including a two-page spread in
Life. The following year her divorce received even more publicity.
She charged that Callaway had called her a 'parasite' and hit her,
pushing her down a flight of stairs.

She then announced her intention of becoming an actress, and
studied drama at Stanford University. After a year she travelled to
France. She lived for six months at Choisel, seeking to develop a
relationship with Ingrid. But after six months she took her own

apartment in Paris and went to work for UNESCO as a secretary. From there she moved to London to study acting.

She had taken up her old name again. It was an intelligent decision in terms of her career since it was the one that had been so widely publicized. Moreover, it symbolized Pia's identification with her mother's career.

Ingrid, however, was not a mother to inspire confidence in her daughter that she, too, could be a successful actress. Pia left Paris full of self-doubt. In London she said that she didn't even dare to take lessons at RADA because at the age of twenty-five she felt that she would be among 'hordes of bright teenagers'. She did dare to admit publicly that she wanted to act. 'I was a coward,' she said then. 'I didn't want to be compared to her. But I've had some offers, and one of these days, when I feel ready, I'll accept one.' Pia was in a curious position. She lived extremely well for a would-be actress, spent much of her money, a good deal of her energy and got nowhere.

Ingrid could have helped her with her career. But when she called her daughter in London, it was with a different sort of offer. 'My mother asked me to go to Rome and take care of the children,' Pia says. 'Their grandmother had died. My mother didn't want to live with them or bring them to France. I had been living in England for a year. I had been lonely. And so I went. I managed the accounts. I took care of things. I tried to be an adult in the family – such as it was.'

According to Petter, Ingrid had also promised to help Pia find movie roles in Italy. However, it was not Ingrid but Roberto who helped Pia win her first movie part. He called his old friend Vittorio De Sica who was directing *Divorce Italian Style*. Pia was given a small part as a cashier. In her one scene she kissed Marcello Mastroianni. It was only a tiny moment, but Pia was so excited that she called Ingrid in London to tell her about it. When Mastroianni's co-star in the film, Sophia Loren, saw the rushes, she said, 'Her beauty is astonishing.'

Pia's second role, as a peasant girl in *Zorba*, was much bigger. Anthony Quinn, the film's star, was a man of considerable charm; he and Pia became good friends. 'Pia was marvellous in our scenes,' Quinn says. 'In many ways she was almost more beautiful than her mother. But she took second place to Ingrid. She couldn't stand up on her own. The mother controlled her.' Ingrid was reported to be 'no doubt . . . interested in Pia's career . . . but not pushing her, and has sent word to Sophia Loren and Quinn that she must not be pampered'. Some people thought that she was jealous of Pia, and did not want the world to know that she was old enough to have a daughter playing roles she once had played. She told friends that she doubted her daughter's acting ability.

Pia did not have Ingrid's drive, but she knew that if she was to become a star, this was her moment. She worried that her first two film performances would be compared not with her mother's first two Swedish films but with later films. On the one hand, she expressed herself embarrassed by the 'undue publicity my tiny roles may get because of Mamma'; on the other hand, she used that relationship to get publicity and promote herself. Indeed, a publicist working on *Divorce Italian Style* contacted George Christy, a successful freelance writer, about doing a piece on Pia. The article, under Pia's byline, appeared in *Good Housekeeping*. It was titled 'My Mother, Ingrid Bergman'. She said that in her early years she was 'estranged, lonely and withdrawn', living in a house 'surrounded with an electrically-wired fence' in which she dreamed 'we were imprisoned like convicts . . . I was disillusioned in childhood, but now the cockleburrs are gone from my heart. At last Mamma and I are together, yet we have learned to be apart.' Pia made no mention of how Ingrid had left her without a word, only that 'unswerving in her honesty, Mama admitted her feelings, and the world whipped her with stinging words'.

In later years, indeed even in Ingrid's autobiography, Pia's judgment of her mother was far more ambivalent. In 1964, however, she appeared to be identifying with her mother partially, in a self-conscious, calculating way. She did not yet understand what it would be like to be cast between her mother and her father, asked by journalists and others to become the arbiter of their pasts. 'I don't want to be the one to defend, to judge one way or another,' she says now. 'I've always been put in that role and I must go on.' She felt that she never said quite what she meant to say, or perhaps she didn't know what to say.

Petter read the magazine article and was profoundly hurt. He wrote a seven-page, single-spaced document refuting the article almost paragraph by paragraph. He pointed out that there had not been an 'electrically-wired fence' on the Benedict Canyon house, only a gate with an electric buzzer, and a five-foot-tall wire fence 'as required by law because of our pool'. He talked about all that he had done for Pia, teaching her 'to dance, to swim, to ski', taking her on trips to Lake Placid, New York, to Puerto Rico and the Virgin Islands. 'I would like to know what disillusion in childhood Pia had suffered that required ventilation in public,' he concluded, comforting himself by believing that 'Pia had very little to do with this whole interview'. Petter could not see that in Pia's mind there had indeed been a great fence around the house in Benedict Canyon. Nor could he understand that despite all he had done for his daughter she was nonetheless a child of divorce; nor that, since she seemed to have learned not to trust people, she might find it necessary to pillage the past, particularly now that she was trying to make her way in the world.

Even if she was not a major talent, Pia might have gone some way in films as the beautiful daughter of Ingrid Bergman, but her scene in *Divorce Italian Style* was cut out and then when *Zorba* proved to be too long her entire role was left out. After all the publicity about her new movie career it was a humiliating start. Left without even one brief moment on film as a memorial to her film career, Pia was living a role stranger than any she might have played onscreen. She was living among the people her father had kept her from so long, and playing surrogate mother for a mother who had once abandoned her. When Ingrid made her periodic forays to Rome, she found it more and more difficult to deal with the problems that her children raised.

Pia stayed on, without a real life of her own. In the spring of 1966 she tested for yet another part, in a film entitled *The Devil in Love*. Once again, all she got out of it was publicity, including a bathing suit picture in *Time*. She decided she had had enough of Rome and her Italian 'movie' career for a while. After three years in Italy, she returned to the United States for what was supposed to be a summer visit. 'I felt I couldn't stay there and take care of her children any longer,' Pia says. 'I realized that the years were going by. The children were getting older. I had been there long enough.'

There was still great value in being Ingrid Bergman's daughter. Pia received an offer from Fiat to make a fourteen-thousand-mile promotional tour of the United States, driving the company's new Fiat 1100. She travelled with ten pieces of luggage, and designer outfits by Fontana. When she arrived in Hollywood, she told a *Modern Screen* reporter, 'I am sincerely ambitious for a career.' But she found no roles in Hollywood either, and when she reached her family in San Francisco, she got a job on a morning television show and began a very different career.

CHAPTER 19

AN ELEGANT FAÇADE

It was Christmas and Lars was away. So much of Ingrid's life had become an elegant façade. Lars was good at the rituals of living, but it was all ritual now. Choisel was more a stage setting for parties, photo sessions and occasional children's visits than a real home. It was a marriage of inconvenience. Lars was always jetting off somewhere and they met sometimes as if they were members of the board flying in for the quarterly meeting. Lars took care of Ingrid by managing her money.

Ingrid could tolerate Lars's absences, but no one wanted to spend Christmas alone; she had only Isabella and Fiorella and the servants with her. She called Lars's secretary, and the secretary called Raymond Gérôme, an actor and director who was one of Ingrid's few friends in Paris, and a close friend of Lars.

Gérôme changed his plans. He took Ingrid and Fiorella to the theatre that evening, and afterwards arranged a dinner party. To the other guests Ingrid was a blessed, beautiful person; they had no idea of the loneliness of her life.

She sat now at Choisel, doing practically nothing. She knew that she was good for Lars's career; he was already successful when she had met him, but now he had developed into perhaps the most successful producer in Europe. His take on *My Fair Lady* alone was enough to make him a rich man; by 1964 had had already grossed over twelve million dollars on the European productions.

The world still considered her the lovely, youthful Ingrid Bergman, but she could feel her age. She knew how badly Lars wanted a child, and she could not give it to him. Worse still, she was beginning to look older than Lars; he was in his prime.

Ingrid might have felt better if she had become enveloped in a new life, a new society, new friends. But although Lars chose to live in France, he had no particular affinity with the French, and cultivated few friends there. As for Ingrid, she was at an age when learning languages becomes more difficult. It was too much effort to strain to speak French as well as she spoke Italian, especially since she spoke Swedish at home.

'Sometimes it was very lonely there,' Isabella remembers. 'We took walks. We'd clean up everything. I had the feeling that you always had to do something.'

When Ingrid was alone at Choisel, the phone didn't ring very often. 'For three or four years people were even surprised that Ingrid was living here,' Gérôme says. 'I think she was surprised by the way she was living in Paris. Ingrid was very humorous about all the Swedish entertaining,' these parties of forty people. She said, "Our habit is to have speeches." But she'd do it.

'She could get out of temper with a tiny matter. I remember once at Choisel she got nervous, her hands got red, and she took tiny steps. I could see she was so upset. She said, "We're out of white wine."

'I was so surprised at her marriage that I said once or twice, "I don't understand it." She said, "There's nothing to understand. You just live it." Both Ingrid and Lars would make a point that was very Swedish; they would say, "Love is ridiculous at our age." She said, "Me with grown-up children."

'Ingrid couldn't stand to be alone any more. One day in Paris I said, "You're lonely. You're a lonely lady in a luxurious estate. Why don't you go to Paris?" She said, "There comes an age when you want to speak your language at night."

'Lars is sort of brilliant, full of references, a good reader, and very enthusiastic about his work in the theatre. He's a very enjoyable companion for a couple of hours. Then he becomes gloomy and grouchy. Lars can be a bully and cruel.

'Ingrid was going through a sort of bad moment in her career. I told Lars, "It's crazy to have Ingrid Bergman sitting at Choisel." He said, "What can I do?" He argued that it was all over for Ingrid. She was left at Choisel fixing sauce béarnaise.'

Ingrid might, indeed, have measured out her days in sauce béarnaise; her career as a romantic lead in films was over. She could laugh about sixty-year-old Cary Grant making love to a woman a third his age. 'Audrey [Hepburn] is now too old for him and in his next picture he will be making love to someone like Jane Fonda,' she said. But she did not want to end her film days like so many ageing stars, the final performances filled with the light of the camera softened in gauze, and then, their whole life a gauze of illusion.

In the summer of 1965 she had an offer to play in Ivan Turgenev's *A Month in the Country* at the Yvonne Arnaud Memorial Theatre in Guildford. There she met Dirk Bogarde who lived nearby. He invited her to stay with him in his country house so that she might not constantly be in the public eye.

The weeks in Guildford were happy. Ingrid played Natalia Petrovna, a lovely, spiritually deprived matron, her life growing dry and untended. Bored with her husband, Yslaev (Geoffrey Chater), she flirts with his friend Mikhail Rakitin (Michael Redgrave) and then with a young tutor, Alexei Belaev (Daniel Massey). Natalia is a jealous, passionate woman. In the end, both Alexei and Mikhail depart. Natalia is left alone with her memories and her husband.

Ingrid dominated the production. *A Month in the Country* was such a success at Guildford that in September it was taken to the Cambridge Theatre in London. There it played for eight months and was one of the biggest hits of the season. According to *The Times*, 'The production would hardly have exerted this special appeal without the presence of Ingrid Bergman, an actress impervious to changes of fashion and whose star quality as an ice goddess with warm human sympathies remains intact after a quarter century in the public eye.' The playgoers were not coming in such droves to see vintage Turgenev. They were coming to see Bergman. They didn't care about the occasional petulant critic who carped that Ingrid's 'performance hardly goes beyond the pictorial'. They didn't care that unlike her British colleagues, Ingrid was not a disciplined stage actress. She was a presence; she was Ilsa and Maria and Sister Benedict and Dr Constance Peterson and Alicia Huberman and Anastasia; she was a quarter century of memories.

In the theatre, Ingrid found an order that was absent in the real world. Everyone knew what had to be done and when to do it, and when her work was over, there was a warm shower of applause. The Queen came one evening with her lady-in-waiting, leaving as quietly as she arrived.

But there were times now when Ingrid questioned the meaning of her life and work. One evening she had dinner with Maximilian Schell, who was starring in John Osborne's stunning play *A Patriot for Me.*

'Where does it all go?' Ingrid asked rhetorically.

'Think what an actor's life used to be,' the Austrian-born actor said. 'All that remained was memories and photos. Now, with film, the art of acting remains.'

'Yes, but what am *I* doing it for?' she asked. 'I just don't know.'

Schell stared at Ingrid. 'I grew up with you. You put on my mind the stamp of a woman, the ideal woman. In my thoughts, you belong to me.'

Was Ingrid consoled? Lars had become little more than an occasional weekend guest. Her children whom she rarely saw were growing up. Robertino now had perfectly coiffed blond hair and matinée idol eyes, an aesthetically pleasing blend of Scandinavia and Italy. He was shy among strangers, masking his apprehension with perfect manners. He was a young man of great charm, who like his father enjoyed fast cars and fine clothes. Unlike Roberto, though, he was not interested in the world outside. Isabella and Isotta were only thirteen years old, but they appeared much older. They were five feet seven inches tall, and were knowledgeable about what many teenagers think is the adult world: travel, restaurants, famous acquaintances. Indeed, they towered so much over boys their own age, in height and experience, that sometimes to their peers they seemed a different generation. That was particularly true of Isabella. She was a vivacious, extroverted, irrepressible child-woman with big warm eyes that saw life as endless possibilities. Almost since birth Isabella had been the dominant twin, and that was even more true as the two girls entered their teen years. Isotta was attractive too, but she did not have the same glowing personality. She was as shy as her sister was outgoing, a studious girl whose work at Santa Giuliana Falconeri, a Catholic girls' school, was always good, but who hardly ever spoke in class.

The twins were growing so fast that when Isabella started complaining about back pain, no one had any idea how serious the condition might be, not even Roberto, king of the hypochondriacs. He took his daughter to a well-known bone specialist, who told him that the condition was indeed serious; Isabella had scoliosis, lateral curvature of the spine.

A Month in the Country had completed its long run and Ingrid flew to Rome, and then, with Roberto and Isabella, travelled to Florence, where a specialist told them that Isabella would require surgery. She would have to wear a body cast for many months, both before and after the operation. Surgery could not be performed for six months, until Isabella's spine was pulled as straight as possible. The machine on which this was done reminded Ingrid of a medieval torture rack. The doctor used his patient's pain as a measure of how far to pull the spine, and thus did not use an anaesthetic.

During the first stretching treatment, Ingrid waited in the hall. She could hear Isabella screaming. When she finally saw her daughter again, she was encased in a plaster cast from hip to neck.

Within a few days Isabella was walking in her cast, and she and her mother went back to Rome. A few weeks later Roberto drove Ingrid and Isabella back to Florence for another stretching. With her body cast, Isabella had to kneel in the car during the long drive. They made another trip to Florence, for a third stretching of the spine.

Finally they went to Florence for the operation itself. The evening before Isabella entered the hospital, Ingrid went with her daughter to a church to light a candle and to pray. She held tightly to Isabella's hand, as if by that gesture she could infuse her with strength and courage. Ingrid was crying as she left the church. She tried to ignore the beggar who accosted her. The beggar saw her tears and followed, whining in supplication, his hand out. As he walked onward, Isabella remained calm, hurrying along beside her mother. The beggar continued moving along next to Ingrid. Suddenly, she turned to the man. 'Here! Here! Take it! Take it!' Ingrid screamed hysterically, her words like a terrible curse. She opened her purse and threw all her money at the beggar, every note, every coin.

The operation took almost seven hours. When it was time for Isabella to be wakened, the nurse slapped her face.

Ingrid passed out in her ex-husband's arms.

In some ways Isabella accepted the illness and dealt with it better than her mother. When Ingrid talked of it years later, she remembered her daughter's courage, but she did not remember that Isabella was sometimes testy and irritable, as is part of any equation of courage. Ingrid loved to tell the story of the boy who drove all the way from Rome to see Isabella and how happy she was.

Isabella remembers the visit differently: 'He came all the way from Rome. He was one of my brother's friends. He had decided to fall in love with a sick girl. I was in the worst mood. I hated him. I didn't want to be with anyone.'

During the year and a half of Isabella's illness, Ingrid took only one professional engagement, an hour-long television version of Jean Cocteau's one-character play *The Human Voice*. But after a few weeks in London in the fall of 1966, she was back in Italy with Isabella. Her daughter did not let the cast limit her life. She wore special dresses that masked it. She walked with a straight posture that seemed to denote pride, not the dictates of the neck-high cast. She even went out dancing, while, as often as not, Isotta stayed home with her mother and the maid.

'That period changed my perception of her,' Isabella says. 'Until then I was very much my father's daughter. But it established the relationship that we had afterwards. I don't know if she regretted that she hadn't spent more time with us. She did always come and visit.'

Ingrid was immensely proud of the time she spent in Italy. Years later, for her autobiography, this was the one episode in her life about which she wrote herself. Isabella's illness had come at a relatively low point in Ingrid's career; moreover, it came at a point when distance was the best way to maintain her marriage. But she had other alternatives and she had indeed made sacrifices for her daughter.

After Isabella's cast was cut off, Ingrid was ready to get back to work. She was about to sign for the lead in a French production of *Anna Karenina*. Instead, she decided to go to Los Angeles and then to Broadway to play Deborah Harford in Eugene O'Neill's final play, *More Stately Mansions*. She had been away from Choisel and Lars for over a year.

She flew into Los Angeles alone on 3 August 1967 to begin rehearsals. The next morning she arrived at the Ahmanson Theater for the first read-through. The Ahmanson was Los Angeles's new cultural mausoleum. There had never been a play performance in the cavernous new theatre; there were none of the echoes of old plays and old players, none of the memories and the ghosts. Ingrid walked onto the great stage, where the cast members and director José Quintero sat in orange plastic chairs. She knew the others only by reputation. Colleen Dewhurst, the other female lead, was one of the great actresses on the American stage; an intense woman, she had a deep, throaty voice that could carry effortlessly to the farthest reaches of the two-thousand-seat theatre. The male lead, Arthur Hill, had co-starred with Dewhurst in the Pulitzer Prize-winning play *All the Way Home*. He looked as if he belonged on a university campus, with a pipe clenched in his teeth, and indeed had brilliantly played a college professor in Edward Albee's *Who's Afraid of Virginia Woolf?*

'Why is everyone here before me?' Ingrid asked. 'Am I late? I'm not late. You're all early.'

When she was nervous she often talked in non sequiturs. 'It's simply astonishing, nine hours' difference in time from Paris, yet I feel fine, I feel all right.'

She sat in the one empty chair.

Quintero was the greatest contemporary English-language interpreter of O'Neill. He approached his task with passion and a scholarly reverence for the great playwright. This would be the first American production of *More Stately Mansions*, and it was a tribute to Ingrid that she should be asked to play in such a company.

For the next month she thought day and night about the play. Deborah Harford is a role for a mature actress of the highest quality. Deborah is a tough-willed matriarch who believes that her son Arthur's bride, Sara, is beneath his station. The dramatic fulcrum of the play is the relationship between mother and daughter-in-law, between the refined, cold, conniving Deborah and the earthy, lusty, ambitious Sara, and their struggle over the heart and soul of Arthur.

In her first scene, Deborah meets her son in the forest after a long absence. As Ingrid remembered, Quintero wanted her to rush on stage and suddenly stop. Ingrid, however, felt that the woman would be worried that she had aged, and would walk almost reluctantly towards her son.

Ingrid was forever mixing up the truths of the stage with the truths of her personal life. When she saw her children after a long period, she made herself up and dressed with particular care. And she indeed crept in hesitating and worried, frightened to see them, fearful that she had aged. When she saw them, she felt her aura of beauty would make up for her infrequent visits; and so, she imagined, it would be with Deborah in *More Stately Mansions.*

Beyond the stage would sit two thousand spectators who had not seen Ingrid for years; for them, too, she felt like creeping into the spotlight, frightened to see them after so many years.

'Next you come right downstage to the footlights. Right down to the steps there, and you sit on the steps there,' the director said.

'But they'll hear my heart going bang-bang-bang,' Ingrid insisted. 'In those very first moments I'm frightened of the audience . . . I'm terrified of the audience. You're close enough to say hello to them. You can hear them talking about you. "She still looks pretty good for her age. How old do you think she is?"'

Ingrid argued with Quintero almost daily, winning some points, losing others. On the first scene they compromised. Ingrid agreed to walk dramatically onstage, but she would stop before walking forward to the footlights. She wrote Lars that Quintero had argued with her.

Opening night, 3 September 1967, finally arrived. This would be not only the first American performance of *More Stately Mansions* and Ingrid's first dramatic performance in America in twenty-one years. It would be a great day in the cultural history of Los Angeles, the opening of a theatre with dimensions beyond anything the city had known. The audience was as star-studded as any that had ever attended a play in Los Angeles. And Lars had flown in for the opening.

Ingrid stood in the wings, waiting to go on. Quintero stood beside her, holding her hand. 'Do it for him!' the director said, and Ingrid rushed forward to the centre of the stage. As she stood there motionless, the audience applauded. It might have been expected that there would be some applause, but not this great salvo. It went on and on, for two minutes, but here, in the early moments of the play, it seemed far longer. Ingrid was overwhelmed. The applause finally ended, and she stood speechless. She couldn't remember her first line. As always, Ruth Roberts was backstage, waiting, and she whispered the words. But Ingrid did not hear, and finally the stage manager shouted her line and Ingrid began:

'What can you expect, Deborah? At your age, a woman must become resigned to wait upon every man's pleasure, even her son's.'

Ingrid did her worthy best as Deborah. There were few actresses in America, however, who could hold an audience the way Dewhurst could. When the play was over, the applause for Dewhurst roared through the great new theatre. Ingrid's reception seemed only an echo, a polite welcome to a hometown favourite, after the applause at her entrance.

Dewhurst was the star of the play, but Ingrid was the star of the evening, and at the party afterwards she was deluged by reporters. She sat holding Dewhurst's hand, answering questions. For every reporter interested in the arts there was another needing a good thirty seconds for the 11 p.m. news.

'If you had your life to lead over again, would you?' asked the television reporter. This was a question she'd been asked a thousand times before.

'Yes, yes, I would,' Ingrid said, as Lars stood nearby. 'Wouldn't you?'

'No,' the journalist said. 'I think your conduct was outrageous.'

'Gentlemen, that is enough,' Lars interjected, leading Ingrid away from the pack of journalists.

Ingrid was besieged not only by reporters but by well-wishers, by vaguely familiar faces that looked at her as if she should recognize them. She was approached, too, by faces from long ago, faces that had aged so that it was like looking into the mirror after many years.

'I hope you understood my card today,' said Alfred Hitchcock, who rarely came out for such evenings. 'Did you?'

Ingrid looked down at the man who had directed more of her movies than anyone else. He appeared far more comfortable with the glare of lights and attention this evening than she was.

'Thank you, I haven't the time to thank you for anything,' Ingrid said. Then she laughed, as if she could make that her transition away from this whole matter.

'Do you know what it is?' Hitchcock insisted, his gaze fixed on Ingrid. '"Best wishes for a faulty stocking."'

'You know . . .' Ingrid laughed.

'Do you know what this is?' Hitchcock would not let her go.

'No.'

'Long run,' Hitchcock said triumphantly.

More Stately Mansions received generally respectful reviews. When it opened on Broadway a month later, it proved as popular with New York theatregoers as it had with those in Los Angeles. The New York critics sounded themes that were familiar since Ingrid had opened in *Liliom* almost three decades before. They questioned her ability to play a character of such cunning and evil. But they praised Ingrid's 'beauty' and 'presence', as if she now transcended any role that she might play. 'Ingrid Bergman . . . is herself a work of art,' wrote Clive Barnes in the *New York Times*. 'She trades heavily on her natural charm and in a sense, her very real inner goodness . . . but makes less of the strangely disparate character of Deborah Harford than you might have hoped.' He was talking not about an actress but about a mythological being who had transcended art and its judgments.

One of those who for years had worshipped at the temple of the mythological Ingrid was Warren Thomas, who had loved her since the days of the Alvin Gang and *Joan of Lorraine*. Warren's mother had died at his birth, and he had lived with his father in a room in a house full of prostitutes. His friends said that Ingrid was his mother fixation, and he had taken 'a vow that one day My Lady would be my friend'. For years, he had sent her flowers and pictures, kept a scrapbook, and whenever she was in town stood waiting to catch a glimpse of his lady. During the New York run of *More Stately Mansions*, he asked to come backstage to take her picture.

'I showed her the scrapbook,' Thomas says. 'She said, "All those years." I said, "I haven't reached my goal yet." I reached out my hand in friendship and she kissed my face. That was it. It started a friendship that grew and grew.'

Ingrid had another guest during much of the run of *More Stately Mansions* in Los Angeles and New York. She felt that her daughter Isotta had been neglected during her sister's illness. Ingrid noticed a bitter cast to her mouth. Isotta insists that she had not felt the least bit jealous of Isabella, only a certain awe at how well her twin sister could manage in her body cast. But for Isotta it was a special time, indeed, to be deposited in Ingrid's dressing room in Los Angeles one evening by her father, to live at the Hampshire House in New York, to have a private tutor and endless adventures.

Soon after Ingrid returned to France, she and Lars went to visit their island. Danholmen was almost a sacred place for Lars, a respite from the world of theatre and telephoning and dealmaking. The island had become famous, and when an occasional small passenger boat passed by, the guide pointed it out. On at least one occasion,

Ingrid stood on a rock and waved at the passengers, much as she had done to the trains that passed Santa Marinella.

This summer she invited Stirling Silliphant, a screenwriter, to come to the island to talk about a film based on the novel *A Walk in the Spring Rain* by Rachel Maddux. Silliphant, who had won an Oscar for his screenplay for *In the Heat of the Night*, had a writing-producing contract with Columbia. From the moment he read the Maddux novel he had wanted to star Ingrid.

Silliphant met Ingrid for the first time at the small wooden dock on Danholmen, as he arrived in Lars's speedboat. He thought it like a scene out of an Ingmar Bergman movie, and his candlelit dinner with Ingrid and Lars as 'the most urbane, delightful evening I think I've ever spent in my life'. Ingrid served fresh bread on a wooden plank, and Lars poured fine French wine, and they ate fish that Lars had caught.

Ingrid listened to the two men talking, but all she wanted to discuss was *her* film.

'Would you like to go out sailing with me tomorrow?' Lars asked.

'Damn it,' Ingrid interrupted. 'What about the script?'

'Yes, I've brought the script,' the screenwriter said, suddenly remembering why he had come to the island. 'But I've only done about a third of it.'

'That's terrible,' Ingrid said.

When Ingrid read what he had brought, she decided to play the part, and Silliphant spent several days on the island. 'I'm going to take you somewhere I've never taken anyone,' Lars said one day. And he sailed Silliphant to a small rock that rose directly out of the water and looked like the back of a giant turtle or a small whale. 'Very few men I know would have the sensitivity to react to this,' Lars said as if he were testing Silliphant. 'And I hope I'm not going to be disappointed.'

Silliphant took off his shoes and jumped out onto the rock, and experienced an extraordinary sensation.

'What do you feel?' Lars asked.

'I feel as if I'm like Jonah, but not in the mouth of the whale but on the back.'

'I love you for saying this. This is where I come. This is my rock.'

Ingrid would not have understood the pleasure Lars took in his rock. And though Silliphant saw Ingrid and Lars's marriage at its best, even here there were things that divided them.

Ingrid insisted that Anthony Quinn should co-star, as the Tennessee mountain man in the film. The Mexican-born Quinn was a fine actor, but he usually played Latin types. The casting made no sense unless you knew that Quinn and Ingrid had been romantically involved. As Ingrid had done with Gary Cooper years before, she wanted to continue her relationship in a second film, and she talked Silliphant into the casting.

After her return to Choisel, Ingrid received a phone call from Mike Frankovich, a Hollywood producer, asking her to star in a film version of the Broadway comedy *Cactus Flower*; she was supposed to play a dental assistant in her mid-thirties, attracted to her philandering boss, Walter Matthau, who has his eyes on a very young woman, Goldie Hawn.

Ingrid had long since declared her intention of no longer playing romantic roles. She was fifty-three years old, almost double Hawn's age. Matthau might look like an ageing bloodhound, but the idea that he would ever choose Ingrid over Goldie could end up the biggest laugh in the film. The producer flew to Paris to convince Ingrid to accept the part.

Ingrid now had two roles simultaneously. One of those with whom she discussed her plans was Ann Todd, her old friend. 'Ingrid said she was leaving to go to the States and she didn't care about her husband or her children,' recalls Todd. 'She said they were secondary.'

In Italy in the old days, the Rossellinis had called Ingrid *bocca da verità*, 'mouth of truth'. She was indeed sometimes inclined to say what others dared hardly think. Yet people were always seeking some greater truth in her words, some greater passion that was not there. She had said what she thought about her marriage, and about her family. It was not that she did not care. She cared, but in her own terms, her own way. She understood the odds against the survival of her marriage, but they were odds she was willing to risk.

In Hollywood, Ingrid took pleasure in the sheer business of making a film; it was 'Goldie' this and 'Walter' that, all kissing and hugging. The public imagined that a film like *Cactus Flower* was a fraternal business, weeks of camaraderie and good times. But careers were to be made or lost on the movie set, and the stars had no time and little interest in developing long-term friendships. Ingrid argued with the director over her lines, seeing that she was not bested by Hawn, in the young television star's film debut. She didn't socialize with Matthau either. 'We weren't close,' Matthau says now. 'I don't think you ever get a chance to get close to anyone you're working with.'

Ingrid's closeness to her male co-stars had usually been based on sexual intimacy and romance. Without that, she had little to say to Matthau. One day Ingrid, Matthau, and the director, Gene Saks, sat over lunch in the executive dining room at Columbia Pictures, observing a play in which she knew neither the characters nor their parts.

'What movie is he in?' she asked, looking at a young man whose long blond hair was neatly pulled back by a barrette.

'He's not in a movie,' Matthau said. 'He's writing one.'

In Ingrid's day writers had looked like writers. She saw another hippie-like young man, and made the logical conclusion. 'Ah, then that one must be a writer,' she said.

'No,' said Saks. 'That's Peter Fonda, the actor.'

'And that little man?' Ingrid said, not venturing a guess at the occupation of the chubby man wearing what appeared to be zipperless pants.

'A vice-president of Columbia Pictures.'

'Hollywood has changed dramatically since I left.'

Soon after she finished *Cactus Flower*, Ingrid was off to the mountains of Tennessee to film *A Walk in the Spring Rain*. Ingrid had convinced Anthony Quinn to accept the role of a mountain man. 'I knew it was wrong for me, but she wanted me for the part and I did it,' says Quinn, who in the film spoke in a peculiar accent more appropriate to the mountains of Shangri-la than to the Great Smokies.

Ingrid and Quinn's last film had been shot in an ancient city of eternal fascination; the Gatlinburg, Tennessee, that Ingrid flew into was a city of motels, fast-food emporiums, and souvenir shops stocked with all the wealth of Taiwan and places east, surrounded by magnificent mountains.

Ingrid discovered soon enough how far Silliphant had gone to provide for her creature comforts. Tennessee was dry so he set up a private cocktail lounge in the rather seedy motel that was to be their home. He imported a Filipino bartender from the Beachcomber restaurant in Los Angeles, along with a myriad of fruit juices, and enough of Ingrid's favourite rum to keep her afloat for a year. He envisioned days of passionate, happy filmmaking and evenings of happy drinking with Ingrid, Quinn, and other members of the team.

Almost from the moment Ingrid met Quinn again, it was obvious that their relationship had as much fizzle as a Coke left open overnight. 'They were like dead lovers,' Silliphant says. 'You could sense the separation. I had banked hopefully that there may have been a resumption of the affair and some of the passion would rub off.'

Ingrid was cast as a professor's wife who with her husband, played by Fritz Weaver, is spending his sabbatical year in the Smoky Mountains; she falls in love with the earthy mountain man. As the rehearsals began, the transcendent question was whether the

professor's wife would physically surrender to the charms of the
mountain man. Ingrid had had affairs during all three of her marriages, but she was not about to have one onscreen. She said that she
was striking out for her own generation in 'the "love bag" as against
the "pornographic bag".' She was convinced that *her* character would
never commit adultery.

'Look at me,' Quinn argued, as Silliphant remembers the scene.
'I'm an animal. Look at me! You mean to tell me this woman
wouldn't succumb to my warmth and my love and my sexual allure?'

'Tony, of course not,' Ingrid said, as if she had never been involved
with the actor. 'She would not.'

'You're wrong,' Quinn insisted.

Silliphant had to please both his stars, and he kept the script
ambiguous. Ingrid could play her part as a virtuous wife, indulging
in a mild and innocent flirtation, while Quinn could play it as if hills
were alive with the sound of rutting. Even during rehearsals Silliphant
realized that before this production was over, he might be needing
his share of Mai Tais and rum toddies. On the evening before the
first day's shooting, he worked until 3 a.m., rewriting the script.
Soon after he woke up he began to hear news from the location that
sounded like battle reports. The more the day wore on, the worse
the reports became. When the assistant director got back to the motel,
he told Silliphant that he was 'in deep shit' and that 'Ingrid is really
pissed'.

There is no guilt like the guilt of the innocent, and Silliphant was
terrified at the thought of what was happening to his film and his
star. When he was told Ingrid wanted to talk to him, he called her
room and invited her down to the closed bar for a private discussion.

'You failed me today,' Ingrid said.

'What do you mean?' Silliphant said.

'I thought you understood how important it is for an actress to
have the writer–producer, the person she started the project with,
there for the first shot,' Ingrid lectured. 'The fact that you weren't
there, that you didn't watch me, has caused me to worry how good
a producer you really are.'

'Boy, that's a heavy charge,' Silliphant said. 'I could try to say I
was exhausted after being up until three, but I can see that's not going
to change your mind.'

'Not at all,' Ingrid said. 'Had you been up all night, you should
have come to the set just long enough to come to me and put your
arms around me and say Ingrid you're brilliant, I love you, I know
you're going to be great; then you could have gone to sleep.'

By now Ingrid was crying. 'I only tell you this because I really care for you, but you have to understand these things. And you'll never learn them unless someone tells you.'

'I'm very grateful to you,' Silliphant said, vowing never to miss an opening shot again.

Ingrid had not always had the treatment from a producer that she insisted was the norm. But she had been in enough films to know that this would be a long, tedious production, and she vented her frustration on the most obvious candidate. Quinn was so fed up with Ingrid and the production that he rented a house to get away. He could not get away from the film itself. Silliphant kept hoping that Ingrid would give in and allow her character to have an affair, but she did not, and the film had as much drama as a Sunday school picnic.

'One of my great tragedies is that I wish I had done a successful picture with Ingrid, because we had such faith in each other,' Quinn says. 'But sometimes in motion pictures you love someone so much, but it doesn't work on the screen. And you don't like somebody and you're wonderful on the screen. The two greatest talents I worked with were Ingrid and Anna Magnani. But I would prefer to work with Anna Magnani, whom I didn't like, than Ingrid, whom I loved.'

Whatever she had intended when she coaxed the actor into taking the part had not worked out. Now after over half a year in America she was ready to return to Lars and to her marriage.

CHAPTER 20

'DARLING, THAT IS YOU CRYING'

Ingrid loved to talk to her husband about her work and, back with Lars, she was full of tales of her half year in America.

Ingrid pretended that she was a woman of perfect candour, but if that were true, her honesty would have begun with her husbands. As in her two previous marriages, Ingrid had had affairs. Her marriage was full of large and small deceits, but to her husband and to the world she acted the loyal and loving wife.

The elegant charade of their marriage extended to Lars too. He was involved in an affair with a beautiful, well-born young Swedish woman. According to Gérôme, months before at a dinner party one of the guests, a Swedish director, had nonchalantly said, 'I was talking to Kristina and . . .' The director assumed that Ingrid must have known about her husband's relationship with Kristina Belfrage. Ingrid did not.

On the evening of her return from the States, Lars told Ingrid about Kristina. Lars's great error was not his betrayal but his admission of betrayal. Ingrid was angry with Lars, but she decided to wait him out, to see if he would end his affair.

So Ingrid Bergman, whom much of the world considered the great symbol of romantic love and courage, settled down into a life of compromise and mistrust rather than face life alone. With Roberto, too, she had been willing to settle for a marriage that was little more than a legal arrangement until public scandal intervened. With Lars, such an arrangement might go on indefinitely, for he was a man of infinite discretion.

Ingrid stayed on at Choisel. Many years before she had left Petter. She had left Roberto too, lost among the broken fragments of his early career, while she went on to new stardom. This time, she was the one alone in the ruins. She felt that she was too old to start again. There are few roles left for ageing actresses, either on stage or off. She had no one but Lars, and she was prepared to make do with a part of him rather than be alone.

Ingrid didn't work during the last half of 1969 and all of 1970. Gérôme tried to talk her into taking an apartment in Paris, but she wouldn't even do that. Lacking insight, she didn't realize how depressed she had become. She was living with the hope of Lars's return to a marriage that she had never profoundly cared about. Now she cared. She needed Lars.

Fiorella Mariani was one of the few people to whom Ingrid could talk openly. Fiorella admired Ingrid immensely; without her aunt by marriage, she never would have dared to start her own career as a theatrical designer. One evening they talked until four in the morning, as they had done so often years before at Santa Marinella.

'Lars is a weak man,' Fiorella remembers saying. 'He's never happy, never satisfied with himself. He's always reaching for something, but without passion. I really feel sorry for him. I like him because I understand his weaknesses.'

'How can you say that?' Ingrid interjected. 'How can you say you like him because of his weaknesses?'

'There's something wrong in his strength, Ingrid. Don't you see?'

Robert Anderson paid a visit in late April 1970. The playwright's feelings for Ingrid had mellowed into friendship. 'Ingrid and Lars were having a bad time,' Anderson says. 'Lars would either not come back or come back and leave in the morning before I was up. I would sit and listen to her stories. She said, "It happens to every middle-aged French housewife." I said, "Do you think of yourself as a middle-aged French housewife?" And she did.'

Lars might have tried to instil confidence in his wife, but instead he acted as if her career had ended, and she had become an appendage to his life.

When finally Ingrid did work again, it was 1971. A British producer, Binkie Beaumont, offered her the part of Lady Cecily Waynflete in George Bernard Shaw's *Captain Brassbound's Conversion*. Ingrid found the play 'boring' and 'unbelievable' – a charitable assessment – but the role delicious. Lady Cecily is an intrepid, highborn British lady. She sets off for Morocco, accompanied by Captain Brassbound. No one is immune to her charms, not anyone of the twenty-three members of the all-male supporting cast.

What an opportunity for a fifty-five-year-old actress whose husband has taken up with a woman half her age, and who feels that her charms are history. Ingrid and twenty-three men. It was a splendid vehicle for the legendary Ingrid Bergman, who had so little to do with the woman sitting at Choisel.

Captain Brassbound's Conversion opened in Brighton before moving to London on 18 February 1971. The play was a resounding popular success, though the most creative aspect of the evening was Ingrid's British accent. The rest of the cast knew that the audience was coming to see not a play but Ingrid.

'She would only play a role if she could identify with the character, that she could see something of herself,' says Joss Ackland, who played Captain Brassbound, and became a good friend. 'Technically, she was hopeless. I would say, "For God's sake, stand still." She was playing a nineteenth-century English woman, which she could never do. But she had such enthusiasm. In this and her other plays she worked with wonderful stage actors. With people like Redgrave, when they talked of her acting, they would just smile.'

Ingrid was the great new star of the season. She was full of life. All the troubles with Lars seemed to be gone. She talked to him on the phone, about the play and about movies she had seen, about other actors and dinner parties. She laughed and gossiped with him, and took comfort in the fact that he was her husband. It was better this way, and Ingrid appreciated Lars's guidance and professional concern.

Life was good again. Ingrid would arrive early for the performance, two hours before curtain time. There in her dressing room, every-thing was right. Her dresser, Louie Hollis, saw to it. Louie was an East Ender; short and stout, she spoke with a cockney accent that Ingrid could sometimes not understand. Louie watched out for the woman she called 'my lady'. It wouldn't do to have her lady drying her hands on towels that others had used; so Louie brought in her own linen towels. She knew how much her lady liked things tidy and clean, and when Ingrid was onstage Louie was always busy, making the little dressing room as neat as a pin.

The Cambridge Theatre wasn't air-conditioned. On hot summer evenings the backstage area felt like an adjunct to the tropics. Every time Ingrid came offstage, Griff James or someone else would be there to lead her to the stage door, where she stepped outside to breathe some real air before hurrying back to catch her next cue.

During the run of *Captain Brassbound's Conversion* Ingrid became very close to Griff. The tall, bespectacled stage manager was not interested in a romantic relationship with Ingrid, but wanted merely to be her friend. He may have looked like a mournful basset hound, but he was a man of quick, subtle wit and great feeling; he cared for Ingrid immensely. He was of Ingrid's generation, without wife or family; he loved the theatre as she did, and had little life beyond it.

After the performance, Griff usually stopped in, while Louie finished her daily routine. Ingrid was not like some of the young actors, rushing off for a date or a drink with friends. Louie claimed

At Hampshire House during *Joan of Lorraine*

Ingrid and Sam Wanamaker in *Joan of Lorraine*

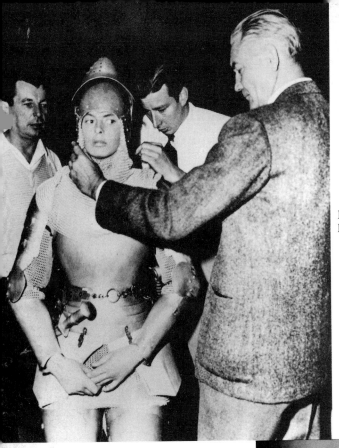

Director Victor Fleming adjusts
Ingrid's armour for *Joan of Arc*

Joan burns at the stake

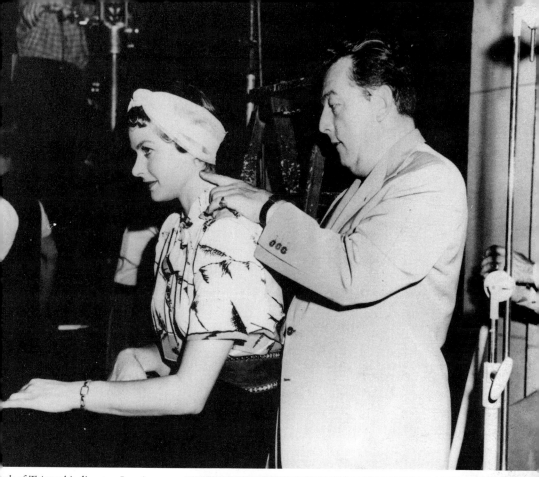

rch of Triumph's director Lewis
ilestone was infatuated with Ingrid

romantic scene with Charles Boyer
from *Arch of Triumph*

Ingrid and Roberto as she arrives in Rome

Ingrid and Roberto at the Excelsior Hotel

Shooting *Stromboli*

In *Stromboli*

When a pregnant Ingrid left
her apartment, a photographer
captured her picture

With Giulietta Masina in
Europa '51

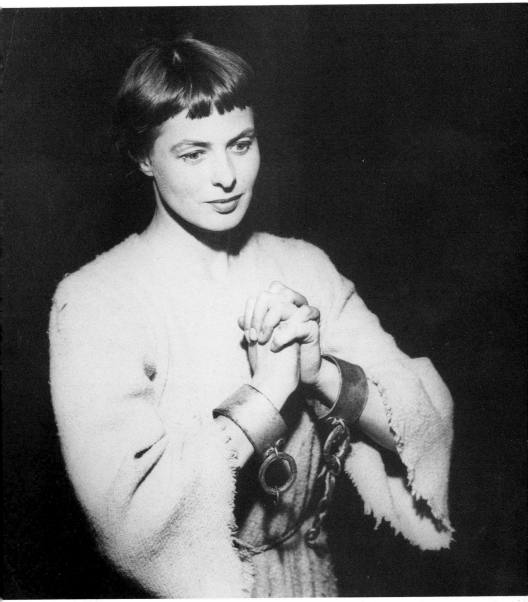

In the Honegger-Claudel oratorio *Joan at the Stake*

With Pia at airport, 1957

Ingrid with Oscar, 1957

Reunited with her three children Isabella, Isotta, and Robertino

New York Press conference, 1957

The dramatic confrontation between Helen Hayes and Ingrid in *Anastasia*

With Lars Schmidt, 1958

With Lars at the Théâtre des Nations
in Paris, 1959

Accompanying her three children back to Italy from Easter holiday in Paris

With Lars

Ingrid with Pia and Hugh O'Brian at the Beverly Hilton

Dancing with Goldie Hawn in *Cactus Flower*

In *A Walk in the Spring Rain,* the chemistry was gone between Ingrid and Anthony Quinn

With Isabella, Pia, and film producer Edgar Lansbury, at the New York premiere of Lansbury's film *Godspell,* in 1973

With Lauren Bacall in *Murder on the Orient Express.* This cameo appearance won Ingrid
her third Academy Award

In his last years, Rossellini looked like a languid cat

Ingrid and Lars's island off the coast of Sweden

The view from Danholmen's living room

Directed by Ingmar Bergman in *Autumn Sonata*

With director Alan Gibson during the screen test for *A Woman Called Golda*

On a sunny day in April 1982, Ingrid came out of her London town house and let the photographers take her picture. The shawl completely covered her swollen arm

'she could go out any night, but she preferred to go home alone'. Actually, her life was here, not only on the stage but in this dressing room too, in the narrow corridors and the darkened theatre. She loved the smell and bustle and warmth of the theatrical life.

To her old friends she was loyal and thoughtful, never forgetting a birthday, forever sending picture postcards. She was well organized, but she sometimes became irritated at the endless rituals of remembrance and caring. When she met new people, she couldn't be bothered remembering names, or even faces. They all became a blur to her, even sometimes people with whom she had worked. One day she was at Burberry's buying a trench coat for Lars when she saw Walter Matthau, her co-star in *Cactus Flower*.

'Walter, it's me, Ingrid,' she said, rushing up to the actor.

'Ingrid *who?*' asked Matthau, who was as notorious as Ingrid for forgetting people's names.

'Ingrid *Bergman*,' Ingrid said, not realizing Matthau was having his little joke.

Captain Brassbound's Conversion was such a success that early in 1972 the play was taken to the States, with an American supporting cast. It was even less appropriate for today's America than for London, but no one seemed to notice. There was no star like Ingrid, no one who still glowed with the magic of the old Hollywood, and had had a life more dramatic than any of her films. She was such a draw that in Washington *Captain Brassbound* was booked into the 2300-seat opera house, which usually staged musicals. On the day that Ingrid addressed a luncheon audience at the National Press Club, the room was jammed with tables and guests. Those turned back made up the largest waiting list for tickets in the club's history. During the luncheon Ingrid sat on a raised platform with other notables. At their tables, the journalists, publicists, and lobbyists filled out questions that were passed forward.

So much had gone on in the two and a half decades since Ingrid had last appeared in Washington; she was a miraculous survivor of an era that most of those in the audience knew only from yellowed news clips. Indeed, the question written on almost half the cards was how Ingrid at the age of fifty-six continued to look so radiant. She laughed and said that she could tell them that she had a good plastic surgeon in Sweden, but that, really, she had always looked young.

As usual, people were seeking in Ingrid concerns and feelings that she didn't have. She told the audience that she had no real interest in politics: 'I have been an entertainer . . . I try to live in a way that I am of help to other people, but that's not politics.' She wasn't going to pretend that she had an intellectual approach to acting: 'I haven't read many of those books about acting. Stanislavsky, I tried to plough through. I think, instinctively, even the first time I read a script I know exactly how the woman is. That is why I turn down many things I don't understand.'

'We are told that the golden age of Hollywood has gone forever,' a questioner said. 'Is this a great loss or a good thing?'

'I think it is in a sense a loss,' Ingrid said. 'But time marches on. I suppose everything has to change. Everything became very glossy and unrealistic, and that was one of the reasons why I left . . . I have to say that when I left for Italy there was a senator in Washington who made a speech against me, and he ended by saying that out of Hollywood's ashes will grow a better Hollywood . . .'

She had meant to say 'out of Ingrid Bergman's ashes', but the Hollywood she'd known had, indeed, gone up in flames the day she left. A new Hollywood and a new Washington had grown up, and the new Washington was ready to make its own atonement for the half-forgotten words of Senator Johnson of Colorado.

Charles Percy of Illinois, a politician astutely aware of the value of publicity, stood up on the floor of the Senate and said: 'Mr President, one of the world's loveliest, most gracious, and most talented women was made the victim of a bitter attack in this chamber twenty-two-years ago. Today I would like to pay long overdue tribute to Ingrid Bergman, a true star in every sense of the word. Our culture would be poorer indeed without her artistry. To the American public she will always hold a place in our hearts as one of the greatest performing artists of our time . . . Miss Bergman is not only welcome in America; we are deeply honoured by her visits here.'

One evening, Ingrid attended a special showing of *Casablanca* by the American Film Institute. She couldn't stand seeing the whole thing again. 'She said, "When I die I hope they won't show it again,"' Griff remembers. Ingrid arrived in time for the last reel and sat in the last row of the balcony.

People watched the film not because it was a dusty cultural artifact, or simply one of the great American films; they watched it as an act of homage. There were Rick's Bars everywhere from Jamaica to Germany. There were people who had seen the film dozens of times, and could recite the dialogue like a catechism. There was hardly a day, hardly an hour, when *Casablanca* wasn't showing somewhere, and Ingrid wasn't wearing her blue in Paris, her white in Rick's, her trench coat at the airport, standing on the tarmac saying goodbye to Rick, goodbye forever. As Rick turned to Louis and said, 'I think this is the beginning of a beautiful friendship,' the audience laughed, and Ingrid laughed with them. She had given up trying to understand why people loved the film so. The audience rose to greet her, and she walked to the front of the crowded theatre. She had talked about *Casablanca* so many times. She had answered the same questions about Bogie, and Henreid and the others more times than she could remember. But she loved to talk about the past, her past, and her responses still sounded as fresh as *Casablanca* itself.

Ingrid went to New York for the run of *Captain Brassbound's Conversion*. Remaining in New York, she played the title role in a children's film, *From the Mixed-up Files of Mrs Basil E. Frankweiler*. She spent considerable time with Pia, who lived in the city and was making her career as a television journalist.

One evening Ingrid visited Joseph Daly at Pia's apartment. Daly was a fast-talking Irish-American who had started out as a salesman for Siren Lingerie. Now he was in real estate, on the make. When Ingrid arrived, Joe told her that a late-breaking news story had detained Pia. Ingrid marched into the living room in her Chanel suit and stood there a moment. As she always did when she was nervous, she talked too rapidly.

A look of horror crossed Daly's face. 'Miss Bergman, there's something I must tell you. We've got a new puppy, and . . .' Ingrid looked down at the rug. She was standing on puppy excrement. She laughed, and was soon down on her knees, scrubbing the rug.

In December 1971 Ingrid attended the couple's wedding. At the wedding dinner dance at the Hotel Carlyle, Ingrid saw Petter for the first time since meeting him with Pia in England. His youthfulness was as striking as hers; he looked at least a decade younger than his sixty-four years. His wife, Agnes, was twenty years younger than him, and they made a handsome couple, alongside their nine-year-old daughter, Brita, one of their four children.

Petter was a prominent neurosurgeon in the United States. In Europe he was a consultant to the Swedish government. Still suspicious of his ex-wife's motives and publicity seeking, he made sure that no pictures were taken of the two of them together.

In June 1973 Ingrid took Robertino with her to the Cannes Film Festival, where she served as president of the jury. She was taken out and paraded around at gatherings and dinners and then set back down in her room, treated the way Mexican peasants carry their favourite saints through the streets of their village before storing them away. Often she was left alone in her suite. She would have liked more invitations, but no one seemed to guess that she might be lonely.

As for her children, none of them finished their higher education. 'From an early age the children learned to be free, to do what they wanted,' says Fiorella. 'They were free but they had no responsibility. Robertino told me when he was taking the matriculation exam, "I hope I fail. If I don't fail, I will have to assume full responsibility."'

So often Isotta had lived in the shadow of her more flamboyant sister. Now she took up with Alberto Acciarito, a son of the working class. Although Isotta at first considered him a prince of the people, some of the family thought him ill-tempered and argumentative. Ingrid was willing to have her daughter live with the young man, and she would even help out, but the last thing she wanted was a marriage.

'This was the only time when I had tension with Father and Mama,' Isotta says. 'They knew that we were fighting a lot and didn't see the point. For a few months I was on my own, not talking to them. We didn't see one another very much because it was embarrassing. I remember Mama sending me a very nice picture of the two of us holding hands in the country. There was a little note saying that we should always be like that, holding hands.' When Isotta went ahead and married Acciarito, for a time her parents didn't see her. Roberto was even less forgiving than Ingrid, but eventually both of them made a tenuous peace with their new son-in-law.

Ingrid didn't know what to do with her children. 'She gave Robertino cars, sports cars,' says Ann Todd. 'I said, "Ingrid, you shouldn't do that." She said, "How else will they love me?"'

For her next role Ingrid accepted the part of Constance in W. Somerset Maugham's *The Constant Wife*. Constance discovers that her husband is having an affair with her best friend; instead of rebuking him she sweetly asks him if she might accept a position as an interior decorator. She is immediately successful in her new job. A year later she leaves for an Italian vacation, taking with her an old beau, who may or may not become her lover. *The Constant Wife* is a witty, amusing play. The London production had an excellent supporting cast and John Gielgud as director. He recognized that Ingrid was hardly the ideal of an aristocratic British lady. In rehearsals, Ingrid spoke the line: 'I wonder what my mother would say about it?' 'Wouldn't it be possible,' Gielgud said wryly, 'to change it to "my *Scandinavian* mother?"'

When the play opened at the Albery Theatre in London's West End, the audiences hardly noticed Ingrid's curious accent, and neither did most of the critics. *The Constant Wife* was one of the biggest hits of the season.

Lars visited London occasionally, and the meanest aspect of his stay was not the talk of his relationship with Kristina but his attitude towards Ingrid's newest and dearest friend, Griff James. From their first meeting Lars had little use for Griff. Lars was a meticulous, elegant dresser, while Griff was a man of backstage, even in his attire. Lars didn't appreciate the qualities that made Griff such good company. It reached the point where Griff made himself scarce when he was about.

One evening in late November, Ingrid returned after the performance to her lovely flat on Mount Street in Mayfair. She could never go to sleep right away, and usually had a few drinks to help her along. She lay in bed leafing through a magazine. She noticed an article about breast cancer, an affliction that seemed almost an epidemic now, affecting Betty Ford, the President's wife, and other famous women. As she read about how women should check their breasts for lumps, she touched her own breasts, and in a desultory way examined herself. Suddenly, on the underside of her left breast, she felt something. A small hard lump. There was no mistaking it. She'd always been perfectly healthy.

It was late. But as she always did when she had a problem, she called Lars in France.

Lars told her to see a doctor immediately. But Ingrid said that she could not. She was in a play.

Ingrid attempted to forget the lump in her breast. She was still a desirable woman, of that she was sure. The idea that she might lose her breast was unthinkable.

Finally she went to see a Harley Street specialist. According to Ingrid he said, 'Yes, you must do something about it, but there's no hurry.' Ingrid could wait to get a biopsy that would reveal if the lump was malignant.

That was the reprieve she wanted. She threw herself into the role of Constance. Each evening was an adventure for the actors who played with her. They never could tell just how she would speak her lines, or where she would stand. A critic who attended a performance in January 1974 reported: 'Miss Bergman's technical performance . . . was way off. Several of her lines went clear out of her head, and many others emerged as sound without sense.' One evening Ingrid was standing in the wings talking to Griff, and she missed her entrance; she swept blithely onstage and said, 'I'm sorry I'm late. I was talking to Griff.' Another evening, she was standing onstage alone at the end of an act when the curtain didn't come down. She simply stood there and laughed and said, 'The curtain should have come down.' Another actress would have come stomping backstage, raging at the stage manager; to Ingrid it was simply amusing and to the audience it was something special, an added memory of their evening with Ingrid Bergman.

The play continued to do spectacular business, and the producer wanted to extend the run well into 1974. When Laurence Evans, Ingrid's agent at ICM's London office, told her this, she confided to him about her illness; it was unthinkable that she should put off the operation any longer. But she did. It was also unthinkable that she should accept a role in a new film, even if it was something as choice as *Murder on the Orient Express*.

In the evenings Ingrid played in *The Constant Wife*. During the day she played in *Murder on the Orient Express*. Sidney Lumet, the director, cast the film with an extraordinary collection of stars, including Albert Finney, Anthony Perkins, Richard Widmark, Sean Connery, Lauren Bacall, Vanessa Redgrave and half a dozen others. Lumet wanted Ingrid to play an ageing Russian princess, the natural role for her after *Anastasia*. When Ingrid saw the script she preferred a small part as a dowdy Swedish missionary, nothing more than a cameo, with twenty-five lines of dialogue. It was unusual for a star of Ingrid's stature to make such a choice, and it led to a brilliant comic performance.

In the late spring, when the run of *The Constant Wife* ended, the doctor wanted Ingrid to go into the hospital for the biopsy, but she decided to fly to New York to see her first grandson, Justin, born to Pia and Joe Daly; there, six months since the original diagnosis, she sought a second opinion from an American doctor.

It did not take the New York specialist very long to realize that Ingrid had already taken incalculable risks; that she would have to have an operation right away.

Ingrid said that it was Lars's birthday on 11 June, and after that she would visit Switzerland. She was treating the matter as if it were a problem between the doctor and the disease, and had nothing to do with her at all. She acted as if she were doing the doctor an enormous favour allowing him to examine her when she had so many more important things to do.

To impress upon Ingrid the seriousness of what he was saying, the American doctor called the Harley Street man, Dr Handley, in London. The two specialists talked awhile. Then the New York doctor handed the phone to Ingrid. Dr Handley told her that she should return to London right away. Ingrid said that she was too busy.

The American doctor could say no more.

*   *   *

Ingrid flew to Europe for Lars's birthday. She called her children and
told them about the operation. 'I have to go into the hospital,' she
told Isotta, who had recently visited her in London and had no idea
about the illness. 'I have a little lump and I have to check what it is.'
Isotta thought that her mother was so healthy that the problem
couldn't be serious.

After the party at Choisel, Ingrid returned to London, and on 15
June 1974, entered the London Clinic as Mrs Schmidt. All four of
her children and Lars flew to London, together in her sickness as they
had rarely been in her health. They waited for Ingrid to come out of
the anaesthesia. Her breast had been removed.

She called Laurence Evans. 'It's all over,' she said, as if she were
talking about a film that had been wrapped.

Soon afterwards Lars appeared in Evans's office to tell him that it
was not all over at all; the tumour was malignant. 'Is it the worst?'
Evans asked. 'No, I don't think so,' Lars said calmly. 'We should be
optimistic.'

To her children, Ingrid had always appeared a woman of formidable
strength; they had grown up with an image of her always off
somewhere doing something marvellous and exciting. It was almost
inconceivable that she should be sick. Ingrid herself acted as if the
discovery that the tumour was malignant was no great matter. On
leaving the London Clinic she and the children flew to Paris to spend
two weeks at Choisel. Ingrid often said that Lars was a better friend
than a husband. In her pain and doubt, she turned to him as she had
not turned to him in love and marriage. He saw her as no one else
did, the anger, the bitterness, the fear. He took control of her illness.

She had heard terrible things about radiation treatment, and she
returned to London for it with foreboding. The doctors had told her
that she might get tired and depressed and want to die. She always
had Isabella or Isotta with her, and they were there when she came
out of the radiation room, to nurse her. Her dresses were remade so
that no one had to know that she had been 'mutilated', as she called
it. And slowly, very slowly, she realized that it was not so terrible,
that the suffering of the treatments did not last, and that life was still
out there to be lived.

Early in 1975 she set out once again, to tour America in *The Constant
Wife*, travelling to Los Angeles, Washington, Boston, and New
York. She had never particularly liked Los Angeles, and a place like
Century City, site of the Shubert Theater, was one of the reasons

she still disliked it. The cluster of tall office buildings hovers over the flatlands of Beverly Hills and West Los Angeles; it is as if a forlorn attempt to make a city had been abandoned leaving an enclave of commerce and culture accessible only by cars that are parked in immense subterranean garages.

When Ingrid was onstage, everything was fine, but an actress, even when she is working, has time on her hands. One Sunday afternoon Ingrid went to a multiscreen movie theatre. 'I've been to four movie houses,' she told Griff later.

'That must have cost you lots of money,' Griff said jokingly.

'Oh, no,' Ingrid replied. 'Three dollars.'

'Oh, Ingrid, you're supposed to pay in each one.'

Ingrid took Griff to see her old haunts. Los Angeles had changed so much that most of the restaurants were gone, or didn't look the same, and Hollywood housed as many derelicts as memories.

She went to see Jean Renoir. Benedict Canyon had grown. There were houses all the way to the top of Mulholland Drive, and the winding road was sometimes blocked with traffic. She used to be able to see Jean and Dido Renoir's house from her own home, but the foliage had grown up. The Renoir home was in a little cul-de-sac; the house had not changed, with its living room as warm and friendly as a French country house, the walls lined with his father's paintings. Jean lay dying, only half aware of the world around him. Ingrid held his hand, and talked to him of good films and old times.

To Ingrid, it sometimes seemed that everybody was sick or dying or dead – Jean, Lewis Milestone, Leo McCarey. Thanks to a bond of silence, almost no one even knew that she was sick.

Alf Kjellin, the Swedish actor and director, came to see her. There was no one left who went back as far as Kjellin. He went back to her arrival at the studio in Stockholm. 'She was at a desperate stage,' Kjellin says. 'She wanted just to be with someone.'

The play was still the thing, though, and the audiences made her forget. And Ingrid was a walker, even in Los Angeles, where a pedestrian is a rare spectacle. After a Saturday matinée in mid-March, Ingrid decided that she and her friends would walk to a French restaurant for dinner. She had not got very far before she stumbled over a stone, twisting her ankle. Her friends helped her limp back to the theatre. A Beverly Hills doctor told Ingrid that she had broken a bone in her left foot. He proceeded to put the foot in a cast.

Ingrid's role did not call for a plaster cast on her leg. Griff phoned the theatre manager to tell him that he would have to cancel the sold-out performance. The manager envisioned a thousand irate playgoers assaulting the box office for refunds. Ingrid decided that broken foot or not, the show must go on.

The stage manager stepped in front of the curtain and told the audience that because Miss Bergman had just broken her foot, the play would start an hour late, giving the cast time to harden.

Ingrid was always playing Ingrid anyway; this evening she played Ingrid with a broken foot playing Lady Cecily. Since the rest of the cast was used to her being the centre of attention, they had no difficulty in following her as the butler pushed her around the stage in a grey swivel chair appropriated from one of the offices. The audience relished every delicious faux pas, every joke, that was being played on Mr Maugham and his old play. Other playgoers soon heard about Ingrid's broken foot; it was a double delight. Ingrid loved the sheer showmanship of the whole business, propelling herself back and forth in her wheelchair. Even when a doctor told her that she could walk, she continued playing from the wheelchair awhile. And when finally she played standing up, she took her bows from the wheelchair.

Ingrid received an Academy Award nomination for her supporting role as the Swedish missionary in *Murder on the Orient Express*. She was sure that the award would go to Valentina Cortese for her performance in François Truffaut's film about making a film, *Day for Night*. That was a real part, and Ingrid's role in *Murder on the Orient Express* was so tiny that it didn't seem possible that she might win. She had come this evening primarily to accept a special honorary award given to Jean Renoir. When she walked onstage she was given a standing ovation. She wore a long, silky dress with wide, long sleeves that made her look rather matronly, but she still exuded that shimmering glow.

'He has left behind him a body of masterpieces on film, just as his father did on canvas,' Ingrid said. She had written the words herself, and she spoke them as firmly as if she were imprinting them on time. 'In the cinema universe, he is a living god. In gratitude, thank you, we love you, Jean.'

When the winner of the best supporting actress award for 1974 was announced, Ingrid heard her name being called. At the Academy Award ceremonies, actors are always saying that they can't believe they won, when they truly feel that any other outcome would have been an outrageous miscarriage of justice. This time, Ingrid truly believed that she should not have won.

'Thank you very much indeed,' she said, accepting her third Academy Award. 'It's always very nice to get an Oscar . . . In the past, Oscar has shown that he's very forgetful and also has the wrong timing because last year when *Day for Night* won [for best foreign film], I couldn't believe that Valentina Cortese was not nominated because she gave the most beautiful performance . . . Therefore . . . it's so ironic that this year she's nominated when the picture won last year.

'I don't quite understand that, but here I am and I'm her rival and I don't like it at all. Please forgive me, Valentina. I didn't mean to . . .'

As Ingrid spoke, Cortese blew a kiss at Ingrid, and Ingrid blew it back. The two other nominees seated in the auditorium, Diane Ladd and Talia Shire, blew no kisses. And Ingrid discovered that an act of graciousness towards one can be considered an act of ungraciousness towards others.

'Oh, we are going to do the crying scene now,' Ingrid said, as she sat regally on a divan. She summoned the make-up man. It was the fall of 1975 and she was at work again in Rome, making *A Matter of Time* with Liza Minnelli and Charles Boyer. She played an aged contessa who had nothing left in the world but memories and a room in a cheap hotel. She was doing her first big dramatic scene with Liza, who played a chambermaid.

Liza was off in a corner. She was going to have to cry too. She stood there thinking of all the bad memories in her life, an expedient that would have made Buddha cry. But then she caught sight of Ingrid, and stopped. Ingrid, who Liza believed cried more beautifully than any actress in films, was having glycerine applied to her eyes!

Liza walked over to the divan. 'What are you doing?' she asked incredulously, as the make-up man continued blowing glycerine until Ingrid's eyes began to sting and run.

'The crying scene,' Ingrid said.

Liza turned back towards her corner. She had only recently met Ingrid, and didn't know what to say.

'Liza, what are *you* doing?' Ingrid asked, calling her back.

'Well, I'm trying to cry.'

'*Really* cry?'

'Yes,' Liza said sheepishly.

'Well, use the glycerine.'

Liza thought a moment. 'Ingrid, but don't you *really* cry?'

'No,' Ingrid said matter-of-factly. 'If I really cried, I'd be unhappy.'

Liza laughed, as if she had made a great discovery. 'When you looked at Humphrey Bogart and had tears in your eyes, that . . .'

'Glycerine.'

'Ingrid, we can't tell this to the world.'

'No, of course we can't. But I'll tell you a secret, and it's something you should remember as an actress. It's not whether you really cry, it's whether the audience thinks you are crying.'

Ingrid and Liza did the scene together, with only Ingrid using glycerine. That evening Liza hurried to see the rushes. Ingrid looked as if she had just been told that her entire family had been wiped out by a mass murderer, and Liza looked as if she had a slight head cold.

Ingrid was glad to be back in Rome making a film, though from the beginning *A Matter of Time* smacked of disaster. Vincente Minnelli had been a fine director once, but that was long ago, and he had this assignment in part because he was Liza's father. And seventy-six-year-old Boyer was in far from a good mood.

Ingrid's twin daughters were working on the film and she saw them every day. Isabella was making her film debut in a tiny role as a nun and Isotta was working in make-up. Ingrid spent long hours at the studio, though the stages were being heated with portable gas burners that sucked the oxygen from the air, and left some of those on the set with headaches.

It almost always took several takes for Ingrid to get a scene right, but she had particular difficulty on *A Matter of Time*. One morning after she had blown a long scene several times, she had lunch with Joel E. Siegel, a young film scholar. 'It's really not my business,' he said, 'but I think there's a typo. There's a word missing. That's why it doesn't make sense.'

Ingrid leaned over towards Siegel: 'It's all rubbish.'

Even if it was all rubbish, there was a human quality to filmmaking in Italy that was totally unlike making movies in Hollywood. Over lunch, Ingrid might sit down with actors, actresses, directors, and producers of half a dozen other films being made at the studio. They discussed all their movies, half a dozen plots and a dozen characters, and exchanged anecdotes. It was as if they were living a dozen lives within the parentheses of a moment. They discussed the past too, and in Ingrid's blessed memory it had lost its pain.

CHAPTER 21

INGRID'S GREAT PERFORMANCE

Ingrid and Roberto were friends once again, and in Rome she saw her former husband fairly often. She could understand Roberto's stunning intellectual soliloquies no more now than she could a quarter century before, but she cared for him. Since the divorce, Roberto had not had the great international success that Ingrid had enjoyed. But he was lionized by a new generation of filmmakers, and several of his films for television were almost as unique and innovative as *Open City* and *Paisan*. He was more in debt than ever, and his relationship with Sonali had finally ended, inevitably over a younger woman, Silvia d'Amico, a film writer. He looked like a fat, languid cat. He would lounge in bed or on a sofa for hours on end, would steam himself in the bath, and then perfume his body. He flew to the United States for conferences, talking of human society as if he, Roberto Rossellini, was living within history, affecting the events and ideas of his time.

On the morning of his seventieth birthday, 8 May 1976, the Roman papers were full of stories about Roberto. Ingrid was in Rome, but she pretended that she was leaving for Paris that day. In the evening Isabella and Isotta took Roberto to his favourite restaurant for a quiet dinner, and there, seated around a U-shaped table covered with fake dollars and lire, sat everyone – Ingrid; Roberto's first wife; his sister; his eldest son; his nieces; his grandchildren – everyone except Robertino, who was in Paris working for Lars.

Roberto took the menu from the white-coated waiter. This was a matter of importance, and he concentrated on the lengthy bill of fare.

'Papa! It's me,' the waiter shouted finally. 'Papa! It's me, Robertino.'

They had always been a family of the great moments. If that life had often served the children poorly, it served the family well now that they were adults, and their visits together were often memorable.

The past was always with Ingrid now. She decided to let Alan Burgess write her authorized biography, sharing the royalties with him. She had known the BBC journalist since she starred in *The Inn of the Sixth Happiness*, based on his book. He was a witty raconteur and she enjoyed her hours with him. Burgess, however, was not the only one who thought he was going to write Ingrid's book; Joe Steele had received a promise from Ingrid as well. She was good at forgetting, and besides, she felt that Joe was getting old and quirky, and was in no condition to write a book.

First, Ingrid had to go through all the papers and clippings and copies of letters that she had kept all these years, and were stored at Choisel. To help her she had Pavo Turtiainen, a young Finn who had worked on and off for her and Lars since 1970. Lars had plucked Pavo out of a restaurant in Helsinki when he served their table impeccably one day. Pavo was a meticulous, infinitely discreet young man, and he worked alongside Ingrid all day.

She decided to start with the pictures, then they began going through the letters, and other material. After two months it became too much for Ingrid – too many memories, too many faded, yellow yesterdays. 'I can't look at it any more,' Ingrid said. She left Pavo alone, to spend two more months organizing the files.

'I'll give you a tape recorder and when you wake up at night you can speak into it,' Burgess told her.

'What, Alan, without an audience?' she laughed. She enjoyed talking about her past, and if she was going to do it in a book, she wanted Burgess there, listening, asking questions. And so they began spending many hours as Ingrid reminisced.

In the fall of 1976, she flew to New York for a visit. Isabella was living there now, working for Italian television as a journalist. One evening Ingrid and Isabella went to Warren Thomas's apartment on the upper West Side to attend a thirtieth-anniversary party for the Alvin Gang. Warren's apartment was a shrine to Ingrid, and her greatest fan considered it a miracle that she would come to his home. He was the annointed, chosen out of the ranks of fandom, and he was aghast that some of the others did not all know how to behave. One of the old Alvin Gang members kept taking Ingrid's picture. Another member, Eleanor, was too shy even to appear, as if to see Ingrid in the flesh might destroy her image. Warren was a kind man, and he arranged for Eleanor to shake Ingrid's hand in her limousine one evening, but as Eleanor was saying hello, other fans arrived, and Eleanor never did get her chance.

Ingrid spent much of her time pretending – that she hadn't had a mastectomy, that she was happy, that she still had a marriage. Choisel was not a home any longer, but a tomb of memories. She was still hoping that somehow things might work out, and even if they didn't, she intended living this life of illusion until the end of her days. But now, in the spring of 1977, Kristina was pregnant. Ingrid needed Lars, and even now Lars did not want to admit that they could not go on together any longer, that it was all over.

She moved into the Raphaël, where she had lived during the days of *Tea and Sympathy*. Soon after she arrived, Roberto called her. He happened to be in Paris for a few days. When he checked in, the doorman had told him that Ingrid was staying there too. Roberto was a good friend in bad times. The mere fact that Ingrid was alone in Paris told him something was wrong. He took Ingrid to dinner that evening, and he put her to bed with a hot-water bottle and aspirins. And then he took her to lunch the next day.

Roberto was strangely reticent, and he knew her, if anything, too well. He did not ask her what was wrong, why she was so depressed, and she did not tell him. He talked almost exclusively of the future. He told her to look ahead.

Roberto kissed Ingrid on the cheek and flew back to Italy. 'Does Ingrid have any problems?' he asked Isabella, in Rome, not admitting to his daughter that he had just seen her.

'Yes, I think Lars and Kristina are going to have a baby,' Isabella said.

Roberto looked very sad. 'He said that Ingrid was like his daughter,' said Francesca Rodolfi, Rossellini's assistant during his last years. 'For Ingrid, Rossellini was the only family. The relationship was tender, like a brother and a sister. He would talk about her like a young girl.'

Roberto was learning his own lessons in loneliness. He had a great hunger still for people, for noise, for discourse, for all the crying, wailing, laughing, arguing sounds of people; but for the first time in years he was without a real family. He had moved into an apartment in Parioli, across the street from Marcella, his first wife. And Marcella took care of Roberto in his last years, as she had so many years before. He asked his niece Fiorella if he could meet a group of her women friends. 'Women can understand,' he said. And so they arrived one evening and they talked and they laughed, Roberto and the young women, and the room was alive with voices.

Ingrid could not bear to sit around in Paris or anywhere else. She accepted the part of rich, eccentric middle-aged Helen Lancaster in N. C. Hunter's *Waters of the Moon* at the Chichester Theatre in England. The play had been a formidable West End success in the early 1950s. If it was a bit dated, there was a double draw to the summer production, for the other female lead was Wendy Hiller.

Ingrid stayed with Ruth Roberts in a charming Sussex cottage. After all these years, Ruth was as devoted as ever to Ingrid, but it was hard sometimes when Ingrid pretended that she was as healthy as when Ruth had first met her.

'What's the matter with her?' Hiller asked during rehearsals, when Ingrid looked terribly tired.

'She's not well, and she won't ask John Clements [the director] if she can go home.'

Dame Wendy was a formidable lady. 'What's the matter, Ingrid?' she asked.

'I think I have shingles,' Ingrid said. 'But I don't want to ask John Clements . . .'

Dame Wendy marched up to the director. 'If you don't let Ingrid go home, and right now, we'll be in a right mess.'

Ingrid went home to the cottage and took two days off. Roberto called one day to say he had been chosen as president of the jury of the Cannes Film Festival, an honour that Ingrid had held four years before. On Friday, 3 June 1977, when Ingrid and Ruth returned to their cottage from lunch, there was a phone message from Fiorella.

Ingrid called Rome. Fiorella told her that Roberto had died of a heart attack. He had been in his apartment getting dressed for an appointment with the head of RAI television when he felt pain in his heart. He telephoned Marcella, and had died in her arms.

Ingrid could not face going on that evening. She telephoned Griff in London and asked him to come down, but he said that he could not.

'I don't know how I can get on the stage, Griff,' Ingrid said.

'Well, you will,' he said gruffly. 'You have to. They don't have understudies.'

Griff's great gift to Ingrid was knowing that in a time like this, a feigned lack of sympathy was best. The more he felt, the more he acted as if he didn't care. At the theatre Dame Wendy didn't sense Ingrid's overwhelming distress. That was Ingrid's great performance that evening.

The next day Lars telephoned to tell her that Kristina had given birth to a baby boy. For Ingrid, the two events, the birth and the death, were linked in her mind, symbols of her aloneness. Soon after Roberto's death, she saw a Swedish newspaper with the headline 'CONGRATULATIONS MR SCHMIDT'. As she read the words, she became angry. Ingrid had had a son born out of wedlock too; none of the papers had saluted the birth of Robertino.

Roberto left nothing but films, memories, and debts. He had 200,000 lire ($200) in the bank, not enough to bury him, and over a million dollars in debts, a monument to his golden tongue. Roberto's funeral was a great cathartic outburst that matched the drama of his life. They carried the body through the streets of the city, and they were all there – the young and the old, the Christian Democrats and the communists, the rich and the poor, the famous and the unknown. And when they laid him to rest, they buried not only Roberto Rossellini but a whole era.

The last time Ingrid had seen Roberto, she told him that Ingmar Bergman, the Swedish director, was planning to do a film with her. He thought it was a wonderful idea.

For years people had talked about Ingmar Bergman directing his compatriot in a film; they were the best-known Swedish artists in the world; they were of the same generation, from a country so small that it sometimes seemed like one great village. Indeed, Ingmar's father, Erik Bergman, a prominent Lutheran minister, had confirmed Ingrid when she was a little girl, and baptized Pia; he was a minister who in his sermons evoked terrifying images of damnation. So could his son.

As a young director Ingmar had known all about the legendary Ingrid Bergman, Hollywood's greatest star. He had seen her films and been drawn to her beauty and her erotic magnetism.

Most directors meeting such an actress would have wanted to work with her right away. But Ingmar worked only with what he considered real actors. 'There are an awful lot of people going around playing in films and the theatre in the absolutely worst sense of the word,' he said. 'They haven't the least talent for acting, but they get by on the strength of their personalities and some special radiation which is extremely hard to define – a form of sensuality, I think, that makes the camera marry them and the audience love them.' In the years since he met Ingrid in Stockholm, he saw her only once in a play. 'She was not very good,' he says. 'She performed like an enthusiastic amateur.'

This was the Ingrid Bergman whom Ingmar asked to be in his film *Autumn Sonata*, playing Charlotte, a world-famous pianist, returning to visit her daughter after a long absence. Many of the others in the cast had appeared with Bergman before. They were part of an ensemble company unique in filmmaking. Liv Ullmann played Charlotte's daughter, Eva. Liv and Ingmar's own daughter, Linn, born during their long relationship, played Eva as a child. Among those with small roles were Gunnar Björnstrand, who had been a classmate of Ingrid's at the Swedish Royal Dramatic School; she had acted with Björnstrand before in a short episode based on the Guy de Maupassant story 'The Necklace' in the eight-part film *Stimulantia* in 1967. There was also Mimi Pollak, who had been a good friend of Ingrid's since the days of her marriage to Lars. The production manager, whose name also happened to be Ingrid Bergman, was Ingmar's wife. Ingmar's former wife, Käbi Laretei, a concert pianist, played the Chopin prelude that Charlotte and Eva play in the film.

When Ingrid first saw the script for *Autumn Sonata*, she was less than impressed. She met Mimi Pollak soon after reading it, and turned her thumb down.

Charlotte is a totally self-absorbed artist, whose art has crowded out everything else in her life. A woman of monumental hubris, she has sought perfection in her art that she cannot find in daily life. Years before, she left her chronically ill child in a home. And she has not visited even her other healthy daughter for seven years.

There are those close to both Ingrid and Ingmar who claim that he wrote Charlotte with Ingrid's life in mind. There is something of Ingrid in Charlotte, but the knowledge of a musician's life comes in part from Käbi Laretei. In Charlotte's affair, there is a hint of his own mother, who was profoundly attracted to a man outside her marriage; and there is surely something of Ingmar himself, an artistic egotist like Charlotte, moulding actors to his purpose and will as if he were writing a novel. Though there is much of Ingrid in Charlotte, Charlotte is not Ingrid. Ingrid did not have Charlotte's self-knowledge, nor did she have her strength of will. And never in her life was she confronted with the reality of her being, as Charlotte was in *Autumn Sonata*.

But Charlotte struck closer to Ingrid's emotional centre than any character she had ever played; the role was the greatest challenge in her career, not only emotionally but physically. She would be acting the part of a strong, wilful woman in the full bloom of health, at a time when her own doctor had discovered a mysterious enlarged gland under her right arm; she would be acting in Swedish, without even the shield of an acquired language between herself and the character; she would be acting with a proud, disciplined group of actors who knew one another very well; and she would be directed by Ingmar Bergman, a man who she had been told was 'diabolical to work with'. Ingrid had spent most of her career entertaining; with Roberto she had tried to make a different sort of film, but he treated actors like puppets with wooden hearts and sawdust souls. She had never had to reach down into herself.

She flew to Stockholm in early September to begin rehearsals at the Swedish Film Institute. The year before, Ingmar had felt humili-

ated by Swedish tax authorities, who removed him from the Royal
Dramatic Theatre and temporarily withdrew his passport; he had
vowed never to make a film in Sweden again. And so, while the film
was being rehearsed for two weeks in Sweden, the shooting would
be at Norsk film studios in Oslo.

On the day Ingrid arrived for the first rehearsal, the rest of the
cast of *Autumn Sonata* was already there, looking as theatrical
as a school board meeting. Ingmar was seated at the long conference table in a blue sweater vest, with paunch, balding pate,
and horn-rimmed glasses. Liv Ullmann, the best-known of the
actors, had the face of a woman who spilled punch at her junior
prom, and years later still remembered the ignominy of that
evening. Ingrid appeared an almost dowdy, matronly woman,
looking all of her sixty-two years. There was a manliness to her
now, a largeness in her body and gesture and step. She had a deep,
cigarette smoker's voice, as if her vocal cords hd been seared by
flames.

Ingmar had decided to add a dimension: to film the filming, a
Bergman film within the Bergman film. And thus the actors were
playing themselves, acting when they were not acting. Ingrid waited
hardly an hour before she did what she usually did at the beginning
of a film; she began to test her director. This time, though, she did
it as if she were protecting more than her role.

'In a way, she didn't understand,' Ingmar says. 'She didn't have
that much imagination. She had this idea that "I am Ingrid Bergman".
The first days were horrible. She had planned the whole performance.
She had planned it in detail. So when I told her, You can't do it this
way, she was furious.

'It frightened her. All actors are frightened, all good actors, and
Ingrid was really a good actor. Good actors know that they have to
go deep inside to find the real emotions and feelings. It's the only
way. She found it impossible. She went to a limit and objected to go
beyond the limit. I had to take her with me by hand and by violence.
We were fighting all the time. Sometimes it was very tiring. She
knew what she wanted and I knew what I wanted. I had to tell her,
This is not you. This is the pianist.'

At the end of the first reading that first day, Liv Ullmann went
into the next room and cried. She was sure that the film would not
work out.

The life and blood and fury of the film is the relationship between
Charlotte and Eva. Most of the rehearsal days were spent working
with Ingrid and Liv. In their great climactic scene, the daughter
confronts the mother with the realities of her life. Charlotte is

devastated. Complaining of her back, she lies down on the floor, and there begins her soliloquy.

'If I lie down on the floor the audience will laugh,' Ingrid said, as if it were Ingrid Bergman on the floor, not Charlotte.

'A pianist when he has a pain lies on the floor,' Ingmar said.

'We were talking about life and death and now I'm supposed to lie down. I feel very awkward.'

'That's exactly how you're supposed to feel.'

Ingmar did not let up. 'You lie down on the floor and you take your stuff with you.'

And then, '"I remember hardly anything from my childhood,"' Ingrid said, reading the script. 'I wonder about that part. Doesn't anyone remember something from their childhood? Couldn't I just say I remember very little from my childhood. It seems a little better.'

'Yes, you can say that,' Ingmar said. 'I think it differs a lot with different people. It's very common that people block it.'

'I don't remember anything before eight or nine,' Liv said.

'I remember very well from childhood,' Ingrid said proudly. 'I remember everything.'

'What she means is from three or four years,' Ingmar said, returning to the script.

'But it's still better to say, "I remember very little,"' Ingrid insisted.

Lying on the floor, Ingrid spoke her lines:

'Nay, I remember so little about my childhood. Neither parent could express affection. Touching was forbidden either as a punishment or as a caress. I was very ignorant about anything that might pertain to love, intimacy, contact, nearness, warmth.

'I found my outlet in music. There was no other place for emotions to show. At times when I lie awake at night, I wonder whether I have really lived . . . I'm older, face and body both aged. I've memories and I've acquired experience and inside all that is just a void.'

On the day of the wardrobe tests, there was another camera in the room. This was the real camera, not the documentary camera, the interloper that had been there since the day Ingrid arrived. And when the new camera focused on her, she seemed to burst into life and colour. She looked like a movie star, or a world-famous pianist off to visit her daughter.

Finally they went to Oslo and another scene familiar to Ingrid: a press conference. Ingrid, Ingmar, Liv, and Sven Nykvist, the cameraman, sat on the platform before fifty or so reporters. Ingrid had almost always been the centre of attention at such gatherings,

but it was Ingmar who was asked most of the questions. Ingrid sat
smoking Gauloises, her hands betraying her nervousness.

The reporters were soon gone, and Ingrid and the others settled
down on the set, alone with the camera and the script. There were
only fifteen people in the whole production company, two thirds of
them women. They hurried around quietly, efficiently, while Ingmar
went to work. The set was closed, not only to visitors, but to life
outside its confines.

For forty days the cast and crew were together, like mountaineers
in a tent during a great storm. Ingrid became friendly with several
of the women in the crew, but still she was somehow isolated from
the others.

She had never had a part that demanded so much of her. Ingmar
coaxed, wooed, led her into herself, using the camera as an instrument
of violation. In one scene Ingrid lay on crumpled sheets in bed. Next
to her lay Lena Nyman, playing her catatonic daughter, Helena. If
people were sick in Ingrid Bergman films, they were sick as she had
been in *The Bells of St Mary's*, with tuberculosis, a few coughs on
the screen; or maybe some picturesque alcoholism, as in *Notorious*
and *Under Capricorn*; this was the kind of disease that Ingrid had never
faced on screen or in life, messy and ugly. It was a disease that
confronted Charlotte's own humanity as a mean and terrible challenge, God's dark joke. Nyman's performance was so strong, so
terrifying in its reality, that it did not seem that she was an actress at
all. Lying there on the rumpled sheets was this horrifying, hopeless
creature who reached out to life in blathering, salivating, half-human
sounds.

Ingrid was sweating. Above, the camera pressed upon her. Above
that camera stood the documentary camera. She lay there, trying to
control her emotions, as if she could not stand to be touched.
Suddenly, she heard a sharp, clanging sound. Someone had dropped
something. Ingrid jumped up, her nerves half shattered.

Ingrid and Ingmar sat on a sofa, talking. 'I live on borrowed time,'
she said.

Ingrid had never mentioned her illness before. Ingmar knew that
it was hard for her, especially at night. Lars had called and said that
it was very bad, and asked him please to hurry; Ingrid needed another
operation.

Ingmar pared the script down; he cut three weeks out of the
shooting; he decided that they would use a double for the outside
shooting, so that Ingrid wouldn't have to go on location; but he

could not cut down on the emotional exertion; he could not cut down on what he was demanding of Ingrid.

Now it was time finally to shoot the climactic confrontation scene between mother and daughter. It is after midnight, the hour of truth. In the dark of night, the two women confront each other. Mousy little Eva rises in a paroxysm of wrath, and with brutal words strikes down her prideful, self-possessed mother, battering her with the truths of their relationship. Ingrid tried the scene again and again, but she couldn't quite grasp it. She didn't understand such confrontation, such brutal truth. She didn't understand her own reaction as Charlotte, begging her daughter for forgiveness and love, is totally exposed. She had never pleaded for love or forgiveness. When she accepted blame, she usually did it proudly, as a burden that she could lift without thought or worry.

Ingmar tried to explain. Then he shot the scene.

'People like you are a menace,' Liv said, in her role as Eva. 'You should be locked away so you can't do any harm.'

As Liv spoke, accusing her mother of abandoning Helena in a nursing home, Ingrid's face was red, as if shame were a colour. 'Look at me, Mama,' Liv said. 'There can only be a single truth and a single lie. There can be no forgiveness.'

'You can't say I'm entirely to blame,' Ingrid said.

'You want exclusive rights. Concessions are ruses for you. You've managed to set up a discount system of life. One day you're bound to find out that your agreement is all on your side. You must come to realize you've been harbouring guilt like everyone else.'

'What . . . what guilt?' Ingrid said. Her eyes were wet with tears, and her face was as damp as if tears were flowing out of her very skin. 'Dearest Eva, can you find it in your heart to show forgiveness. I'll try to change myself. You'll teach me. We'll take time with each other. But help me. I can't go on any longer. Your hatred is so terrible. I haven't realized how – how selfish and childish I've been. Can't you hug me? Or if you would touch me at least. Help me!'

'Ingrid was an anarchist, an erratic anarchist,' says Ingmar. 'When she took away any make-up and showed her naked face in the midnight scene, that was the anarchist. That was the anarchist who doesn't think of seeing her past face.

'I remember one day Liv and Ingrid standing in front of a mirror, staring at themselves. It was a time when they were both looking terrible. Ingrid said, "I don't think Liv and I will have any more engagements, but you and Sven will have your awards."'

CHAPTER 22

'OH, WENDY, IT'S ONLY A PLAY'

Immediately after her last scene in *Autumn Sonata*, Ingrid flew to London. In a few weeks the lump under her arm had grown as big as an egg. She was put in the hospital, where she remained only three days, long enough to have the growth removed, and to learn that it was malignant.

Each morning Griff took her in a taxi to the Middlesex Hospital for a 9 o'clock appointment. 'She'd enter through this door that said "Nuclear Medicine" and she'd emerge a half hour later,' Griff says. Inside, Ingrid lay under a supervoltage X-ray machine that generated 22 million electron volts. Then Griff took her by another taxi to the 10.30 rehearsals at the Phoenix Theatre for the West End revival of N. C. Hunter's *Waters of the Moon*. Ingrid played Helen Lancaster, a rich, spoiled woman whose Rolls-Royce becomes stuck in a snow-drift, marooning her, along with her husband and daughter.

Griff never asked what happened behind the door marked 'Nuclear Medicine' and Ingrid never told him. If anything, Griff joked even more mercilessly with Ingrid, chiding her, putting her down. Griff could not imagine *his* Ingrid ever faltering, ever being dreadfully sick, ever dying. But he watched over her during the long hours of rehearsals, never letting her know how closely. Actors can be merci-less in their self-absorption, and when Ingrid grew terribly fatigued, the others hardly noticed. Ingrid said nothing, but continued the best she could. It was Griff who made Patrick Garland, the director, call a halt.

Ingrid still had Lars. She had made up with him, and had met Kristina and the baby. He still managed her money and property, and took care of all the details she had never been able to manage. She talked to him practically every day. Once, from Los Angeles, she called him in Paris to ask how much she should tip at her hotel. Lars pointed out that Ingrid's phone call would cost more than any tip, but she wanted to leave knowing that she had done the right thing.

She did have a new man in her life, John Van Eyssen, an American film executive living in London. Van Eyssen was a civilized, solicitous divorcé who made few demands on Ingrid. 'Obviously, I loved her,' Van Eyssen says. 'We had a wonderful relationship. We laughed a great deal. I thought of her as a great, marvellous person. The big laugh. She bore no grudges. She bore no ill will. If people didn't like her, *tant pis*. If things were really bad she would laugh.'

The opening night of the tryout at Brighton was one of those dreadful evenings that make actors such a superstitious breed. Everything went wrong. At the end of the first act, Wendy Hiller was supposed to play the piano while Ingrid and the rest of the cast danced. Hiller plunked her fingers on the piano keys, setting off a deafening silence. She started again, but still the tape machine didn't supply the music. The audience began whispering.

'I'm terribly sorry, but the piano does not seem to work,' Ingrid said. 'Please forgive us, but we have to bring the curtain down for a moment.'

The next day Garland and the cast went through a postmortem discussion. Wendy Hiller was three years older than Ingrid, but even at sixty-five she was the eternal perfectionist. She fumed with anger. 'Oh, Wendy,' Ingrid said quietly, 'it's only a play.'

When *Waters of the Moon* opened at the Haymarket Theatre on 28 January 1978, the tape recorder was working, and the play became the great new hit of the season. Dame Wendy received better notices than Ingrid, but it was for Ingrid that there were queues at the box office. The two actresses were forever joking about Wendy's notices and Ingrid's fans. One day early in the run, Wendy came up to Ingrid in her dressing room. 'If anyone else stops me in the street and says, "Ah, Miss Hiller, isn't it a lovely play and isn't Miss Bergman beautiful," I shall say Miss Bergman is not beautiful. She's a dreadful woman and terrible to play with.' The next day Ingrid handed her co-star an azalea, from 'the dreadful Bergman woman'. She went to the front of the theatre where the management had posted quotes from critics celebrating Wendy's performance. She had herself photographed sneering as broadly as a villain in a silent film, and distributed the picture to Wendy and other members of the company.

Like most actors in London, Ingrid had always wanted to play the Haymarket, an historic 1820 building. With its exquisite portico, crystal chandeliers, gold leaf, and blue upholstery, the Haymarket Theatre is the most elegant in London. Backstage, however, is a very different sort of relic of the nineteenth century, quarters so threadbare and cramped that they seem to propel the actors on stage in relief. For her dressing room Ingrid had chosen not the star's quarter, number 10, upstairs, but number 1, downstairs, a rectangular room the size of a small bedroom. The austere white and cream-coloured dressing room was lit by two lamps hanging on cords from old gas fixtures. Outside her door, the bare wooden staircase looked almost worn through.

On matinée days, Ingrid and Griff went to dinner together at a little Italian pizza restaurant that they had discovered. Usually, before the performance, she sat in her dressing room, writing letters, chatting with Griff or members of the company.

Louie was seventy years old and retired. But she had come back to serve 'my lady'. As her dresser, Louie knew about Ingrid's illness, but she never said anything, and tried to be as chipper and gay as always. She had been there the day Ruth Roberts had come, and after Ruth left, seen Ingrid sitting on the floor crying, looking at her pictures in their silver frames: her mother, her father, her aunt.

'Louie, they're all dead,' Ingrid said.

'What was wrong with them?' Louie asked.

'Cancer.'

'I do hope that you dodge it,' Louie said. 'We don't want that.'

Although Ingrid and Wendy kept up their good-natured repartee, the British actress found it frustrating to work with her. Dame Wendy had no star persona. When she trundled off to Buckinghamshire after a performance, pushing her way through the fans waiting primarily to see Ingrid, it might have been the nice old lady who ran the teashop on the corner. Hiller was her role. When she was at her best, in a great role in a great play, the audience knew that it was seeing something that was born and lived and died within the time span of a performance. She needed the disciplining confines of a script. She needed a director who had shaped the play. She needed to work with actors who knew their lines and followed the director's biddings. Now, on this great stage where she had appeared five times before, with some of the greatest actors in the British theatre, she was acting with Ingrid, out of whose mouth came the most peculiar words and phrases, and who wandered the stage like Ahab.

'It was a bit of a dicey situation,' Dame Wendy says, 'telling an international star for God's sake keep still.' She complained to Griff who spoke to Ingrid, but his admonitions only seemed to make it worse. After one performance in which Ingrid had uttered several lines of gibberish, Wendy called Patrick Garland. 'You must come in. She's speaking Chinese again.'

The director came to the theatre to talk to his star. Ingrid only laughed. 'I had a chat with Lars in the morning and spoke Swedish. The children came in the afternoon and I spoke Italian. And my French friends came in the early evening. I just got quickly through the play and went to bed.'

Garland had directed enough plays in his day to know that even if Ingrid forgot half her lines, the audience hardly cared. After one performance, an American director came to congratulate Garland. 'It was a beautiful play,' he said. 'And what a wonderful idea to have that pin spotlight on Ingrid during the entire play. This one figure always emblazed by a tiny spotlight.'

'But there wasn't any spotlight,' Garland said.

Garland had learned from Griff that Ingrid had cancer. 'If she has a period of fatigue, understand,' Griff said. Garland knew all the jokes about Ingrid forgetting her lines during *The Constant Wife*, and he could hardly believe that she was sick. She had such vitality.

A few days before the play closed, Louie was helping Ingrid into her last-act costume. As she always did, Ingrid took hold of her dresser's shoulder, to steady herself. Louie saw that Ingrid's face was clenched in a grimace.

'Whatever is the matter,' Louie asked.

'It's started again,' Ingrid said, feeling the pain that she had hoped was gone forever. This time, however, she felt it somewhere new in her body, in her right breast.

Ingrid had always experienced the end of a play or a film like a death in the family. *Waters of the Moon* could truly be her last play. On Saturday evening, 1 July 1978, the house was full, as it had been from the first night. At the end the audience applauded as if by the sheer force of their appreciation they could make the evening last forever. But the applause finally died down, and the curtain closed for good, and Ingrid walked back to her dressing room.

Louie was busy packing things away. She could see that Ingrid 'seemed out of it, she was in such a state'. Louie folded the hand towels that she had brought in for Ingrid's use.

'Don't do that, Louie,' Ingrid said. 'Don't do that, little Lou.'

Louie stopped working. Ingrid took off her make-up and dressed. Ingrid said goodbye to the rest of the cast, embracing them and wishing them well. Finally they were gone too.

'Why don't you go home?' Louie said.

'No, I don't want to.'

The car that was supposed to take Ingrid home did not arrive. She walked back into the theatre to see it for the last time. She expected to see the stage all dark and quiet, but there was a flurry of activity, as the stagehands struck the sets. In her whole life in the theatre, she had never seen this. In a few hours, all the props and fixtures that had defined her life for months would be carted off. The new sets would go up, and on Monday evening there would be a whole new world on the stage.

'I didn't know all this went on,' she told Griff.

Anthony Peek, the deputy theatre manager, came out and sat with Ingrid for a while. He talked about how successful the play had been, six months without an empty seat. He told her of the Japanese tourists who had attended, to see her and hear her voice, though they could not understand a word. Ingrid stored such compliments in her memory the way she pasted clippings in scrapbooks. But memories are memories, even those as fresh as this evening's performance. Soon the stage was bare; the stagehands were gone. It was time to dim the lights.

Soon after the play closed, Ingrid entered the London Clinic. When Dr William Slack opened her right breast, he found that it was malignant and he performed a mastectomy. Once again Ingrid made her daily trips to the Middlesex Hospital for radiotherapy. She felt better. Nevertheless, the doctors made her cancel her American tour of *Waters of the Moon*, and the news of her illness was out.

She had time on her hands now, but how much time? She had bought a red-brick house at No. 9 Cheney Gardens in Chelsea. Her apartment, reached by a small private elevator, was pleasantly, if rather modestly furnished, with her three Oscars the most notable adornment in the living room. Nearby was a dressmaker, a greengrocer and the Beehive Pub. She loved to stroll down the King's Road looking at the outrageous clothes in shop windows, and at the young people with their purple hair and chains.

In October, she flew to New York to dub *Autumn Sonata* into English. She spent time with Pia, who was a theatre and film critic for NBC-TV. Ingrid's visit with her eldest daughter in her spacious apartment on Central Park West was not quite like a scene from *Autumn Sonata*, but the pain and memories were still terribly alive.

'Mother thought she was going to live in New York for a while,' says Isabella. 'Pia said, "You can always stay here." But Pia said that Mother complained that the children didn't eat with a knife and fork or didn't eat vegetables. Apparently there was some sort of tension. Pia said that next time you come maybe you should stay in a hotel.'

The critics rhapsodized over her performance in *Autumn Sonata*. She was nominated for an Academy Award as best actress; had she won, she would have been the only person ever to have received four Academy Awards for acting. She had consolation in the New York Film Critics Award as best actress and the Donatello, Italy's version of the Oscar.

In the spring of 1979, she flew to Hollywood. Jean Renoir had died a few weeks earlier, and she had driven up to Benedict Canyon to see his widow. She went out to the Motion Picture Home and visited Joe Steele.

Steele's dream had been to redo his biography of Ingrid. He thought he had her approval but she had gone ahead with her own project. Steele and his collaborator, Bill Davidson, lost their publisher's interest. Although Ingrid reportedly helped Steele financially, he felt betrayed, and without the project to sustain him he deteriorated rapidly and died.

In Los Angeles, Ingrid participated in an evening in which the American Film Institute gave Alfred Hitchcock its Lifetime Achievement Award. She had expected to say a few words, introduce a few people, and sit down, but the day before, George Stevens, Jr, the director, told her that she would be mistress of ceremonies. It was not the kind of thing she liked to do, especially at the last moment. But it was Hitch, and they pushed and pushed, and she agreed.

On the evening of the tribute, Ben Benjamin, an ICM agent who handled Ingrid's affairs in Hollywood, drove to the Beverly Wilshire Hotel to pick Ingrid up. Benjamin called Ingrid's suite, and she said that she needed some help from his wife, Carla, who was waiting in the car. So Carla Benjamin went to Ingrid's suite and found her there unable to finish hooking her dress.

They were all there that evening at the Beverly Hilton Hotel. The old stars and the new stars: Cary Grant, James Stewart, Jane Wyman, Olivia de Havilland, Christopher Reeve, Walter Matthau, Michael Caine, Barbra Streisand. And Hitchcock. At 79 he now had a pacemaker, arthritis, a drinking problem, and was more than a hundred pounds overweight. He waddled into the International Ballroom in tiny mincing steps, like a child just learning to walk, his scowl lost in the jowls of his face. It seemed a merciless act to have brought him here. He sat down between Alma, his invalid wife, and Cary Grant at a dinner table that included Ingrid, James Stewart, Sidney Bernstein, and Lew Wasserman of ICM. They were all old friends, but Hitchcock sat as if alone, his face devoid of emotion.

As mistress of ceremonies, Ingrid was an ebullient, radiant presence. Looking at her and then at Hitchcock was like looking at life and death, youth and age. Through most of the evening Hitchcock rarely stirred out of his somnolence. At the end, when he had received his award and made his little speech, Ingrid spoke a last time.

'We must leave you now, but thanks to film, Hitch's work never will,' she said. 'Now there's just one little thing I want to add before we finish this evening.'

She looked down at Hitch.

'You remember that agonizing shot when you had built some kind of elevator. It was a basket or something with you and the cameraman. And you were shooting this vast party in *Notorious*. And you came zooming down with your elevator and all the way down into my hand, where you saw the key in a close-up.

'Now, well, you know that Cary stole that key after the scene. Yes. And he kept it. He kept it for about ten years. And one day he put it in my hand. And he said, "I've kept this long enough. Now it's for you. For good luck." I've kept it for twenty years. And in this very same hand there is the key.'

As Ingrid held the key up, the audience applauded. Even Hitchcock struck his hands together. Then Ingrid had a terrible realization. She was holding up the wrong key.

'It has given me a lot of good luck and quite a few good movies too. And now I'm going to give it to you with a prayer that it will open some very good doors for you too. God bless you, dear Hitch. I'm coming to give you the key.'

Ingrid swept across the room as she had in so many movies. She hugged Hitchcock and as she gave him the key, the old man smiled.

Afterwards she mailed Hitchcock the right key, along with an apology. In his earlier days Hitchcock would have found the mix-up richly amusing, an anecdote to be told and retold. But he did not answer the letter. She wrote him a second letter, and a third. Finally he replied with a one-line message: 'I got the key.'

A few months later, when Ingrid returned to Hollywood, she went once again to visit Hitchcock. 'He took my hands,' she said, 'and tears streamed down his face and he said, "Ingrid, I'm going to die," and I said, "But of course you are going to die sometime, Hitch – we are all going to die." And then I told him that I, too, had recently been very ill, and that I had thought about it too. And for a moment the logic of that seemed to make him more peaceful.'

In July 1979, Ingrid had a visit from Petter. He was cooperating with Alan Burgess on her biography, giving him material, letters, and countless interviews. Burgess had come highly recommended by George and Phyllis Seaton, and the British journalist had, in Petter's words, 'somehow become a sort of "father confessor" for both sides'.

'As soon as Petter knew I was writing a book about Ingrid Bergman, he was interested in meeting her,' Burgess says. 'I said to Ingrid, "Would you like to meet him?" She said, "I don't know. I suppose so."'

According to Petter, Burgess had asked him to meet with Ingrid, at her request. He says, 'I knew that if I said no it would be in the papers that Dr Lindstrom refused to see his former wife who is ill with cancer.'

At times, Petter could be hopelessly naive about human relationships. He had already heard rumours that Ingrid had editorial control over the book, but Burgess kept insisting that Petter would have *his* say. And he continued to give the author information and assistance, seeking his vindication in what in fact was Ingrid's authorized biography.

Ingrid was not alone when Petter entered her house in Chelsea one July afternoon. Burgess was there as well, because Ingrid feared that it might be an unpleasant reunion, but Ingrid and Petter seemed to hit it off so well that Burgess soon made his exit. Indeed, Ingrid invited him to return. That second day, Petter looked at Ingrid's swollen arm and suggested that she wear a stockinette. After his visit he wrote her, enclosing samples of stockinettes, and recent photos of Stöde, where they had married so many years before. He addressed her as 'Dear Grandma' and offered her more medical information: 'The swelling and edema of an arm after the kind of treatment you have had is caused by obstruction or coagulation of veins and lymph vessels and therefore the swelling might come and go.'

Petter wrote about their past together as well, confronting Ingrid once again with matters such as the Capa and Adler affairs, Pia's trips to London, and the details of the Messina meeting. 'It is understandable if some of the details and dates of the past are not so clear to us,' he wrote. 'In the past I never published anything to correct the abundant interviews published to make me look rather despicable. However, it seemed best to clarify a few issues that came up at our recent meetings in London.'

Ingrid answered Petter's letter immediately, writing in longhand on airmail paper. She did not view their mutual past as if she were a historian, arguing data, facts, and detail; she regarded her past as her lover, to be enjoyed, reminisced about. As she always did with what was unpleasant, she pushed it aside, and went on to happier matters. She didn't even mention Petter's questions. She thanked him for sending recent photos of Stöde; 'Stöde is just as I remember it when we drove up there the first time.'

Ingrid filled that summer with travel so that, as she wrote Petter, she had no time for illness. In August she went to Sweden and travelled by train, bus, and ferryboat, and not only to Danholmen but to Stockholm.

Her children's lives were moving on, and that gave her more occasion to travel. Isotta was pregnant. Then Isabella called to say that she was planning to marry Martin Scorsese, the Italian-American film director. Isabella had met Scorsese when she interviewed him in New York City, as part of her work for Italian television. Scorsese was a great admirer of Isabella's father, and the two of them quickly became involved.

'Does he move you?' Ingrid asked.

'What do you mean?' Isabella asked.

'Does he *move* you?' Ingrid asked again.

'Yes, Mother, he moves me completely.'

In October, Ingrid flew to Rome to attend the wedding. It was a wedding that seemed out of a movie: the celebrated director marrying the lovely daughter of Roberto Rossellini and Ingrid Bergman.

In November, Ingrid flew to Los Angeles for a tribute put on by the Variety Clubs of America to raise money for a new hospital wing. These tributes had become a minor growth industry in Hollywood, a predictable formula that was at least as calculating as it was sentimental. On the evening that Ingrid walked onto Sound Stage 9 at Warner Brothers, a formally dressed group had assembled on the old Rick's Café set.

Ingrid wore a long-sleeved, neck-high, floor-length white gown. Around her neck was a diamond-and-emerald-studded necklace worth as much as half a million dollars, a gift from Lars. This was the first time she was wearing it in public, at her former husband's insistence. Midway into the programme, she received an award from the Swedish consul. He pinned the ribbon around her neck, totally covering the jewels.

'Ingrid worked very hard on her speech for the tribute,' said her cousin Britt, who had flown in for the evening. 'She wanted to make one big performance. During the tribute she said, "Why is Goldie Hawn talking? I hardly talked to her during the filming of *Cactus Flower*."'

At least Goldie Hawn had worked with Ingrid. Most of those eulogizing her knew her hardly at all. Of those who did Lewis Milestone sat in a wheelchair in a corner, unable even to rise to salute her; Ruth Roberts was here, but she, too, was sickly and old.

It was forty years since Ingrid had first arrived in California, thirty years since she had left. Hollywood had changed, and the people Ingrid had known in the 1940s were for the most part dead or dying. It was not Ingrid being eulogized this evening, but a golden glorious image that even now she could step back and examine as if it were another person.

At the end of the evening, Ingrid got up to make her speech. 'I thought I should give you a surprise,' she said. 'You don't know how long I have been in the film industry. You see, when my father had discovered that something new had happened and that was motion pictures, he was so enthusiastic that he went on my birthday and rented a camera that he cranked by hand.'

A tiny baby in her mother's arms. A little girl on her second birthday pushing a wheelbarrow. A young mother holding her daughter. A little girl at a graveside.

'I was always polite, at least on the screen,' Ingrid said. 'I am three years old, coming to my mother's grave. That's why I was so happy to have those shots, so at least I can see her move.'

The images flickered on. A little girl greeting her relatives from Germany. A bigger girl with her cousin Britt. Ingrid and Greta, her father's lover. A teenager getting off a small boat near her vacation home.

Ingrid spoke as proudly as if these were images from her famous movies, and she was the creator of the character on the screen. There was, indeed, a truth in these home movies beyond anything that had been said at the tribute. There had been such a feeling of warmth and family and security in the first pictures. But then the mother is dead, and the camera draws back. There are relatives and friends in the pictures, Ingrid not the centre any longer. Then finally a child–woman alone in a heavy coat getting off a small boat.

'I came off a quite small boat,' Ingrid said, 'and ten years later I came off a much bigger boat to the harbour of New York.'

When Ingrid was in Los Angeles, she and Griff went to visit the Farmer's Market. It was one of the places she had always liked in Los Angeles, one of the places she had taken Roberto. The market had become something of a tourist trap, but Ingrid ignored that, and enjoyed her lunch. During the meal Griff jumped up and ran over to a nearby newsstand. In the racks were piles of *National Enquirers* with the headline 'INGRID BERGMAN HAS CANCER'. Griff turned the papers over and returned to the table, hoping Ingrid hadn't noticed.

Ingrid and Burgess drove down to San Diego to visit Petter. A few months before, Petter had talked to Kay Brown in New York. 'Kay mentioned that she and Ingrid would visit me,' Petter wrote Burgess later. 'That was quite a surprise, since I had not extended any such invitation to them. Kay got a cold and couldn't come to California, but by then you telephoned me [the day before] saying that you and Ingrid were coming to visit me in San Diego. This seemed strange indeed. However, I could hardly refuse to see Ingrid if she indeed came to visit, just as I could not say no when you told me last June in London that Ingrid wanted to see me there. How would that have come out in Ingrid's interviews that her former husband, a physician and a Professor of Surgery, refused to see her when she was suffering from cancer, and when she was in his vicinity. After your arrival here with Ingrid last November, I frankly asked you why Ingrid had come to visit me. Equally frankly you answered that Ingrid wanted to see my children and wanted to include a report about her visit here in your forthcoming book. In other words, that trip of hers to San Diego was mainly for publicity reasons.'

Burgess's version is that Petter had invited Ingrid's longtime agent down to San Diego after the Variety Club tribute, and Kay had assumed that Ingrid was invited as well. Burgess, moreover, says that his book was finished and he was going to San Diego to give Petter part of the manuscript to read. 'I had no intention of writing about the trip,' he says.

Burgess had not yet written the conclusion of the book, though. It would have been an almost irresistible bit of drama to end not with the Variety Club tribute, as he did, but with Ingrid's sentimental journey southward to Petter, and a reconciliation with her former husband. 'It was my idea of getting these two people together,' says Burgess. 'They were both decent characters. Petter didn't object to it. He was overjoyed when she got here.'

Petter was not interested in sentimental reconciliations. Since their divorce he had achieved what by any measure was the American dream. His second wife offered him a kind of companionship that Ingrid had never given him. Not only did he have a lovely fellow doctor as a wife, three healthy, well-mannered sons and a daughter, and a home with a pool and sauna, but he was still a vital man, a practising physician with an international reputation. He looked a good fifteen years younger than his seventy-two years, this man whom Ingrid had once considered too old for her.

An observer might think that Petter had it all. Yet when he spoke of events of thirty years before, it was as if they had just happened; there were those who thought that he was obsessed with his former wife. Some of those who had heard Petter's stories, such as Alan Burgess, believed that Petter had never loved Ingrid, that it had all been pride and possession. Others who had heard the same stories thought that he had never stopped loving her.

Even after all these years, Petter was still on occasion being reminded of his first marriage. Earlier in the year, a two-part article in a leading Swedish magazine, *Husmodern*, had been full of errors and half truths that he felt slandered him and his life. There were also articles that quoted Pia about her hard times as a child. His eldest daughter insisted that she had been misquoted, but her remarks were painful to Petter and complicated their relationship. If he was to tell his side of the story that time was now.

Ingrid and Burgess settled into rooms at the Coronado. The next day they arrived at Petter's house, on a bluff overlooking the Pacific Ocean. It was Thanksgiving. Petter invited Ingrid and Burgess for dinner.

Ingrid was drinking a great deal. Petter could see that she was in some pain. He knew that there was a special kind of sling that would help. The next day he took her to a medical supply house to have it made for her.

Ingrid wrote Petter and Agnes a warm thank you note from the Hotel Pierre in New York. She said that it had been a 'joy' to visit Petter's family. 'I miss the delicious air in San Diego!'

Whatever hope Ingrid might have had for a reconciliation with Petter ended the moment he read the pages that Burgess had left with him. Although there was a lengthy interview with Petter, on most of the major points Burgess had sided with Ingrid's version.

Burgess wrote Petter that he was sorry Petter was upset about the material he had read. He said that he realized Petter had given him a great deal of material that he hadn't gone through carefully. He promised to do so and add it to the book.

Ingrid tried to smooth things over with Petter by simply ignoring the problem of the book. On 26 March 1980, she wrote him a gay little note addressed to 'Dear Grandpa', thanking him for more photos of his family and wishing him a happy Easter. On that same day, Petter wrote a long letter to Ingrid addressed to 'Dear Grandma'.

'The past thirty years you yourself and your representatives have never stopped publishing some very bad reports about me, some pure lies, other gross distortions,' he began in the five-page, single-spaced communication. 'I never responded, never gave an interview regarding you or our relationship in spite of all the invitations and pressures . . . Time has changed. Someone recently reminded me of the old saying that if a lie is repeated often enough it becomes truth . . . I have submitted extensive records and comments to Alan and I suggest that you read them all.'

Petter learned soon afterwards that what Burgess had told him was an objective biography would be published in the fall of 1980 as Ingrid's autobiography. He felt doubly deceived, and he and Pia both asked that their letters be removed. Although Petter could not be expected to believe such an unlikely tale, it was the publisher, Delacorte Press, that convinced Ingrid that she should expand her first-person interviews and put her name on the book as an autobiography.

The curious form of the book allowed Ingrid, in Burgess's words, 'to say what she wanted to say in the first person and have me, the narrator, say what she didn't want to say or couldn't really say'. It was even less likely, now, that Ingrid was going to allow *her* book to become a running debate with Petter, giving him the right to reply to anything he felt was 'inaccurate or distorted', as Burgess had promised him in writing in 1978.

'Dear Alan Burgess, who I thought I knew,' Petter wrote Burgess on 29 July 1980.

> I have difficulty admitting that I might have made a mistake when I relied on you and trusted all your verbal and written promises regarding your book . . . I have received a copy of a letter of yours where you talk about slander to which you feel you have been exposed and where you imply some possible legal action from your side. It might be of some interest to you to see how you and your 'heroine', as you call her, would appear in court under cross-examinations. Since I.B. recently telephoned from London to the Husmodern Magazine in Stockholm that she never had felt better in her whole life, I assure that she will be in good condition to appear in court, and not only in the many public appearances which evidently have been scheduled for promotion of your book.
>
> By this time you too have probably seen enough of the contradictions and the fairy tales I.B. is capable of during her neverending play acting. As I have explained to you, it was my impression over several years that I.B. was basically an honest and kind person, and with a good sense of humor, although totally obsessed with her career and her publicity. Nothing else really concerned her.

Petter and Pia separately contacted Harriet Pilpel, a prominent New York literary attorney, who in turn contacted Delacorte Books about removing their letters and interviews. Petter was on strong moral if not legal grounds. Ingrid did not see it that way, and she took the restrained legal letters as personal attacks.

'I was deluged with legal problems,' remembers Jeanne Bernkopf, the editor. 'Our answer was to paraphrase the letters. But on the interviews with Petter, I finally said just remove them . . . I called Alan and said, "Every single piece of information, take it out."'

Ingrid thought that with Petter out of the way, everyone would be happy with the book. But she soon discovered the mixed joys of authorship. Irene Selznick was upset at Ingrid's portrayal of her in the book and equally bothered by Ingrid's treatment of Sidney Bernstein. Before setting off on her publicity tour, Ingrid wrote in her trip diary that Irene complained that her two best friends had been left out. She realized that she had upset most of the people mentioned in the book and those not mentioned as well.

To promote *My Story*, Ingrid travelled extensively in both the United States and Europe in the last months of 1980, and she was received not as another celebrity plugging a bestseller, but as a great star, a great dying star. When she could, she watched her taped interviews on television. She was as self-critical as she had ever been. But she viewed an interview a success when there was no mention of Petter, whom she called in her diary 'Dr L', and no ugly intrusion into her illness.

In Paris, one sunny afternoon, she noticed a poster with her name on it, advertising a newspaper story about '*La dernière lutte contre la morte*' [The last fight against death]. She bought the paper and sat down at a sidewalk café to read about herself and her illness. Afterwards, she wrote in her diary that the whole story was about a woman dying of a dread disease; there were photographs of her in bed, taken from her movies; not a word was true.

CHAPTER 23

'I DON'T WANT THE FILM
TO BE OVER'

In November 1980, Harve Bennett, a Paramount producer, got together a group of people in his office to discuss the casting of his new project, a television miniseries based on the life of Golda Meir. It was his secretary, Silvia Rubinstein who suggested Ingrid Bergman.

Before contacting Ingrid, Bennett checked things out as best he could. Golda was a sacred name to most Jews. There had been a terrible brouhaha over Vanessa Redgrave, an avowed supporter of the Palestinian Arabs, playing a Jewish concentration camp inmate in the television film *Playing for Time*. He didn't want any of that. He learned that 'some people thought the Jewish community would be offended by Ingrid playing the part'. But people in Hollywood always run scared.

Bennett had Marilyn Hall on his side. She had been involved with the project from the beginning, and she had as good contacts with the Jewish community as anyone. She was married to Monty Hall, a TV game show host, and was a formidable fund-raiser for Jewish organizations. She phoned Mike Frankovich, the producer of *Cactus Flower*, and asked him to call Ingrid in London.

When Frankovich called from Hollywood, Ingrid gave him an emphatic no. Golda was not Ingrid's new Joan of Arc, a role she identified with and had dreamed of playing. Ingrid knew very little about Golda except that she was tiny, Jewish, and recently deceased. People would not accept a Golda who was tall, Protestant, and spoke with a Swedish accent. That was the end of that.

Though her arm had become increasingly swollen, Ingrid couldn't stand the idea of simply sitting around waiting for visits from her children and friends. Early in 1981 she set off on her first trip to Israel with her cousin Britt.

Although this was purely a tourist trip, Ingrid couldn't help but think sometimes of Golda Meir. Beyond that, she was being wooed, sometimes in ways she didn't quite realize. Marilyn Hall had called Teddy Kollek, the mayor of Jerusalem; he spent several hours showing Ingrid films of Golda, and talking about the early years of Israel.

Ingrid received a call from Gene Corman, the on-location producer of *A Woman Called Golda*, who was in Israel making another film but had time to woo Ingrid. 'Apart from being a motion picture producer, I'm a movie fan, and I'd love to have dinner with you.'

When he saw Ingrid walk into the lobby of the King David Hotel in Tel Aviv, he was stunned. The illness had eaten away her beauty. Then, as they sat in the candlelight of the hotel bar, an extraordinary thing happened. Through the flickering light he saw Ingrid again, the Ingrid of *Casablanca* and *Saratoga Trunk* and *Anastasia*, the Ingrid of his youth.

Corman told her all that he knew about Golda. This was no simple Hollywood heroine he was talking about. Here was a Golda Meir who had left her husband and children to pursue her career; who had lovers while she was married; who had struggled not only for Israel but for herself, for her own recognition and success. Yet here was a Golda Meir who when she was prime minister might be found in the kitchen cooking dinner. Here, finally, was a Golda Meir who died after a long struggle with leukaemia.

As Corman sketched the outline of Golda's life, he could see tears in Ingrid's eyes, and when he was finished she asked him for some books about Golda.

Politicians and movie stars have a great deal in common, and the more Ingrid read about Golda, the more the character resonated within her. Here was this world figure, a creator not only of Israel but of her own image. And here was this little lady who some-how had the ego and ambition to crawl out of her marriage and family life and rise to international heights that few women had ever reached.

In deciding whether to play Golda, Ingrid was not unlike a politician deciding whether to run again. She talked to practically every-one about Golda. Laurence Evans, her British agent, thought that she was wrong for the part. Sidney Bernstein was opposed too, as worried about dangers in Israel as about the role itself. Initially, Kay Brown had not been enthusiastic either, but she knew Ingrid so well that she realized that anything that would get her working again was good.

When Ingrid returned to London, the script for *A Woman Called Golda* was waiting for her. Although she had been very interested in the film, she decided to turn it down. Ingrid wrote Bennett on 9 April 1981 that she so greatly revered Golda Meir and held her in such respect that she couldn't possibly play her in a film.

A month later Ingrid attended a large dinner given by the International Variety Clubs, the charity that the year before had given her a tribute. Seated next to her was Marilyn Hall, whose husband, Monty, was the honorary chairman. Marilyn spent the evening trying to get Ingrid to change her mind.

'The main reason she gave was how could the Israelis accept her when her mother was German,' Marilyn says. There were other questions in Ingrid's past that were far larger. No one has a memory like the Jews, and there were surely those in Israel who knew a good deal about Ingrid's short-lived career for UFA, and the film she made in Nazi Germany in 1938. She also had reason to be worried that Petter would make some statement.

That evening in the ballroom at the Grosvenor House, Ingrid made other excuses. 'The life of Golda is too fresh in people's minds,' she said. 'If it was someone like Isadora Duncan I would take a chance.' And she admitted, 'You know, I know nothing about Israel. I'm not political.'

At the end of the evening, Marilyn agreed to send a driver to pick up the script. When no one showed up at Ingrid's town house, she called Marilyn at the hotel.

'Oh, I'm very sorry about the driver . . .'

'That doesn't matter,' Ingrid said brusquely. 'If for my purpose I wanted to play Golda Meir and felt that I could, I would be willing to play the part. Why don't you come over to my flat and we'll talk about it.'

Marilyn came and Ingrid talked eagerly about the role. On the table sat the script that she had wanted to return. There were marks all over it, and pages turned down. 'You know you can't insure me,' Ingrid said. 'And I'll have to have a screen test.'

The last time Ingrid had made a real screen test was for *For Whom the Bell Tolls*, but she wanted one this time. She made reference to the heavy make-up she would wear as Golda. 'I have never played underneath a mask in my life. I want to see if I can do it.'

Bennett made plans to fly to London for the test. The executive producer had seen recent photos of Ingrid, and he felt that it would not be that difficult to make her look like Golda. 'It occurred to me that the problem was her own self-perception,' Bennett says. 'She did not see the changes in herself any more than any of us do who think of ourselves at an earlier age. She would not perceive herself as resembling Golda Meir.'

To help prepare her, Ingrid was sent voice and video tapes, including a lengthy BBC interview. Golda's voice alone contained the story of her life. One could hear the expanses of Russia, where she was born; the irony and humour of Yiddish; the brashness of big-city, beer-making, tough-talking Milwaukee, where she lived as a young woman; and the struggles of life in Palestine, to which she came as a Zionist.

In her career, Ingrid had played in five languages – Swedish, German, English, Italian, and French – but always with *her* accent. Yet if Ingrid couldn't get Golda's voice right, she could get nothing of the role right. She practised in the shower, and in the kitchen. She played the tapes, pacing back and forth in her living room.

On the day of the screen test, Ingrid arrived at the small studio. She went into the make-up room, where Wally Schneiderman began his work. He had been in the business for almost forty years, and was one of the finest make-up men in films. He had saved pictures of Golda in his files, with hopes that one day he would have this assignment. With modern film stock, he didn't need the heavy make-up he once would have used. Highlights and shadows would be enough, alone with a grey wig. As Ingrid watched critically, he brushed her face with make-up, and applied a small bridge on her nose.

When Ingrid walked back into the studio, there was a momentary hush. It was no longer Ingrid Bergman but a woman who had the feel and walk and look of Golda Meir. A fine actress can look fat when she is thin, and short when she is tall, and what was most amazing was that Ingrid didn't even seem big any longer, but appeared to be a tiny, dumpy old lady. Ingrid looked at Frederick Young standing there behind the camera. She walked up to Young and embraced him. Freddy had shot *Indiscreet* and *The Inn of the Sixth Happiness*, and they talked awhile about old times. Ingrid felt comfortable working with people she knew; Freddy was the only person here with whom she had worked before, hired for this one day. Most of the others treated her with overwhelming deference and caution, as if a harsh word might shatter her.

While Alan Gibson, the director, was blocking the shots with a stand-in, Ingrid sat in a chair, chain-smoking. Corman noticed that her hands were shaking. The producer thought: 'What have we done?' He walked up to Ingrid, knelt beside her, and attempted some soothing, aimless conversation.

'You know I'm nervous,' Ingrid said.

'Ingrid, we are all very excited to have you, and you are so dedicated that you want a screen test.'

As Corman talked, the camera was dollied in closer and closer. Ingrid looked past the producer, to the camera.

'Oh, you know I see an old friend,' she said.

'If you're ready we'll begin now, Ingrid,' Gibson said in his gentle voice.

Ingrid did four scenes that day, showing Golda at different stages in her life. Another actress would play Golda as a young woman, but 66-year-old Ingrid would have to play Golda from middle age to almost 80. There was no one there that day who was not impressed. But as always, the proof was in the film, and it was not until the following afternoon that Ingrid arrived at the Paramount offices to see the test.

The lights went off, and the first scene played upon the small screen. The camera had always loved Ingrid, loved her when she blushed and glowed with youthful loveliness in her first colour test for Selznick forty-two years before, loved her as Sister Benedict and as Anastasia. And as the camera moved in, framing her face, it loved her still as homely old Golda, loved the nuances and lines in her face, loved the sadness and depth.

There was no sound in the room except for an occasional nervous cough. When the footage ended, Ingrid asked that it be screened once more. And when she had seen the test again, and the lights came on, she turned in her seat, tears glistened in her eyes. 'If you want me, I'm yours,' she said, and then Corman and Bennett and Gibson had tears in their eyes too.

Ingrid invited everyone over to her flat to celebrate and drink champagne. She had only one bottle of champagne in the apartment, but the others had brought several bottles more. Ingrid drank glass after glass, and the others matched her as best they could. 'Do you have any comments?' she asked.

Bennett had a comment, but if it hadn't been for the champagne he would not have made it. When he watched the screen test, he had thought back to his boyhood days, going to the synagogue and hearing the cantor sing with a sob in his voice. Ingrid had a sob in her voice, a way of talking that made one want to cry. It had made him want to cry watching *Casablanca* and *For Whom the Bell Tolls*. It made him want to cry in the screening room, but he had had the feeling that if Golda had seen it, she would have said, 'I'm not so sentimental.'

'I have only one thing to say.'

'Yes,' Ingrid said, suddenly sober.

'Watch the self-pity.'

'You noticed?'

'Yeah.'

'Yes, yes, yes, I can control that,' she said.

Ingrid wasn't going to let anything stand in the way of her performance. When Nastassja Kinski was suggested for the part of the young Golda, Ingrid felt that a lesser-known actress would be prefer-able. The suggestion was made that Isabella play the young Golda, but Ingrid dismissed that as well. Instead, the fine Australian actress Judy Davis was hired for the part.

On 4 September 1981, Ingrid flew from London to Tel Aviv, accompanied by Margaret Johnstone, who from now on would spend more time with her than anyone else. Margaret was a tall, big-boned woman who looked more like a Swedish farmer's wife than the British-born masseuse and expert cook that she was.

Ingrid had called on Margaret to give her a massage when she returned to England after the American run of *The Constant Wife*. Ingrid could not hide her illness from a masseuse, and the two women talked about the disease. 'I've gone through woes and so have you,' Margaret said, and showed Ingrid a scar from a non-malignant growth. In the months that followed, Ingrid had become more dependent on Margaret, not only for massages but for cooking and companionship and errands. For Margaret, it was an exciting new world, and she was delighted to be asked to go to Israel with Ingrid.

Ingrid knew that the film would be made under the most punishing of schedules. This was not a theatrical picture, after all, but a four-hour television miniseries, filmed at three times the pace of a Holly-wood feature. Moreover, it was not even network television, but a syndicated programme, with a decidedly smaller budget.

In Israel, *A Woman Called Golda* was an event of importance; everyone in the country had an opinion about Golda Meir. Making the film in Israel was like a portrait painter attempting to sketch a likeness while family members, neighbours, enemies, and assorted kibitzers stood criticizing every brush stroke. In this case, however, the producers allowed the onlookers to pick up a brush and paint a few lines. Moshe Dayan, the former defence minister and war hero, was worried about how he would be portrayed. He was shown his lines, and he tinkered with them until he felt he came out well.

Golda's children wanted nothing to do with the film. They had expressed their concerns that Golda's love life would be portrayed. That was taken care of in the script by giving Golda a relationship with only one, composite figure, Ariel, and making a veiled suggestion that he and Golda might have been lovers. The producers had the full cooperation of the Israeli government, and the script was far from a balanced portrait of the Zionists' fight for the birth of Israel. Although there was much in the film about Arab terrorists, nothing was said about the terrorism of the Irgun and the Stern gang or about the life of the Palestinians.

The film, then, was not about the brutal business of history. Nor was it about the human price of power. Philip Gillon wrote in the *Jerusalem Post* that Golda, along with Ben-Gurion, 'was a good hater . . . We saw nothing of their capacity to hate in the film . . . Golda emerges as that ambitious young girl who marries the wrong man but goes on to become an implacable, strong Momma plying the kiddies with ghastly Jewish delicacies'.

Ingrid saved the film. 'I have a feeling that what I perceived, as the producer, and Harold Gast, as the writer, and Alan Gibson, as the director, was a romanticized version of Golda, our ideal,' says Bennett. 'But I think Ingrid reached beyond that.'

In her first few days in Israel, Ingrid immersed herself even further in Golda's life. She spent a day at the Rad Film Archives and another at United Studios, looking at an Israeli version of *This Is Your Life* about Golda. She went to Jerusalem to watch a three-hour documentary at a television station. She spent an afternoon with Lou Kaddar, Golda's longtime secretary and confidante. She met Moshe Dayan a few days before he died.

Ingrid did not complain when she was shown the small, nondescript trailer that would be her dressing room. Here every morning Schneiderman spent an hour and a quarter making her up, before letting the hairdresser come in to fit on one of the four wigs. Schneiderman used less make-up than he had for the screen test, and no longer employed a bridge for the nose. Ingrid had lost a lot of weight, and she wore special padding around her legs.

Ingrid had to play a Golda as a fortyish mother and as a nearly eighty-year-old grandmother dying of leukaemia. That would have been challenge enough, but she had to play the role with a right arm that had become grotesquely swollen. When she was not being filmed, she rested her arm on a telescoping stand above her head.

For Alan Greenberg, the Israeli cameraman, the challenge was extraordinary. He could see how the heat of the lights bothered Ingrid, and he tried to keep the lights to a minimum. The costuming department had fitted Ingrid with long-sleeved dresses, but Greenberg had to make the audience unaware that Ingrid had an enormous, almost immovable arm. One evening early in the shooting, he sat watching the rushes along with Ingrid and other members of the production. 'She was supposed to be young, but she looked very old,' Greenberg remembers. 'Her attitude was very bad when she saw how she looked. I didn't sleep all that night. But from that I learned how to work with her.'

When the filming began, Ingrid got up in the morning at 5.45. She left the hotel an hour later and was dressed and made up, on the set ready to shoot by 8.30. Even on an air-conditioned set, her rubberized padding would have been unpleasant, but in the heat and sun of Israel, it was like sitting all day in a sauna. In the morning she was usually vivacious, but when Schneiderman touched up her make-up in the afternoon, he could see the fatigue written all over her face.

Margaret was staying with Ingrid in her suite in Tel Aviv. She knew better than anyone how tired Ingrid was becoming. 'Let's switch to a later start,' Margaret suggested.

'Oh no, they're on a tight budget and schedule,' Ingrid said, unwilling to complicate the filming.

When Sidney Bernstein came for a visit, he became upset that Ingrid was having to get up practically at dawn. Margaret called Corman and from then on Ingrid started several hours later each morning. The great unspoken worry was that she could not complete the film.

The heat was insufferable and Ingrid was growing weaker by the day. Though she did not complain, she had rarely had to put up with such conditions, and never with such a schedule. She tried to rest in the trailer, but the air-conditioning kept going off, and it heated up like an oven.

One day when it was close to one hundred degrees, and a dog left in a closed car would die in a few hours, Ingrid shot a scene in a car in Jerusalem. The car was jammed with a driver, the camerman, and lights, and by the time Ingrid returned from the drive on a road parallel to the Knesset, she was exceedingly tired and irritable. She took out her anger on the one person not involved with the film. Margaret.

The next shot that day was in a café overlooking the Wailing Wall. 'I don't know if I can make it,' Ingrid told Corman. She sat in a chair with a coat around her, while the scene was set up. Mayor Teddy Kollek happened to be visiting the set that afternoon, but Corman asked him not to talk to Ingrid.

The shot was made, and Ingrid finally arrived back at the Solomon Sheraton Hotel. When Margaret entered the suite she found Ingrid out on the balcony.

'Darling, I'm sorry if things have been difficult for you today, but I know you understand that I want to die with my boots on.'

Despite the rigours of her role, Ingrid found time to do interviews and accept invitations. One evening she was the honoured guest at the opening of the Israeli film archives. Ingrid made a few remarks before a showing of *For Whom the Bell Tolls*, and then sat down next to Monty Hall. *For Whom the Bell Tolls* was Ingrid's first colour film, and her youthful beauty is astounding. She glows with health and well-being, and her suntanned, tawny skin seems the colour of life itself. Ingrid watched for a few minutes, and then turned to Hall: 'You'll have to forgive me. I can't stand it.'

She kept losing more weight, and the padding she wore covered a shrivelled frame. Golda had leukaemia for the last fourteen years of her life. In one scene a doctor tells her of the disease. Ingrid was the same age as Golda in the scene, and the scene resonated with meanings within meanings.

'How much longer do I have?' Ingrid asked, playing with such understatement and poignancy that a mere whisper had more power than a scream.

'I'd say you have a good few years ahead of you.'

'Well, I'm 66. How long can I expect to live anyway?'

As Ingrid spoke the lines, Greenberg turned his head away from the scene he was filming. 'I just can't watch her,' he said softly to Gibson.

In the following scene, Golda tells Lou Kaddar that she is ill, but does not tell her that she has leukaemia. 'But I don't understand why she would do that,' Ingrid protested to Gibson.

'Because she realizes its impact on other people,' the director said.

Ingrid thought a moment. 'That's right,' she said, and went ahead with the scene.

Ingrid had seen the famous picture of Golda when she hears herself named prime minister and puts both her hands over her face in a gesture of amazement. The edema of Ingrid's right arm and hand seemed to mandate a double. On the morning of the shooting, Corman had lined up a middle-aged woman whose hands would be shot. The night before, however, Ingrid had strapped her right arm up high above her head, trying to drain the fluid. She slept very little, but when she got up, the hand appeared almost normal.

Corman shot the scene as soon as Ingrid emerged from her trailer. She had to say nothing, only to raise her hands to her face, and when it was over and Corman said 'Print,' Ingrid exclaimed, 'I did it!'

Ingrid was weakening so fast, that by the time Lars and Isabella arrived for a visit, it was impossible to hide the physical deterioration. Several times in the last months Lars had thought Ingrid was about to die, but she had reserves of sheer strength that amazed him.

Lars was the one person to whom Ingrid confided all her complaints. One day Ingrid, Lars, and Isabella visited the Wailing Wall in Jerusalem. 'See, you're standing between two wailing walls,' Ingrid said.

Lars laughed, but he was profoundly worried. As soon as the

shooting finished in Israel, Ingrid was supposed to fly to Los Angeles to shoot the American scenes. But Lars doubted if she was up to such a long trip. Corman and Gibson decided that they would have to finish the film in London.

On the eve of Ingrid's return to England, a grand party was held at the Tel Aviv Hilton. There were belly dancers, and live music, and mounds of food, and even a camel, and Ingrid stayed on and on. The next morning the El Al flight to London was delayed four hours. When Ingrid, Margaret, Gibson and Schneiderman finally arrived at the airport, they learned that the airline had gone on strike.

That evening they flew out of Tel Aviv on the only connection available, an Air France airbus. Ingrid refused the one first-class seat available, and stayed with her colleagues instead. By the time the plane reached Nice, she was very tired. She wanted to get off and go to sleep, but the baggage had been checked to Paris. It was after one o'clock by the time the group checked into a Paris hotel, and the restaurant was closed. Ingrid was exhausted, but she still could laugh that because of a broken shoe strap Margaret had walked into the hotel in her bare feet.

The last scene to be shot takes place in 1948. Golda, who has gone to the United States to raise money for arms, learns that war has already begun in the Middle East, while she is thousands of miles away. Ingrid arrived for the scene in White's Hotel at Lancaster Gate. As the camera tracked slowly in on her face, Ingrid was to speak the line: 'In another seventy-two hours it will all be over.'

The camera moved in and stopped, focusing on Ingrid's face. She sat there. Silence. The camera rolled on.

'My God,' Ingrid said. 'I forgot it . . . I don't want the film to be over.'

CHAPTER 24

'I'M ALONE'

As soon as the film was wrapped up Ingrid retired to her house in Cheney Gardens and into herself, venturing out as little as possible. When Lars came to visit, he was sure once again that this was the beginning of the end. He told Ingrid that she must call Margaret to say that she wasn't feeling well, and needed her help. He phoned Margaret from the airport at seven o'clock in the morning to see if Ingrid had called. On his next visit, a few days later, Lars asked Margaret to take care of Ingrid full time. Ingrid said, 'You don't know what you've taken on. Old ladies can be quite difficult.'

At Christmas she flew to Choisel to spend the holidays with Lars and members of her family. 'She was very sad,' Isabella remembers. 'I could tell she felt it was the last time . . . I knew she was very lost, talking about death at the party. She couldn't go to sleep. She said, "What is the best way to go?" I felt she was talking about suicide. She showed me articles about euthanasia.'

When Ingrid returned to London, Margaret moved into the house. Margaret was endlessly solicitous, but Ingrid did not find it easy having her in the house twenty-four hours a day. She didn't do things the way Ingrid did them. She tried to manage Ingrid's life.

The rich are not allowed merely to die. Although Dr Edward MacLellan was dubious about chemotherapy in Ingrid's case, she went to St Thomas's Hospital in Lambeth for five week-long visits during the next four months. To prevent the loss of her hair, ice packs were placed on the scalp before each treatment, freezing the roots.

Chemotherapy is war on the body, and Ingrid suffered greatly from her treatments, experiencing acute nausea and extremes of temperature. For all the agony, the therapy did no good, and after each session Ingrid seemed to sink more into herself.

She would spend long hours before the television screen. When she wrote letters, she did not let on how she felt. She was sometimes full of bravado, as if she were a character in somebody's play. On 14 March she wrote Oriana Fallaci, the Italian journalist, about her arm:

'I call him my dog, I joke with him: "You are a dog, a nasty sick dog. Come on, let's go walking."'

Lars instructed Margaret to get Ingrid out of the house. 'I would use Lars's name,' Margaret says. 'She never complained, but she must have thought I was awfully hard. Sometimes we'd go to the movies . . .' Ingrid loved the movies, but she couldn't stand what she considered the foul-mouthed, vulgar realism of many new films, and if she didn't like what she was seeing after a few minutes, she would march right back up the aisle.

Ingrid did not have many friends, but the friends she had were good ones, and Griff was the best of them all. Ingrid didn't have to play 'Ingrid Bergman' with Griff. She would call him and usually he came over right away. And they would talk and laugh, and he would scold her, or make fun.

Once, they talked about dying. 'You'll come to my funeral,' Griff said. 'I'm going to the greatest prop corner in the sky.'

'I want Prokofiev's *Romeo and Juliet* played at *my* funeral,' Ingrid said.

'I want the music from *Gone With the Wind* at mine.'

'You shall have it,' Ingrid said, and feigned anger, 'even though it's not from an Ingrid Bergman movie.'

Lars called every day, wherever he was. There were those who said that Lars felt guilty about Ingrid, but guilt was perhaps too small a word for all that he felt. He had his son now, but his relationship with Kristina had not worked out. He was at an age when most men would have slowed down, particularly one of Lars's wealth, but he continued his restless journeyings, as if he knew that he no longer belonged anywhere.

One day early in April, Lars called from Stockholm.

'Isn't there anything you would like?' Lars asked.

'I would like a *fastlagsbullar*,' Ingrid said, naming the marzipan bun that in Sweden is served with warm milk for Easter.

Lars arranged for four buns to be sent express to London, with a chauffeur waiting in London to deliver them to Ingrid.

When she went to the theatre Ingrid always took a seat on the aisle, so nothing would touch her arm. 'She was so happy at the theatre,' Ann Todd says. 'I think she liked hearing clapping.'

Ingrid could not stand to have people take notice of her, now that she looked as she did. One evening she and Ann arrived at a theatre, to find a contingent of photographers waiting under the marquee. Ingrid ordered the chauffeur to turn around and go back to Chelsea.

'Come on, what does it matter?' Anne said. 'We can get through this.'

The two actresses ran the gauntlet of photographers, but Ingrid was furious as the theatre manager led them to their seats. 'Who told the press I was coming?' Ingrid asked accusingly.

'No one,' the man said mildly. 'They're waiting for Princess Margaret.'

Ingrid and Ann laughed at that story again and again. But there came a day when there were indeed photographers waiting for Ingrid. In mid-April, when she decided that she was not strong enough to go to New York for the first screening of *Golda*, the tabloids announced that Ingrid was fighting for her life. 'INGRID BERGMAN BATTLES FOR LIFE', announced the *Daily Mirror* on its front page. 'STAR INGRID IN FIGHT FOR LIFE', said the *Express*.

Outside on the pavement in Cheney Gardens, the photographers began their watch. They had telephoto lenses and Ingrid didn't even dare go near the front window. She had experienced nothing like this since her days in the clinic in Rome, when the *paparazzi* were waiting for a birth, not a death. 'They wait there to see my body,' she told Fiorella, who was visiting.

One lovely April morning, Shirley Green, a British friend of Marilyn Hall's, arrived to deliver a gift of Ingrid's favourite perfume, L'Air du Temps. When Griff opened the door the photographers pressed forward.

'Go away, you vultures,' Griff said. 'Go take photos of Elizabeth Taylor.'

'She's too boring,' one of the photographers yelled.

If Ingrid did not intend to spend her days blockaded in her town house, she would have to go outside and let the photographers have all the photos they wanted. And so that day she called Ann Todd and had her come over to help make her up. She wore a wool cape that masked her enlarged arm, and she sat on a bench near the Thames and let the photographers have their way. 'I am not as young as I used to be,' she said. 'But my health is fine. I am not dying.'

Finally Ingrid had something to look forward to: Isabella and Isotta's thirtieth birthday party in New York, on 18 June 1982.

Isabella was starting a new career, as a model. Ingrid couldn't get over the money Isabella could earn simply by posing, not having to memorize a line. Isotta was living in New York too, her marriage at an end.

Ingrid prepared for the trip as she would for a great performance. She wanted to look as good as possible for the children. She went to Franka, her designer, and had new outfits made. On 15 June, she flew to New York on the Concorde, accompanied by Robertino. 'She was very tired,' Robertino remembers. 'She was really skinny. But always a sense of humour.' She stayed at the Wyndham Hotel. One day Ingrid and Isotta were in an elevator with two elderly ladies, who inspected her as if she were a disreputable forgery. 'Is that her?' one lady whispered. 'It can't be her,' the second lady whispered back. 'She's so old.'

One of those who saw Ingrid in New York was Steven Weiss, an investment banker, who was close to Lars and had once dated Pia. 'We talked about her death,' Weiss says. 'Death was part of her. She said she could deal with it. She'd overwhelm you with her honesty, but I'm not sure that she realized the inner parts of her life. I think if you really analysed it, you could say that she never felt comfortable with anything but her career. She was not entirely emotionally involved with her three husbands. She was so honest and candid, and yet she seemed to be shielding herself from things. Even with her children she didn't have time for the little things. Ingrid was Ingrid. She was almost an island unto herself.'

The birthday party was Ingrid's party, and she helped plan the evening. She had learned that Pavo, the young Finn who had worked at Choisel, was in town. She hired him to prepare a smorgasbord. A Salvation Army choir would come and sing 'Happy Birthday'.

That evening Ingrid made up with particular care. She wore a long-sleeved high-necked dress, with a sling the same colour. She had a hard time even sitting in the limousine, but she smiled out at the faces that peered in the windows. When she arrived at Pia's apartment on Central Park West, photographers waited outside. And Warren Thomas was there too, waiting outside for her this day as he had been waiting for her for more than three decades.

The relatives and friends had gathered in the spacious living room overlooking the park. Ingrid tried to appear completely relaxed, but her arm was a constant irritation, affected by the least touch or jostling.

Ingrid had an exquisite sense of the proper gift. She gave the twins two old pearl necklaces that had been her mother's. And she also gave them a picture of their Swedish grandmother wearing the pearls. Even here among her family, she was not comfortable speaking extemporaneously, but read remarks she said she had found, written by Peter Ustinov.

'Youth is not a time of life – it is a state of mind,' she said. 'So long as your heart receives messages of beauty, cheer, courage, grandeur, and power from the earth, from man, and from the Infinite, so long you are young. When the wires are all down and your heart

is covered with the snows of pessimism, then you are old and may
God have mercy on your soul.'

It was a memorable party, and its prospect had sustained Ingrid
for many weeks. Even at such a gloriously sentimental gathering,
she still had thoughts of Petter. 'A lot of Rossellinis were in New
York from Italy,' she wrote Bang Alving in Sweden. 'I wonder what
Petter would have said if he had seen them all invade his daughter's
home.'

Ingrid stayed on in New York longer than she had planned. On 3
July she finally flew back to London, to be met by Griff and Margaret.

Ingrid had always loved the summers. The days of July and August
had been a time for the island and the children, for champagne and
laughter, a short respite from work. Now the summer was a time of
heat and long days, of a life that stretched out before her without
work or purpose.

One day Fiorella visited and, receiving a phone call, was informed
that a friend had committed suicide.

'He died the way he wanted to live,' Fiorella said.

'What courage,' Ingrid said, and Fiorella thought that Ingrid was
thinking of killing herself.

Fiorella was not the only one worried that Ingrid might be contemplating suicide. 'Ingrid had some mild sleeping problems,' Margaret
says. 'Lars used to bring these pills that came from Switzerland. Lars
said when he brought them, "We must hide these because she has
said if she ever has enough pills . . ."'

'At the end she was very sad, you know,' Isabella says. 'She felt
extremely depressed. I think she would have killed herself. I think
that made Griff and Margaret be there all the time. I think she didn't
do it because she didn't want to have another scandal. I think she
would have been very happy if there had been an accident, if she fell
down the stairs or something. But they were afraid that she would
create a situation.

'Mother didn't want to have people there who had pity for her.
That's why I went every three weeks, but not for longer, because if
she just perceived I was there for that she would have been outraged.
She would have been so violent if I was there just for that. If you
just sat around watching TV, she would get angry. "What are you
doing watching TV! Why don't you do something! I hate you just
looking at me."'

Isotta made visits to London too. 'For Mama it was a constant
struggle. I'd see her very depressed. Sometimes I'd go to London
and she wanted to die. Sometimes, she'd say, "I can't go on. I have

no strength." What do you say? What do you tell? She didn't want us. As a mother she didn't want me there bored sitting. After a week she would say, "Go home." We knew that we would be scolded. Very often she said, "If I become very sick so I'm helpless, I'm going to jump out of the window." But I knew that it wasn't true. She was touched with life. She said, "I don't want to leave, but I can't go on." Mama loved life.'

Ingrid wanted to spare her children as much of the pain as she could. And yet to her cousin Britt she expressed a different opinion. 'When the girls were visiting her, she said they always had something to do,' Britt said. 'I have a feeling she felt a little lonely.'

Margaret and Griff believed that they had been delegated a burden that members of the family should have shared more fully. The most difficult aspect of the family life were the phone calls to Ingrid from Isotta's estranged husband, allegedly threatening Ingrid.

One day Marilyn Hall called Ingrid in London. *Golda* had been a spectacular success on American television, but Hall was calling her as a friend.

'Margaret has the flu,' Ingrid said. 'My cousin Britt was here, but she had to fly back to Sweden.'

'You're not alone?' Hall asked.

'Yes, I'm alone. And it's hot as hell.'

'Why don't you have an air-conditioner?'

'I won't need it next year.'

'Where are your children?'

'They're not here. I'm alone.'

She had always been alone. And it was out of her aloneness that everything had come. She had risen out of the aloneness of her room at Aunt Hulda's to begin her career in the theatre. She had been alone in America, with people that she only partially understood. She had been alone with Petter, and she had fled from him. She had fled into roles, and into the arms of lovers, into other marriages and other lands. She had fled from the aloneness of Choisel, the aloneness of inactivity. She spent hours talking and thinking of her past. She was not reflecting back on her life to justify it or draw meaning from it, as much as to sanctify it.

Her friends talked about the future the way a nurse fluffs up a pillow. They talked about a visit to Martha Gellhorn's cottage in Wales, though Ingrid could not possibly travel so far. They talked about attending the Edinburgh Festival in September, though no one was sure that she would live that long.

'How are you feeling, darling?' Ann Todd asked one summer evening, on what turned out to be their last outing together.

'I'm fine,' Ingrid said. 'It's just this pain in my back that troubles me.'

'Perhaps you've been sitting in a draught.'

'Yes, I expect that's what it is.'

For a Swede, July is high summer, and for Ingrid, the summer had always meant the island of Danholmen. July was over now, and the crowds had thinned at Fjällbacka, but the sun was almost as high, and the sea was still warm. As weak as she was, Ingrid wanted to visit the island. And so on Monday, 10 August, she flew to Stockholm, moving through the airports in a wheelchair. Britt was there in Stockholm, waiting for her.

For Lars, Danholmen was a magical antidote. He kept Ingrid's clothes and possessions in a bedroom there, as if he and Ingrid were still married. He said that anyone got right on the island, and he could see how good the sun and the sky were for Ingrid. At first, she was not strong enough to make her daily walk around the island, but her skin freshened with colour and she grew stronger. Sitting on the island watching the windsurfers sailing the sea as if sail and sailor were one, she said that she wished she had done that at least once, she wished she had sailed around Danholmen the way Lars and his friends did so often.

Lars called Lasse Lundberg, a good friend who ran a sailing school in Fjällbacka, and said, 'Ingrid's bad, but let's have a party Saturday night.' They came, Lasse and his wife, Ingela, bringing the crayfish that Ingrid loved so much. Ingrid felt comfortable with the Lundbergs, and they were the only guests besides Britt and Lars, and Pavo.

There are few sunsets in the world like those along the coast of Sweden in summer. For a while the horizon seems to be in flames, and then the skyline glows, and nighttime arrives not as blackness but as a soft half light. Scores of times Ingrid had sat watching the sun go down, as if she and Lars and their guests were the only people in the world. And watch it she did this day, and talked of the past.

'When he was little I would always tell Robertino bedtime stories,' Ingrid said, laughing to herself. 'One time I said, "Please tell *me* one." He said, "Well, there was this poor little boy. He lived with his poor parents in a poor house. He was so poor he had to leave home. He took his Rolls-Royce and drove away."'

Ingrid had told that story before, but everyone laughed.

'This reminds me of the Last Supper in the Bible,' Ingrid said. Everyone laughed again.

Lars left the island the day before Ingrid. Pavo and Britt would close down Danholmen. It was not like Lars, and Pavo felt that his employer could not stand to be there when Ingrid sailed away for the last time.

Ingrid was planning to spend a few days in Stockholm before returning to London. She was so weak now, and her condition was so painful, that it was clear that she should fly to the Swedish capital, but she would hear nothing of that. She didn't want any photographers to take pictures of her the way she looked now. She insisted that she be driven.

On the day that they left Danholmen, the sky grew grey and threatening. Britt and Pavo helped Ingrid down to the small fishing boat. Ingrid and Britt sat in the stern of the boat, protected by a blue awning. Pavo looked up at the black clouds and thought that perhaps he should wait. But he decided to leave, and as they sailed towards the mainland, the storm fell upon the sea.

In Fjällbacka, Ingrid said goodbye to Lasse and Ingela and got in the back seat of Lars's Citroën. Pavo drove as quickly and smoothly to the capital as he could, stopping only for a picnic lunch.

In Stockholm, Ingrid stayed in Britt's small apartment, only a few blocks from the apartment where they had lived as teenagers. As sick as she was, she went out to visit old friends, to remember old times. In this district she had walked as a young girl, looking up at the marquees of the theatres.

On her last evening in Stockholm, 23 August, Ingrid and Britt travelled to Mälarstrand, overlooking the water, not far from the town hall. There, in a large apartment high above the street, lived Greta Danielsson and her husband. All that remained of the beauty that had captivated Ingrid's father over half a century before were two sparkling eyes, and a kindness and warmth that time had only enhanced.

When Ingrid arrived, Greta thought that unlike all that she had heard, Ingrid was still beautiful, unmarked by the illness. They talked of old times, and Greta remembered the visit Ingrid had made to Örebro, in the lake country, when Greta was living there with her young doctor husband. They lived in an apartment overlooking the marketplace, and the townspeople had stood in the street, crying for Ingrid to come out on the balcony. And Ingrid had said, 'I'm not a royal person', but she had gone out on the balcony and the townspeople had cheered.

Greta realized now that Ingrid had come to say goodbye.

'I am not afraid to die,' Ingrid said. 'I've had a rich life. I am content.'

Ingrid told Griff, 'I said goodbye to everyone', as if she had everything in order, just the way she tucked her stockings in her shoes at night.

Ingrid's sixty-seventh birthday would be on Sunday, 29 August 1982, less than a week away. On Saturday morning, as she was getting out of the bath, she felt a pain unlike anything she had felt before. The cancer had advanced to her spine, collapsing her twelfth vertebra.

To ease her pain, Dr MacLellan gave her injections of diamorphine, a form of heroin. For the first time in the seven years of her illness, Ingrid was bedridden, with little prospect of ever rising to her feet again.

All week there had been phone calls back and forth between Ingrid and her children, and she had kept insisting that they not bother coming to London. But it was still strange, knowing Ingrid and her sense of occasion, that none of her children were there for her birthday.

'I'm so tired, darling,' she told Ann Todd on the phone. 'I'm so tired.'

'How lovely, Ingrid, how lovely. You just go to sleep.'

On Sunday morning there were several calls, calls from friends who did not know how sick Ingrid had become, calls wishing her a happy birthday, but Ingrid flitted in and out of consciousness. Dr MacLellan visited and discovered that her right lung was not working any longer, and only the upper third of her left lung had not collapsed. The doctor told them that the end was near.

Ingrid knew that Griff was coming to wish her a happy birthday. 'Do I look all right?' she asked Margaret. 'Give me my brush and make-up.'

Griff arrived at the town house and so did Lars, carrying a box of flowers. They stood over Ingrid's bed, Lars and Griff, Margaret and Britt, and they toasted her in champagne. They brushed her lips with champagne too, and she smiled, and then they left her and the room was quiet. In the evening, when Britt and Margaret went to bed, the only sound was Ingrid's laboured breathing.

Britt was in the next room, sleeping fitfully. At 3.30 she realized that she could no longer hear Ingrid's breathing. She went into the bedroom and saw that there were tiny beads of blood on Ingrid's lips. She took a mirror and placed it upon Ingrid's lips, although she knew already that she was dead.

CHAPTER 25

THE ENDLESS SEA

In October they came to Saint Martin's-in-the-Fields to say goodbye to Ingrid, twelve hundred of them in all. The children were there: Pia, Robertino, Isabella and Isotta. Lars was there, and so were the Rossellinis, Fiorella and Marcella and Franco and others. Britt was there, as were many others from Sweden. Gérôme had come over from Paris. Liv Ullmann was there too, and Sir John Gielgud and Dame Wendy Hiller and Joss Ackland. Warren Thomas was one of them now, one of the family and friends. And some of Ingrid's other fans came, those who had seen many of her forty-five films, her plays and her television performances.

Words of Shakespeare and Saint-Exupéry were read in her honour. Birgit Nilsson sang a Beethoven song. A children's choir marched down the aisle of the great church and sang 'This Old Man' from *The Inn of the Sixth Happiness*. But there was nothing that was as touching as the moment when, from a distant corner of the church, a violin played the strains of 'As Time Goes By'.

Ingrid had ascended into myth. The woman who had lived, the woman of bone and blood, of ambition and self-absorption, of courage and cunning, was no more. That person lived on, however, in the lives of those she had known. There was no one, though, who had shared all of her joy and emotion, all of her solitude and fear. For some, like Griff or Margaret or Warren, her loss was as deep as if they had lost part of their own body, and they mourned her as if she were their own blood. For Pia, her mother was as ambiguous a legacy in death as in life, and she seemed to live in an emotional no-man's-land between the memory of her mother and the living presence of her father. When she accepted her mother's Emmy for *Golda*, no one who heard her that evening would have imagined how complex her feelings were towards Ingrid. For Ingrid's other children, the memory of their mother was far sweeter, and they did what they could to serve her memory.

Ingrid's death did not free Petter of his regret that years before he had not spoken out to tell of an Ingrid Bergman the world did not know. As for Lars, he lived on his own island, an island more isolated than Danholmen. He had become the curator of Ingrid's image, and he loved her in memory as he had not loved her in the flesh.

In June, Lars invited a small group of relatives and friends to Danholmen. They walked to a tiny bay, carrying baskets of flowers that they had collected on the island. They stood on the grey rocks, looking out to sea.

Lars and Isotta sailed out into the water in a small boat, with Lasse and a Swedish priest. There they cast Ingrid's ashes into the water, while those on shore threw their baskets into the surf.

The sea was calm and the baskets slowly drifted out. They finally reached a fisherman tending his lobster pots. The fisherman did not know why the water was full of flowers, but he did not touch the baskets, and the flowers drifted farther out and disappeared in the endless sea.

The Count of the Monk's Bridge/*Munkbrogreven*
Svensk Filmindustri, 1934
Produced by AB Fribergs Filmbyra
Directed by Edvin Adolphson and Sigurd Wallen
Screenplay by Gösta Stevens, from the play *Greven fran Gamla Sta'n*
  by Arthur and Siegfried Fischer
Cast: Valdemar Dahlquist, Sigurd Wallen, Eric Abrahamson, Weyler
  Hildebrand, Artur Cederborg, Edvin Adolphson, Ingrid Bergman,
  Tollie Zellman, Julia Caesar, Arthur Fischer, Emil Fjellstrom,
  Viktor Andersson

Ocean Breakers/*Branningar*
Svensk Filmindustri, 1935
Produced by Film AB Skandinavien
Directed by Ivar Johansson
Screenplay by Ivar Johansson, from an idea by Henning Ohlsson
Cast: Tore Svennberg, Sten Lindgren, Carl Strom, Ingrid Bergman,
  Brof Ohlsson, Knut Frankman, Karin Swenson, Weyler Hilde-
  brand, Georg Skarstedt, Henning Ohlsson, Vera Lindby, Viktor
  Ost, Emmy Albiin, Viktor Andersson, Helga Brofeldt, Carl
  Browallius, Olle Grenberg, Holger Lowenadler, E. Rosen

The Family Swedenheilms/*Swedenhielms*
Svensk Filmindustri, 1935
Produced by AB Svensk Filmindustri
Directed by Gustav Molander
Screenplay by Stina Bergman, from the play by Hjalmar Bergman
Cast: Ingrid Bergman, Gösta Ekman, Karin Swanström, Häkan
  Westergren, Björn Berglund, Tutta Rolf, Sigurd Wallen, Nils
  Ericsson, Adèle Söderholm, Mona Geijer-Falkner, Hjalmar Peters,
  Sven Jerring

Walpurgis Night/*Valborgsmassoafton*
Svensk Filmindustri, 1935
Produced by AB Svenskfilmindustri

Directed by Gustaf Edgren
Screenplay by Oscar Rydquist and Gustav Edgren
Cast: Lars Hanson, Karin Carlsson, Victor Sjöström, Ingrid Bergman, Erik Berglund, Sture Lagerwall, Georg Blickingberg, Stig Järrel, Richard Lund, Linnéa Hillberg, Marie-Louise Sorbon

On the Sunny Side/*Pa Solsidan*
Svensk Filmindustri, 1936
Produced by Aktiebolaget Wivefilm
Directed by Gustav Molander
Screenplay by Oscar Hemberg and Gösta Stevens, from the play by Helge Krog
Cast: Lars Hanson, Ingrid Bergman, Karin Swanström, Edvin Adolphson, Einar Axelson, Marianne Lofgren, Carl Browallius, Bullen Berglund, Eddie Figge, Olga Andersson, Viktor Andersson, Eric Gustafsson

Intermezzo
Svensk Filmindustri, 1936
Produced by AB Svenskfilmindustri
Directed by Gustav Molander
Screenplay by Gustav Molander and Gösta Stevens, from an original story by Gustav Molander
Cast: Gösta Ekman, Ingrid Bergman, Inga Tidblad, Hasse Ekman, Erik Berglund, Hugo Björne, Emma Meissner, Britt Hagman, Anders Henrikson, George Fant, Folke Helleberg, Millan Bolander, Carl Ström

Dollar
Svensk Filmindustri, 1938
Produced by AB Svenskfilmindustri
Directed by Gustav Molander
Screenplay by Stina Bergman and Gustav Molander, from the comedy by Hjalmar Bergman
Cast: Georg Rydeberg, Ingrid Bergman, Kotti Chave, Häkan Westergren, Birgit Tengroth, Elsa Burnett, Edvin Adolphson, Gösta Cederlund, Erik Rosén, Carl Ström, Axel Högel, Millan Bolander

A Woman's Face/*En Kvinnas Ansikte*
Svensk Filmindustri, 1938
Produced by AB Svensk Filmindustri
Directed by Gustav Molander

Screenplay by Gösta Stevens, from the screenplay *Il Était une Fois* by François de Croisset

Cast: Ingrid Bergman, Anders Henriksson, Karin Kavli, Magnus Kesster, Erik Berglund, Gösta Cederlund, Georg Rydeberg, Bror Bügler, Tore Svennberg, Göran Bernhard, Gunnar Sjöberg, Hilda Borgström, Sigurd Wallen

The Four Companions/*Die Vier Gellen*
UFA, 1938
Produced by UFA in Germany
Directed by Carl Fröhlich
Screenplay by Jochen Huth, from his play
Cast: Ingrid Bergman, Sabine Peters, Carlsta Löck, Hans Söhnker, Ursula Herking, Leo Slezak, Erich Ponto, Heinz Welzel, Willi Rose, Karl Haubenreisser, Wilhelm P. Krüger, Lotte Braun

Only One Night/*En Enda Natta*
Svensk Filmindustri, 1939
Produced by AB Svensk Filmindustri
Directed by Gustav Molander
Screenplay by Gösta Stevens, from the story 'En Eneste Natt' by Harold Tandrup
Cast: Ingrid Bergman, Edvin Adolphson, Aino Taube, Olof Sandborg, Erik Berglund, Marianne Löfgren, Magnus Kesster, Sophus Dahl, Ragna Breda, John Eklöf, Tor Borong, Viktor Andersson, Ka Nerell

Intermezzo: A Love Story
Selznick International–United Artists, 1939
Produced by David O. Selznick
Directed by Gregory Ratoff
Screenplay by George O'Neil, based on the Swedish scenario by Gustav Molander and Gösta Stevens
Cast: Leslie Howard, Ingrid Bergman, Edna Best, John Halliday, Cecil Kellaway, Enid Bennett, Ann Todd, Douglas Scott, Eleanor Wesselhoeft, Moira Flynn

A Night in June/*Juninatten*
Svensk Filmindustri, 1940
Produced by AB Svensk Filmindustri
Directed by Per Lindberg
Screenplay by Ragnar Hyltén-Cavaallius and Per Lindbert, from a story by Tora Nordström-Bonnier

Cast: Ingrid Bergman, Edvin Adolphson, Aino Taube, Olof Sand-burg, Erik Berglund, Marianne Löfgren, Maghus Kesster, Sophus Dahl, Ragna Breda, John Eklöf, Tor Borong

Liliom
A play by Ferenc Molnár, adapted by Benjamin Glazer
Produced by Vinton Freedley
Staged by Benno Schneider
Opened at the Forty-fourth Street Theater, New York, 25 March 1940
Cast: Burgess Meredith, Ingrid Bergman, Margaret Wycherly, John Emery, Ann Mason, Elia Kazan, Beatrice Pearson, Elaine Perry

Adam Had Four Sons
Columbia, 1941
Produced by Robert Sherwood
Directed by Gregory Ratoff
Screenplay by William Hurlbutt and Michael Blankfort
Cast: Ingrid Bergman, Warner Baxter, Susan Hayward, Fay Wray, Richard Denning, Johnny Downs, Robert Shaw, Charles Lind, Helen Westley, June Lockhart, Pete Sosso, Gilbert Emery, Renie Riano, Clarence Muse, Billy Ray, Steven Muller, Wallace Chad-well, Bobby Walberg

Rage in Heaven
Metro-Goldwyn-Mayer, 1941
Produced by Gottfried Reinhardt
Directed by W. S. Van Dyke II
Screenplay by Christopher Isherwood and Robert Thoeren, based on the novel by James Hilton
Cast: Robert Montgomery, Ingrid Bergman, George Sanders, Lucile Watson, Oscar Homolka, Philip Merivale, Matthew Boulton, Aubrey Mather, Frederic Worlock, Francis Compton, Gilbert Em-ery, Ludwig Hart

Dr Jekyll and Mr Hyde
Metro-Goldwyn-Mayer, 1941
Produced and directed by Victor Fleming
Screenplay by John Lee Mahin, based on the story by Robert Louis Stevenson
Cast: Ingrid Bergman, Spencer Tracy, Lana Turner, Ian Hunter, Donald Crisp, Barton MacLane, C. Aubrey Smith, Sara Allgood, Peter Godfrey, Frederick Worlock, William Tannen, Francis

Robinson, Denis Green, Billy Bevan, Forrester Harvey, Lumsden Hare, Lawrence Grant, John Barclay

Anna Christie
A play by Eugene O'Neill
Produced by the Selznick Company
Directed by John Houseman and Alfred de Liagre, Jr
Opened at the Lobero Theater, Santa Barbara, 30 July 1941; also played in San Francisco and New Jersey
Cast: Ingrid Bergman, Damian O'Flynn, Jessie Bosley, J. Edward Bromberg, John Miller, Peter Bronte, Edmund Glover, Walter Brooke, William Alland

Casablanca
Warner Brothers, 1942
Produced by Hal B. Wallis
Directed by Michael Curtiz
Screenplay by Julius J. and Philip G. Epstein and Howard Koch, from the play *Everybody Comes to Rick's* by Murray Burnett and Joan Alison
Cast: Humphrey Bogart, Ingrid Bergman, Paul Henreid, Claude Rains, Conrad Veidt, Sydney Greenstreet, Peter Lorre, S. Z. Sakall, Madeleine LeBeau, Dooley Wilson, Joy Page, John Qualen, Leonid Kinsky, Helmut Dantine, Curt Bois, Marcel Dalio, Corrina Mura, Ludwig Stossel, Ilka Gruning, Charles La Torre, Frank Puglia, Dan Seymour

Swedes in America
Office of War Information, 1943
Produced by the Office of War Information's Overseas Bureau
Directed by Irving Lerner
Cast: Ingrid Bergman and the Charles Swensons and their family of Chisago, Minnesota, and neighbours

For Whom the Bell Tolls
Paramount, 1943
Produced and directed by Sam Wood
Screenplay by Dudley Nichols, from the novel by Ernest Hemingway
Cast: Gary Cooper, Ingrid Bergman, Akim Tamiroff, Katina Paxinou, Joseph Calleia, Vladimir Sokoloff, Arturo de Cordova, Mikhail Rusumny, Eduardo Ciannelli, Fortunio Bonanova, Duncan Renaldo, Alexander Granach, Leonid Snegoff, George Coulouris, Frank Puglia, Pedro de Cordoba, Michael Visaroff,

Konstantin Shayne, Martin Garralaga, Jean Del Val, Jack Mylong, Feodor Chaliapin, Mayo Newhall, Michael Dalmatoff, Antonio Vidal, Robert Tafur, Armand Roland

Gaslight
Metro-Goldwyn-Mayer, 1944
Produced by Arthur Hornblow, Jr
Directed by George Cukor
Screenplay by John Van Druten, Walter Reisch, and John L. Balderston, based on the play *Angel Street* by Patrick Hamilton
Cast: Charles Boyer, Ingrid Bergman, Joseph Cotten, Dame May Whitty, Angela Lansbury, Barbara Everest, Emil Rameau, Edmund Breon, Halliwell Hobbes, Tom Stevenson, Heather Thatcher, Lawrence Grossmith

Saratoga Trunk
Warner Brothers, 1945
Produced by Hal B. Wallis
Directed by Sam Wood
Screenplay by Casey Robinson, based on the novel by Edna Ferber
Cast: Gary Cooper, Ingrid Bergman, Flora Robson, Jerry Austin, Florence Bates, John Warburton, John Abbott, Curt Bois, Ethel Griffies, Minor Watson, Louis Payne, Fred Essler, Adrienne D'Ambricourt, Helen Freeman, Sophie Huxley, Maria Shelton, Sarah Edwards, Jacqueline de Wit, Thurston Hall, William B. Davidson, Theodore Von Eltz, Glenn Strange, Monte Blue, Georges Renavent, Alice Fleming, Alan Bridge, Ruby Dandridge, Ralph Dunn

The Bells of St Mary's
RKO Radio, 1945
Produced and directed by Leo McCarey for Rainbow Productions
Screenplay by Dudley Nichols, from a story by Leo McCarey
Cast: Bing Crosby, Ingrid Bergman, Henry Travers, William Gargan, Ruth Donnelly, Joan Carroll, Martha Sleeper, Rhys Williams, Dickie Tyler, Una O'Connor, Bobby Fresco, Aina Constant, Gwen Crawford, Matt McHugh, Edna Wonacott, Jimmy Crane, Minerva Urecal, Pietro Sosso, Cora Shannon, Joseph Palma, Jimmy Dundee, Dewey Robinson

Spellbound
Selznick-United Artists, 1945
Produced by David O. Selznick

Directed by Alfred Hitchcock
Screenplay by Ben Hecht, adapted by Angus MacPhail from the
novel *The House of Doctor Edwardes* by Francis Beeding
Cast: Ingrid Bergman, Gregory Peck, Michael Chekhov, Jean Acker,
Donald Curtis, Rhonda Fleming, Leo G. Carroll, Norman Lloyd,
John Emery, Paul Harvey, Steven Geray, Erskine Sanford, Janet
Scott, Victor Kilian, Wallace Ford, Dave Willock, Bill Goodwin,
George Meader, Matt Moore, Harry Brown, Art Baker, Regis
Toomey, Joel Davis, Clarence Straight, Teddy Infuhr, Richard
Bartell, Addison Richards, Edward Fielding

Notorious
RKO Radio, 1946
Produced and directed by Alfred Hitchcock
Screenplay by Ben Hecht
Cast: Cary Grant, Ingrid Bergman, Claude Rains, Louis Calhern,
Madame Konstantin, Ivan Triesault, Reinhold Schunzel, Moroni
Olsen, Alex Minotis, Wally Brown, Ricardo Costa, Sir Charles
Mendl, Eberhard Krumschmidt, Fay Baker

Joan of Lorraine
A play by Maxwell Anderson
Presented by The Playwrights Company
Directed by Margo Jones
Alvin Theater, New York, 1946
Cast: Ingrid Bergman, Sam Wanamaker, Kenneth Tobey, Gilmore
Brush, Romney Brent, Roger De Koven, Kevin McCarthy, Joseph
Wiseman

Arch of Triumph
Enterprise-United Artists, 1948
Produced by David Lewis for Enterprise Studios
Directed by Lewis Milestone
Screenplay by Lewis Milestone and Harry Brown, based on the novel
by Erich Maria Remarque
Cast: Ingrid Bergman, Charles Boyer, Charles Laughton, Louis
Calhern, Roman Bohnen, Stephen Bekassy, Ruth Nelson, Curt
Bois, J. Edward Bromberg, Michael Romanoff, Art Smith, John
Laurenz, Leon Lenoir, Franco Corsaro, Nino Pepitoni, Vladimir
Rashevsky, Alvin Hammer, Jay Gilpin, Ilia Khmara, Andre Mar-
sauden, Hazel Brooks, Byron Foulger, William Conrad, Peter
Virgo, Feodor Chaliapin

Joan of Arc
Sierra Pictures–RKO Radio, 1948
Produced by Walter Wanger
Directed by Victor Fleming
Screenplay by Maxwell Anderson and Andrew Solt, adapted from the play *Joan of Lorraine* by Maxwell Anderson
Cast: Ingrid Bergman, José Ferrer, George Coulouris, Richard Derr, Selena Royle, Jimmy Lydon, Francis L. Sullivan, Irene Rich, Gene Lockhart, Nicholas Joy, Richard Ney, Colin Keith-Johnston, Leif Erickson, John Emery, John Ireland, Ward Bond, J. Carroll Naish, Hurd Hatfield, Cecil Kellaway, Philip Bourneuf, Sheppard Strudwick, Taylor Holmes

Under Capricorn
Warner Brothers, 1949
Produced by Transatlantic Pictures
Directed by Alfred Hitchcock
Screenplay by James Bridie, from Hume Cronyn's adaptation of the play by John Colton and Margaret Linden and the novel by Helen Simpson
Cast: Ingrid Bergman, Joseph Cotten, Michael Wilding, Margaret Leighton, Cecil Parker, Denis O'Dea, Jack Watling

Stromboli
RKO Radio, 1950
Produced and directed by Roberto Rossellini
Story by Roberto Rossellini in collaboration with Art Cohn and Renzo Cesana
Cast: Ingrid Bergman, Mario Vitale, Renzo Cesana, Mario Sponza

The Greatest Love/*Europa '51*
I.F.E. Releasing Corp., 1951; 1954 (USA release)
A Ponti–De Laurentiis Production
Produced and directed by Roberto Rossellini
Screenplay by Roberto Rossellini, Sandro de Leo, Mario Pannuzio, Ivo Perilli, and Brunello Rondi, from Roberto Rossellini's original story
Cast: Ingrid Bergman, Alexander Knox, Ettore Giannini, Giulietta Masina, Teresa Pellati, Sandro Franchina, William Tubbs, Alfred Browne

Joan of Arc at the Stake
Oratorio by Arthur Honegger, written by Paul Claudel

Produced and directed by Roberto Rossellini
Teatro San Carlo, Naples, 1953, and elsewhere
Cast: Ingrid Bergman, Tullio Carminati, Marcella Pobbe, Florence
  Quartarar, Miriam Pirazzini, Giacinto Prandelli

We, the Women/*Siamo Donne*
Titanus, 1953
The Chicken, the third of five segments, stories and screenplays by
  Cesare Zavattini; Luigi Chiarini collaborated on the screenplay
Directed by Roberto Rossellini
Cast: Ingrid Bergman, Anna Magnani, Isa Miranda, Alida Valli,
  Emma Danieli, Anna Amendola

Joan at the Stake/*Giovanna d'Arco al Rogo*
1953
Produced and directed by Roberto Rossellini
Screenplay by Roberto Rossellini, based on the story and dialogue
  of Paul Claudel and the oratorio of Paul Claudel and Arthur
  Honegger
Cast: Ingrid Bergman, Tullio Carminati, Giacinto Prandelli,
  Augusto Romani, Plinio Clabassi, Saturno Melitti

Journey to Italy/*Viaggio in Italia*
Titanus, 1954
Produced by Roberto Rossellini in association with Sveva-Junior
  Films
Directed by Roberto Rossellini
Story and screenplay by Roberto Rossellini and Vitaliano Brancati
Cast: Ingrid Bergman, George Sanders, Paul Muller, Anna Pro-
  clamer, Maria Mauban, Leslie Daniels, Natalia Rai, Jackie Frost

Fear/*Angst*
Minerva Films, 1955
Produced by Minerva Films
Directed by Roberto Rossellini
Screenplay by Roberto Rossellini, Sergio Amidei, and Franz Graf
  Treuberg, based on the novel *Der Angst* by Stefan Zweig
Cast: Ingrid Bergman, Mathias Wiemann, Renate Mannhardt, Kurt
  Kreuger, Elise Aulinger

Anastasia
20th Century-Fox, 1956
Produced by Buddy Adler

Directed by Anatole Litvak
Screenplay by Arthur Laurents, adapted by Guy Bolton from a play
by Marcel Maurette
Cast: Ingrid Bergman, Yul Brynner, Helen Hayes, Akim Tamiroff,
Martita Hunt, Felix Aylmer, Sacha Piteoff, Ivan Desny, Natalie
Schafer, Gregoire Gromoff, Karel Stepanek, Ina De La Haye,
Katherine Kath

Tea and Sympathy
A play by Robert Anderson, French adaptation by Roger-Ferdinand
Presented by Elvire Popesco and Hubert de Malet
Directed by Jean Mecure
Opened at Théâtre de Paris, 2 December 1956
Cast: Ingrid Bergman, Jean-Loup Philippe, Yves Vincent, Georges
Berger, Simone Paris, Bernard Lajarrige, Guy Sarrazin, Guy
Kerner, Bernard Klein, Jean Mondani, Pierre Derone

Paris Does Strange Things/*Elena et les Hommes*
Warner Brothers, 1957
Produced and directed by Jean Renoir
Screenplay by Jean Renoir, based on his story
Cast: Ingrid Bergman, Mel Ferrer, Jean Marais, Juliette Greco,
Marjane, George Higgins, J. Richard

Indiscreet
Warner Brothers, 1958
Produced and directed by Stanley Donen for Grandon Productions
Screenplay by Norman Krasna, based on his play *Kind Sir*
Cast: Cary Grant, Ingrid Bergman, Cecil Parker, Phyllis Calvert,
David Kossoff, Megs Jenkins, Oliver Johnston, Middleton
Woods

The Inn of the Sixth Happiness
20th Century-Fox, 1958
Produced by Buddy Adler
Directed by Mark Robson
Screenplay by Isobel Lennart, based on the novel *The Small Woman*
by Alan Burgess
Cast: Ingrid Bergman, Curt Jurgens, Robert Donat, Michael David,
Athene Seyler, Ronald Squire, Moultrie Kelsall, Richard Wattis,
Peter Chong, Tsai Chin, Edith Sharpe, Joan Young, Lian Shin
Yang, Noel Hood, Burt Kwouk

The Turn of the Screw
NBC-TV, 1959
Executive producer, Hubbell Robinson, Jr
Directed by John Frankenheimer
Adapted for television by James Costigan, from the novella by Henry James
Cast: Ingrid Bergman, Hayward Morse, Alexandra Wager, Isobel Elsom, Laurinda Barrett, Paul Stevens

Goodbye Again/*Aimez-Vous Brahms?*
United Artists, 1961
Produced and directed by Anatole Litvak
Screenplay by Samuel Taylor, based on the novel *Aimez-vous Brahms?* by Françoise Sagan
Cast: Ingrid Bergman, Yves Montand, Anthony Perkins, Jessie Royce Landis, Jackie Lane, Pierre Dux, Jean Clarke, Peter Bull, Michele Mercier, Uta Taeger, Andre Randall, David Horne, Lee Patrick, A. Duperoux, Raymond Gérôme, Jean Hebey, Michel Garland, Paul Uny, Colin Mann, Diahann Carroll

Twenty-four Hours in a Woman's Life
CBS-TV, 1961
Executive producer, Lars Schmidt
Directed by Silvio Narizzano
Screenplay by John Mortimer, based on a story by Stefan Zweig
Cast: Ingrid Bergman, Rip Torn, John Williams, Lili Darvas, Helena de Crespo, Jerry Orbach

Hedda Gabler
A play by Henrik Ibsen, translated by Gilbert Sigaux
Produced by Lars Schmidt
Dircted by Raymond Rouleau
Opened at Théâtre Montparnasse, Paris, 10 December 1962
Cast: Ingrid Bergman, Claude Dauphin, Jean Servais, Jacques Dacomine

Hedda Gabler
CBS-TV, 1963
Produced by David Susskind, Lars Schmidt, and Norman Rutherford
Directed by Alex Segal
Adapted for television by Phil Reisman, Jr, from Eva Le Gallienne's translation of the Henrik Ibsen play

Cast: Ingrid Bergman, Michael Redgrave, Ralph Richardson, Trevor Howard, Dilys Hemlett, Ursula Jeans, Beatrice Varley

The Visit
20th Century-Fox, 1964
Produced by Julian Derode
Directed by Bernhard Wicki
Screenplay by Ben Barzman, based on the play by Friedrich Duerrenmatt
Cast: Ingrid Bergman, Anthony Quinn, Irina Demick, Valentina Cortese, Ernest Schroeder, Paolo Stoppa, Hans-Christian Bleck, Romolo Valli

The Yellow Rolls-Royce
Metro-Goldwyn-Mayer, 1965
Produced by Anatole De Grunwald
Directed by Anthony Asquith
Screenplay by Terence Rattigan
Cast: Ingrid Bergman, Omar Sharif, Joyce Grenfell, Wally Cox

A Month in the Country
A play by Ivan Turgenev
Produced and directed by Michael Redgrave
Opened at the Yvonne Arnaud Memorial Theatre in Guildford, England, in June 1965, before moving to the Cambridge Theatre in London
Cast: Ingrid Bergman, Michael Redgrave, Fay Compton, Daniel Massey, Max Adrian, Jennifer Hilary, Geoffrey Chater, Peter Pratt

Stimulantia
Omnia Films, 1967
An eight-part film. Ingrid Bergman appeared in the episode *The Necklace (Smycket)*, written and directed by Gustav Molander from the story by Guy de Maupassant
Cast: Ingrid Bergman, Gunnar Björnstrand, Gunnel Brostrom

More Stately Mansions
A play by Eugene O'Neill
Staged by José Quintero
Opened at the Ahmanson Theater in Los Angeles, September 1967 and at the Broadhurst Theater in New York, October
Cast: Ingrid Bergman, Colleen Dewhurst, Arthur Hill, Fred Stewart,

Barry McCallum, Vincent Dowling, Helen Craig, John Marriott, Lawrence Linville, Kermit Murdock

The Human Voice
ABC–TV, 1967
Produced by David Susskind and Lars Schmidt for Stage 67
Directed by Ted Kotcheff
Adapted for television by Clive Exton, from a translation by Carl Wildman of a story by Jean Cocteau
Cast: Ingrid Bergman

Cactus Flower
Columbia, 1969
Produced by M. J. Frankovich
Directed by Gene Saks
Screenplay by I. A. L. Diamond, from the play by Abe Burrows
Cast: Ingrid Bergman, Walter Matthau, Goldie Hawn, Jack Weston, Rick Lenz, Vito Scotti, Irene Hervey, Eve Bruce, Irwin Charone, Matthew Saks

A Walk in the Spring Rain
Columbia, 1970
Produced by Stirling Silliphant
Directed by Guy Green
Screenplay by Stirling Silliphant, from the novel by Rachel Maddux
Cast: Ingrid Bergman, Anthony Quinn, Fritz Weaver, Katherine Crawford, Tom Fielding, Virginia Gregg, Mitchell Silberman

Captain Brassbound's Conversion
A play by George Bernard Shaw
Produced in the United States by Roger Stevens and Arthur Cantor
Played in England and the United States, 1971 and 1972
American Cast: Ingrid Bergman, Leo Leyden, Geoff Garland, Yusef Bulos, Eric Berry, Zito Kozan, Joss Ackland

From the Mixed-up Files of Mrs Basil E. Frankweiler
Cinema 5, 1973
Produced by Charles G. Mortimer, Jr
Directed by Fielder Cook
Screenplay by Blanche Hanalis, based on the novel by E. L. Konigsburg
Cast: Ingrid Bergman, Sally Prager, Johnny Doran, George Rose, Georgann Johnson, Richard Mulligan, Madeline Kahn

Murder on the Orient Express

Paramount Pictures, 1974
Produced by John Brabourne and Richard Goodwin
Directed by Sidney Lumet
Screenplay by Paul Dehn, based on the novel by Agatha Christie
Cast: Ingrid Bergman, Albert Finney, Lauren Bacall, Martin Balsam, Jacqueline Bisset, Jean-Pierre Cassel, Sean Connery, John Gielgud, Wendy Hiller, Anthony Perkins, Vanessa Redgrave, Rachel Roberts, Richard Widmark, Michael York, Colin Blakeley, George Coulouris, Denis Quilley

The Constant Wife

A play by W. Somerset Maugham
Produced by Arthur Cantor
Directed by John Gielgud
London and Shubert Theater, New York, 1975
Cast: Ingrid Bergman, Jack Gwillim, Brenda Forbes, Carolyn Lagerfelt, Marti Stevens

A Matter of Time

American International Pictures, 1976
Produced by Jack H. Skirball and J. Edmund Grainger
Directed by Vincente Minnelli
Screenplay by John Gay, based on the novel *The Film of the Memory of Maurice Druon*
Cast: Ingrid Bergman, Liza Minnelli, Charles Boyer, Isabella Rossellini, Spiros Andros, Tina Aumont, Fernando Rey

Autumn Sonata

New World Pictures, 1978
Produced, written, and directed by Ingmar Bergman
Cast: Ingrid Bergman, Liv Ullmann, Lena Nyman, Halvar Björk, Arne Bang-Hansen, George Lokkeberg, Gunnar Björnstrand, Erland Josephson, Linn Ullmann, Knut Wigert, Evan von Hanno, Marianne Aminoff, Mimi Pollak

Waters of the Moon

Played at Chichester Theatre's summer season and at Haymarket Theatre, London, 1979
Produced by Duncan C. Weldon and Louis Michaels
Directed by Patrick Garland
Cast: Ingrid Bergman, Wendy Hiller, Doris Hare, Frances Cuka,

Derek Godfrey, Charles Lloyd Pack, Paul Hardwick, Brigette Kahn, Carmen Silvera, Paula Geoffrey

A Woman Called Golda

Paramount Television, 1982
Executive Producer: Harve Bennett
Associate Producer: Marilyn Hall
Producer: Gene Gorman
Written by Harold Gast and Steven Gethers
Cast: Ingrid Bergman, Ned Beatty, Franklin Cover, Judy Davis, Anne Jackson, Roberto Loggia, Leonard Nimoy, Jack Thompson, Anthony Bate, Ron Berglas, Bruce Boa, David de Keyser, Barry Foster, Nigel Hawthorne, Louis Mahoney

SELECTED BIBLIOGRAPHY

Magazine and newspaper articles are cited in the notes.

Adler, Larry. *It Ain't Necessarily So*. London: Collins, 1984.

Adolphson, Edvin. *Ea berätar*. Stockholm: Bonniers, 1972.

Anobile, Richard, Jr. *Casablanca*. New York: Universe Books, 1974.

Arce, Hector. *Gary Cooper*. New York: Bantam Books, 1980.

Austin, Paul Britten. *On Being Swedish: Reflections Towards a Better Understanding of the Swedish Character*. London: Secker and Warburg, 1968.

Avallone, Michael. *A Woman Called Golda*. New York: Leisure Books, 1982.

Bacon, James. *Made in Hollywood*. New York: Warner Books, 1977.

Barnett, Lincoln. *Writing on Life: Sixteen Close-Ups*. New York: William Sloane Associates, 1951.

Barzini, Luigi. *From Caesar to the Mafia: Sketches of Italian Life*. New York: The Library Press, 1971.

Behlmer, Rudy. *America's Favorite Movies Behind the Scenes*. New York: Frederick Ungar, 1982.

Behlmer, Rudy, ed. *Memo from Selznick*. New York: Grove Press, 1972.

Benchley, Nathaniel. *Humphrey Bogart*. Boston: Little Brown, 1975.

Béranger, Jean. *La Grande Aventure du Cinéma Suédois*. Paris: La Terrain Vague, 1956.

Berenson, Bernard. *The Passionate Sightseer: From the Diaries 1947–1956*. New York: Simon & Schuster, 1960.

Bergman, Ingmar. *The Marriage Scenarios*. New York: Pantheon Books, 1974.

Bergman, Ingrid, and Burgess, Alan. *Ingrid Bergman: My Story*. New York: Delacorte, 1981.

Boccardi, Luciana, ed. *Dossier Ingrid Bergman: Una Vita per il Cinema*. Venice, 1983.

Bondanella, Peter. *Italian Cinema from Neorealism to the Present*. New York: Frederick Ungar, 1983.

Bowers, Ronald. *The Selznick Players*. New York: A. S. Barnes, 1976.

Brown, Curtis, F. *Ingrid Bergman*. New York: Galahad, 1973.

Capa, Robert. *Slightly out of Focus.* New York: Henry Holt, 1947.

Chierichetti, David. *Hollywood Costume Design.* New York: Harmony Books, 1977.

Cowie, Peter. *Ingmar Bergman, A Critical Biography.* New York: Scribner, 1982.

——. *Swedish Cinema.* London: A Zwemmer, 1966.

Davidson, William. *The Real and the Unreal.* New York: Harper, 1961.

Dyer, Richard. *Stars.* London: British Film Institute, 1982.

Francisco, Charles. *You Must Remember This . . . The Filming of Casablanca.* Englewood Cliffs, N.J.: Prentice-Hall, 1980.

Frank, Gerold. *Zsa Zsa Gabor: My Story.* Cleveland and New York: World, 1960.

Guarner, Luis José. *Roberto Rossellini.* Translated by Elisabeth Cameron. New York: Praeger, 1970.

Henreid, Paul, with Fast, Julius. *Ladies' Man: An Autobiography.* New York: St Martin's Press, 1984.

Higham, Charles, and Greenberg, Joel. *Hollywood in the Forties.* New York: A. S. Barnes, 1968.

Hotchner, A. E. *Choice People.* New York: Morrow, 1984.

Myams, Joe. *Bogie: The Biography of Humphrey Bogart.* New York: New American Library, 1966.

Ibsen, Henrik. *Plays: Two.* London: Methuen, 1982.

Katz, Roberto. *Death in Rome.* New York: Macmillan, 1967.

Koch, Howard. *As Time Goes By.* New York: Harcourt Brace Jovanovich, 1979.

——. *Casablanca: Script and Legend.* Woodstock: Overlook Press, 1973.

Lamarr, Hedy. *Ecstasy and Me: My Life as a Woman.* New York: Bartholomew House, 1966.

Lambert, Gavin. *GWTW: The Making of Gone with the Wind.* Boston: Little Brown, 1973.

Liehm, Mira. *Passion and Defiance: Film in Italy from 1942 to the Present.* Berkeley: University of California Press, 1984.

Locock, C. D., trans. *A Selection from Modern Swedish Poetry.* New York: Macmillan, 1929.

Madsen, Alex. *William Wyler, the Authorized Biography.* New York: Thomas Y. Crowell, 1973.

McBride, Joseph, ed. *Persistence of Vision.* Madison: Wisconsin Film Society Press, 1968.

Millichap, Joseph R. *Lewis Milestone.* Boston: Twayne Publishers, 1981.

Moberg, Vilhelm. *A History of the Swedish People: From Prehistory to the Renaissance*. New York: Pantheon, 1972.

——. *A History of the Swedish People: From the Renaissance to the Revolution*. New York: Pantheon, 1973.

Oakley, Stewart. *A Short History of Sweden*. New York: Praeger, 1966.

Orwell, George. *A Life: Bernard Crick*. New York: Penguin, 1982.

Overbey, David, ed. and trans. *Springtime in Italy: A Reader on Neo-Realism*. Hamden, Conn.: Anchor Books, 1978.

Procaci, Giuliano. *History of the Italian People*. New York: Harper & Row, 1968.

Quirk, Lawrence J., ed. *The Films of Ingrid Bergman*. Secaucus. N.J.: Citadel Press, 1970.

Ranvaud, Don. *Roberto Rossellini*. London: Blackrose Press, 1981.

Rhode, Eric. *A History of the Cinema from Its Origins to 1970*. Harmondsworth: Penguin Books, 1979.

Rosenzweig, Sidney. *Casablanca and Other Major Films of Michael Curtiz*. Ann Arbor, Mich.: UMI Research Press, 1982.

Roncoroni, Stefano, ed. *The War Trilogy of Roberto Rossellini*. Translated by Judith Green. London: Loorriner Publishing, 1973.

Sanders, George. *Memoirs of a Professional Cad*. New York: Putnam, 1960.

Scott, Franklin D. *Sweden: The Nation's History*. Minneapolis: University of Minnesota Press, 1977.

Selznick, Irene. *A Private View*. New York: Alfred A. Knopf, 1983.

Shipton, David. *The Great Movie Stars: The Golden Years*. New York: Hill and Wang, 1979.

Sklar, Robert. *Movie-Made America: A Cultural History of American Movies*. New York: Vintage, 1975.

Skoglund, Gunnar. *God Min I Brokigt Spel*. Stockholm: Norstedt, 1983.

Smith, Dennis Mack. *Mussolini: A Biography*. New York: Vintage, 1983.

Spoto, Donald. *The Dark Side of Genius: The Life of Alfred Hitchcock*. Boston: Little Brown, 1983.

Steele, Joseph Henry. *Ingrid Bergman: An Intimate Portrait*. New York: Delacorte, 1959.

Stern, Michael. *No Innocence Abroad*. New York: Random House, 1952.

Strindberg, August. *Plays: Two*. Translated by Michael Meyer. London: Methuen, 1982.

Swindell, Larry. *The Reluctant Lover: Charles Boyer*. Garden City, N.Y.: Doubleday, 1983.

Tannenbaum, Edward R. *The Fascist Experience: Italian Society and Culture 1922–1945*. New York: Basic Books, 1972.

Taylor, John Russell. *Ingrid Bergman*. New York: St Martin's, 1983.

——. *Strangers in Paradise: The Hollywood Émigrés 1933–1950*. New York: Holt, Rinehart & Winston, 1983.

Tengroth, Birgit. *Livs Levande*. Stockholm, 1952.

Thomas, Bob. *Selznick*. New York: Doubleday, 1970.

Todd, Ann. *The Eighth Veil*. New York: Putnam, 1981.

Travelyan, Raleigh. *Rome '44: The Battle for the Eternal City*. New York: Viking, 1982.

Verdone, Mario. *Roberto Rossellini*. Paris: Éditions Seghers, 1963.

Von Heidenstam, O. G. *Swedish Life in Town and Country*. New York: Putnam, 1904.

Von Zaneigbergk, Eva. *Stockholm to Delight You*. Stockholm: Bonniers, 1960.

Walker, Alexander. *Stardom: The Hollywood Phenomenon*. New York: Stein and Day, 1970.

Wallis, Hal, and Higham, Charles. *Star Maker*. New York: Berkley, 1981.

Warner, Marina. *Joan of Arc: The Image of Female Heroism*. New York: Penguin Books, 1981.

Welch, David. *Propaganda and the German Cinema*. Oxford: Clarendon Press, 1983.

Whelan, Richard. *Robert Capa*. New York: Alfred A. Knopf, 1985.

Winquist, Sven, and Jungstedt, Torsten. *Svenskt Filmskadespelar Lexikon*. Sweden: Bokfolaget Forum AB, 1973.

Yeadon, David. *Backroad Journey of Southern Europe*. New York: Harper & Row, 1981.

Research Notes

In researching *As Time Goes By*, I believe that I talked to almost every major living figure in Ingrid Bergman's life. I have relied primarily on interviews that I conducted and on documents such as letters, diaries, contracts, etc. that I have personally seen. I have occasionally quoted from books, newspapers, and magazines. Although I have read most of the celebrity journalism, gossip columnists, and fan magazines about Ingrid, I have used such sources only as examples of Ingrid's image.

I have used Miss Bergman's autobiography as my primary source for her own version of herself, for there she is quoted accurately.

In the notes that follow I have highlighted the sources of important facts, quotes, and material. To keep this to a reasonable length, I have not cited each instance that I have quoted a major figure from my interviews. Letters and memos from the Selznick organization are from the Selznick archives at the University of Texas. Newspaper and magazine articles are cited below. Books are listed by author's names and are fully cited in the selective bibliography.

page

Chapter 1: 'Papa, Papa, That's What I'm Going to Do'

1   Description of Strandvägen in nineteenth century: Soder, pp. 76–81.
1   *the silver shoe and the photo constituted:* interview with Disa Lauhren, Stockholm.
1   Biographical information about the Bergman family from family history and genealogy in Swedish in Miss Bergman's possession at the time of her death.
2   *Friedel's senior:* Although Ingrid told Steele that her father was 18 years older, her tombstone in Stockholm and family genealogical records show that Justus was born in 1871 and Friedel in 1884.
2   *No. 21, modelled after a palace:* Soder, p. 81.
3   *'Is Mrs . . .':* interview with Lauhren, Stockholm.
4   *'She was a . . .':* interview with Lauhren, Stockholm.
5   *'I think . . .':* interview with Greta Danielsson, Stockholm. Danielsson was then called by her maiden name, Haugran.
5   *'We fell in love and . . .':* interview with Danielsson.
6   *He handed:* interview with Danielsson
6   *'She was like a sister':* interview with Britt Engstrom, Stockholm.
7   Description of the Red Mill: interview with Torsten Jungstedt, Stockholm.
7   *'If you remember . . .':* interview with Lauhren, Stockholm.
7   *'My father was . . .':* interview with Engstrom, Stockholm.
8   *'I never had . . .':* interview with Engstrom, Stockholm.
8   *'I think she . . .':* interview with Danielsson.
8   ostrich farm: interview with Jungstedt.

8   *'age of lethargy':* quoted in Béranger.
8   *the cinema was:* interview with Rune Waldekranz, Stockholm.
10   *the boy in:* Steele, p. 18.
10   *'with only minor slips':* 'Smorgasbord Circuit', by Irving Wallace, *Collier's*, Dec.
     21, 1946, pp. 12, 96

Chapter 2: 'Oh, She Starts Well, Doesn't She?'

12   *'When I was . . .':* interview with Dr Petter Lindstrom. Unless noted otherwise,
     all quotes from Lindstrom are from a series of interviews conducted in Santa
     Monica and San Diego.
13   *'She was absolutely . . .':* interview with Engstrom.
14   *few memories:* interviews with Hasso, Los Angeles; Sundstrom and Bjornstrand,
     Stockholm.
15   *'had destroyed a scene . . .':* quoted in Adolphson, pp. 213–214.
16   *'I was crushed . . .':* quoted in Tengroth, pp. 111–117.
16   *'And who's this?':* quoted in Adolphson, pp. 213–214.
17   *'More as an . . .':* interview with Dahlqvist, Malmo.
22   *'How happy I . . .':* quoted in Tengroth, pp. 111–117.
23   *'Little golden kitten . . .':* quoted from undated letter, IB to PL.
23   *'How many hours . . .':* quoted from *Dagens Nyheter* article by Barbro Alving,
     July 11, 1937.
24   *'MOST BEAUTIFUL AND . . .':* quoted from Alving, op. cit.

Chapter 3: Destined for Hollywood

26   *'Men make . . .':* quoted in BB, p. 51
26   *'I had the . . .':* interview with Holm, Stockholm.
27   *'Gustav Molander, the director . . .':* interview with Dahlqvist.
28   *'rubber truncheons and . . .':* quoted in Crick, p. 364.
29   *She refused:* BB, pp. 51–52.
30   *'As I recall it . . .':* interview with Kay Brown, New York.
30   *'Miss Reissar has long . . .':* letter Brown to David O. Selznick (henceforth
     DOS) July 26, 1938, Selznick archives (henceforth SA).
31   *'Keep it most . . .':* memo DOS to Brown, Aug. 15, 1938, SA.
31   *'would still be . . .':* cable DOS to Brown, Aug. 16, 1938, SA.
31   *'a cold shudder . . .':* DOS to Brown, Aug. 16, 1938, quoted in Behlmer, p.
     123.
32   Description of Stockholm and *'This feeling of . . .':* letter Jenia Reissar to
     Brown, SA.
32   *'It was as soon . . .':* interview with Reissar, London.
32   *'Under no circumstances . . .':* letter Reissar to Brown, Oct. 4, 1938, SA.
33   *'To almost every question . . .':* letter Reissar to Brown, Jan. 28, 1939, SA.
34   *'when I arrived in . . .':* letter Brown to O'Shea, Feb. 24, 1939, SA.
35   Terms of contract: contract dated Feb. 14, 1939, SA.
35   *'SOMEWHAT UNATTRACTIVE AND . . .':* cable DOS to Brown, Feb. 12, 1939,
     SA.
36   *'utterly disappointed':* quoted in cable Brown to O'Shea, Mar. 16, 1939, SA.
36   *'My wife, who since . . .':* letter Lindstrom to Brown, Mar. 15, 1939, SA.
36   *'IF WE ARE . . .':* cable DOS to Brown, Apr. 6, 1939.

Chapter 4: 'A Figure to Take into Account'

38 *April 20, 1939:* Although IB wrote in her autobiography that she arrived May 6, 1939, the Selznick archives show otherwise.
38 '*I think that . . .*': letter DOS to Brown, Feb. 27, 1939, SA.
38 '*eligibles*': letter Brown to DOS, Apr. 24, 1939, SA.
39 '*I got in . . .*': interview with Neuberger, New York City.
39 *Irene greeted:* BB, pp. 64–65. Irene Selznick says that this story is not true and that Miss Bergman told her she made up the story to give Alan Burgess a good anecdote in her autobiography. Burgess denies this and indeed Ingrid told the story to reporters years before her autobiography was written.
40 Description of first meeting with Selznick based on BB, pp. 65–69.
41 '*revolutionary instructions . . .*': letter DOS to IB, Nov. 3, 1945, SA.
41 '*We have enough trouble . . .*': quoted in Irene Selznick, p. 225.
43 '*a combination . . .*': quoted in 'Big Girl', by Kyle Crichton, *Collier's*, Sept. 14, 1940, p. 13.
43 '*Yi! Yi!*': quoted in Crichton, p. 13.
43 *tower of babel:* interview with Finnochio, Los Angeles.
43 '*This in turn . . .*': memo DOS to Ratoff/cc Toland, June 22, 1939, SA.
44 '*I don't hear . . .*': letter Brown to Lewton, July 17, 1939, SA.
44 '*I was told . . .*': interview with Sandler, Los Angeles.
45 '*She was the most . . .*': letter DOS to Brown, July 28, 1939, SA.
46 *That had all been called off:* memo DOS to Calvert, July 28, 1939, SA.
46 *To avoid:* memo Calvert to Hebert, July 31, 1939, SA.
46 *so sad:* cable IB to DOS, Aug. 9, 1939, SA.

Chapter 5: A Wilful Ignorance

47 *Pia cried and would not:* letter IB to Irene Selznick, Sept. 7, 1939, SA.
47 *Parsons alleged:* Los Angeles Examiner, Sept. 21, 1939.
47 '*this thing could . . .*': memo DOS to Birdwell, Sept. 26, 1939, SA.
47 *neither any political:* cable IB to Selznick, Sept. 29, 1939, SA.
47 '*they have a claim . . .*': memo Brown to O'Shea, Oct. 11, 1939, SA.
48 '*frightening American . . .*': letter IB to DOS, Sept. 29, 1939, SA.
48 '*I always . . .*': letter DOS to IB, Oct. 16, 1939, SA.
49 '*her angelic nature . . .*': memo DOS to Brown, Oct. 17, 1939, SA.
49 *she did not feel:* letter IB to Brown, Oct. 28, 1939, SA.
50 *Ingrid danced:* quoted in BB, p.83.
50 Description of the *Rex* based on *The New York Times*, Jan. 13, 1940.
50 *Gellhorn noticed:* interview with Martha Gellhorn, England.
50 '*Don't talk too much . . .*': quoted in BB, p. 83. Also Myer Beck from memo Brown to DOS, Feb. 9, 1940, SA.
52 '*I noticed a distinct . . .*': memo DOS to Brown, Feb. 6, 1940, SA.
52 '*I can't see . . .*': memo Brown to DOS, Feb. 9, 1940, SA.
53 *According to Kay:* interview with Brown, New York City.
53 '*not unduly . . .*': cable Brown to DOS, Mar. 20, 1940, SA.
54 '*Thank God . . .*': letter IB to DOS, Mar. 27, 1940, SA.
54 '*The theatre was . . .*': New York World Telegram, Mar. 30, 1940.
55 '*Oh, you've . . .*': Crichton, p. 30.
56 '*reluctance about . . .*': O'Shea to DOS, May 23, 1940, SA.
56 '*stubborn as . . .*': memo O'Shea to DOS, June 21, 1940, SA.
56 '*It is outrageous . . .*': memo DOS to O'Shea, June 24, 1940, SA.

Chapter 6: 'The Bars of My Cage are Broken'

59   'addicted to . . .': interview with Pober, Hollywood.
59   seven hours later: MGM archives.
59   'There are people . . .': interview with Isherwood, Santa Monica.
60   'I know I can . . .': interview with Dr Ray Daum, Austin, Tex.
61   Ingrid was the: memo DOS to Brown, Dec. 10, 1940, SA.
62   Selznick commissioned: memo DOS to Brown, Dec. 10, 1940, SA.
62   'I suggested . . .': interview with Gellhorn.
63   'dumb': memo DOS to Brown, Jan. 31, 1940, SA.
64   'shy and . . .': interview with Schram, Los Angeles.
64   in 1934: 'Cameraman Asks for Divorce After Love Balm Suit', Los Angeles
     Daily News, Mar. 14, 1934.
65   'was deeply . . .': quoted in BB, p. 102.
65   'I watched . . .': interview with Houseman, Brentwood.
65   'that in all his career . . .': quoted in letter DOS to Benny Thau, Mar. 4, 1941,
     SA.
65   Never achieved . . .: quoted in BB, pp. 102–103.
65   'he wasn't in . . .': quoted in BB, p. 102.
65   'Six years is . . .': letter Fleming to IB, undated 1947.
66   'He adored . . .': interview with de Havilland, Venice, Italy.
67   'like the Ideal . . .': New York Journal American, Aug. 26, 1941.
67   'Garbo of the 40s': New York Post, Aug. 26, 1941.
67   'EVERY EVENING . . .': cable Lindstrom to DOS, Sept. 5, 1941, SA.

Chapter 7: Money, Fame, and Power

68   'really sweet': letter IB to Ruth Roberts, quoted in BB, p. 106.
68   'The Lindstroms had . . .': by Homer C. Hosmer, Rochester Times-Union.
69   'Don't get upset . . .': letter IB to DOS, Sept. 29, 1941.
69   'a very poor looser . . .': memo O'Shea to DOS, Oct. 11, 1941, SA.
69   'was all wrong . . .': cable DOS to O'Shea, Oct. 31, 1941, SA.
69   'another reason . . .': letter IB to DOS, Nov. 7, 1941, SA.
69   'I really feel . . .': letter Lindstrom to Brown, Oct. 24, 1941, SA.
70   'With your . . .': letter IB to DOS, Nov. 7, 1941, SA.
71   'We talked about . . .': interview with McCann, Rochester, N.Y.
72   'a frightening one . . .': memo Selznick to Brown, Jan. 28, 1942, SA.
72   'I should be very . . .': letter Lindstrom to Brown, Oct. 24, 1941, SA.
72   'genius of . . .': memo Brown to DOS, Mar. 16, 1942, SA.
72   'I've heard some . . .': SA, Mar. 24, 1942.
73   'I wish you . . .': memo DOS to Brown, Mar. 31, 1942, SA.
73   'squawking about . . .': memo DOS to Brown, Mar. 31, 1942, SA.
73   'she was so . . .': memo Brown to DOS, Apr. 2, 1942, SA.
73   'that Swedish . . .': memo DOS to Brown, Apr. 7, 1942, SA.
74   'fainting . . .': cable IB to DOS, Apr. 20, 1942, SA.
74   In February: memo Wallis to Trilling, Feb. 14, 1942, Warner archives at the
     University of Southern California (henceforth WA).
74   On April 1: memo Wallis to Curtiz, Apr. 1, 1942, WA.
74   'an agent at . . .': Wallis and Charles Higham, p. 94.
74   'Selznick was always . . .': interview with Wallis, Beverly Hills.
74   'What will we . . .': 'Casablanca: The Enduring Oscar-Winner', by David

Zimman, *The Newsday Magazine*, Apr. 10, 1983; also interview with Julius Epstein, Los Angeles.

75   '*I said Casablanca . . .*': interview with Epstein, Los Angeles.
75   Terms of the deal: Francisco, pp. 106–107 and WA.
75   '*all the more . . .*': confidential memo DOS to O'Shea, Mar. 17, 1942, SA.
76   *right hand:* interoffice memo Alex Everlove to Ken Whitmore, WA.
76   '*Long live . . .*': quoted in 'Champion Language Assassin', by Pete Martin, *Saturday Evening Post*, Aug. 2, 1947.
76   First-day shooting from production notes, WA.
76   '*be careful . . .*': memo Virginia Olds to DOS, May 28, 1942, SA.
77   '*along with . . .*': interview with Wallis.
77   '*a bit of a ham*': memo Trilling to Wallis, May 1, 1942, WA.
78   *her role:* BB, p.115.
78   '*the pre-action . . .*': interoffice memo Paul Nathan to Aeneas MacKenzie, Jan. 3, 1942, WA.
79   '*You must remember . . .*': song by Herman Hupfeld.
79   '*I didn't do . . .*': quoted in Benchley, p. 112.
80   '*This is . . .*': quoted in Benchley, p. 104.
80   '*I think . . .*': interview with William, Los Angeles.
80   '*Oh, God! . . .*': quoted in *Ladies' Man* by Paul Henreid, p. 126.
81   Refugee backgrounds from Warner production and publicity files, WA.
81   '*In Europe . . .*': quoted in Martin, p. 63

Chapter 8: A Tigress Who Has Made a Kill

83   '*absolute nonsense*': memo DOS to O'Shea, July 27, 1942, SA.
83   *Ingrid always insisted:* BB, p. 117.
83   '*Buddy DeSylva . . .*': quoted in *Hollywood Reporter*, July 29, 1942.
84   *Ingrid wanted to try:* instructions re IB test from DOS, July 28, 1942, SA.
84   *They would: Hollywood Reporter*, Aug. 3, 1942.
84   '*Are you . . .*': quoted in Henreid, pp. 131–132.
85   '*triumphant vitality . . .*': quoted in Henreid, p. 131.
86   '*Edith Head, the . . .*': Chierichetti, p. 62.
86   '*happy to . . .*': cable Roberts to O'Shea, Aug. 7, 1942, SA.
86   '*climbed on all . . .*': letter IB to O'Shea, Aug. 10, 1942, SA.
87   '*beautiful man*': quoted in BB, p. 214.
87   '*Tell him . . .*': letter IB to O'Shea, Aug. 10, 1942, SA.
88   '*you don't . . .*': letter IB to Irene Selznick, Aug. 29, 1942, SA.
88   '*In a lifetime . . .*': unsent cable DOS to Lindstrom, Aug. 6, 1942, SA.
89   '*I must handle . . .*': cable DOS to Flagg, Dec. 28, 1942.
90   '*deepest appreciation*': cable Steele to MacFadden, Feb. 15, 1943, SA.
90   '*Dear Boss!*': letter IB to DOS, Dec. 31, 1942, SA.
90   Terms of deal: memo Obringer to Wallis, May 19, 1943, WA.
91   '*Cooper wanted . . .*': interview with Wallis.
91   '*I feel rather . . .*': memo DOS to Flagg, Dec. 29, 1942, SA.
91   '*self-effacement*': Steele, p. 4.
92   '*Sometimes I . . .*': quoted in 'Bergman, the Beautiful', *Movieland*, January 1944.
92   The censors: letter from Obringer to Jack Warner, Mar. 19, 1943, WA.
92   *driving together:* interview with Frank Barrena, Los Angeles.
93   '*I want to . . .*': Warner publicity release, WA.

93   *'In my whole . . .'*: quoted in Bacon, p. 60.
94   *She sailed:* BB, p. 122.
94   *'hit the Bell . . .'*: *Time*, Aug. 2, 1943.
95   *'Ingrid was . . .'*: interview with Keyes.
95   *'I am going . . .'*: letter IB to DOS and Irene Selznick, Aug. 29, 1943, SA.
95   *'flesh-peddler'*: quoted in Irene Selznick, p. 258.
96   *Selznick wrote:* letter DOS to Lindstrom, Nov. 17, 1943, SA.
97   *'The worst . . .'*: letter IB to DOS, Dec. 27, 1943, SA.

Chapter 9: A Hollywood Career

98   *number one actress:* letter from *Box Office Digest* to DOS announcing IB as No. 1 actress for previous year, July 27, 1944, SA.
98   *Irene told her:* BB, p. 136.
99   *little Pia:* interview with Dido Renoir, Beverly Hills.
100 *'Petter was a . . .'*: interview with Gregory Peck, Los Angeles.
100 *'I got out . . .'*: interview with Pia Lindstrom, New York.
100 *'Lindstrom is . . .'*: quoted in Davidson, pp. 158–159.
101 *'Ingrid always . . .'*: interview with Kjellin, Los Angeles.
101 *sent the script:* note, June 14, 1944, SA.
102 *'getting herself . . .'*: memo DOS to Colby, June 22, 1944, SA.
102 *'didn't believe . . .'*: quoted in Spoto, p. 275.
102 *first shot:* interview with Norman Lloyd, Los Angeles.
103 *'rather erotic story'*: Spoto, p. 248.
104 *permission to stay:* quoted in 'Portrait of Ingrid Bergman', by Joseph Henry Steele, *Photoplay*, April 1945, p. 36.
104 *'imperious, like . . .'*: interview with William, Los Angeles.
105 *Selznick did not:* memo DOS to O'Shea, Dec. 9, 1944, SA.
105 RKO deal: memo, RKO archives; also interview with Peck.
105 *extra $25,000:* memo DOS to O'Shea, Jan. 23, 1945, SA.
106 *arrested twice:* Los Angeles newspaper clippings for Feb. 25, Mar. 30, and Apr. 13, 1945, in files of Academy of Motion Picture Arts and Sciences.
107 *'Goodbye, goodbye . . .'*: letter IB to DOS, June 13, 1945, SA.
107 *'That is such . . .'*: interview with Adler, London. See also Adler, p. 140.
108 *'Ingrid wasn't . . .'*: interview with Adler.
108 Scene in hunting lodge based on interview with and letter from Robert L. Orbach.
108 *'What a pity . . .'*: interview with Adler; and Adler, p. 141.
109 Description of Capa's career based on Whelan and Capa.
110 *'The fabrication . . .'*: quoted in Whelan, p. 100.
110 *'The next day . . .'*: interview with Adler.
110 *One evening:* interview with Adler.
111 *'I'm shot! . . .'*: interview with Adler; and BB, p. 152.
111 *'One evening . . .'*: interview with Adler.

Chapter 10: The Loneliness of a Bad Marriage

113 *'Ingrid said . . .'*: interview with Neuwald.
114 *'Hitchcock said . . .'*: interview with Grant, Beverly Hills.
114 *'a fiction, fresh . . .'*: Spoto, p. 292.
115 *$175,000 and:* Steele, p. 286.

116 'fantastic distortion': letter DOS to O'Melveny, Oct. 26, 1945, SA.
116 'was extremely . . .': memo Hungate to O'Shea, SA.
116 frantically wired: cable Reissar to DOS, Nov. 16, 1945, SA.
116 'without moving . . .': cable O'Shea to DOS, Dec. 16, 1945, SA.
118 'psychic subterfuge': Steele, p. 79.
118 'What do you . . .': quoted in Davidson, p. 160.
118 'Should we . . .': quoted in Laurence Stallings, Esquire, August 1950.
119 One evening: interview with Grant.
119 One evening: Steele, p. 90.
120 Even Bertolt Brecht: interview with Lloyd.
121 'Ingrid loved . . .': interview with Lloyd.
121 'I'm sure . . .': interview with Michel Bernheim.
121 'Why aren't . . .': interview with Lloyd.
121 'One day . . .': interview with Adler.
122 'That's Ingrid . . .': quoted in 'My Mother, Ingrid Bergman', by Pia Lindstrom as told to George Christy, Good Housekeeping, October 1964.

Chapter 11: A Secular Saint

125 'aura . . . partly . . .': quoted in 'Sonnet to a Lady', by Sam Wanamaker, in unnamed magazine, circa 1947, in Ingrid Bergman collection at Lincoln Center Library of the Performing Arts.
125 For several weeks: interviews with Frederick O'Neal and Billy Rowe, New York.
126 'If I had . . .': AP, Oct. 28, 1946.
126 emotional crisis: Steele, p. 115.
126 'My white rose . . .': quoted in Whelan, p. 233.
127 'Sometimes I think . . .': quoted in 'Ingrid of Lorraine', by Lincoln Barrett, Life, Mar. 24, 1947.
127 'so pure, so . . .': 'How Ingrid Became Joan', by Maxwell Anderson, Photoplay, April 1947.
127 'as Miss Bergman . . .': 'Backstage with Miss Bergman', by S. J. Woolf, New York Times Magazine, Dec. 29, 1946.
126 a group: interview with Frank Edwards, Beverly Hills, and Warren Thomas.

127 One evening: interview with Lloyd.
128 15 percent: 'Miss Bernstein Promises to Return', New York Times, May 11, 1947.
129 'Come back . . .': interview with Bernheim, Los Angeles.
129 'It's not . . .': interview with Pia Lindstrom.
130 'I would like . . .': letter Lindstrom to Wyler, Jan. 31, 1947.
130 'Lindstrom really was . . .': quoted in Davidson, p. 158.
130 $175,000 plus: deal memo in RKO archives.
130 'Tears are just . . .': letter Fleming to IB, undated 1947.
130 'damn embarrassing': quoted in Steele, p. 139.
130 she shouldn't think: letter IB to Roberts, quoted in BB, p. 177.
131 'There's no fool . . .': letter Fleming to IB, quoted in BB, p. 180.
132 fifteen or so: interviews with Edwards and Thomas.
132 Ingrid put: Steele, p. 148.
132 Charades were: interview with Celeste Holm, Washington, D.C.
133 'That little . . .': quoted in Steele, p. 155.

133   *'Ingrid was supposed . . .'*: interview with Adler.

134   *'David, your . . .'*: quoted in Lambert, p. 86.

134   *One evening:* 'The Real Ingrid Bergman Story', by Laurence Stallings, *Esquire*, August 1950.

135   *Fleming deferred:* production notes in RKO archives.

135   *'I remember . . .'*: interview with Jose Ferrer, Los Angeles.

135   The horse: interview with Howard.

136   *'Every actress . . .'*: interview with Ferrer.

136   *for Christmas:* memo Heniigson to Wanger, Dec. 17, 1947, RKO.

138   *'I would not . . .'*: interview with Adler.

138   *'We are drinking . . .'*: letter IB to Roberts, quoted in BB, p. 191.

Chapter 12: 'Ti Amo'

139   *The film was not:* based on an examination of Los Angeles newspapers for the spring of 1948 at the Los Angeles Public Library.

139   *She saw it:* Steele, p. 92, and *New York Times* film advertisements for spring 1946. Also PL says that he never saw the film with IB.

140   *'She told me . . .'*: quoted in Irene Selznick, pp. 374–375.

140   *'If you need . . .'*: quoted in BB, p. 4.

140   *signed a letter:* letter IB to Milestone, Apr. 19, 1947, in archives at Library of Academy of Motion Picture Arts and Sciences.

140   *'beautiful present'*: quoted in Overbey, pp. 102–103.

141   *sister Marcella:* interview with Marcella Mariani, Rome.

142   *'From the time . . .'*: interview with Reissar, London.

142   *particularly thrilled:* letter Rossellini to DOS, SA.

142   *'This danger . . .'*: letter DOS to Reissar, June 19, 1948, SA.

143   *'What a . . .'*: letter IB to Lindstrom, July 19, 1948.

144   *She wrote:* letter IB to Roberts, Aug. 6, 1948, quoted in BB, p. 185.

144   *'He creates . . .'*: quoted in *No Innocence Abroad*, by Michael Stern, p. 171.

145   *'a phenomenon of . . .'*: interview with Father Lisandrini, Rome.

145   *One day Roberto:* interview with Helen Tubbs, New York.

146   *congratulating her:* cable Rossellini to Jones, SA.

146   *'Personally, I . . .'*: letter Reissar to DOS, Sept. 28, 1948, SA.

146   *'Swedish women . . .'*: quoted in Steele, p. 168.

147   *Gallup's polls: The Hollywood Reporter*, Nov. 16, 1948.

148   *Steele could:* Steele, p. 159.

149   *'I'm going . . .'*: quoted in Steele, p. 168; also interview with Lindstrom quoting Lopart.

149   *One evening:* interview with Helen Tubbs.

149   *Ingrid had prepared:* interviews with Veger and Lindstrom.

149   *'I was uncontrollably . . .'*: quoted in Davidson, p. 162.

150   *'As time wore . . .'*: quoted in Hedy Lamarr, pp. 101–102.

150   *'I can't understand . . .'*: interview with Sam Goldwyn, Jr., Los Angeles.

151   *'Roberto was . . .'*: quoted in Davidson, p. 162.

151   Ingrid's and Roberto's contracts on *Stromboli*, based on Steele, p. 169, plus divorce proceedings in 1950.

151   *a Hollywood column:* 'The Bergman Bombshell', by Louella Parsons, *Photoplay*, July 1949.

152   *One evening:* interview with Celeste Holm.

152   *Ingrid wrote:* BB, pp. 204–205.

Chapter 13: The Prince of Disorder

154 *Visiting with:* interview with Ferrer.
154 '*was not . . .*': quoted in Selznick, p. 375.
154 '*She fell . . .*': quoted in Irene Selznick, p. 375; also interview with Irene Selznick.
155 *most popular:* Tannenbaum, p. 237.
155 *The American:* Painter-Downs, *The New Yorker*, Nov. 20, 1948.
155 '*it was a . . .*': BB, p. 207.
156 '*Here is . . .*': interview with Tubbs.
156 '*Did Ingrid . . .*': interview with d'Amicos.
156 *Roberto scheduled:* 'Ingrid Bergman Meets the Press in Rome, and Near-Riot Ensues', Associated Press, Mar. 22, 1949.
157 *She saw only:* interview with d'Amicos.
157 '*charming like a . . .*': interview with Marcella Mariani.
158 *Petter lilla:* letter IB to Lindstrom, Exhibit A, 1952 trial.
159 '*I was worried . . .*': interview with Marcella Mariani.
159 '*Sure, we . . .*': quoted in Davidson, p. 163
160 '*a spectacular . . .*': BB, p. 220.
161 '*I have seen . . .*': quoted in 'Ingrid's Love Affair', by Michael Wilson in the British *People*, Dec. 3, 1950.
161 '*The actors . . .*': interview with Neuwald.
162 '*A little higher . . .*': quoted in Wilson, Dec. 3, 1949.
162 *9 and 12 April:* quoted in BB, p. 221.
162 *Pia was anticipating:* interview with George Diehl, Arizona, and Lindstrom.
162 '*I had to be . . .*': interview with Cassini, Milan.
163 '*A wife that . . .*': letter Lindstrom to IB, quoted in BB, p. 221.
163 '*I think . . .*': interview with Neuwald.
163 '*Sometime afterward . . .*': Stern, pp. 174–175.
164 '*endangering my . . .*': cable Wanger to IB, quoted in BB, p. 237.
165 '*Kay is . . .*': interview with Marcella Mariani.
165 *Kay warned:* BB, pp. 243–244.
165 '*At Stromboli . . .*': interview with Brown, New York.
166 *A century earlier:* Berenson, pp. 67–68.
167 '*Nightmare*': quoted in BB, p. 245.
167 '*an Italian farce*': interview with Brown.
168 '*She looked . . .*': quoted in Davidson, p. 163.
168 *until 6 May:* 'Ingrid's Mate Boards Plane', United Press, Rome, May 6, 1949.
169 '*Petter called . . .*': interview with Engstrom, Stockholm.
170 *She wrote him:* letter IB to Lindstrom, quoted in BB, p. 248.
170 '*My mission was . . .*': court testimony quoted in *Los Angeles Examiner*, June 17, 1952.
170 '*I said . . .*': court testimony quoted in *Los Angeles Times*, June 18, 1952.
171 '*Ingrid took no part . . .*': quoted in Wilson, in *People*, Nov. 27, 1950.
172 *He told her:* Steele, p. 205.
172 '*When they . . .*': interview with Father Lisandrini.
172 '*In the beginning . . .*': letter IB to Steele, quoted in Steele, p. 255.
173 '*in the midst . . .*': quoted in Overbey, p. 107.
173 '*was trembling . . .*': Wilson, *People*, Dec. 4, 1950.
174 '*NO ONE REALIZES . . .*': Steele, p. 205, and BB, p. 255.
175 *Steele stayed up:* Steele, pp. 207–213.

Chapter 14: The Edge of a Volcano

176   *he pointed out:* Steele, p. 219.
176   *It was not:* quoted in BB, p. 257.
178   *'I took a . . .':* quoted in 'Ingrid Bares Her Troubles', *Los Angeles Times*, Aug.
      10, 1949.
178   *Was Ingrid pregnant?:* BB, p. 258.
179   *gaiety fell:* Steele, p. 229.
179   *even refused:* Los Angeles Daily News, Aug. 16, 1949.
179   *you know if:* letter IB to Anna-Britta, Sept. 3, 1949, quoted in 'Ingrid and Pia
      Tell Their Own Stories', article in Lewis Sweyd Collection at U.S.C.
179   *'From what . . .':* interview with Franco Rossellini, Rome.
180   *Since her:* 'The Real Love Story', by Cholly Knickerbocker, *New York Journal
      American*, Sept. 21, 1949.
181   *'friends in . . .':* interview with Cassini.
181   *Strangely unaffected:* Steele, p. 238.
181   *wrote an article for Collier's:* interview with Sandler.
182   *'spokesman for . . .':* Los Angeles Herald Examiner, Sept. 23, 1949.
182   *Ingrid wrote:* letter IB to Lindstrom, quoted in BB, p. 261.
182   List of assets based on court documents in divorce proceedings.
182   *As Steele learned:* Steele, p. 283.
183   *'STRANGE . . .':* New York Mirror, Oct. 10, 1949.
183   *Steele thought:* Steele, p. 242.
184   *and told her:* Steele, p. 242.
184   *Pia asked:* letter IB to Steele, quoted in Steele, p. 250.
184   *'The experience . . .':* interview with Pia Lindstrom.
184   *None of:* letter IB to Steele, Dec. 1, 1949, quoted in Steele, p. 257.
185   *'There is . . .':* letter IB to Steele, Nov. 25 and 26, 1949, quoted in Steele, pp.
      254–255.
185   *he warned:* letter Steele to IB, Steele, pp. 256–257.
186   *Steele said:* Steele, pp. 259–260.
186   *'Few women . . .':* Los Angeles Examiner, Dec. 12, 1949.
186   *As Gregory:* interview with Peck.
188   *'Whether she . . .':* The New York Times, Dec. 15, 1949.
189   *She told Ingrid;* letter IB to Steele, quoted in Steele, p. 275.
190   *'The guards . . .':* letter IB to Steele, quoted in Steele, p. 277.
190   *'five-million-lire . . .':* 'Letter from Rome', by Genet, *The New Yorker*, Apr. 8,
      1950.

Chapter 15: A Child of Love

192   *'living publicly . . .':* 'Vatican Attack on Rossellini', *Daily Telegraph*, Feb. 16,
      1950.
192   *'while thousands . . .':* quoted in London News, Feb. 12, 1950.
192   *In Annapolis:* Washington Post, Feb. 10, 1950.
193   *'low level . . .':* quoted in The Worker, Feb. 22, 1950.
194   *almost hysterical:* BB, p. 276.
195   *'Most of the . . .':* letter IB to Steele, quoted in Steele, p. 284.
195   *'Maestro!':* quoted in BB, pp. 280–281.
196   *On another occasion:* interviews with Ann Todd, London, and David Lean,
      Beverly Hills.
196   *'I saw her . . .':* interview with Fellini, Rome.

196 *'Ingrid's reaction . . .'*: interview with Masina, Rome.
197 *'We were like . . .'*: interview with Fiorella Mariani, Rome.
197 *'with a very . . .'*: letter DOS to Reissar, June 13, 1950, SA.
198 *She said that:* letter IB to Steele, Steele, p. 295.
198 *'Let's go . . .'*: interview with a prominent Italian director. The story of Rossellini's sexual unhappiness with Ingrid was confirmed in separate interviews with two of his closest associates.
198 *'a woman without passion':* interview with Rodolfi.
198 *'While she was . . .'*: interview with Father Lisandrini.
199 *'express to her . . .'*: deposition, August 1980.
200 *$80,000 in:* Steele, p. 282, and newspaper accounts.
201 *property settlement:* property settlement filed in court documents.
201 *in court proceedings: Los Angeles Examiner,* June 24, 1952.
201 *'of August 9 . . .'*: letter Pacht to Bautzer, Aug. 17, 1950.
202 *'No, I have no . . .'*: *The New York Times,* Nov. 2, 1950.
202 *'Mr Borre . . .'*: letter Brinn to Lindstrom, Nov. 17, 1950.
203 *'You and your . . .'*: letter Lindstrom to IB, Mar. 20, 1951.
203 *She remembered:* BB, p. 289.
203 *Fiorella Mariani:* interview with Fiorella Mariani.
204 *Roberto did:* newspaper clipping from unnamed London paper for July 7, 1951, in British Film Institute library.
204 *Lean said:* quoted in BB, p. 290.
204 *'I had . . .'*: interview with Todd.
204 *'I recall . . .'*: affidavit filed in Superior Court of California, June 4, 1952.
205 *'Yes, this is . . .'*: UPI, Aug. 30, 1951, *Los Angeles Daily News,* p. 4.
205 *'I remember . . .'*: quoted in Davidson, p. 159.
205 *One evening:* AP, 'Rome Crowd Boos Ingrid', *Los Angeles Herald,* June 16, 1951.
206 *'Ingrid was like . . .'*: interview with Masina.
207 *The world is more:* quoted in *Bianco e Nero* No. 2, 1952, pp. 15–16, translated by Judith White.
208 *'I don't think . . .'*: interview with Bautzer, Los Angeles.
208 *'I don't want . . .'*: *Los Angeles Times,* June 5, 1952.
209 *did not mention:* Pia Lindstrom's diary.
209 *'Will the judge . . .'*: interview with Seaton, Beverly Hills; also affadavit.
209 *'Friday the thirteenth!':* quoted in *Los Angeles Examiner,* June 14, 1952.
210 *'one of the . . .'*: interview with Bautzer.
210 *'perhaps she had . . .'*: quoted in 'Ingrid Sobs at Loss of Pia's Love', *New York Daily News,* June 17, 1952.
211 *'back from saying . . .'*: *Los Angeles Examiner* and *Los Angeles Times,* June 27, 1952; also *The Los Angeles Mirror,* June 26, 1952.
212 *would fight:* letter IB to Pia Lindstrom, BB, p. 300.

Chapter 16: The Donna of Santa Marinella

213 *On a grand:* interview with Fiorella Mariani.
213 *'how Roberto . . .'*: interview with Serpe, Beverly Hills.
214 *'Father would say . . .'*: interview with Isabella Rossellini.
214 *'Children, it's . . .'*: interview with Father Lisandrini.
214 *Sam Spiegel: Daily Telegraph,* June 25, 1952.
214 *Graham Greene:* 'Behind Bergman's Closed Doors', by Hedda Hopper, *Modern Screen,* May 1952.

214   'I was in . . .': interview with Lollobrigida, Venice.

215   'We'd talk . . .': interview with Fiorella Mariani.

215   'She told . . .': interview with Renzo Rossellini, New York.

216   'I want to . . .': quoted in Frank.

217   not much laughter: letter IB to Steele, Steele, p. 312.

217   'Go down . . .': interview with Tubbs.

218   'through with films': quoted in 'Ingrid Bergman to Quit Films', New York Times, Mar. 16, 1953.

218   family moved into: Hollywood Reporter, May 8, 1953.

219   'How do things . . .': quoted in 'The Enduring Courage of Ingrid Bergman', by A. E. Hotchner, McCall's, May 1982, reprinted Hotchner.

219   'the Joan of Ingrid . . .': Svenska Dagbladet (Swedish Daily News), Feb. 18, 1955.

220   the criticism: Vecko-Journalen (The Weekly Journal), Feb 26, 1955.

220   'tried to break . . .': quoted in Davidson, pp. 169–170.

220   'I summoned . . .': quoted in Davidson, p. 170.

221   My editor: quoted in Davidson, p. 171.

221   'When you did . . .': interview with Father Lisandrini.

222   Miss Bergman and: quoted in Quirk, pp. 143–144.

222   'If a good . . .': letter IB to Steele, quoted in Steele, p. 315.

222   'I give you . . .': interview with Dido Renoir.

222   'splitting artistically': quoted in AP, Citizen News, June 7, 1955.

223   'never seen . . .': Los Angeles Times, June 29, 1955.

223   Ingrid waved: BB, p. 282

223   'From the beginning . . .': interview with Fellini.

Chapter 17: 'Welcome Home, Miss Bergman'

224   'Why are . . .': interview with Ferrer, Beverly Hills.

225   a figure of: Variety, Dec. 21, 1955; Mirror, Dec. 21, 1955.

225   he soon left: Daily Mail, June 27, 1956.

225   'Roberto's India . . .': interview with Fiorella Mariani.

226   'I think that . . .': interview with Helen Hayes, New York.

227   fifteen curtain calls: AP, New York Times, Dec. 4, 1956.

227   'his face was . . .': quoted in Davidson, p. 173.

228   'Phyllis and I . . .': interview with Anderson, New York City.

229   'When I look . . .': interview with Rossellini, Monte Carlo.

230   'Now I know . . .': quoted in The New York Times, Aug. 5, 1956.

230   The results: Newsweek, Aug. 13, 1956.

231   'I was very sad . . .': interview with Pia Lindstrom.

231   'Then we'll . . .': letter IB to Steele, quoted in Steele, p. 326.

231   Description of Alvin gang based on interviews with Frank Edwards, Los Angeles, and Warren Thomas.

232   'Miss Bergman . . .': quoted in PBS documentary on Ingrid Bergman.

232   'at least fifty . . .': quoted in 'Dick Williams', New York Mirror-News, Jan. 23, 1957.

233   'well-nigh rhapsodic': 'Ingrid's Return', Newsweek, Jan. 28, 1957.

233   'I had given . . .': interview with Anderson.

233   'nice': UP, Jan. 21, 1957.

234   Dear Bob: letter IB to Anderson.

234   'I seldom went . . .': interview with Grant.

235 *Lars said:* interview with Schmidt, Paris.

235 *He said that:* quoted in Steele, p. 331.

235 *Indian film starlet:* quoted in UPI, *Los Angeles Herald Express*, May 27, 1957.

235 *'There was . . .':* interview with Tonti, Rome.

236 *'My wife and . . .':* quoted in *Los Angeles Times*, May 21, 1957.

236 *'There were nights . . .':* quoted in Davidson, p. 173.

236 *She wrote Steele:* letter IB to Steele, quoted in Steele, p. 332.

237 *it was all lies:* BB, p. 353.

237 *The one person:* BB, p. 354.

238 *'That summer . . .':* quoted in 'My Mother, Ingrid Bergman', by Pia Lindstrom as told to George Christy in *Good Housekeeping*, October 1964.

238 *'It is rubbish . . .':* INS and AP, Oct. 21, 1957.

238 *According to Ingrid:* BB, pp. 356–357.

239 *$976 a month:* New York Times*, Nov. 8, 1957.

239 *'Ingrid, take also . . .':* interview with Father Lisandrini.

Chapter 18: A Man of Perfect Manners

240 *'Why don't you . . .':* UP, 'Ingrid Sad on Arrival in London', Nov. 12, 1957.

240 *Ingrid's deal:* production memo, WA.

240 *'Mother had . . .':* interview with Isotta Rossellini, New York.

240 *'By the time . . .':* letter IB to Steele, quoted in Steele, p. 338.

241 *'She was so . . .':* interview with Donen, Beverly Hills.

241 *'We had . . .':* interview with Grant.

241 *Anderson wrote:* interview with Anderson.

242 *She flew to Rome: New York Times,* Dec. 24, 1957.

242 *They greeted the:* publicist's letter, WA.

242 Biography of Schmidt based primarily on 'Hardly Anybody Knows Him – That's the Way He Wants It', by Dora Jane Hamblin, *Life*, Oct. 16, 1964; interview with Hamblin, Rome; and interview with Schmidt, Paris.

243 *'The house was . . .':* interview with Schmidt.

243 *'Ingrid said . . .':* interview with Schmidt.

244 *She believed:* letter IB to Steele, Steele, p. 343.

244 *'We reach . . .':* UPI, *Los Angeles Times*, July 12, 1958.

244 *'The children . . .':* UPI, *Los Angeles Times*, July 12, 1958.

245 *suspicious of a:* letter IB to Liana Ferri, Oct. 5, 1958, quoted in BB, p. 368.

245 *'some of . . .':* interview with Franco Rossellini, Rome.

245 *For months:* 'Inside Hollywood', by Herb Stein, *Daily Racing Form*, Los Angeles, June 3, 1959; also *The Morning Telegraph*, June 22, 1959.

246 *privately she condemned:* interview with Danny Selznick, Washington, D.C.

246 *'I met an . . .':* interview with Schmidt.

247 *'My sense was . . .':* interview with Hamblin.

248 *'We were . . .':* interview with Schmidt.

248 *'I may . . .':* interview with Isabella Rossellini.

248 *'Separation is not . . .':* interview with Schmidt.

248 *The court ruled:* AP, *The New York Times*, Jan. 25, 1959.

248 *To ensure:* AP, Jan. 24, 1959.

249 *'We lived . . .':* interview with Isabella Rossellini.

249 *One weekend he:* interviews with Isabella and Isotta Rossellini.

250 *'That's something . . .':* quoted in *Los Angeles Times*, Apr. 4, 1959.

250 *In April she:* AP, Apr. 17, 1959.

250   Description of court hearings based on *Washington Post*, Sept. 10, 1959: *Newsweek*, Sept. 21, 1959; AP, Sept. 9, 1959.

251   *She went up: The New Yorker*, Oct. 10, 1959.

251   *'It's no good! . . .'*: quoted in *Newsweek*, Oct. 19, 1959.

251   *'I don't see . . .'*: quoted in *New York News Syndicate*, Oct. 14, 1959.

252   *flew out of:* Reuters, Oct. 17, 1959.

252   *'Everyone swam . . .'*: interview with Isabella Rossellini.

252   *'I would have . . .'*: quoted in *Los Angeles Times*, Nov. 25, 1960.

253   *'he could steal . . .'*: quoted in 'Hedda Hopper', *Los Angeles Times*, Nov. 25, 1960.

253   *'I wanted . . .'*: quoted in 'Erskine Johnson' column, *Los Angeles Mirror*, Feb. 10, 1961.

253   *'Ingrid started . . .'*: interview with Perkins, Los Angeles.

253   *'She would have . . .'*: quoted in 'Psycho II', by Brad Darrach, *People*, June 13, 1983.

253   *'a presumably . . .'*: interview with Perkins. Brad Darrach, the author of the *People* article, stands by his story.

253   *'What's the . . .'*: interview with Perkins.

255   *It was Anthony:* interview with Anthony Quinn conducted by Vesna Obradovic Leamer, Washington.

255   *'Ingrid begged . . .'*: interview with Quinn.

256   *'Somehow in . . .'*: interview with Nichols, Boston.

256   *'At the Cannes . . .'*: *Daily Express*, June 27, 1964.

257   Salaries on *The Yellow Rolls-Royce* based on figures in the production file, WA.

257   *'She said to . . .'*: interview with Nichols.

257   *'My uncle . . .'*: interview with Fiorella Mariani.

258   *'Roberto was a . . .'*: interview with Senroy, Rome.

258   *She charged:* UPI, Dec. 12, 1961.

259   *'I was a . . .'*: quoted in *Newsweek*, Nov. 25, 1963.

259   *'My mother asked . . .'*: interview with Pia Lindstrom.

259   *'Her beauty . . .'*: quoted in *New York Daily News*, June 27, 1964.

259   *'Pia was . . .'*: interview with Quinn.

259   *'no doubt . . .'*: *New York Daily News*, June 27, 1964.

260   *'undue publicity . . .'*: quoted in *Good Housekeeping*, October 1964.

260   *'I don't want . . .'*: interview with Pia Lindstrom.

261   *'I felt . . .'*: interview with Pia Lindstrom.

261   *Pia received: Los Angeles Herald-Examiner*, July 31, 1965.

261   *'I am sincerely . . .'*: quoted in *Modern Screen*, November 1965.

Chapter 19: An Elegant Facade

262   *She called Lars's:* interview with Gérôme, Paris.

262   *His take on: Life*, Oct. 16, 1964.

263   *'Sometimes it was . . .'*: interview with Isabella Rossellini.

264   *'Where does it . . .'*: interview with Schell, Venice.

266   *'Here! . . .'*: interview with Isabella Rossellini.

266   *'He came . . .'*: interview with Isabella Rossellini.

267   *'Why is everyone . . .'*: quoted in *Los Angeles Times West Magazine*, Sept. 10, 1967.

269   *Ingrid's reception: The New York Times*, Sept. 14, 1967.

269   *'I hope you . . .'*: PBS documentary on Ingrid Bergman.

270   *'I showed her . . .'*: interview with Thomas.

270   *Isotta insists:* interview with Isotta Rossellini.
270   *On at least:* interview with Stig Nahlbom.
271   *'the most urbane . . .':* interview with Silliphant, Beverly Hills.
272   *'Ingrid said she . . .':* interview with Todd, London.
272   *'We weren't close':* interview with Matthau, Venice.
273   *'What movie . . .':* quoted in 'Ingrid Bergman: The New Happiness in Her
       Life', by Muriel Davidson, *Good Housekeeping*, May 1969.
273   *'I knew it . . .':* interview with Quinn.
273   *'They were like . . .':* interview with Silliphant.
274   *'the "love bag" . . .':* quoted in *Los Angeles Herald-Examiner*, June 7, 1969.
275   *'One of my . . .':* interview with Quinn.

Chapter 20: 'Darling, That Is You Crying'

277   *'Lars is a . . .':* interview with Fiorella Mariani.
277   *'Ingrid and Lars . . .':* interview with Anderson.
278   *'She would only play . . .':* interview with Ackland, London.
278   *Louie watched out:* interview with Hollis, London.
279   *'Walter, it's me . . .':* interview with Matthau.
280   *Ingrid arrived:* Washington Post, Mar. 28, 1972.
281   *'Miss Bergman . . .':* interview with Daly, Venice.
281   *'From an early . . .':* interview with Fiorella Mariani, Rome.
282   *'This was the . . .':* interview with Isotta Rossellini.
282   *'She gave . . .':* interview with Todd.
283   *'Yes, you must . . .':* quoted in BB, p. 447; also *The Daily Express* four-part
       series on the death of Ingrid Bergman by Michael Thornton, Sept. 27, 1982,
       to Sept. 30, 1982.
283   *'Miss Bergman's . . .':* Los Angeles Times, Jan. 16, 1974.
283   *'I'm sorry . . .':* interview with James.
285   *'I have to . . .':* interview with Isotta Rossellini.
285   *'It's all . . .':* interview with Evans.
286   *'I've been to four . . .':* interview with James, Venice and London.
286   *'She was at . . .':* interview with Kjellin.
286   *'What are you . . .':* interview with Minnelli, Venice.
289   *'It's really not . . .':* interview with Siegel, Washington, D.C.

Chapter 21: Ingrid's Great Performance

291   *Joe Steele had received:* interviews with Bill Davidson and Danny Selznick.
291   *To help her she had:* interview with Turtiainen, New York.
291   *'I can't look . . .':* interview with Turtiainen.
291   *'I'll give . . .':* interview with Burgess, Houston.
291   *Ingrid and Isabella went:* interviews with Thomas and Isabella Rossellini.
292   *'Does Ingrid . . .':* interview with Isabella Rossellini.
292   *'He said that . . .':* interview with Rodolfi, Rome.
292   *'Women can . . .':* interview with Fiorella Mariani.
293   *'What's the matter . . .':* interview with Hiller.
293   *'I don't know . . .':* interview with James.
293   *didn't sense:* interview with Hiller.
294   *drawn to her beauty:* BB, p. 467.
294   *'There are an . . .':* quoted in introduction to Winquist and Jungstedt.
294   *'She was not . . .':* interview with Bergman, Sweden.

296 *On the day:* description based on the private documentary made during the shooting of *Autumn Sonata.*

296 *'In a way . . .':* interview with Ingmar Bergman.

297 *'If I lie down . . .':* based on the documentary.

298 *'I live on . . .':* interview with Ingmar Bergman.

299 *'People like you . . .':* based on the dubbed English-language version of *Autumn Sonata.* The English-language printed version of the script is substantially different and somewhat wooden in places.

299 *'Ingrid was . . .':* interview with Ingmar Bergman.

Chapter 22: 'Oh, Wendy, It's Only a Play'

300 *'She'd enter . . .':* interview with James.

300 *Once, from:* interview with Schmidt.

301 *'Obviously, I loved . . .':* interview with Van Eyssen.

301 *'Oh, Wendy':* interview with Garland.

301 *'If anyone . . .':* interview with Hiller.

302 *'Louie, they're . . .':* interview with Hollis.

302 *'It was a bit . . .':* interview with Hiller.

302 *'You must . . .':* interview with Garland.

303 *'Whatever is . . .':* interview with Hollis.

304 *He talked:* interview with Peek.

304 *'Mother thought . . .':* interview with Isabella Rossellini. Pia Lindstrom has no comment to make about this incident.

305 *Steele and his collaborator:* interview with Davidson and Lindstrom.

305 *Benjamin called:* interview with Benjamin, Beverly Hills.

305 *'We must leave you now . . .':* videotape of tribute viewed at American Film Institute in Los Angeles.

306 *She was holding:* interview with Isabella Rossellini.

306 *'He took my hands':* quoted in Spoto, p. 552.

306 *'As soon as . . .':* interview with Burgess, Houston.

307 *'Dear Grandma':* letter Lindstrom to IB.

308 *'Does he move . . .':* interview with Isabella Rossellini.

308 *'Ingrid worked . . .':* interview with Engstrom.

309 *'I thought . . .':* videotape of tribute.

309 *Griff turned:* interview with James.

309 *'Kay mentioned . . .':* letter Lindstrom to Burgess.

310 *'I had no . . .':* interview with Burgess.

311 *been a 'joy':* letter IB to Lindstrom.

311 *he was sorry:* letter Burgess to Lindstrom.

311 *'The past . . .':* letter Lindstrom to IB, Mar. 26, 1980.

312 *it was the publisher:* interviews with Ross Claiborne and Jeanne Bernkopf, New York.

312 *'to say what . . .':* interview with Burgess.

312 *'I was deluged . . .':* interview with Bernkopf.

313 *Irene Selznick was upset:* IB diary, viewed at home of Isabella Rossellini.

Chapter 23: 'I Don't Want the Film to be Over'

314 *got together:* interviews with Harve Bennett and Silvia Rubinstein, Los Angeles.

314 *She phoned:* interview with Hall, Beverly Hills.

314   *Ingrid couldn't help:* interview with Engstrom.
315   *he was stunned:* interview with Corman, Los Angeles.
315   *Laurence Evans:* interview with Evans.
315   *she so greatly:* letter IB to Bennett, Apr. 9, 1981.
316   *'You know, I . . .':* interview with Hall, Beverly Hills.
317   *He had saved:* interview with Schneiderman, London.
318   *'I have only . . .':* interview with Bennett.
319   *'I've gone through . . .':* interview with Johnstone, London.
320   *'was a good hater . . .':* 'An Unworthy Script', by Philip Gillon, *The Jerusalem Post International Edition,* undated clipping obtained from Paramount Studios.
320   *Schneiderman used:* interview with Schneiderman, London.
320   *For Alan Greenberg:* interview with Greenberg, Los Angeles.
322   *'You'll have to . . .':* interview with Monty Hall.
322   *Several times:* interview with Schmidt.
322   *'See, you're standing . . .':* interview with Isabella Rossellini.

Chapter 24: 'I'm Alone'

324   *Lars asked Margaret:* interview with Johnstone.
324   *'She was very . . .':* interview with Isabella Rossellini.
324   *Although Dr Edward MacLellan:* Thornton, *Daily Express,* Sept. 30, 1982.
325   *'I want . . .':* interview with James.
325   *'Isn't there . . .':* interview with Engstrom.
325   *'She was . . .':* interview with Todd.
326   *'They wait . . .':* interview with Fiorella Mariani.
326   *arrived to:* interview with Green, Beverly Hills.
327   *'Is that . . .':* interview with Isotta Rossellini.
327   *'We talked about . . .':* interview with Weiss, New York.
327   *Thomas was there:* interview with Thomas.
328   *'A lot of . . .':* letter IB to Alving, July 6, 1982, reproduced in the Swedish magazine *Saxons.*
328   *'He died . . .':* interview with Fiorella Mariani.
328   *'Ingrid had . . .':* interview with Johnstone.
328   *'At the end . . .':* interview with Isabella Rossellini.
328   *'For Mama . . .':* interview with Isotta Rossellini.
329   *'When the girls . . .':* interview with Engstrom.
329   *'Margaret has . . .':* interview with Hall.
329   *'How are you . . .':* interview with Todd.
330   *'Ingrid's bad . . .':* interview with Lasse Lundberg, Fjällbacka.
330   *'When he was . . .':* interviews with Lasse and Ingela Lundberg.
331   *Britt and Pavo:* interview with Turtiainen.
331   *Greta thought:* interview with Danielsson.
332   *'I said goodbye . . .':* interview with James.
332   *'I'm so . . .':* interview with Todd.
332   *'Do I look . . .':* interview with Johnstone.

Chapter 25: The Endless Sea

333   *they came:* *The Times of London,* Oct. 15, 1982.
334   *They walked:* interviews with Schmidt and Lasse and Ingela Lundberg.

Acknowledgments

Although this is not an authorized biography, I believe that everyone close to Ingrid Bergman cooperated. For thirty-five years, journalists and authors have asked Dr Petter Lindstrom for interviews, and he has always backed away. He agreed to talk to me with only the promise that I would attempt to write about Ingrid's and his marriage in an objective fashion.

Miss Bergman's third husband, Lars Schmidt, was extremely helpful, as well. Not only did I have two worthwhile interviews with Mr Schmidt in Paris, but he invited me to visit the island of Danholmen in Sweden.

Miss Bergman's children were equally forthcoming. I met Robertino at the tribute to his mother at Venice on the first anniversary of her death. Isabella, Isotta, and Pia all put up with my endless questions. I would like especially to thank Isabella, who spent many hours with me, and could not have been more helpful.

There are journalists in five countries who shared their expertise with me. Costanzo Costantini, of *Il Messaggero*, is a distinguished journalist and author, a congenial host and guide to Roman culture and life. Logan Bentley, an American journalist in Rome was very generous too. In Paris, Gisele Galante opened the files of *Paris Match*. In Stockholm, Marie Anne Johnson was a wonderful guide to Sweden; Stig Nahlbom, the well-known columnist for *Expressen*, was generous with his time and insights. Torsten Jungstedt, the film historian and television personality, was extraordinarily helpful. He even arranged to fly to Stöde, in southern Sweden, to do a radio interview with Åke Dahlquist, the cameraman, at a time when he could act as my translator. Alan Burgess, the author of Ingrid's autobiography, spent a long afternoon and evening with me in Houston, Texas; many authors would not have been so gracious to a colleague involved in a project similar to their recent book. In Hollywood, Bill Davidson talked about his experiences writing about Ingrid. Tag Gallagher, a film scholar writing a biography of Roberto Rossellini, was very kind.

I made two lengthy trips to Europe, and wherever I travelled, Ingrid's family and friends were helpful. In Rome, Fiorella Mariani, Marcella Mariani, and Franco Rossellini were marvellous introductions to the Rossellini side of the family. Federico Fellini was full of brilliant metaphor, and was gracious enough to invite me to his home to interview his wife, the distinguished actress Giulietta Masina. In Paris, Raymond Gerome provided memorable insights into Ingrid. In London, Griff James, Margaret Johnstone, and Ann Todd were generous with their time and memories, as were many others. In Stockholm, I particularly remember time spent with Greta Danielsson and Britt Engstrom, but I cannot possibly thank all the people there or anywhere else for their help. I would also like to thank Iris Love, the archaeologist, for her help in Venice.

There is a voluminous printed record of Ingrid's life and career, and I explored archives and libraries in four countries. It took me ten days to go through the

Bergman material at the David O. Selznick collection at the Humanities Research Center of the University of Texas, a time made infinitely more enjoyable and easier thanks to Dr Ray Daum. The staff at the Lincoln Center Library for the Performing Arts was helpful. So was the staff at the Margaret Hedrick Library of the Academy of Motion Picture Arts and Sciences in Beverly Hills. I received gracious assistance at the Warner Brothers collection at the University of Southern California, the archives of RKO Pictures, Inc., in Los Angeles, and the American Film Institute in Los Angeles. I would also like to thank MGM for allowing me to look at their archival material, and Mary Anne Dolan, editor of the *Los Angeles Herald-Examiner*, for permitting me to see the newspaper's files. I did useful research at the Library of Congress, the graduate research library at UCLA, the Santa Monica Public Library, and the Los Angeles Public Library. I also received help from the Rochester Public Library and the Rochester *Times-Union* library. The Warner Brothers retirees organization allowed me to solicit their members for memories of Ingrid.

I was able to screen several rarely seen Ingrid Bergman films at the UCLA film archives. Ollie Rosberg was very helpful at the Swedish Film Institute in Sweden, as was the staff at Svensk Filmindustri. Material at the British Film Institute in London was very useful. I also would like to thank William Hifner, the librarian at the *Washington Post*, for his assistance.

My wife, Vesna Obradovic Leamer, was my researcher in the United States and my interpreter in Italy, as well as my first and finest critic. That the book was such a pleasure to write has much to do with her, and I have dedicated the book to her. Any author would dream of having Larry Ashmead as an editor, and this is the second time that I have been so fortunate. Craig Nelson, a young editor at Harper & Row, offered his uniformly perceptive comments on the manuscript, as well. Margaret Wimberger, now herself an assistant editor at Harper & Row, handled all the details of this project with acumen and good cheer. I also must thank Kenneth P. Norwick, my literary attorney, who is both an outstanding attorney and a man of highest principle. And I am grateful to my agent in Britain, June Hall.

When I finished interviewing Ingmar Bergman, he said: 'I could have told you stories, but I told you the truth.' I am indebted to the Swedish director for his perceptions and for allowing me to view his private documentary on the making of *Autumn Sonata*.

I am grateful to all Ingrid Bergman's other friends, associates, relatives, who told me not only stories but what they considered the truth. They include: Joss Ackland, Larry Adler, Robert Anderson, Frith Banbury, Frank Barrena, Kate Barrett, Greg Bautzer, Ben and Carla Benjamin, Harve Bennett, Michel Bernheim, Jeanne Bernk-opf, Gunnar Bjornstrand, Kay Brown, Igor Cassini, George Christy, Ross Clai-borne, Richard Coe, Claudette Colbert, Bob Colman, Gene Corman, Åke Dahlquist, Joe Daly, Silvia d'Amicos, Suso Cecchi d'Amicos, Brad Darrach, Olivia de Havil-land, Giuseppe De Santis, Madame de Sica, George Diehl, Stanley Donen, Frank Edwards, Julius Epstein, Laurence Evans, José Ferrer, Mel Ferrer, Armiene Field, Silvia Field, Rhonda Fleming, Joan Fontaine, Franka, Charles Futoran, Patrick Garland, Martha Gellhorn, Alan Gibson, David Golding, Sam Goldwyn, Jr., Cary Grant, Shirley Green, Alan Greenberg, Marilyn and Monty Hall, Dora Jane Hamblin, Doris Hare, Signe Hasso, Helen Hayes, Charlton Heston, Wendy Hiller, Louie Hollis, Celeste Holm, Elsa Holm, John Houseman, Noel Howard, Paul Hume, Christopher Isherwood.

Marion Keyes, Alf Kjellin, David Ladd, Disa Lauhren, David Lean, Reginald LeBorg, Francesco Leseur, Judge Mildred Lillie, Father Lisandrini, Carlo Lizzani, Norman and Peggy Lloyd, Gina Lollobrigida, Lasse and Ingela Lundberg, Marcel Machu, Aldo Martini, Giulietta Masina, Elia McCann, Fiorella Mariani, Marcella

Mariani, Walter Matthau, Liza Minnelli, Gunilla Mohlin, Roger Moore, Stig Nahlbom, Elsa and Vincent Nepture, Elsa Neuberger, Ellen Neuwald, Mark Nichols, Leonard Nimoy, Tom J. A. Olsson, Frederick O'Neal, Roberto Orbach, Guya Palavachini, Malcolm Peattie, Gregory Peck, Major Peek, Mimi Pollak, Anthony Quinn, Senator Charles Percy, Anthony Perkins, Rae Pober.

Jenia Reissar, Madame Renoir, Tony Reyes, Don Roberts, Francisco Rodolfi, Toby Rowland, Franco Rossellini, Lina Rossellini, Renzo Rossellini, Billy Rowe, Silvia Rubinstein, Ake Sandler, Carl Schaeffer, Wally Schneiderman, Maximilian Schell, Martin Scorsese, Phyllis Seaton, Danny Selznick of Monday Productions, Irene Selznick, Sonali Senroy, Ralph Serpe, Stirling Silliphant, Catharine Stackkelberg, Frank Sundstrom, Warren Thomas, Umberto Tirelli, Eva Tissell, Aldo Tonti, Helen Tubbs, Pavo Turtiainen, Raf Vallone, John Van Eyssen, Peter Veger, John Veitch, Rune Waldekranz, Hal Wallis, Stephen Weiss, Sandra Westin, Richard Whelan, Bob William.

Index